PROFESSIONAL BUSINESS CONNECTIVITY SERVICES IN SHAREPOINT® 2010

PROFESSIONAL

Business Connectivity Services in SharePoint® 2010

PROFESSIONAL

Business Connectivity Services in SharePoint® 2010

Scot P. Hillier
Brad Stevenson

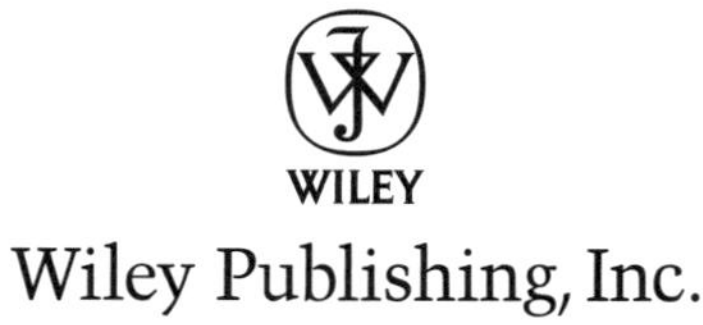

Wiley Publishing, Inc.

Professional Business Connectivity Services in SharePoint® 2010

Published by
Wiley Publishing, Inc.
10475 Crosspoint Boulevard
Indianapolis, IN 46256
www.wiley.com

Published simultaneously in Canada

ISBN: 978-0-470-61790-8
ISBN: 978-1-118-04381-3 (ebk)
ISBN: 978-1-118-04380-6 (ebk)
ISBN: 978-1-118-04379-0 (ebk)

Manufactured in the United States of America

10 9 8 7 6 5 4 3 2 1

For general information on our other products and services please contact our Customer Care Department within the United States at (877) 762-2974, outside the United States at (317) 572-3993 or fax (317) 572-4002.

Wiley also publishes its books in a variety of electronic formats. Some content that appears in print may not be available in electronic books.

Library of Congress Control Number: 2010942336

As always, to Nancy

—Scot Hillier

To my lovely wife, Laura, and my wonderful parents,
Geoff and Anita

—Brad Stevenson

ABOUT THE AUTHORS

SCOT HILLIER is an independent consultant and Microsoft SharePoint Most Valuable Professional focused on creating solutions for Information Workers with SharePoint, Office, and related .NET technologies. He is the author/coauthor of 15 books and DVDs on Microsoft technologies including this book and "Professional SharePoint 2010 Development." Scot splits his time between consulting on SharePoint projects, speaking at Tech Ed and SharePoint Connections, and delivering training for SharePoint developers through Critical Path Training. Scot is a former U. S. Navy submarine officer and graduate of the Virginia Military Institute. Scot can be reached at `scot@shillier.com`.

BRAD STEVENSON is a Senior Lead Program Manager at Microsoft, where his involvement with the SharePoint product group dates back to the 2003 release. Brad led UI development in the Business Connectivity Services team for the SharePoint 2010 release. He has spoken on the subject of SharePoint upgrade and connection to external data at various events and national conferences including Office Advisory Councils, TechReady, and the Microsoft SharePoint Conference. Brad hails from Victoria, Canada and holds a degree in computer science and business from the University of Victoria. Prior to joining Microsoft, Brad worked in the software industry in several countries including New Zealand, England, Canada and the United States. He lives in Seattle, Washington with his wife Laura.

ABOUT THE TECHNICAL EDITOR

TODD BAGINSKI is an independent consultant and Microsoft SharePoint Most Valuable Professional who uses SharePoint, Silverlight, Office, and .NET technologies to create websites and custom solutions for information workers. Todd is the content author and presenter for the BCS portion of the SharePoint MCM program and a regular speaker at the TechEd, SharePoint Connections, and Microsoft SharePoint conferences. Todd is a very active person who enjoys spending time with his family and skiing every chance he gets. Todd can be reached at `todd@toddbaginski.com`.

CREDITS

ACQUISITIONS EDITOR
Paul Reese

PROJECT EDITOR
Rosanne Koneval

TECHNICAL EDITOR
Todd Baginski

PRODUCTION EDITOR
Daniel Scribner

COPY EDITOR
Sadie Kleinman

EDITORIAL DIRECTOR
Robyn B. Siesky

EDITORIAL MANAGER
Mary Beth Wakefield

FREELANCER EDITORIAL MANAGER
Rosemarie Graham

ASSOCIATE DIRECTOR OF MARKETING
David Mayhew

PRODUCTION MANAGER
Tim Tate

VICE PRESIDENT AND EXECUTIVE GROUP PUBLISHER
Richard Swadley

VICE PRESIDENT AND EXECUTIVE PUBLISHER
Barry Pruett

ASSOCIATE PUBLISHER
Jim Minatel

PROJECT COORDINATOR, COVER
Katherine Crocker

PROOFREADER
Publication Services, Inc.

INDEXER
Ron Strauss

COVER DESIGNER
Michael E. Trent

COVER IMAGE
© Francesco Ridolfi/istockphoto.com

ACKNOWLEDGMENTS

THERE ARE MANY, MANY PEOPLE to thank for the successful completion of this book starting with my co-author, Brad Stevenson. I met Brad (whose initials are actually "BCS," no kidding) at the very beginning of 2009 when we started the effort to create training materials around what was then called Line-of-Business Integration (LOBi). Brad spent a significant amount of time explaining the vision and functionality of the new technology in a little kitchen area. Along with Boris Scholl, who led the Visual Studio effort, they got me hooked. I knew immediately that I wanted to write a book about it. Securing Brad as a co-author was a selfish move because I got to use his vision as a foundation for the book.

Next on the list to thank is our outstanding technical reviewer, Todd Baginski. Todd has been around BCS\BDC for a long time, and is a recognized expert in the SharePoint community. He did foundational work on the MetaMan model-generating product. Thanks for all your insights, Todd.

Along with Brad and Todd, the BCS, Search, and Visual Studio teams at Microsoft have been very generous with their time. Thank you to Mohammed Nazeeruddin (aka "Nazeer"), Russell Palmer, Thomas Mechelke, Arshish Kapadia, Nan Xie, Nitin Ved, Uma Subramanian, David Koronthaly, JD Klaka, Dwayne Codrington, Betty Yip, Dan Stanciu, and Alex Croicu. My apologies to anyone I might have missed; I pestered many people.

Outside of Microsoft, I also received input from key people in the SharePoint community. Thanks to those who reviewed chapters and provided some feedback. I'd like to send out a special thanks to Spence Harbar, who did a detailed review of Chapter 8. I probably still haven't explained Kerberos to his liking, but I tried.

There are also many people to thank at Wrox. Thanks first to Rosanne Koneval for leading the editing of the book. Thanks to Paul Reese and Jim Minatel for accepting the idea and providing a good working environment. Additional thanks to everyone else involved in the project.

Finally, no one can be successful without the loving support of family. Through every book, travel assignment, and late night, my wife Nancy has been there. Here's looking forward to building a nice house on that 20 acre parcel when the time comes. Ashley and Matt, you have grown up while I've written all these books. Ashley on to graduate school, Matt on to college. Wow! Hopefully, there will still be time for a family vacation at Massanutten every now and then.

Thank you to everyone.

—Scot Hillier

CONTENTS

INTRODUCTION

THE CREATION OF BUSINESS CONNECTIVITY SERVICES (BCS) for Microsoft SharePoint Foundation 2010 and Microsoft SharePoint Server 2010 involved a massive investment of people and resources by Microsoft. The result of this investment is a set of services, components, and technologies that have significant implications for the entire SharePoint community. Gradually, the impact of BCS is beginning to sink in as developers peel back its layers and put it to work, but most people do not yet understand how deeply they will be affected.

At this writing, many people in the community have seen BCS presentations and demonstrations. The typical presentation involves a message that says "use BCS to integrate systems such as CRM and ERP with SharePoint." The typical demonstration involves a no-code solution created in SharePoint Designer that rapidly integrates External Data, creates an External List, and synchronizes that list with Microsoft Outlook. While the typical presentation and demonstration fits well into an hour and looks sexy, it often misses the point. Business Connectivity Services is not simply middleware to use with existing systems, it is the data layer on top of which every SharePoint solution that uses External Data should be built.

When SharePoint developers architect solutions, they often discuss the differences between lists and databases. Lists are great for creating data structures that are easily editable by end users, but they lack the storage efficiency offered by databases. So what if you are trying to create an application that needs the capacity and efficiency of a database for storage, but you want it integrated with SharePoint? In the past, developers often simply created ASP.Net applications and deployed them to the LAYOUTS directory or built custom web parts that connected directly to a SQL Server database. BCS changes all of that.

Because BCS offers an integration layer capable of connecting SharePoint to External Data, developers should now consider it as the primary pattern for developing applications in SharePoint. If your SharePoint solution needs data storage with capabilities beyond those of a standard list, you should use BCS to create that solution. For making this effort, you will be rewarded with a host of capabilities that a custom ASP.NET application will never have such as enterprise search, External Data columns, user profile integration, client synchronization, off-line support, and Microsoft Word integration.

This book presents BCS from a developer's perspective. The idea behind the book is to present all of the power and capabilities of BCS along with guidance for using them in custom application development. After you fully understand BCS, you'll never think of SharePoint solutions the same way again.

WHO THIS BOOK IS FOR

This book is for professional SharePoint developers. While many of the solutions in this book can be created with no code using the SharePoint Designer, we assume that the reader is an accomplished C# developer with experience using the Microsoft SharePoint object model. Discussions involving related technologies such as web parts and workflows all assume the reader has general knowledge of the subject.

HOW THIS BOOK IS STRUCTURED

This book is organized to present a structured view of BCS development. Early chapters present no-code BCS solutions that utilize the SharePoint Designer. Later chapters present solutions that require Visual Studio 2010. Along the way, the book also divides server-side and client-side capabilities that can be used in solutions. The following is a brief description of each chapter:

Chapter 1: Business Connectivity Services — This chapter provides an overview of BCS, its relationship to other components of SharePoint, and its role in the business environment. The chapter concludes with a simple no-code solution.

Chapter 2: Using BCS Solutions in SharePoint 2010 — This chapter presents the integration points between existing BCS solutions and SharePoint 2010. Readers will learn how to make use of facilities such as External Lists, External Data columns, External Data web parts, and user profile integration.

Chapter 3: Using BCS Solution in Office 2010 — This chapter presents the integration points between existing BCS solutions and Microsoft Office 2010. Microsoft Outlook and the client cache are covered in detail along with the SharePoint Workspace and Microsoft Word.

Chapter 4: Creating BCS Solutions with the SharePoint Designer — This chapter provides full coverage of creating BCS solutions through the SharePoint Designer. This chapter includes coverage of intermediate topics such as form deign and workflow integration.

Chapter 5: Programming BCS Solutions in SharePoint 2010 — This chapter provides coverage of the server-side object models available in BCS. Readers will learn to create custom solutions for SharePoint 2010 using these models.

Chapter 6: Programming BCS Solutions in Office 2010 — This chapter provides coverage of the client-side object models available in BCS. Readers will learn to create custom solutions for Office 2010 using these models.

Chapter 7: Developing and Using Connectors — This chapter provides complete coverage of connector development in Visual Studio 2010. These connectors are used when developers need more control over communication with external Systems.

Chapter 8: Working with BCS Security — This chapter provides a detailed examination of security in BCS solutions. Coverage includes both classic and claims mode considerations for SharePoint 2010.

Chapter 9: Working with Enterprise Search — This chapter shows how to create solutions that use enterprise search with External Systems. The chapter presents fundamental search information as well as advanced development topics.

WHAT YOU NEED TO USE THIS BOOK

To use this book successfully, readers should have a development or test SharePoint environment where they can work through chapters. Sample code is provided with each chapter, and readers may wish to install and examine the code while reading.

CONVENTIONS

To help you get the most from the text and keep track of what's happening, we've used a number of conventions throughout the book.

Boxes like this one hold important, not-to-be forgotten information that is directly relevant to the surrounding text.

Notes, tips, hints, tricks, and asides to the current discussion are offset and placed in italics like this.

As for styles in the text:

- We *italicize* new terms and important words when we introduce them.
- We show keyboard strokes like this: Ctrl+A.
- We show file names, URLs, and code within the text like so: `persistence.properties`.
- We present code in two different ways:

```
We use a monofont type with no highlighting for most code examples.
We use bold to emphasize code that is particularly important in the present
context or to show changes from a previous code snippet.
```

SOURCE CODE

As you work through the examples in this book, you may choose either to type in all the code manually or to use the source code files that accompany the book. All of the source code used in this book is available for download at `www.wrox.com`. Once at the site, simply locate the book's title (either by using the Search box or by using one of the title lists) and click the Download Code link on the book's detail page to obtain all the source code for the book.

Because many books have similar titles, you may find it easiest to search by ISBN; this book's ISBN is 978-0-470-61790-8.

Once you download the code, just decompress it with your favorite compression tool. Alternately, you can go to the main Wrox code download page at `www.wrox.com/dynamic/books/download.aspx` to see the code available for this book and all other Wrox books.

ERRATA

We make every effort to ensure that there are no errors in the text or in the code. However, no one is perfect, and mistakes do occur. If you find an error in one of our books, like a spelling mistake or faulty piece of code, we would be very grateful for your feedback. By sending in errata you may save another reader hours of frustration and at the same time you will be helping us provide even higher quality information.

To find the errata page for this book, go to `www.wrox.com` and locate the title using the Search box or one of the title lists. Then, on the book details page, click the Book Errata link. On this page you can view all errata that has been submitted for this book and posted by Wrox editors. A complete book list including links to each book's errata is also available at `www.wrox.com/misc-pages/booklist.shtml`.

If you don't spot "your" error on the Book Errata page, go to `www.wrox.com/contact/techsupport.shtml` and complete the form there to send us the error you have found. We'll check the information and, if appropriate, post a message to the book's errata page and fix the problem in subsequent editions of the book.

P2P.WROX.COM

For author and peer discussion, join the P2P forums at `p2p.wrox.com`. The forums are a Web-based system for you to post messages relating to Wrox books and related technologies and interact with other readers and technology users. The forums offer a subscription feature to e-mail you topics of interest of your choosing when new posts are made to the forums. Wrox authors, editors, other industry experts, and your fellow readers are present on these forums.

At `http://p2p.wrox.com` you will find a number of different forums that will help you not only as you read this book, but also as you develop your own applications. To join the forums, just follow these steps:

1. Go to `p2p.wrox.com` and click the Register link.
2. Read the terms of use and click Agree.

3. Complete the required information to join as well as any optional information you wish to provide and click Submit.
4. You will receive an e-mail with information describing how to verify your account and complete the joining process.

You can read messages in the forums without joining P2P but in order to post your own messages, you must join.

Once you join, you can post new messages and respond to messages other users post. You can read messages at any time on the Web. If you would like to have new messages from a particular forum e-mailed to you, click the Subscribe to this Forum icon by the forum name in the forum listing.

For more information about how to use the Wrox P2P, be sure to read the P2P FAQs for answers to questions about how the forum software works as well as many common questions specific to P2P and Wrox books. To read the FAQs, click the FAQ link on any P2P page.

PROFESSIONAL

Business Connectivity Services in SharePoint® 2010

1

Business Connectivity Services

WHAT'S IN THIS CHAPTER?

- Understand the challenges of integrating external systems
- Understand the BCS architecture
- Learn to create a simple BCS solution

In today's diverse business environment, information workers need access to different types of data that reside in multiple locations. Structured data exists in an organization's enterprise applications, such as customer relationship management (CRM), product life-cycle management (PLM), and enterprise resource planning (ERP) applications, or is consumed from Web 2.0 services such as Microsoft Dynamics CRM Online or Salesforce.com. Unstructured data is created in productivity applications such as those in Microsoft Office, in team and collaboration applications such as Microsoft SharePoint, and in Web 2.0 services such as wikis or blogs.

Information workers spend much of their time using productivity applications, yet need to access structured data in order to make decisions and perform their jobs. This requires them to frequently switch between applications, which lowers productivity and can result in stale or incorrect information. To address these problems, many organizations have created custom applications and portals. These may solve some of the problems, but in turn can create a different set of business challenges:

- **Interoperability:** A custom application will typically involve a user interface to support a single business function, such as managing customer data or editing product information. Such applications traditionally encapsulate the application's user interface, business logic, and data in a single software package. However, because it is built to serve a single purpose, this type of stand-alone application creates an "island" of data and is not designed to facilitate interoperability.
- **Low-fidelity interfaces:** Consolidated business portals provide data from various business applications to information workers. They adequately present a high-level

view, but do not address the need to drill down and analyze data or collaborate on the data with other workers. Content creation is difficult with Web applications, and the page-based Web model can lack a wider business process context and suffer from variations in user experience.

- **High cost to build, train, support, and upgrade:** Custom applications don't leverage existing software investments; you have to start from scratch each time, solving difficult connectivity, deployment, and UI problems. These applications don't bring data to a familiar work environment, so users must navigate to a new software destination (which takes work and time) and learn a new user interface. Custom applications typically use proprietary interfaces that may accomplish the original purpose efficiently, but that makes it difficult to repurpose or extend the applications to meet new requirements, because they depend on the programming interfaces of other business applications.

Clearly there are limitations to using custom applications . . . but are there better approaches?

CHALLENGES INTEGRATING EXTERNAL DATA

Instead of creating a custom application to expose external data to information workers, why not integrate the External Systems directly into productivity applications such as SharePoint and Office?

For example, imagine an organization that relies on an event-planning solution with external data stored in a proprietary database. Rather than create a new special calendaring application that users must learn, why not create an Office solution that allows users to do their calendaring in Outlook, where they do the majority of their scheduling already?

EXTERNAL DATA

This refers to structured, business-critical data that is external to SharePoint. Examples include sales data such as customers, orders, and products, employee data such as salary and contact information, and financial data such as loan applications and credit history.

EXTERNAL SYSTEM

An application that manages and presents external data is referred to as an External System. Examples of External Systems include line-of-business (LOB) systems such as Siebel, Oracle, and SAP. External Systems can also encompass back-end, back office, front office, and custom applications as well as Web 2.0 services.

SharePoint/Office integration is ideal for information workers, but presents its own set of challenges to solution developers charged with actually performing the integration.

SharePoint solutions are often closely related to the data and processes contained in External Systems. For example, a document library containing invoices may contain metadata also found in the ERP system, or be addressed to a customer whose information is also in the CRM system. Without some way of using data from External Systems, the SharePoint solution would be forced to duplicate information.

Duplication of data leads to another problem: how do users know which version is up-to-date? If they regularly work with the SharePoint data but have to cross-reference it with data in the External System, this creates significant maintenance overhead that could slow adoption and ultimately result in a higher total cost of ownership.

User Challenges

In addition to the data challenges related to SharePoint, there are challenges involved in integrating external data with Office 2010 documents. When salespeople create a quote, for example, they often look up customer contact information in a CRM system, copy it to the clipboard, and then paste it into the document. This duplication of effort obviously increases the time it takes to create documents. Furthermore, salespeople must be connected to the network in order to access the CRM system; they cannot easily create quotes while offline.

Users are often frustrated because systems such as CRM or ERP and productivity software do not seem to "talk" to each other. It's difficult to create a sales proposal document that combines data from both systems. Too often there is a lack of integration among the systems that are important to users.

IT Challenges

Information Technology workers want to deploy applications that efficiently meet end user needs, yet still meet security, reliability, and regulatory compliance requirements. Writing custom code to integrate external data, whether it's into a custom application or into SharePoint or Office, brings up a lot of questions. For example, is the custom application reliable? Can it be modified by business units? Can it be easily upgraded and enhanced to meet new requirements or serve more users? Does it build on and leverage strategic software assets?

Microsoft Business Connectivity Services (BCS) can help address all three classes of challenges. By using BCS to handle the "heavy lifting" — connectivity infrastructure, deployment, and UI entry points — you leave yourself free to focus on customizations specific to the business problems at hand.

INTRODUCING BUSINESS CONNECTIVITY SERVICES

Business Connectivity Services (BCS) makes it easy to integrate external data into SharePoint 2010 and Office 2010 by providing infrastructure to help solve many of the data, user, and IT problems inherent in data integration solutions. Today professional developers are needed to build this class of solution; with BCS, a broader range of users — from power users to IT staff to developers — can work together, leveraging BCS capabilities to enable rich interaction with the external data in applications that end users are already familiar with. Professional developers are freed up to focus on building reusable data connections and UI components that can be shared with power users and BUIT staff who are assembling end-to-end solutions. By expanding the set of users directly involved in building and customizing a solution, you can remove the central IT bottleneck and solve more business problems.

BCS solutions map External System capabilities to standardized interfaces to define how to interact with a system's external data. As a result, solution developers don't have to learn the nuances of each LOB system; they can deliver powerful solutions faster. BCS also facilitates deployment and maintenance of scalable and secure solutions through integration with Visual Studio ClickOnce technology. This allows you to connect SharePoint solutions with Office client computers.

In a nutshell, BCS is all about connecting end users with enterprise data that they need to do their jobs — without requiring that they leave the familiar user interfaces of the applications they use today: SharePoint and Office. This makes it easier for end users to gain insight into the underlying data, make decisions, and take action within the context of the problem at hand.

SharePoint provides a range of different capabilities, from sharing information seamlessly and securely to searching for people and information. One of the groups of capabilities is referred to as *composites*; BCS is the centerpiece of this group. Composites refer to the ability to create powerful collaboration and information-sharing solutions that balance self-service with ease of management. You can assemble these solutions without code, building on the extensible platform capabilities of SharePoint 2010 and Office 2010. BCS is meant to achieve three things:

- Extend the reach and usage of external data
- Make external data actionable and available
- Create collaborative solutions easily through the reuse of components

Evolution of the Business Data Catalog

BCS builds upon the capabilities delivered in the Business Data Catalog (BDC) functionality of Microsoft Office SharePoint Server 2007. BDC enhanced the capabilities of SharePoint as a platform for developing composite applications by providing a simple, declarative mechanism to connect SharePoint 2007 to any database ADO.NET can connect to, or to any SOAP web service. BDC entities, Business Data web parts, and Business Data list columns were designed to provide a read-only window into External Systems.

In SharePoint 2010, BCS provides much deeper integration of external data directly into the SharePoint and Office UIs in a fully read-write fashion. External Content Types (ECTs) allow solution designers to describe both the structure of the External System and how that data should behave within SharePoint and Office.

If you have not previously worked with the Business Data Catalog, don't worry; no prior experience is required to understand or use BCS in SharePoint or Office solutions.

EXTERNAL CONTENT TYPE

The External Content Type (ECT) is perhaps the most important BCS concept. An External Content Type is the SharePoint and Office representation of a real business entity, such as a customer, order, or employee.

The evolution of the BDC Entity introduced in Microsoft Office SharePoint Server 2007, an ECT is a metadata description of the connectivity settings, data structures, and stereotyped operations — like create, read, update, and delete — that allow access to business entities as exposed by External Systems. In addition to describing the new stereotyped operations now supporting read/write access to external data, External Content Types in SharePoint 2010 can also describe SharePoint and Office integration behaviors, such as mappings to native Office item types — contact, task, appointment, and post. ECTs also describe where data should be available: offline in Outlook 2010, SharePoint Workspace 2010, or only online within SharePoint.

SharePoint 2010 features like External Lists, web parts, list columns, and search are all based on External Content Types.

Note: *Visual Studio 2010 still uses the term* entity *instead of* External Content Type *to maintain consistency with the BDC Runtime Object Model classes and methods. In this context the two terms refer to the same concept.*

BCS and Other Integration Services

BCS is the premier choice for integrating external data into SharePoint and Office, but it's certainly not the only Microsoft offering in the larger "data integration" space. How does it differ from other options and how can BCS add value on top of them?

BizTalk Server is a useful starting point: which aspects of BizTalk can I use or reuse with BCS? Core BizTalk functionality is aimed at lower-level business process automation — performing Electronic Data Interchange (EDI) operations or very complex orchestrations in which transaction integrity trumps latency. BCS can thus consume BizTalk orchestrations that are exposed as WCF or SOAP web services. If you have existing BizTalk orchestrations it may make sense to evaluate how much additional work would be required to "flatten" them and provide them in a format that BCS can consume.

The most common BizTalk functionality that can be used with BCS is the BizTalk adapters. An adapter is a WCF-based component that can act as a communication broker between SharePoint/Office and an External System. The adapter consists of design-time components and runtime components for receive and send operations, respectively. With a WCF endpoint hosted on an IIS server that stands in front of the External System, data can be presented in a consistent fashion for consumption by BCS. The BizTalk adapters simplify connectivity to Oracle databases, Oracle

E-Business Suite, Siebel, and SAP, among other types of External Systems. The adapters can be licensed separately from the full functionality of BizTalk Server.

CONNECTING TO SAP

Although BizTalk provides an SAP adapter, when evaluating options to connect to SAP you will want to investigate Duet Enterprise for Microsoft SharePoint and SAP. Out-of-the-box SAP services can be difficult for applications to consume directly — they are complex and very granular. Duet Enterprise builds directly on top of BCS to provide additional infrastructure and end user capabilities within SharePoint and Office. Duet Enterprise also provides new claims-enabled Windows Communication Foundation (WCF) services and components on the SAP end to simplify retrieval and presentation of data.

Next is the Entity Data Model (EDM), which is the conceptual schema of data used by the ADO.NET Entity framework. At a high level, EDM tries to accomplish some of the same things as BCS: it abstracts the structure of External Systems and enables developers to build applications that are not hard-coded to work with a particular system. EDM is limited to ADO.NET databases as the source for external data, but can be combined with powerful data query components such as Language Integrated Query (LINQ) to easily fetch data from databases modeled with EDM.

When considering how EDM and BCS can work together, it's easiest to think of EDM fulfilling the role of the data contract and BCS providing the service layer and UI integration endpoints. If you have an existing EDM file that describes the structure of one or more databases, you can easily use BCS to execute simple .NET code that describes the LINQ calls necessary to fetch data. For each EDM EntityType an External Content TypeECT will be defined. The LINQ calls to perform create, read, update, and delete (CRUD) stereotyped operations will be described in the ECT, along with the fields that make up the EntityType.

Another integration option is WCF RIA Services, which aims to simplify the challenges inherent in creating Rich Internet Applications (RIAs) that use Silverlight to move data across the Web. WCF RIA Services act as an infrastructure to make it easier for developers to write application logic to interact with Windows Communication Foundation (WCF) services, EDM models, or other data sources.

Like BCS, WCF RIA Services enables developers to create stereotyped operations to abstract common interactions with External Systems (such as CRUD). You can centralize business or application logic by adding it to your assembly, and easily present the data using a Silverlight application in either server environments (such as the SharePoint Silverlight Web Part) or client environments (such as the Office client task pane).

If you already use or plan to use applications built on WCF RIA Services, BCS can leverage some of those investments to facilitate deep integration with SharePoint and Office. This allows you to combine the advantages of WCF RIA Services (a well-defined location for business logic between data input elements such as forms and the data stack itself) and those of BCS (deep UI integration in both SharePoint and Office). The simplest way to do this is by creating a BCS.NET assembly connector to consume data entities, operations, and business logic from your WCF RIA Services solution's domain service.

To illustrate how these technologies can work together, let's look at a simple end-to-end example: connecting to a database to present customer data in SharePoint.

1. We start in Visual Studio by using EDM to model our Customer data.
2. We then create a Silverlight project and enable WCF RIA Services to present data from our database to end users.
3. We add business logic to our project; this lives in the domain service that the Silverlight part connects to when retrieving/submitting data.
4. Next, we publish the project to SharePoint as a WSP package. This will be installed as a full-trust solution.
5. We then create a site and a web part page, add SharePoint's Silverlight Web Part to the page, and configure it to host our Silverlight application.

An information worker can now browse to a SharePoint page and interact with the Silverlight application to view, create, update, or delete customers in an external database.

Now let's add BCS to the picture. We will start by opening Visual Studio to create a few additional artifacts.

1. We create a .NET assembly connector where we'll specify the LINQ calls to create, read, update, or delete data from our Customers database, as well as specifying the fields that make up a customer.
2. We publish the project to SharePoint, which will export it as a WSP package and install it as a full-trust solution. This will register a new `Customer` External Content Type with BCS.

With a minimal amount of extra effort, we've enhanced our solution to allow end users to easily create SharePoint lists that show customers, search for customers, and connect customer lists to Outlook and SharePoint Workspace. If necessary we could write additional code to present customer data in other Office applications by using VSTO add-in support.

ARCHITECTURE OVERVIEW

BCS is an umbrella term for a set of technologies that brings data from External Systems into SharePoint Server 2010 and Office 2010. It spans tools, connectivity infrastructure, and UI components on both the server and client. The term Business Data Connectivity, or BDC (same acronym as in 2007, but *Connectivity* instead of *Catalog*) is used to refer to the connectivity runtime. This BDC runtime is identical on the server and client, an ECT can be interpreted in either SharePoint or Office client, and the same External System called to retrieve data.

Figure 1-1 shows the set of BCS connectivity and UI capabilities across SharePoint and Office.

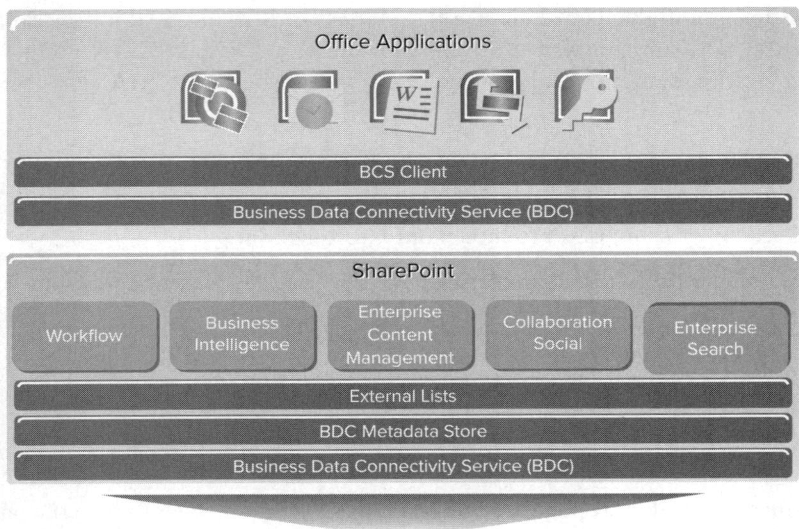

FIGURE 1-1

External Systems hold the data that we want to surface. The systems can be Web Services, WCF Services, SQL Server, custom line-of-business databases, or Web 2.0 services. BCS provides a different connector for each class of External System: WCF/Web Service, Database, .NET Connectivity Assembly, and Custom. The final two connectors enable you to write code to connect to virtually any type of data source, ranging from individual files (such as text files, CSV files, and Excel spreadsheets) to complex External Systems.

The BDC Metadata Store is a database that holds XML Metadata Model files. Each of these files contains one or more External Content Types and describes how to connect to and interact with an External System.

METADATA MODEL

The BDC Metadata Model contains External Content Type definitions, any associations between the ECTs (such as customer and order), and security permissions for the various ECTs. The model is automatically generated when you save an ECT in SharePoint Designer 2010 or Visual Studio 2010. Alternatively, you can create the model using third-party tools, manually in your XML editor of choice, or programmatically on the SharePoint server by using the BCS Administration object model.

The Business Data Connectivity Service (BDC) is the runtime object model invoked when a user request to interact with an External System is received. The BDC runtime reads ECTs from the BDC Metadata Store and routes calls through the appropriate connector (WCF/WS, DB, .NET Connectivity Assembly, Custom) to access the data source.

The BDC runtime may also call other SharePoint services before making a call to an External System. The Secure Store Service (which securely stores credential sets for External Systems and associates those credential sets with identities of individuals or with group identities) and the SharePoint Secure Token Service (which is used to request a security token that can be passed to a Claims-enabled External System) are two such examples.

Users can create External Lists and configure External Data web parts to work with data that BCS exposes. Once an External List is available, numerous other SharePoint capabilities can interact with it, including Workflow, Search, and InfoPath forms. These are described in more detail in Chapter 2.

Users can also connect External Lists to computers with Office 2010 installed. In supported Office client applications (SharePoint Workspace, Outlook, and Word) the BCS Client components act as connectors between the BDC runtime service and Office applications.

External data and Secure Store Service data are cached on client computers, the former being stored in a SQL CE database and the latter being stored in the Windows Credential Manager Service. The BDC client runtime uses a local cached copy of the Metadata Model containing the ECTs to connect directly to External Systems. Connections are made to SharePoint only when the user checks for updates to the ClickOnce package. Chapter 3 expands on BCS integration with Office 2010.

KEY CAPABILITIES

BCS provides a wide range of features across SharePoint 2010 and Office 2010, but, broadly speaking, they can be grouped into three areas:

- Presentation
- Connectivity
- Tooling

Presentation

The goal of the presentation features in BCS is to extend the SharePoint and Office user experience and capabilities to handle external data and processes. Let's start within SharePoint to understand the out-of-the-box capabilities that are at your disposal to present external data.

- **External List:** A type of SharePoint list that points to an External Content Type as its data source, but looks and feels like any other SharePoint list. When a user browses to an External List, data is retrieved directly from the External System. Supports full CRUD capabilities.

- **External Data Column:** A column that can be added to an existing list or document library and bound to one or more fields from an External System. When the column is added, a read-only copy of the data is made in SharePoint. Note that External Data Columns were referred to in SharePoint 2007 as Business Data Columns, or Business Data in Lists.
- **External Data Web Parts:** Five web parts (Item, List, Related List, Actions, and Item Builder) that can be added to any SharePoint web part page to display external data. The parts are read-only but can easily be extended to leverage External Lists and actions to enable write-back scenarios. External Data web parts are sometimes referred to in SharePoint 2010 UI and documentation as the Business Data web parts, the same name used in SharePoint 2007.
- **Chart Web Part:** A powerful web part with rich customization capabilities that can be used to visually present charts and graphs of SharePoint data or external data.
- **Enterprise Search:** Allows end users to search External Systems from within the SharePoint Search Center. Search scopes can be created to target a specific set of external data.
- **External Data in User Profiles:** Enables an administrator to append fields from External Systems to data from your corporate Active Directory and store the results in the SharePoint user profile database. Once defined, the value of any user profile field can be sent to the External System when data is retrieved at runtime.
- **InfoPath:** Can be used to replace the standard SharePoint forms for an External List. Once customized, the same InfoPath form can be presented in both SharePoint and SharePoint Workspace.

Most of the SharePoint presentation features in the preceding list are covered in detail in Chapter 2. Search is covered in detail in Chapter 9.

BCS also provides a broad set of capabilities within Office client applications to present external data:

- **SharePoint Workspace (SPW):** View and interact with any in a rich client application, regardless of whether users are online or offline. Sort, filter, group, or search external data, and view item details in InfoPath forms.
- **Outlook:** View and interact with External Lists whose structure maps closely to the Office item types that Outlook supports. (Appointment, Contact, Post, and Task.)
- **Word:** Create or edit a Word document or template in a SharePoint document library that has one or more external data columns. Add Quick Parts to enable end users to select and embed external data into their document.
- **Access:** Create a read-only link table to surface external data inside an Access rich client application. Be aware that data in these applications cannot be viewed when it is hosted by Access Services in the browser.

The Office presentation features described in the preceding list are covered in detail in Chapter 3.

Connectivity

BCS provides read/write-capable connectivity from both SharePoint and Office to WCF/Web Services, ADO.NET databases, and custom sources through .NET assemblies or Custom connectors. Figure 1-2 highlights the server and client connectivity components that make up BCS.

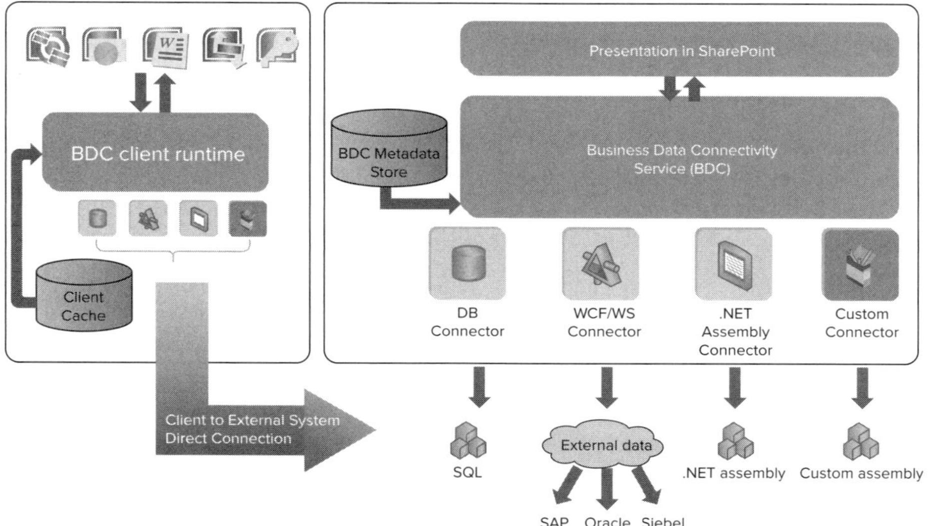

FIGURE 1-2

BDC runtime services on both server and client allow a direct connection to a wide variety of External Systems. In SharePoint all operations are performed synchronously, with the user receiving immediate feedback as to whether the request was successful. In Office client applications the user can be online (i.e., able to connect to the External System) or offline. When the user is offline, operations are queued in the client cache, and when connectivity is reestablished the operations are committed. The client cache is a SQL CE database that is able to store Metadata Models as well as external data.

In order to control and limit the load placed on External Systems, both client and server BDC runtimes have the ability to throttle connections to these systems. Connections can be throttled at a global level (with an upper limit on total connections) as well as according to connection type (with an upper limit on rows that can be returned from a database, or a timeout value for a WCF/web service request). Default values are specified for these settings for both SharePoint and Office, which can be modified or disabled by an administrator.

In SharePoint 2007, BDC supported only single-item operations, such as retrieving and displaying a customer in a Business Data web part. With SharePoint 2010, BDC allows for batch and bulk operation support, which enables multiple items to be read in a single call, dramatically reducing round-trips to the External System.

SharePoint Search 2010 uses BCS to crawl and index external data, and offers full-text search regardless of where the data resides. Search also uses the BDC service to perform security trimming of external data when a query is executed. External data can be incrementally crawled to identify items that have changed, and proprietary External Systems can be crawled through the use of BCS.NET assembly connectors or custom connectors.

Tooling

BCS provides an integrated tooling experience that scales from simple solutions to advanced code-based applications, with capabilities to enable packaging of SharePoint solutions for deployment to Office client computers.

In SharePoint Designer 2010, SPD users can discover and use external data. They can create ECTs to describe External Systems that are relatively flat in structure and simple to understand, define associations between ECTs, create External Lists, add InfoPath forms to these lists, and perform other operations critical to building most BCS solutions. SharePoint Designer is most useful for the following operations:

- Create connections to External Systems such as:
  - Database
  - WCF or Web services
- Map operations for an External System
  - Create, read, update, delete
  - Associations
- Re-use existing connections to External Systems
  - .NET type
- Surface external data
  - In SharePoint External Lists
  - In Outlook as Appointments, Contacts, Posts, or Tasks

Visual Studio 2010 is optimized for creating and publishing code-based components to SharePoint. By using the new Business Data Connectivity project type, developers can easily do the following:

- Create a .NET Assembly Connector to
  - Aggregate data across multiple External Systems
  - Perform custom data transformations
  - Execute custom business logic/rules (such as by triggering a workflow)
  - Query data from data sources the out-of-the-box connectors do not support

- Enhance and expand solutions created in SharePoint Designer
- Bring external data into other Office client applications (such as Excel) with VSTO add-ins

Visual Studio offers a simple drag-and-drop experience to create External Content Types as part of a .NET assembly connector. Empty stereotypes are automatically defined for the CRUD methods; the developer simply fills in the code. Developers can switch between Visual and XML views of the ECT definitions, and press F5 when finished to import the ECTs to SharePoint in the form of a WSP. From there it's easy to create an External List and see things "running" end to end. You can even add a breakpoint to your code and step through the code as your External List loads data.

BCS provides automatic packaging and deployment for solutions. When a user navigates to an External List and clicks a button to take it offline to SharePoint Workspace or Outlook, BCS packages all related artifacts into a single, versioned ClickOnce package that is saved to a sub-folder of the External List. The user is redirected to this package and ClickOnce is launched to deploy it to the client machine. Where required, solutions can also be "pushed" to desktops via tools such as SMS.

BCS also plugs into common SharePoint tools such as backup and restore, site migration, and upgrade from previous versions, just as many other SharePoint services do.

BCS in SharePoint and Office SKUs

With the SharePoint 2007 release, Business Data Catalog functionality was available only in the Microsoft Office SharePoint Server Enterprise Edition SKU. For SharePoint 2010 the connectivity and administration are available in SharePoint Foundation. There continues to be a tiered story for the SharePoint Server 2010 SKUs, which are differentiated based on the Client Access License (CAL) purchased for each user. Table 1-1 lists the three SharePoint SKUs, and notes which BCS features are available in each. All features available in SharePoint Foundation are included in both SharePoint Server SKUs. All features in SharePoint Server with Standard CAL are included in SharePoint Server with Enterprise CAL.

TABLE 1-1: BCS Capabilities in SharePoint 2010

SKU	FEATURES
SharePoint Foundation	BDC runtime OM, Connectors (WCF/WS, DB, .NET Assembly Connector, Custom), BDC Metadata Store, External Lists, External Data column, BDC Administration pages, BDC administration OM, Workflow
SharePoint Server with Standard CAL	Secure Store Service OM and Administration pages
SharePoint Server with Enterprise CAL	External Data Search, Profile pages, External Data web parts, Rich Client Extensions (i.e., Office 2010 connectivity for External Lists), InfoPath forms

For Office 2010, BCS is included in the Professional Plus suite (often referred to as Pro Plus) and its stand-alone derivatives such as Outlook 2010, Word 2010, Access 2010, and Excel 2010. BCS is not available in other suites, such as Standard, nor in stand-alone applications that are not present in Professional Plus, such as Visio or Project. There is no tiered functionality in Office as in SharePoint — if BCS components are installed you get all the BCS client features:

- BDC runtime
- SQL CE cache
- BCS client runtime

Connecting an External List to SharePoint Workspace or Outlook obviously requires that the appropriate host application be installed. Building an advanced code-based solution that targets an application that BCS doesn't support out of the box (such as Excel 2010) is possible, provided that either the Pro Plus suite or a corresponding stand-alone application is installed.

CREATING SIMPLE BCS SOLUTIONS

BCS solutions can be complex, or so simple that they don't even use code. Using the capabilities of SPD and SharePoint you can easily create External Content Types and External Lists. This external data can then be edited in SharePoint or Office clients. In this section you'll walk through a simple BCS solution based on the AdventureWorksLT SQL Server database. The database contains two tables of sales-related data; Figure 1-3 shows the Customer table. The goal of the walkthrough is to create lists of customers and products in SharePoint and make those lists available in Outlook and SharePoint Workspace respectively.

	CustomerID	NameStyle	Title	FirstName	MiddleName	LastName	Suffix	CompanyName	SalesPerson	E
1	1	0	Mr.	Orlando	N.	Gee	NULL	A Bike Store	adventure-works\pamela0	c
2	2	0	Mr.	Keith	NULL	Harris	NULL	Progressive Sports	adventure-works\david8	k
3	3	0	Ms.	Donna	F.	Carreras	NULL	Advanced Bike Components	adventure-works\jillian0	c
4	4	0	Ms.	Janet	M.	Gates	NULL	Modular Cycle Systems	adventure-works\jillian0	j
5	5	0	Mr.	Lucy	NULL	Harrington	NULL	Metropolitan Sports Supply	adventure-works\shu0	l
6	6	0	Ms.	Rosmarie	J.	Carroll	NULL	Aerobic Exercise Company	adventure-works\linda3	r
7	7	0	Mr.	Dominic	P.	Gash	NULL	Associated Bikes	adventure-works\shu0	c
8	10	0	Ms.	Kathleen	M.	Garza	NULL	Rural Cycle Emporium	adventure-works\josé1	k
9	11	0	Ms.	Katherine	NULL	Harding	NULL	Sharp Bikes	adventure-works\josé1	k
10	12	0	Mr.	Johnny	A.	Caprio	Jr.	Bikes and Motorbikes	adventure-works\garrett1	j

FIGURE 1-3

Creating External Content Types

The solution begins with the definition of External Content Types to define the schema, and operations to perform on the external data. Whether your BCS solution ultimately uses code or not, you will almost always define the ECTs using SharePoint Designer. The tooling in SPD for creating ECTs was designed to be sophisticated enough to be used by professional developers across all types of BCS solutions. To begin, open a SharePoint site in SPD and select External Content Types from the list of Site Objects, as in Figure 1-4.

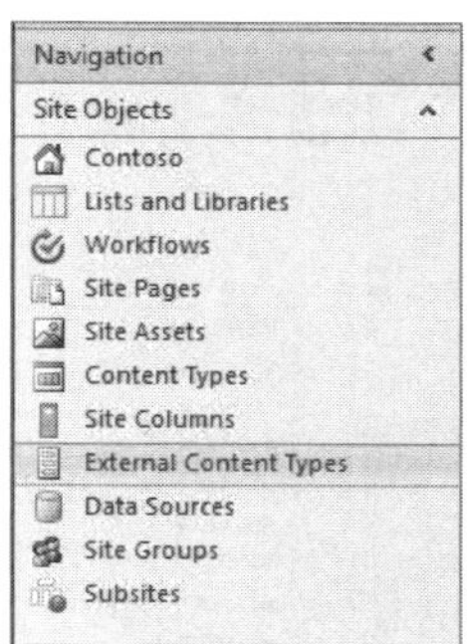

FIGURE 1-4

The External Content Type gallery displays the set of existing ECTs; clicking the External Content Type button in the New section of the ribbon begins the creation process. The ECT summary page prompts you for basic properties such as programmatic name, display name, namespace, and version. Office Item Type, shown in Figure 1-5, defines how the ECT should be presented when taken offline to Outlook 2010. The default option, Generic List, means that the ECT doesn't map to any Office item type and will be available to take offline in SPW but not Outlook. For this walkthrough choose Contact, as the fields of the Customer table map well to the properties of an Outlook contact.

Clicking the link to discover external data sources and then choosing Add Connection opens a dialog where you select the type of system that you are connecting to: WCF/Web Service, .NET Assembly Connector, or SQL Server. Choosing SQL Server allows you to enter the database server and database name, as shown in Figure 1-6.

FIGURE 1-5

FIGURE 1-6

The list of database tables is now displayed in the Data Source Explorer tab. Expand the Customer table to view its structure; right-click the table to define an individual create, read, update, or delete method. As we are modeling a database in this example, we can save time by selecting Create All Operations, shown in Figure 1-7, which will condense the process into one three-step wizard.

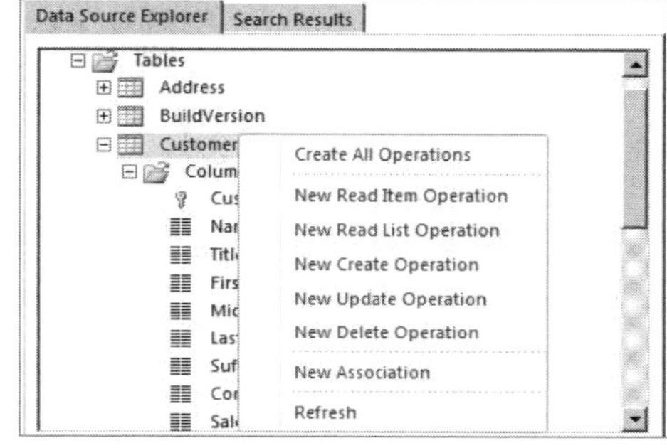

FIGURE 1-7

On the second step of the wizard you will need to map fields from the Customer table to Outlook contact properties. For this example, map `FirstName`, `LastName`, `CompanyName`, and `EmailAddress` to the Outlook properties of the same name. Additionally, map `Phone` to `Business Telephone Number`. Do this by selecting the database field in the left column and the corresponding Office property from the drop-down menu in the right column, as shown in Figure 1-8. Note that several properties, such as `SalesPerson` and `ModifiedDate`, remain unmapped. Click Finish to exit the wizard.

Data Source Elements	Properties	
CustomerID	Data Source Element:	Phone
NameStyle	.NET Type:	System.String
Title	Map to Identifier:	☐
FirstName	Identifier:	
MiddleName	Field:	Phone
LastName	Display Name:	Phone
Suffix	Foreign Identifier:	(Click to Add)
CompanyName	Required:	☐
SalesPerson	Read-Only:	☐
EmailAddress	Office Property:	Business Telephone Number (BusinessT...
Phone	Show In Picker:	☐
PasswordHash	Timestamp Field:	☐
PasswordSalt		
rowguid		
ModifiedDate		

FIGURE 1-8

Complete the process by clicking Save in SPD to publish the ECT to the BDC Metadata Store.

Creating External Lists

External Lists can be created through the browser or in SPD. For this walkthrough, click the Create Lists & Forms button in the ribbon and give the list a name, as in Figure 1-9. You can optionally add InfoPath forms to the list by selecting the checkbox at the bottom of the dialog.

The new External List can be viewed in the browser, as shown in Figure 1-10. Users can create, view, edit, and delete items because all of these operations were defined as part of the ECT.

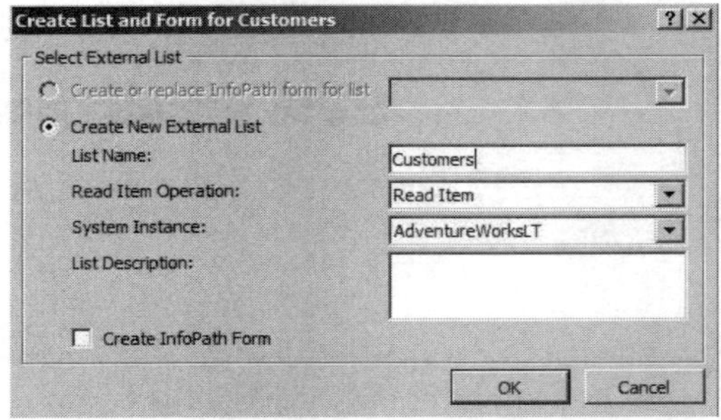

FIGURE 1-9

CustomerID	NameStyle	Title	FirstName	MiddleName	LastName	Suffix	CompanyName
1	No	Mr.	Orlando	N.	Gee		A Bike Store
2	No	Mr.	Keith		Harris		Progressive Sports
3	No	Ms.	Donna	F.	Carreras		Advanced Bike Components
View Item	No	Ms.	Janet	M.	Gates		Modular Cycle Systems
Edit Item / Delete Item	No	Mr.	Lucy		Harrington		Metropolitan Sports Supply

FIGURE 1-10

Connecting External Lists to Office 2010

SharePoint Server 2010 with the Enterprise Client Access License supports connecting External Lists to SharePoint Workspace 2010, and where applicable to Outlook 2010. In the List tab of the External List's ribbon, a Connect to Outlook button enables synchronization to Outlook. A Visual Studio ClickOnce package is automatically created and accessed to present the installation screen shown in Figure 1-11.

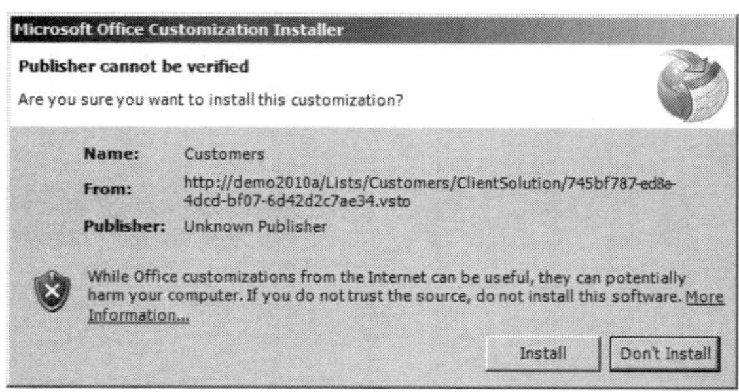

FIGURE 1-11

Outlook is launched if it's not currently running and a new Customers folder is created in the SharePoint External Lists PST store. Synchronization of data from the SQL Server database happens almost immediately and items are presented to the user. As a result of the Customers ECTs being mapped to the Contact Office Item Type, the items are shown in the business card view in Outlook, as illustrated in Figure 1-12. Double-clicking an item to open the inspector view reveals fields such as `LastName` and `Phone` that were mapped to Outlook properties. You can view those properties that were not mapped, such as `SalesPerson` and `ModifiedDate`, by clicking the Customers Details button in the ribbon.

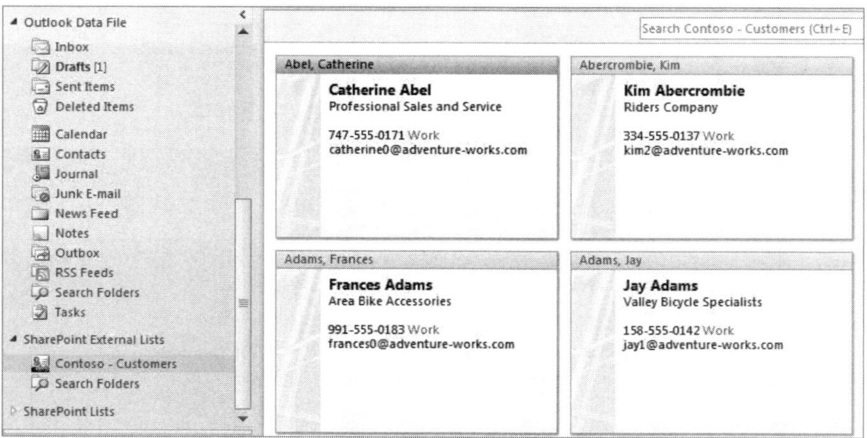

FIGURE 1-12

All External Lists, not just those that mirror the schema of an Office Item Type, can be synchronized with SharePoint Workspace. For the purposes of this walkthrough, an additional ECT and an External List have been prepared to show data from the Products database table. The preparation steps were identical to those for the Customer sample, with the exception of Office item type. Because products do not map closely to an appointment, contact, post, or task item, Generic List was selected. As in Figure 1-13, from the Products External List, click the Sync to SharePoint Workspace button in the List tab of the ribbon.

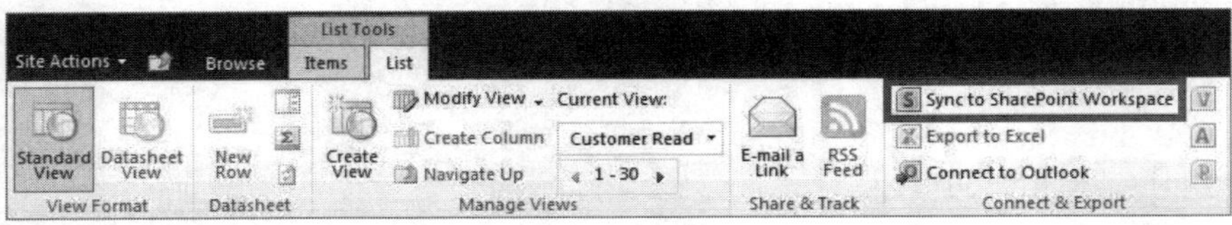

FIGURE 1-13

Again, a Visual Studio ClickOnce package is created and accessed to install the necessary ECT, form, and data subscription components. Figure 1-14 shows the Products External List in the SharePoint Workspace.

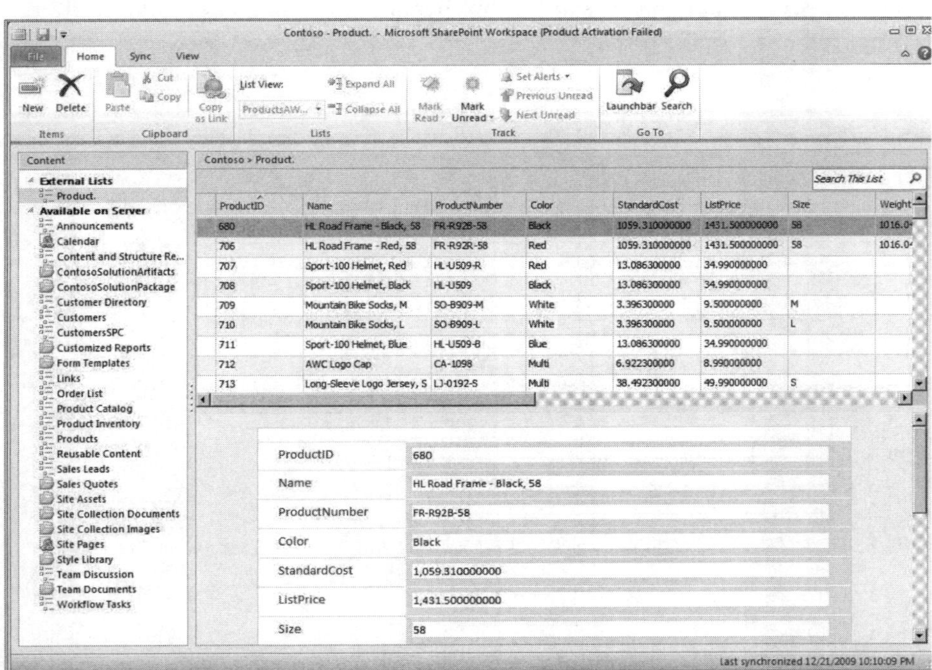

FIGURE 1-14

TYPES OF SOLUTIONS

Solutions that leverage Business Connectivity Services typically fall into one of three high-level categories:

- Simple solutions that leverage out-of-the-box capabilities
- Intermediate declarative solutions
- Advanced code-based solutions

The first two do not require the use of code, although they can reuse code-based components that have been published by developers. Reuse is important for two reasons:

- Dramatically more users can assemble and customize these types of solutions compared to solutions that require coding, freeing up developers and IT organizations to focus their resources on solving more complex problems.
- Central IT retains control over the types of actions that these solutions can perform, which leads to fewer management headaches. Reuse also has a side benefit of making it easier to convert solutions to central IT-supported apps in the future if that is desired.

The third solution category, advanced solutions, is entirely code-based. Visual Studio is the preferred tool for composing and publishing reusable components or entire end-to-end solutions.

Figure 1-15 shows the three different types of BCS solutions, the types of users who create them, the tools used to create them, and common scenarios that can be accomplished with each. The arrows indicate the ability to enhance a simple solution to become an intermediate solution, as well as the ability to share components from advanced solutions for re-use in intermediate solutions.

Let's review the characteristics and benefits of each type of solution.

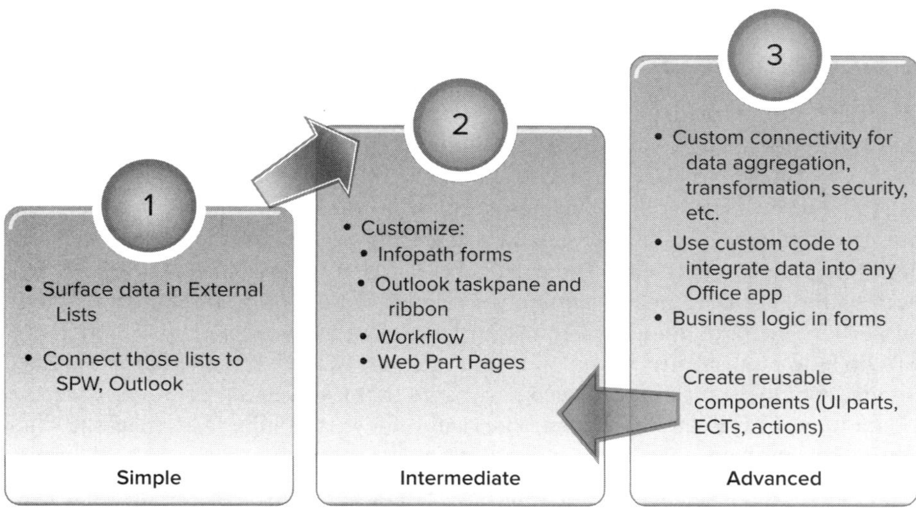
1
• Surface data in External Lists
• Connect those lists to SPW, Outlook
Simple
2
• Customize:
• Infopath forms
• Outlook taskpane and ribbon
• Workflow
• Web Part Pages
Intermediate
3
• Custom connectivity for data aggregation, transformation, security, etc.
• Use custom code to integrate data into any Office app
• Business logic in forms
Create reusable components (UI parts, ECTs, actions)
Advanced

FIGURE 1-15

Simple Solution Leveraging Out-of-the-Box Capabilities

In SharePoint Foundation 2010 you can surface external data in an External List or on a web part page via the Business Data web parts or the Chart Web Part. You can also add an External Data column to a standard SharePoint list or document library. That column can then be exposed as a Quick Part in Word 2010.

In Outlook 2010 you can take an External List offline from SharePoint Server 2010 with Enterprise Client Access License and allow users to interact with the external data from within Outlook. Users see the same formatting (contact, appointment, task, or post) as for regular Outlook items and can use the same gestures to interact with them. This type of solution runs under the native BCS Outlook add-in, which is installed with Office 2010 and loaded at Outlook startup.

In SharePoint Workspace 2010 you can take an External List offline from SharePoint Server 2010 with Enterprise Client Access License and allow users to interact with the external data from within SharePoint Workspace. Business Connectivity Services does not provide an extensible programming model to extend this type of simple solution, but you can associate an InfoPath form with the External List. This opens up the ability to customize the form and present the customized form on both the server and the client in SharePoint Workspace.

Users in Outlook and SharePoint Workspace can synchronize data directly with the External System(s) automatically (the default interval is every three hours) or by explicitly clicking an action. They can also explicitly check for schema updates to the External List, which will result in a new ClickOnce package being deployed to the machine if the structure of the External List, its forms, or its views have changed.

Tooling for simple solutions mostly involves creating External Content Types, which is typically done with SharePoint Designer but can involve Visual Studio, or an XML editor if necessary. From there you can create an External List using the browser or SharePoint Designer and click a button in the SharePoint ribbon to connect it to Outlook or SharePoint Workspace. Web part pages and external data columns can be created using the browser or SharePoint Designer.

Intermediate Declarative Solution

The most common types of intermediate solutions are simple solutions that have been further customized to add capabilities. These additional capabilities include InfoPath forms, SharePoint workflow, and SharePoint web part pages. You can customize InfoPath forms that present External Data by changing the look and feel, adding declarative rules/business logic, or adding code behind. The latter requires that the form be published as an admin-deployed form to the server — Chapter 4 walks you through this process end to end. You can also create or add capabilities to SharePoint workflows through SharePoint Designer by configuring the out-of-the-box SharePoint List activity to read data from, or write data to, an External List, or by reusing a custom workflow activity built in Visual Studio (and published to SharePoint) that interacts with External Lists or the BDC runtime object model. Finally, you can create web part pages that leverage out-of-the-box web parts (Business Data Item, List, Related List, Actions, Item Builder, and Filter as well as the Chart Web Part) and optionally configure part-to-part connections to send data among them. You can customize the look and feel of parts by editing the XSLT of each part in the web part tool pane.

Another type of intermediate customization involves external data in Outlook 2010. For example, you can show related order information in a custom task pane when a user has a Business Contact inspector open.

Starting with basic Outlook elements you can customize the view that is shown for a folder of external data. Do this by opening the folder in Outlook and using the standard commands to build and save a new view. BCS provides a command to save the customized view to SharePoint and place it in a sub-folder of the External List, making it available to future users who connect the list to Outlook.

Additional Outlook customizations are slightly more complex than other intermediate customizations and require that you create XML files — such as Solution Manifest (`OIR.Config`), Subscription, Ribbon, and Layouts — and then create a ClickOnce package by using BCS SDK tools. Users can then deploy the solution in Outlook by installing the ClickOnce package. In such a solution, you can define custom task panes and present external data to users via external data parts (either out-of-the-box parts or code-based custom parts) hosted in a task pane. You can also define ribbon files and custom actions (exposed in the ribbon or in an external data part) that either trigger code or launch a browser pointing to a URL. Finally, you can customize Outlook forms by starting with the auto-generated forms that BCS provides, tweaking them, and saving/exporting the file(s). Customizations here leverage Business Connectivity Services' rich client runtime (including the BCS Outlook add-in), which presents the elements defined in the XML files at runtime.

The final type of intermediate solution is referred to as a *data-only solution*. As the name implies, this is used to tell BCS to fetch data from an External System and store it in the client cache. No UI is created to view/administer the data in Outlook. This is useful when combined with an advanced solution that integrates with an Office application, such as Excel or PowerPoint, as advanced solutions are not capable of communicating with BCS to populate the client cache.

A variety of tools, including InfoPath Designer (for forms), SharePoint Designer (for workflows), a browser (for SharePoint web part pages), and Outlook (for customized forms and views), can be used to build intermediate solutions.

To create the XML files needed for your Outlook declarative solution, you can use any XML editor. Visual Studio provides IntelliSense, which can be helpful when you are creating these XML files. Business Connectivity Services provides a Solution Packaging Tool as part of the SDK, which you can use to create a ClickOnce package for Outlook declarative solutions. Chapter 6 describes the schema of these XML files, and provides sample files to get you started.

Advanced Code-Based Solution

Advanced solutions can involve the creation of reusable components (.NET assembly connector to aggregate or transform data from External Systems, custom web parts, custom workflow activities, code behind for InfoPath forms, and code-based actions or external data parts for use in Outlook declarative solutions) or an entire end-to-end solution that leverages the Business Data Connectivity object model. The rest of this section discusses the different options and considerations for end-to-end solutions.

A code-based .NET Framework solution created with a tool such as Visual Studio can use any element of the public Business Connectivity Services object model and can enable users to interact with external data. It can register with the Business Data Connectivity (BDC) service by using the BDC runtime object model to present data in SharePoint or an Office 2010 application that supports VSTO add-ins. Creating a custom client application that is not hosted in a Microsoft Office application to surface external data is not supported.

External Data can be retrieved directly from the External System while a client application is connected to it, or External Data can be retrieved locally from the BCS rich client cache to enable offline scenarios. To populate the cache with External Data, one or more External Lists can be taken offline to SharePoint Workspace or Outlook, or a Declarative Data Only solution can be deployed to the client machine. Developers wishing to deploy a Data Only and an advanced solution together as a single unit can chain the ClickOnce packages together by referencing the second package in the Post Deployment Action (PDA) of the first package. Advanced solutions can be used to extend BCS to Office applications that are not supported out of the box, such as Excel and PowerPoint.

In a code-based end-to-end solution, the developer controls the user interface, packaging, and deployment. This type of solution cannot make use of Business Connectivity Services' rich client runtime, which is used by simple and intermediate solutions to integrate data into Office applications.

The only exception to the preceding rules about populating the cache with data, and advanced solutions owning all UI elements, is advanced solutions that target Outlook. These solutions are able to provide a Subscription file that defines the data that should be pulled into the client cache, and an `OIR.config` file that describes the structure of folders that should be created in Outlook. Additional UI customizations such as customizing the ribbon, showing data in a task pane, and providing custom forms are the responsibility of the solution developer and will require additional code.

Code-based solutions are developed with a tool such as Visual Studio 2010. A BDC project type is available to facilitate the creation of .NET assembly connectors. Learn how to create a .NET assembly connector in Chapter 7.

To summarize, a broad spectrum of solutions can be built using BCS. These range from simple solutions that rely on out-of-the-box capabilities with little or no customization to intermediate solutions that involve customizing a wide range of features in SharePoint and Office 2010. Advanced solutions involve the creation of code via Visual Studio, and can either be complete end-to-end solutions or provide reusable code-based components that can be included in intermediate solutions.

SOLUTION PACKAGING

As noted previously, BCS lets you package SharePoint solutions into ClickOnce applications for deployment to Office 2010 machines. This functionality is completely transparent for simple solutions — the package for an External List is created on demand when a user clicks Connect to Outlook or Sync to SharePoint Workspace. The same mechanism is used to install declarative or advanced solutions, but the ClickOnce package must be created in advance by the solution developer. Microsoft provides a Software Development Kit (SDK) tool to streamline the process of creating a declarative or advanced solution package.

ClickOnce Package

Regardless of who creates it or how it is created, the ClickOnce package must contain a Metadata Model file that includes one or more ECTs. As shown in Table 1-2, additional elements are optional and depend on the type of solution and which Office application will host it.

TABLE 1-2: ClickOnce Package Contents by Solution Type

COMPONENT	DESCRIPTION	SIMPLE	DECLARATIVE	ADVANCED
Metadata Model	Contains ECTs, describes how to connect to External Systems	Required	Required	Required
Subscription	Describes the set of data (i.e. views) with which to populate the client cache	Automatically created on client after deployment	Required	Not supported
InfoPath forms	Shown in SharePoint workspace; can contain declarative validation logic or code behind	Automatically created on client after deployment	Optional (for showing data in Outlook task pane or custom form region)	Requires code
`OIR.config` file	Basic Outlook UI structure	Automatically created on client after deployment	Required (except for Data Only)	Required if targeting Outlook
Outlook view customizations	Defines the columns and sort/filter/group settings for an external data folder	Optional	Optional	Requires code
Outlook UI customizations	Outlook Forms[3] forms, ribbon files, custom task pane layouts, UI controls to show in forms/task panes	Not supported	Optional	Requires code

Where it is noted in the table that code is required, it is the responsibility of the solution developer to include the element in the package and register/display the artifact in the host application at runtime.

Deployment Concepts

When a user clicks a link or action that points to a ClickOnce package, the initial deployment process begins. The user sees an initial trust prompt, as shown in Figure 1-11, of the Simple Solution walkthrough. By default this prompt shows an unknown publisher; you can change this by registering a certificate on the SharePoint farm. This process is described in Chapter 5.

Elements of a solution will almost certainly change after initial deployment to a given group of users. The schema of the External System(s) could change, necessitating modifications of the ECTs and model file, InfoPath or Outlook forms, or other solution elements.

Simple solutions provide a semi-automated mechanism for processing updates to a solution — whenever a user clicks the Connect to Outlook or Sync to SharePoint Workspace button on an External List, BCS checks to see if there is an existing solution. If not, a new ClickOnce package is generated; if so, the version of each server-side artifact (Metadata Model, InfoPath forms, External List views) is checked to see if it has changed. If there are no changes, the existing package is current and made available for download; if there are changes, a new version of the package is created. Similar logic is executed if a user clicks Check for Updates from a BCS folder in Outlook or chooses to sync an External List in SharePoint Workspace.

Declarative and advanced solutions hosted in Outlook, like simple solutions, give users the ability to explicitly check for updates from a BCS folder in Outlook. However, neither declarative nor advanced solutions can be auto-generated; thus the solution developer must manually replace the ClickOnce package with a newer version.

Data only declarative solutions and advanced solutions hosted in applications other than Outlook must provide their own logic to check for updates or simply rely on "push" mechanisms to update client machines.

SECURITY

There are two key components to security: authentication and authorization. When connecting to External Systems, BCS must be flexible enough to understand several different authentication modes. In the simplest case, BCS may be passing Windows credentials from the user (whether in SharePoint or in an Office application) through to the External System. However, most real-world applications have more complex requirements such as proprietary authentication mechanisms including tokens or claims.

From an authorization perspective, SharePoint objects can be secured, BCS provides the ability to secure ECTs and models, and External Systems control permissions to the data itself. It is important to understand how these layers work together and to implement the minimum set of permissions necessary to enable users to be productive.

In order for BCS solutions to be secure and easy to deploy, they must gracefully deal with a wide range of authentication and authorization scenarios. These scenarios are discussed in more detail in Chapter 8; what follows is a brief overview of the key concepts.

Authentication Overview

The most common BCS authentication scenario involves a database or web service as the External System. These systems are typically internal to the organization and use either Windows authentication or username/password authentication. In these scenarios BCS supports two authentication models: *Trusted Subsystem and Impersonation and Delegation*. In the Trusted Subsystem model BCS uses a single account to access the External System regardless of the end user's identity. With Impersonation and Delegation, BCS attempts to impersonate the end user and access the External System.

The authentication mode that BCS uses to connect to an External System is defined by the `AuthenticationMode` element in the XML Metadata Model file that defines one or more External Content Types. There are five possible values for the `AuthenticationMode` element:

- `Passthrough` falls under the Impersonation and Delegation authentication model and results in BCS using the credentials of the currently logged-in user to access the External System. `Passthrough` works well for simple scenarios (such as the walkthrough earlier in this chapter) in which the External System is hosted on the same computer as SharePoint; it falls short for most real-world scenarios because of the "double-hop" problem, which is discussed in Chapter 8.

`RevertToSelf` falls under the Trusted Subsystem authentication model and results in BCS using the credentials of the application pool to access the External System. Although `RevertToSelf` can solve the double-hop problem, all user requests to the External System will be made using the same account. While appropriate for some scenarios, this makes it impossible for the External System to grant an employee rights to view a certain set of data and a manager rights to view additional details. It also makes it difficult or impossible to track which users made changes to the External System. The final three values — `WindowsCredentials`, `RdbCredentials`, and `Credentials` — are used to pass a separate set of credentials from the Secure Store Service (SSS). The SSS is a flexible credential management service that supports both the Trusted Subsystem and the Impersonation and Delegation authentication models. If you map all end-user credentials to a single group account in SSS, you can support the Trusted Subsystem authentication model. Alternatively, if you map end-user credentials to a unique set of credentials per user, SSS is supporting the Impersonation and Delegation authentication model. SSS is capable of managing three different types of credentials (Windows, SQL, and username/password), which correspond to `WindowsCredentials`, `RdbCredentials`, and `Credentials` respectively.

Claims and OAuth

BCS can also use claims to authenticate against External Systems that support it. The External System must both support claims and trust the SharePoint claims provider. A common scenario is a custom WCF service that implements claims authentication and exposes data from one or more databases. To implement claims authentication, `AuthenticationMode` should be set to `Passthrough`. As noted previously, this will cause BCS to authenticate with the current user's credentials. In this scenario, however, the External System's WCF service will request a Security Assertion Markup Language (SAML) token, which is necessary to authenticate in a claims environment. When BCS receives the request for the SAML token, it contacts the Secure Token Service (STS), an application service that runs in the SharePoint farm. The SharePoint STS examines the end-user credentials and issues a SAML token. This SAML token is then used by BCS's WCF connector to authenticate against the WCF service.

OAuth is a common authentication mechanism that is used by web-based applications and services. It is a token-based standard in which a user provides log-in information and is issued a token that grants access to a particular website for a specific set of resources for a specified duration. The SDK provides a working BCS code sample that shows how to connect to an External System that uses OAuth.

Office Client

Much of this section refers to scenarios that involve accessing External Systems from SharePoint — what changes when a user is trying to authenticate from an Office client application? One of the goals of BCS is to provide a symmetrical runtime experience on both server and client — the same Metadata Model and ECTs are made available in both locations and user requests are sent directly to the External System — but there are some scenarios in which different client settings will be required. It is for this reason that you can specify client-specific settings as part of your ECTs and Metadata Models. This gives you the flexibility to choose the authentication mode most appropriate for each environment.

`Passthrough` authentication will result in the client's passing the user's current Windows credentials through to the External System. If the External System is a claims-enabled WCF service, a request will be made to the SharePoint STS to obtain a token that can then be passed from the client to the External System. This is one of the few scenarios in which a request for external data from a client requires that SharePoint be accessible.

`RevertToSelf` is not useful for client scenarios — unlike on the server, the client is not impersonating the identity of a user to process a request and thus there is no identity to revert to. Client requests made with this setting in the Metadata Model will act the same as `Passthrough` requests.

Secure Store can be used on the client and credentials will be persisted in the Windows Credential Manager store. It is important to note, however, that credentials that are encrypted in the SSS within SharePoint are not transferred to Office client applications — users must re-enter the credentials locally. A key consideration with SSS is whether to use individual or group accounts. All users can be mapped to a group account on the server, whose credentials can be managed by an administrator. When a BCS solution that requires these group credentials is connected to an Office client application, the end user will be prompted for those credentials, which he or she is unlikely to have access to. Individual credential mapping is a cleaner approach when you are using SSS with client applications — end users will still be prompted to enter credentials if those credentials don't exist or have expired in the Credential Manager store, but the users are more likely to know what they need to enter.

Authorization Overview

Authentication is only the first part of accessing data from External Systems. After the user is authenticated BCS must determine whether the user is authorized to call a particular operation on an ECT. BCS has four different permissions that may be assigned. These are Edit, Execute, Set Permissions, and Selectable in Clients. The Edit right grants the ability to create, delete, and update BCS metadata. The Execute right grants the ability to make a call to an External System. The Set Permissions right grants the ability to assign rights to other users, and the Selectable in Clients right provides access to utilities such as the External Content Type picker. These rights can be assigned at the model, system, entity/ECT, and operation levels through the Central Administration UI for the BDC application service.

In addition to the authentication and authorization scenarios described earlier, it is possible to add custom code to a .NET Assembly Connector or Custom connector to address requirements unique to a particular scenario or External System. Two important considerations here include:

- The context in which your code is running: by the time the request reaches the BDC runtime you may not have direct access to the SharePoint or Office context in which the user initiated the action.
- Are you building a client-server solution that relies on resources that exist only in SharePoint? For example, client machines cannot fetch the credentials of the SharePoint application pool account.

SUMMARY

In short, there are many challenges when it comes to integrating external data. Business Connectivity Services helps to address those challenges by providing a powerful and quick way to connect that data into SharePoint and Office 2010. BCS can also work alongside and extend other integration service offerings such as BizTalk, EDM, and WCF RIA Services.

External Content Types (ECTs) are the critical building block of BCS: they define how to connect to an External System to retrieve data for a particular object such as a Customer. The definitions include the methods to call when to read or update data, the fields that constitute a single Customer record, and how that Customer should behave within the SharePoint and Office environments.

The core capabilities of BCS can be divided into three areas: presentation, connectivity, and tooling. External Lists are the primary presentation mechanism for data in SharePoint, while SharePoint Workspace and Outlook are the primary Office applications. BCS can natively connect to databases, SOAP web services, and WCF services; you can also define your own custom connection to aggregate or transform data by creating a .NET assembly connector or custom connector. SharePoint Designer offers a graphical, wizard-based experience for creating ECTs, External Lists and InfoPath forms. Visual Studio can be used to create code-based components from scratch, or to enhance ECTs created or modified in SPD.

All the core BCS runtime and administration infrastructure is available in SharePoint Foundation, as are the External List capabilities. SharePoint Server adds web parts and Secure Store functionality, as well as the ability to connect External Lists to Office client applications.

BCS provides support for several different authentication schemes, including Trusted Subsystem and Impersonation and Delegation. You can also connect to a Claims-enabled WCF service to exchange SAML tokens or, by writing code, connect to a token-based service that uses OAuth.

At this point you understand the fundamental BCS concepts and have seen a sample end-to-end scenario. Chapter 2 takes an in-depth look at the different BCS components within SharePoint — from the administration and runtime infrastructure to the External Lists and web parts that end users interact with.

2

Using BCS Solutions in SharePoint 2010

WHAT'S IN THIS CHAPTER

- Understand server-side components
- Learn to administer the BDC Service
- Understand External Lists and web parts
- Learn to use Workflow with BCS

External Content Types form the backbone of BCS solutions by defining how SharePoint and Office interact with External Systems. Once you have created ECTs you can use them in SharePoint in a variety of ways. External Lists are the simplest way to surface External Data, but there are several other options in SharePoint. ECTs can be used to display data in web parts, add External Data to existing lists, interface with workflows, or act as a data source for custom components. This chapter takes a detailed look at BCS in SharePoint, from the Business Data Connectivity components that act as the plumbing to process requests for External Data, to the rich set of out-of-the-box components that enable you to present this data to end users. After reading this chapter you will understand the purpose of each component as well as how they all work together, and you will be ready to use SharePoint Designer to begin building BCS solutions.

UNDERSTANDING BUSINESS DATA CONNECTIVITY

As discussed in Chapter 1, Business Data Connectivity (BDC) is a term that encompasses the infrastructure, runtime, and administration components of BCS. Both the server and the client have BDC components, which are complementary, so you can use a similar approach to creating

BCS solutions whether you are focused on the server, the client, or both. On the server, the BDC components consist of the BDC Service Application, the BDC Service Application Proxy, the Metadata Store, and the BDC Server Runtime. On the client, the BDC components consist of a metadata cache, a dispatcher, a sync agent, and the BDC Client Runtime. Client components are explored in more detail in Chapter 3.

We begin by looking at External Content Types and how they relate to the BDC Metadata Model, and then examine the various components of the BDC Service Application and how you manage them.

Introducing the BDC Metadata Model

For each External Data element that you want to make available to end users through BCS, an External Content Type must be created. An ECT (referred to in SharePoint 2007 as an entity) is simply a series of XML fragments that describe how to interact with an External System. At a high level, an ECT can be thought of as:

- A table, or a view from a database
- A result set from a T-SQL statement, or
- A result set from a web method call

For example, a `Product` ECT might specify that `ProductID`, `Description`, `Category`, and `Cost` fields be returned from an ERP system when a particular `Product` record is requested by passing in `ProductID`.

Additionally, an ECT defines the operations that can be performed against the External System. These operations can be mapped to a set of stereotyped Methods that BDC understands. A detailed list of Methods supported by BDC can be found in Chapter 4. The five most common stereotyped Methods enable you to perform CRUD operations (Create, Read a single item, Update, Delete, and Query for a list of items) and can be generated with SharePoint Designer. They are:

- `Finder` (read list)
- `SpecificFinder` (read item)
- `Creator` (create)
- `Updater` (update)
- `Deleter` (delete)

In certain scenarios you may want to represent a subset of operations for an External System (such as read and update, but not create or delete). This is allowed; in most cases you must at minimum define a `SpecificFinder` method. This will enable scenarios that involve only retrieving items, such as External Data columns in lists, and the Business Data Item web part. Scenarios that also present a list of items (such as External Lists, or the Business Data List web part) will additionally require that a `Finder` method be defined.

Data structures such as the External Content Type and its stereotyped Methods (which define the available operations) and `TypeDescriptors` (which define the fields) abstract out complex details about an External System. These are collectively referred to as *Metadata Objects*, and make up the *BDC Metadata Model*. The Metadata Model, a single XML file, abstracts the underlying physical sources and provides a consistent way to interact with different kinds of External Systems. In SharePoint 2007 the Metadata Model was referred to as an application definition file, commonly abbreviated "appdef" or "app def."

There are multiple ways to create Metadata Model files. When you are using SharePoint Designer to define a new ECT, a Metadata Model is automatically created, assigned a GUID-based name, and uploaded to the Metadata Store. The ECT is contained within that model file. Alternatively, you can upload a model to the Metadata Store on the SharePoint server using the Central Administration pages or BDC Administration OM.

Once a Metadata Model has been saved to the Metadata Store, External Content Types defined in the model can then be used by out-of-the-box components or custom components to present External Data to end users. Note that Metadata Model names must be unique within a Business Connectivity Services service application.

"External Content Type" Versus "Entity"

You will see both terms referenced throughout this book; treat them as synonymous.

External Content Type *(ECT) is used in SharePoint Designer, SharePoint UI (External Lists, External Data columns, and External Data web parts), and the BDC Server administration UI. Like a standard Content Type within SharePoint, an External Content Type is intended to define a reusable element that defines schema and behavior.*

In order to maintain backward compatibility with Microsoft Office SharePoint Server 2007, both the BDC Runtime and Administration Object Models continue to use the term Entity *instead of* ECT. *Thus applications (such as Visual Studio) and artifacts (such as the Metadata Model) that deal with lower-level constructs also use the term* Entity.

In addition to defining the schema of External Data and the methods necessary to perform CRUD operations against it, the BDC Metadata Model can contain other useful metadata such as the following:

- **Associations:** Relationships between External Content Types. An association points to a method on the External System that accepts one or more ECT instances as input and returns a set of ECT instances of another type of External Data. A typical example of such a method is a `GetOrdersByCustomer` method on the `Customer` ECT that accepts a `CustomerID` as input and returns a list of orders.
- **Filters:** `Limit`, `Wildcard`, `UserContext`, and other filter types that pass values to the External System to facilitate fetching the smallest set of external items that match the user's criteria.

- **Default settings:** The values that should be used in communicating with the External System, in the absence of specific user input. These are most commonly associated with filters.
- **Actions:** A hyperlink to a URL in which information about an external item can be passed as input to the target page in the form of a query string parameter.

This additional metadata is extremely powerful, as it can be leveraged through BDC Runtime object model calls such as `Entity.FindFiltered` and `Entity.FindAssociated`. This makes it simple to get the External Data you need in a consistent way from multiple heterogeneous External Systems. Detailed examples using various BDC metadata objects are contained throughout the book.

BDC Metadata Store

BDC Metadata Models are stored in a relational database and loaded into memory before they are interpreted by the BDC Runtime. The database tables and stored procedures for holding, reading, and modifying the BDC Metadata Model constitute the BDC Metadata Store (also called the Metadata catalog). This component exists only on server deployments of Business Connectivity Services. To edit a Metadata Model that has been saved to the Metadata Store, you may do either of the following:

- Export the model, make the necessary modifications to the XML file, and re-import it (through the BDC Service Application's Central Administration UI or by using PowerShell).
- Use the BDC Administration object model to edit individual elements.

Editing the Metadata Store database directly is not supported. For Office client deployments, the Metadata Store is replaced by an in-memory copy of the BDC Metadata Model obtained from the client cache — a Microsoft SQL Server Compact Edition database. Chapter 3 covers this architecture in detail.

Resource Files

In addition to the Metadata Model file that contains the base XML metadata for a system, a second type of XML file (referred to as a *Resource file*) can optionally be used to isolate specific metadata elements that commonly change. These include:

- **Localized names:** Names for metadata objects in a particular locale. For example, English, French, and Spanish field names for an ECT and its filter parameters.
- **Properties:** Properties for metadata objects. For example, authentication mode, ECT version, and data source connection settings.
- **Permissions:** Access control lists (ACLs) for metadata objects. For example, the security group containing users who have rights to retrieve customer information.

Although the preceding information can be added directly to the Metadata Model file, separating some or all of these elements into a distinct Resource file can be useful in certain situations.

When uploading a new Metadata Model, BDC deletes the existing metadata and replaces it with the new file. This can lead to additional testing/validation effort, as well as requiring a full crawl of External Systems described in the model by the Search indexer. If you import Resource files containing localized names, properties, or permissions, however, BDC merges the contents of the Resource file with existing metadata.

Resource files are useful, for example, if you have an existing model for an ERP system. If your External System's connection information changes, or you wish to add support for additional languages to your application, you can easily create a Resource file containing new connection settings for the External System(s) or localized names for properties. Resource files are also useful for moving among development, staging, and production environments by isolating the settings that are specific to a given environment and making them easier to identify and change. Chapter 5 shows how to create Resource files.

Versioning

Metadata Model files as a whole are not versioned, but External Content Types within a model file are. `Version` is a property of the `Entity` (External Content Type) metadata object; it's a string property of the form `1.0.0.0`. The following code shows the `Version` property on an `Entity` inside a Metadata Model:

```
<?xml version="1.0" encoding="utf-16" standalone="yes"?>
<Model>
  ...
    <Entities>
      <Entity Namespace="http://www.contoso.com" Version="1.0.0.0"
       EstimatedInstanceCount="10000" Name="Product"
       DefaultDisplayName="Product">
      </Entity>
    </Entities>
  ...
</Model>
```

Saving an ECT from SharePoint Designer will automatically increment the fourth digit of the version by one (e.g., changing `1.0.0.0` to `1.0.0.1`) regardless of the type of change made. Importing a model through the Central Administration UI will not auto-increment the version; it is up to you to edit this property in the file itself. Model import will fail if an ECT with the same name and version already exists in the Metadata Store. The first two digits are typically incremented when a "breaking change" occurs (for example, the data type of a field has changed, or a required field has been added); the last two digits are used to signify "non-breaking changes" (for example, to the default value for a filter).

The `Version` property exists primarily to enable you to track changes within your solution components, but it is checked by InfoPath when an External List form is accessed. When an InfoPath form is created for an External List, the version of the ECT associated with the list is stored as a property in the form. When the form is accessed by an end user (in SharePoint or within the Office client), the current version of the ECT is retrieved from the metadata cache; if the first and second digits match, the form can be opened. If the first or second digits have changed, the ECT schema is assumed to have changed in a fashion that would "break" the form and prevent a user from successfully submitting a change to the External System. InfoPath will display an error on form open; the form must then be opened in InfoPath Designer and republished.

To simplify the process of identifying what has changed, InfoPath Designer will automatically refresh the form's data source on form open — this will retrieve the latest ECT schema from the Metadata Store. The designer of the form should manually adjust form elements as required based on the changes that have occurred. (For example, by dragging a new required field onto a view or removing a field that has been deleted in the External System.)

The Metadata Store can contain multiple versions of an ECT, but only one of them can be active at a given time. The version shown in the Administration UI is the active version, although it may not be the latest, as you can activate older versions. You can also manipulate ECT versions through PowerShell.

It is a best practice to minimize the number of inactive ECTs in your BDC Service(s) — these can lead to clutter and confusion in the Central Administration UI and, in certain cases, to profile pages having redundant web parts added to them. Before importing a Metadata Model, first delete obsolete versions of that model. SharePoint Designer will automatically delete previous ECT versions when saving an ECT.

BDC Service Application

The BDC Service Application is installed as part of SharePoint setup and can be administered through the Central Administration site. The Service Application is comprised of several components, including the BDC Metadata Store database, where settings such as Metadata Model files are stored. Figure 2-1 shows the basic architecture of the BDC Service Application.

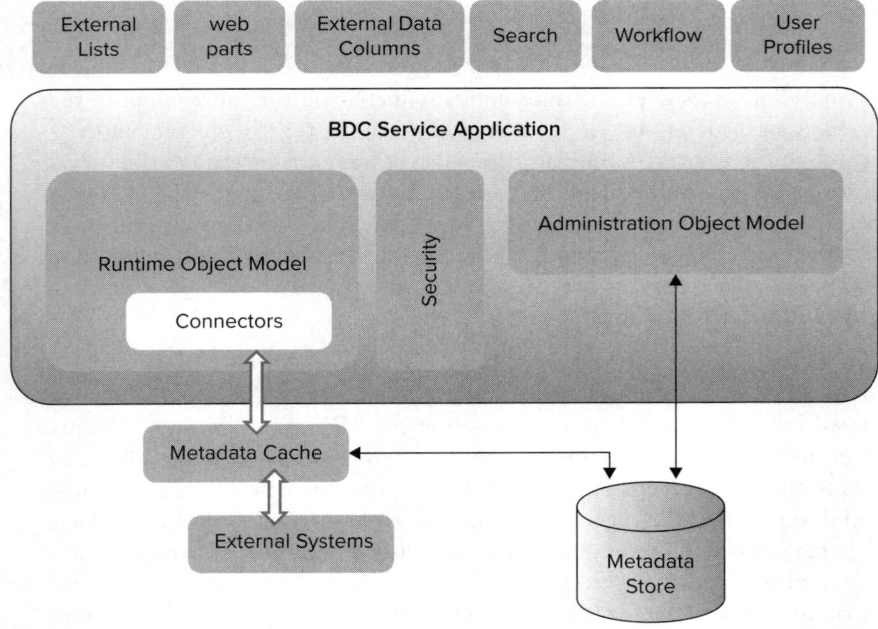

FIGURE 2-1

When an end user browses to a SharePoint page, a connection is established to a front-end SharePoint server. If that page hosts a component that uses BCS to access External Data, the appropriate Metadata Model settings and External Data Connectors are used to access the External System(s) and retrieve data through the BDC Runtime object model.

To optimize performance, a metadata cache is maintained by the BDC Service so that the service can quickly access ECT data without having to read it directly from the Metadata Store database. This metadata cache is updated every 60 seconds to ensure that the latest settings are available to the farm. It is important to note that the BDC Metadata Store does not contain rows of External Data; it contains only metadata about External Systems. The metadata cache refresh interval cannot be modified.

For multi-server SharePoint farm deployments, the BDC runtime OM is hosted on front-end SharePoint servers, while the other components of the BDC Service Application typically reside on one or more application servers.

Managing the BDC Service Application

The BDC Service is part of the Service Application framework in SharePoint and can be managed just like other services such as Search, InfoPath, and User Profiles. You can access the management user interface for the BDC Service through the Central Administration site by selecting Application Management ➪ Manage Service Applications. Most tasks can also be scripted using Windows PowerShell. Figure 2-2 shows the main BDC Service Application management page in Central Administration, located at `http://server:port/_admin/BDC/ViewBDCApplication.aspx`.

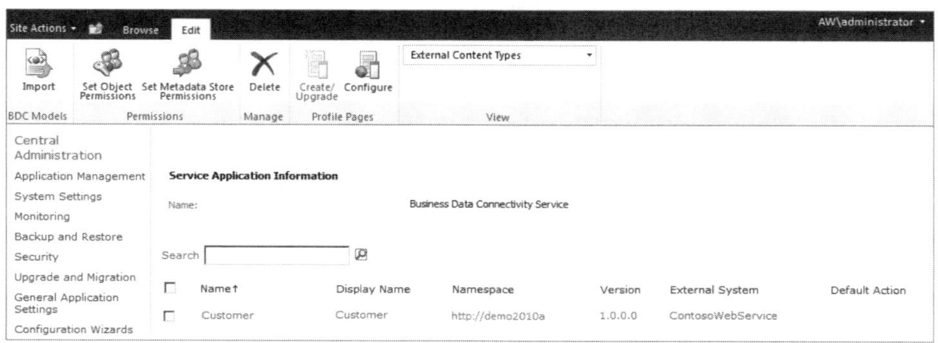

FIGURE 2-2

You can perform the following common tasks to manage components of the BDC Service:

- Set permissions.
- Import and export Metadata Models and Resource files.
- Manage External Content Types:
    - View all ECTs for a BDC Service app.
    - View all ECTs for a Metadata Model file.

 - View details of a given ECT.
 - Delete an ECT.
 - Add an action to an ECT.
 - Define a location for storing profile pages.
 - Create or update the profile page for an ECT.
 - Set permissions.
- Manage External Systems and External System instances.

Permissions

In order to manage any aspect of the BDC Service, a user must have rights to access the BDC Service and Metadata Store. For farm installations, these rights are *not* automatically granted to the account that was used to run SharePoint setup — you must configure permissions for the service. Farm administrators or existing administrators of this instance of the BDC Service can grant BDC Service permissions to other users. To assign one or more administrators to the BDC Service, navigate to an instance of a BDC Service Application within the Central Administration site and click the Edit tab of the ribbon. Click the Assign Administrators action within the Permissions group. Figure 2-3 shows the Set Metadata Store Permissions page used to grant access to an instance of a BDC Service Application.

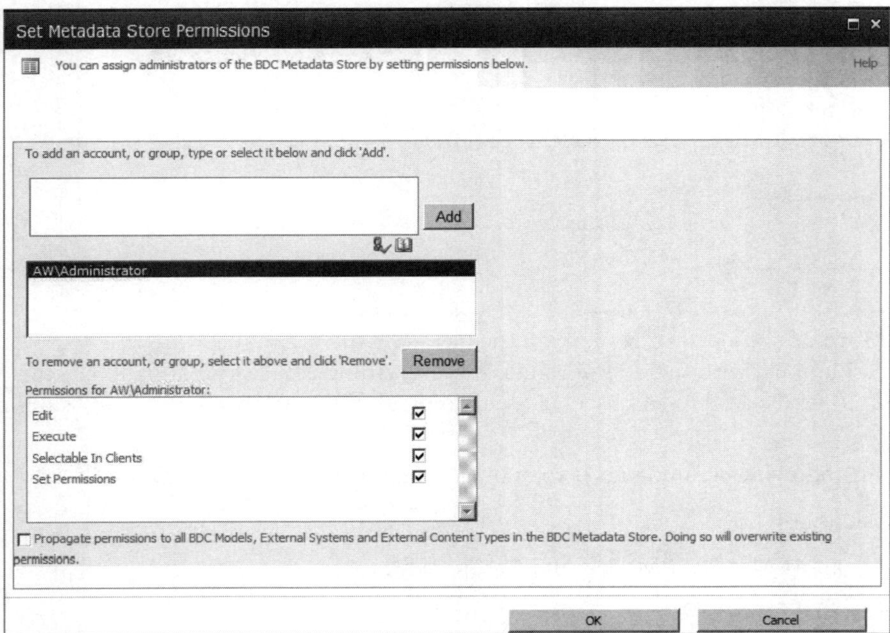

FIGURE 2-3

This page enables you to specify individual users, security groups, or claims that will be able to access this BDC Service Application. There are four rights that can be granted to each user, group, or claim:

1. **Edit:** Allows the editing of existing, or the creation of new, External Systems, BDC Metadata Models, and External Content Types
2. **Execute:** Allows the execution of operations (create, read, update, delete, and query) on External Content Types
3. **Selectable in clients:** Allows the user to select External Content Types via the ECT picker control and use them as data sources when creating External Lists, or when adding/configuring External Data columns, web parts, etc.
4. **Set permissions:** Allows the user to grant access to others to manage External Content Types, External Systems, and BDC Metadata Models

It is worth noting that after typing or picking an account or group, you must click the Add button to move the account to the second text box, which then allows you to select the different permissions options. Entering an account and clicking OK to submit the page will *not* set any default permissions.

The final checkbox on the page, labeled "Propagate permissions to all BDC Metadata Models, External Systems and External Content Types in the BDC Metadata Store," must be selected if you wish to grant rights to existing elements of the BDC Service Application. For example, to grant a user access to update an item in an existing External List called Products, you would grant Execute permissions and select the checkbox to propagate permissions.

The preceding steps can be used to grant access to the BDC Service Application and all elements below it, including Metadata Models, External Systems, and External Content Types. It is also possible to control permissions at each level in this hierarchy by navigating to the appropriate node and using the Set Object Permissions action in the ribbon.

There are three groups of users that may require BDC permissions: SharePoint administrators, power users and developers building BCS solutions (referred to jointly as *BCS developers*), and end users. A SharePoint administrator will grant the necessary permissions to the BCS developers at a particular level in the metadata hierarchy (for example, at the level of everything under a particular external system, or of the entire Metadata Store). BCS developers can now create and edit new ECTs/Metadata Models at and below this level in the metadata hierarchy. They are able to build and test their BCS solutions, with full admin rights over everything they are creating. Once the solutions are ready to be released to end users, a SharePoint administrator will edit permissions on the ECTs/Metadata Models so end users are able to access the data.

Editing ECT Permissions in SharePoint Designer

When you are modifying an External Content Type in SPD, permissions specific to that ECT in the Metadata Catalog are reset. To avoid having to reapply these permissions each time, set permissions at the BDC Service level instead.

Model Import

Importing a BDC Metadata Model is the easiest way to add it, and its related External Content Types, to a Metadata Store. To import a BDC Metadata Model or Resource file you must have either farm administrator rights or Edit rights for an instance of the BDC Service Application. Figure 2-4 shows the Import BDC Metadata Model page, which can be accessed from a BDC Service Application page: in the "BDC Metadata Models" group of the Edit tab, click Import.

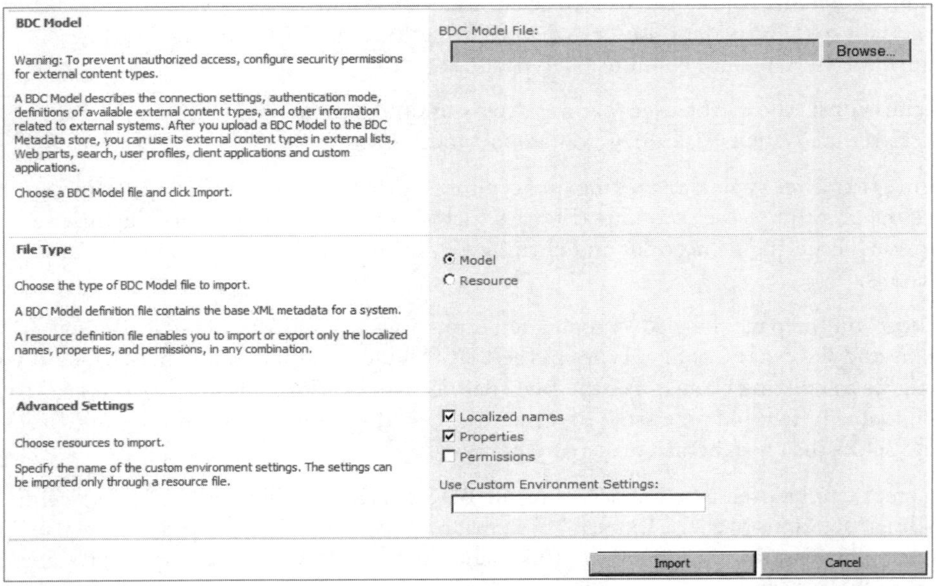

FIGURE 2-4

Use the Browse button to locate the BDC Metadata Model or Resource file, or enter the path in the corresponding text box. Next, specify its file type: Model or Resource.

If you are importing a Resource file you must select one or more types of resource to import:

- **Localized names:** Import localized names for the External Content Types in a particular location. Imported localized names are merged with existing localized names.
- **Properties:** Import properties for External Content Types. Imported properties are merged with existing property descriptions.
- **Permissions:** Import permissions for External Content Types. If permissions for an External Content Type already exist in the access control list stored by the BDC Service, their values are overwritten with those supplied in the imported file. For example, User 1 has access to the External Content Type called Products. If you import permissions that specify that only User 2 has access to Products, the previous permissions for Products will be deleted and new permissions will be stored that specify only User 2 has access.

You can optionally save the group of imported resource settings for future export to a file. To do this, type a unique name for this group of settings in the Use Custom Environment Settings field.

Model Export

Exporting a BDC Metadata Model or Resource file is useful for common tasks like moving an application from a development environment to a production environment. To export a BDC Metadata Model or Resource file you must have either farm administrator rights or Edit rights for an instance of the BDC Service Application. To access the Model Export page click the Edit tab in an instance of a BDC Service application. In the View group click "BDC Metadata Models." On the subsequent BDC Metadata Models page, select the model or resource file to export and click Export. Figure 2-5 shows the Model Export page.

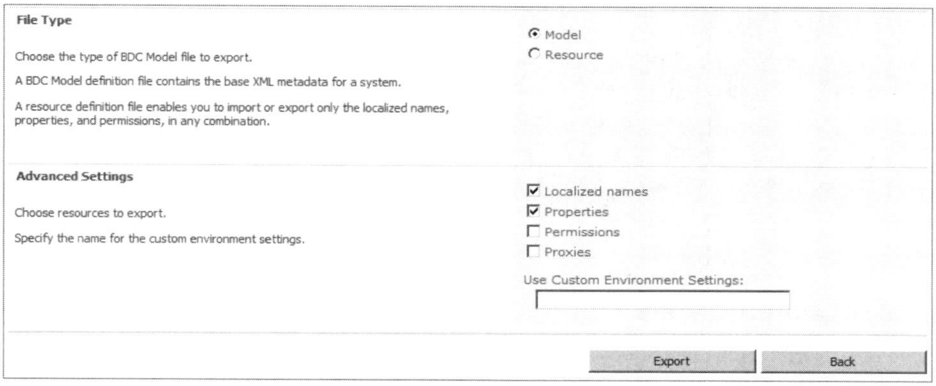

FIGURE 2-5

The File Type section is used to select the type of file you are exporting, either a BDC Metadata Model or a Resource file.

If you are exporting a Resource file, in the Advanced Settings area select one or more types of resource to export:

- Localized names for the External Content Type(s)
- Properties for the External Content Type(s)
- Permissions for the External Content Type(s)
- Proxies for the selected External Content Type(s) that enable BDC to connect to the external system

If you previously saved a set of resources for later use by specifying a value in the Use Custom Environment Settings field, you can type the unique name of the file that contains these environment-specific settings in the Use Custom Environment Settings field and it will be exported.

Clicking Export will prompt you for a location in which to save the BDC Metadata Model or Resource file.

You can also export one or more ECTs into a Metadata Model file through the BDC Administration OM or through SharePoint Designer. More details on SharePoint Designer can be found in Chapter 4.

EXPORTING FROM SHAREPOINT DESIGNER VERSUS CENTRAL ADMIN

You cannot upload an ECT to the BDC Metadata Store unless it is part of a BDC Metadata Model file. Thus, when you create a new ECT using SPD, BCS automatically creates a model file and provides a GUID as its name. That model is not intended to be exported and used in the same scenarios as handcrafted model files (such as for editing properties and then importing, or for sharing across SharePoint farms). The only way to export External Content Types that have been created via SPD is through the Export button in SPD itself.

It's also worth noting that SPD will export permissions by default, whereas Central Administration gives you the option to export permissions, but this option is not selected by default. As discussed earlier in this section, the Model Export page has four checkboxes near the bottom under Advanced Settings. SPD will generate a model with all four boxes selected and export it, whereas Central Administration selects only the top two boxes (Localized Names and Properties) by default.

Managing External Content Types

To manage settings for a particular External Content Type, while in an instance of the BDC Service, click the Edit tab in the ribbon. In the View group, click External Content Types. You can select an ECT to act on by clicking the arrow next to the ECT name. Some actions, such as Delete, allow you to multi-select by selecting multiple checkboxes and then clicking the appropriate command in the ribbon.

Figure 2-6 shows the View External Content Types page and the actions available on a given ECT.

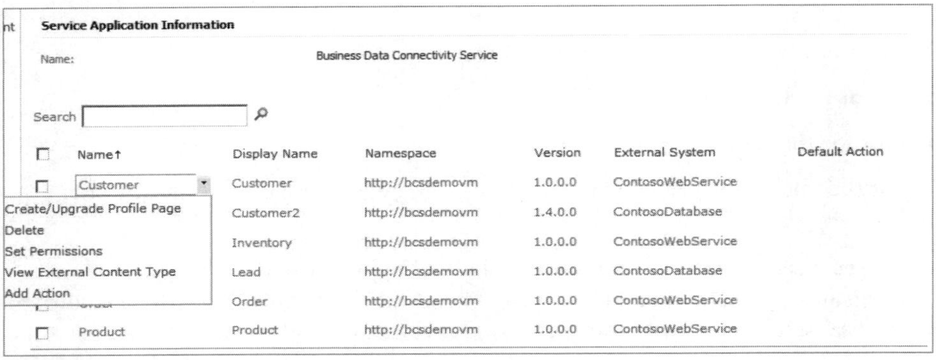

FIGURE 2-6

Managing Actions

External Data actions open a web page that can interpret information about an external item and provide useful information about that item. Actions are an outstanding means of integrating with existing web-based systems that rely on query string parameters. Each action is associated with a particular ECT; it has a name and a target URL. An action can also provide one or more dynamic parameters that are passed to the target web page in the query string; this enables the target page to provide contextually relevant information based on the external item that the user is working with.

For example, the following XML fragment is from a BDC Metadata Model file that contains an action with two parameters:

```
<Actions>
  <Action
    Name="Map This Customer"
    Position="1"
    IsOpenedInNewWindow="true"
Url="http://www.bing.com/maps/default.aspx?where1={0},{1}"
    ImageUrl="">
    <ActionParameters>
      <ActionParameter Name="AddressLine1" Index="0" />
      <ActionParameter Name="AddressLine2" Index="1" />
      </ActionParameters>
  </Action>
</Actions>
```

Now when a user navigates to the Customers External List created in Chapter 1, he or she sees an additional action available for each row in the list: Map This Customer. Clicking that action for a particular row in the list will result in BCS displaying the selected customer's address using Bing maps. The URL is constructed at runtime by a concatenation of the base URL for Bing with each `ActionParameter` element and its value. If the value is a string that contains spaces, each space is replaced with a +.

Thus at runtime the format is
`URL?ActionParameter0=ActionParameter0Value&ActionParameter1=ActionParameter1Value`

The actual URL for the customer shown in the screenshot is `http://www.bing.com/maps/default.aspx?where1=3761+N+14th+St,Tacoma,WA`.

Figure 2-7 shows the target Bing Maps page and the fully constructed URL, including values for the address of the selected customer.

You can create and modify External Data actions through the BDC Service administration pages, such as by defining permissions for the action, setting input parameters, and marking one action per ECT as the default. Actions can also be added directly to a Metadata Model file and imported to the BDC Service. Figure 2-8 shows the administration page used to add an action to an ECT.

FIGURE 2-7

Name

Type a name for the action.

Action Name

URL

Type the URL to navigate to when you click on the action. If you want the URL to vary depending on the item to which it applies, add one or more parameters, then assign a property to each parameter below. Type a number in braces such as {0} where you want to insert a parameter in the URL.

Navigate To This URL

Example: http://example.com/edit.aspx?id={0}

Launch the action in a new Web browser window (applies to External Data Web Parts only):

○ Yes ◉ No

URL Parameters

Assign a property to each parameter in the URL.

Parameter Property

Add Parameter

Icon

Choose an icon to display next to the action.

◉ No icon

○ Standard icon Delete

○ The image at this URL

Default action

Select the check box if you want this to be the default action.

☐ Default action

External lists created before adding an action will not list this action automatically. Only new external lists will display the action in the context menu.

OK Cancel

FIGURE 2-8

The structure and basic capabilities of actions haven't changed since Microsoft Office SharePoint Server 2007, but actions can be leveraged in more places with BCS. When an External List is created, all the actions for the list's corresponding ECT are copied and created as User Custom Actions on the list itself. These actions are surfaced in the menu for each item in the list, but not in the ribbon. Figure 2-9 shows standard actions (View Item, Edit Item, Delete Item) as well as an External Data action (View Profile) surfaced in an External List's item-level menu.

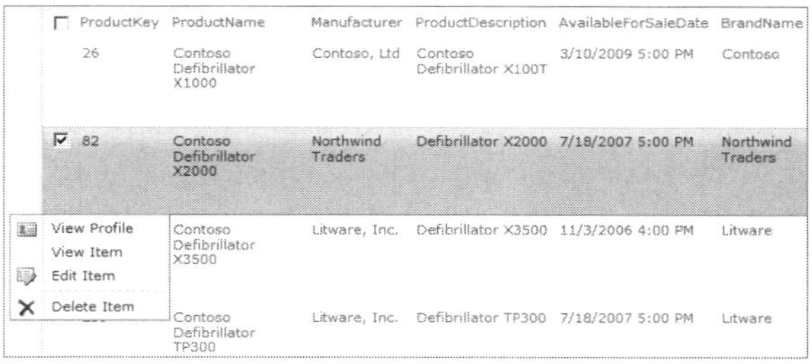

FIGURE 2-9

SharePoint Designer can be used to manage External List actions; this is discussed in Chapter 4. The BDC Administration OM can also be used to manage actions; this is discussed in Chapter 5.

Permissions defined on an External Data action are not automatically carried over to the corresponding user custom action, as there is no direct mapping for an ACL from the Metadata Model to list-level permissions. Here's one way to think about this: the External Data action is used as a template for the user custom action — the latter is created based on the settings of the former, but from that point forward it is its own object, and has its own permissions settings. If you wish to conditionally hide and show user custom actions at runtime, you can do this through standard SharePoint event receivers. (This approach works for both regular and External Lists.)

User custom actions, the component that all SharePoint lists (including External Lists) use to render and execute actions, understand a limited set of runtime parameters (such as list ID, site URL, and item ID). To enable the rich set of user-defined runtime parameters that External Data actions support, an action redirector page was built to act as an intermediary translation tier. Each action on an External List points to the action redirector page. (You can access this page via the `_layouts` path from any site.) This page takes a set of input parameters that are used to identify the corresponding External Data action (in the BDC Metadata Store) that should be executed. The structure of that action, including its runtime parameters, is then retrieved and populated based on the current context in the External List. The user is then redirected to the target URL with all input parameters filled in.

As a result of the action parameters' being retrieved at runtime, you can add and remove parameters as needed through the BDC Service administration pages. Those changes will automatically be picked up by External Lists that refer to the actions in question. If new External Data actions are added or removed, or properties of existing actions are modified in the BDC Service, however, existing External Lists will not be updated to reflect these changes. You can use the SharePoint list OM to programmatically update External Lists.

Adding a new action to an External List that points to an External Data action is a straightforward process with SharePoint Designer and is described in Chapter 4. The same task can be performed with the administration object model, which is covered in Chapter 5.

You can leverage the action redirector page from a custom web part or other component by constructing a URL that contains the correct set of input parameters. These vary slightly based on the scenario; the possible combinations are listed below.

When you are executing an action on the current item (as opposed to a related item that needs to be retrieved separately) the following parameters are required:

- `EntityNamespace`
- `EntityName`
- `LobSystemInstanceName`
- `ItemID`
- `ActionName` (if not specified, the default action for this ECT is executed)

The Action Redirector page retrieves the appropriate action and its parameters, retrieves the External Data item based on the supplied `ItemID`, constructs the URL with values filled in for each parameter, and redirects the user to the target URL.

Here is an example of a URL pointing to the ActionRedirector: `http://server/site/_layouts/ActionRedirect.aspx?EntityNamespace=AdventureWorks&EntityName=Product&LOBSystemInstanceName=AdventureWorks&ItemID=__bg801237742218323547&ActionName=Map%20This%20Customer`.

When you are executing an action on an item associated with the current item, the following parameters are required:

- `ParentEntityNamespace`
- `ParentEntityName`
- `ParentLobSystemInstanceName`
- `ParentSpecificFinderName`
- `ParentAssociationName`
- `EntityNamespace`
- `EntityName`
- `LobSystemInstanceName`
- `ItemID`
- `ActionName` (if not specified, the default action for this ECT is executed)

The Action Redirector page retrieves the appropriate action and its parameters, retrieves the related External Data item, constructs the URL with values filled in for each parameter, and redirects the user to the target URL.

Managing Profile Pages

A profile page is a SharePoint web part page that displays information about an external item. Profile pages are what users will see when clicking through on a search result for an external item, and are designed to show a 360-degree view of the item and items associated with it. One profile page can be created per ECT; parameters are passed to the page at runtime to determine which specific item to retrieve information for. When you create a profile page a View Profile action is automatically added to the corresponding ECT to make it easy for users to navigate to the page from a web part, External List, or other component that displays data for the ECT.

Profile pages automatically add the following web parts when a page is created. These parts can be customized or removed, as with any SharePoint web part page.

- **Business Data Item Builder:** This part retrieves information about the external item to be displayed from the URL and passes it to other parts on the page. It is not shown to end users at runtime.
- **Business Data Item:** This part shows details for the external item.
- **Business Data Related List:** One instance of this part is added for each association with the selected item. For example, if you are viewing details about a particular customer and the Customer ECT defines a relationship with the Orders ECT and the Sales Team ECT, two Related List parts are added to the page: one to show orders for that customer and one to show the members of the sales team who work with that customer.

These web parts are also connected to pass information within the page — the Item web part passes the ID of the item it's displaying to each of the Related List web parts, which then make calls to the External System to retrieve a list of related items. Figure 2-10 shows a Product Category profile page containing the Item Builder (hidden), Item, and Related List web parts.

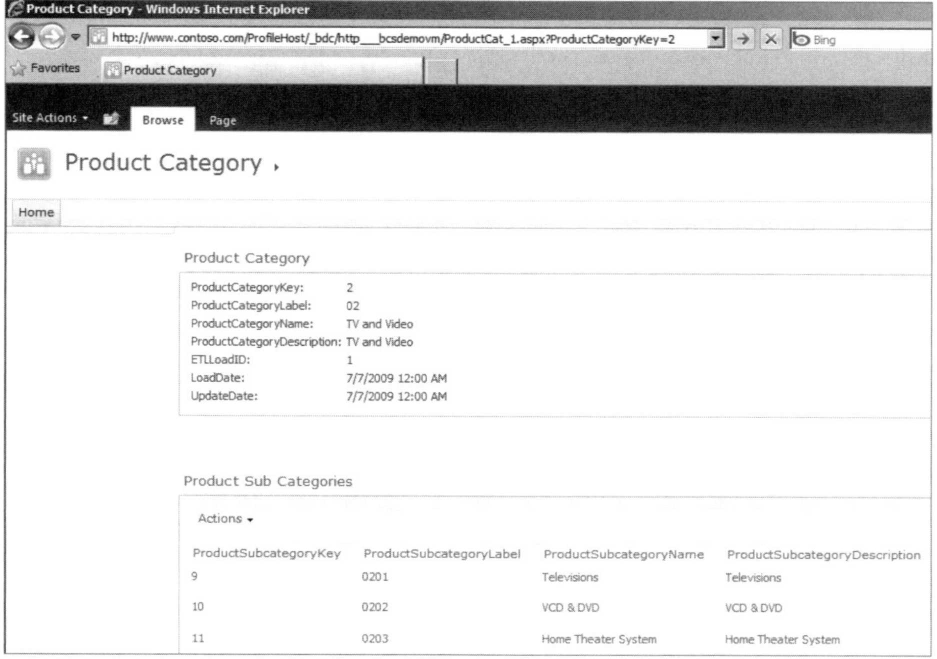

FIGURE 2-10

BCS allows profile pages to be stored in any SharePoint site. Before you can create a profile page you must first set the ECT Profile Page Host site. You can do this from the BDC Service administration pages by selecting Configure in the Profile Pages ribbon group and entering a URL such as `http://server/site`. (In Figure 2-10 the URL is `http://www.contoso.com/ProfileHost`.) This URL can be changed at any time, but profile pages hosted at the old location will remain there. A document library named `_bdc` is created at the specified site. As profile pages are created, a sub-folder will be created for each ECT namespace and the profile page for that ECT will be added to the sub-folder. Ensure that permissions on your Profile Page Host site are set to allow Design rights to users who need to create profile pages.

To create a profile page, select the External Content Type that you wish to create the page for and click Create/Upgrade in the Profile Pages ribbon group. The page is created and stored in the appropriate location, and a View Profile action is added to the ECT. If the ECT does not have any other actions, View Profile is marked as the default. This behavior is different from that of SharePoint 2007, in which a View Profile action and profile page were *automatically* created for each application definition file (i.e., Metadata Model) that was imported.

Figure 2-11 shows the View External Content Types administration page and highlights the relevant profile page actions.

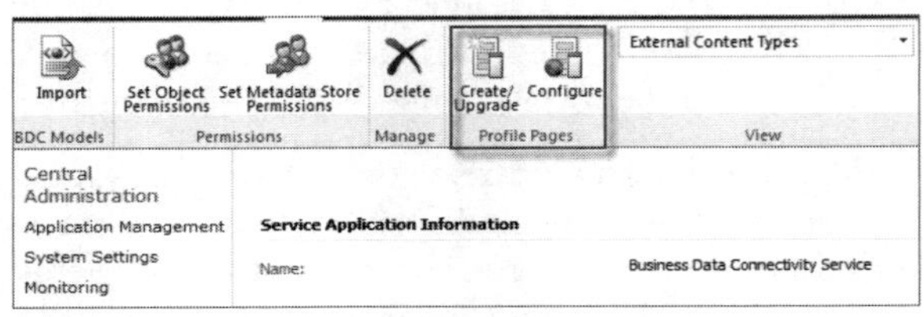

FIGURE 2-11

You can disable profile page creation by unchecking the Enable Profile Page Creation box on the ECT Profile Page Host dialog.

The BDC Admin OM also enables you to set the Profile Page Host URL and create individual profile pages.

Throttling

When you are creating applications that interact with External Systems, you must ensure optimal performance by setting limits on how many users can retrieve data at the same time, and on how many items can be retrieved in a single query. BCS allows administrators to define throttling limits per instance of a BDC Service Application.

Throttles can be created at several levels. First, you can limit the total number of concurrent connections made to External Systems. Additionally, for each connection type (also referred to as *proxy*), you can adjust five different throttle settings to limit the number of connections made and the amount of data returned from External Systems. Table 2-1 lists each throttle and its default settings.

TABLE 2-1: BDC Service Application Throttle Settings

TYPE	DESCRIPTION	SCOPE	DEFAULT	MAXIMUM
Connections	Total number of connections allowed to External Systems	Global	100	500
Items	Number of rows returned from a database query	Database	2,000	25,000
Timeout	Database connection timeout	Database	60 sec.	600 sec.
Size	Size of returned data	WCF	3 MB	150 MB
Timeout	Web service connection timeout	WCF	60 sec.	600 sec.

If a throttle limit is exceeded by a request to the BDC runtime, end users will see a generic error message. (External Lists will display an "Unable to display this web part" error, followed by a Correlation ID. Search the server log files for the Correlation ID to see the detailed throttling error, which will look like this:

```
Error while executing web part:
Microsoft.BusinessData.Runtime.ExceededLimitException:
Database Connector has throttled the response. The response
from database contains more than '2000' rows. The maximum number
of rows that can be read through Database Connector is '2000'.
The limit can be changed via the
'Set-SPBusinessDataCatalogThrottleConfig' cmdlet.
```

You manage throttles using PowerShell scripts. The following code displays the current throttle settings:

```
Add-PSSnapin Microsoft.SharePoint.PowerShell -ErrorAction SilentlyContinue
$bdc = Get-SPServiceApplicationProxy |
  Where {$_ -match "Business Data Connectivity"}

Get-SPBusinessDataCatalogThrottleConfig -ThrottleType Connections -Scope Global ➥
-ServiceApplicationProxy $bdc
Get-SPBusinessDataCatalogThrottleConfig -ThrottleType Items -Scope Database ➥
-ServiceApplicationProxy $bdc
Get-SPBusinessDataCatalogThrottleConfig -ThrottleType Timeout -Scope Database ➥
-ServiceApplicationProxy $bdc
Get-SPBusinessDataCatalogThrottleConfig -ThrottleType Size -Scope Wcf ➥
-ServiceApplicationProxy $bdc
Get-SPBusinessDataCatalogThrottleConfig -ThrottleType Timeout -Scope Wcf ➥
-ServiceApplicationProxy $bdc
```

Each of the throttle settings may be modified using PowerShell. The following code shows how to change the number of items that can be returned from a database:

```
Add-PSSnapin Microsoft.SharePoint.PowerShell -ErrorAction SilentlyContinue
$bdc = Get-SPServiceApplicationProxy |
  Where {$_ -match "Business Data Connectivity"}

$throttle = Get-SPBusinessDataCatalogThrottleConfig
  -ThrottleType Items -Scope Database ↵
-ServiceApplicationProxy $bdc
Set-SPBusinessDataCatalogThrottleConfig -Maximum 3000
  -Default 1000 -Identity $throttle
```

Alternatively, you can disable any throttle. The following code shows how to disable the connections throttle:

```
Add-PSSnapin Microsoft.SharePoint.PowerShell -ErrorAction SilentlyContinue
$bdc = Get-SPServiceApplicationProxy |
  Where {$_ -match "Business Data Connectivity"}

$throttle = Get-SPBusinessDataCatalogThrottleConfig -ThrottleType Connections ↵
-Scope Global -ServiceApplicationProxy $bdc
Set-SPBusinessDataCatalogThrottleConfig -Enforced $false -Identity $throttle
```

BDC Server OM

The BDC Server Runtime consists of the runtime object model, the administration object model, and the security infrastructure. The runtime object model provides access to External Data, while the administration object model provides objects that enable you to manage ECTs in the Metadata Store.

The runtime object model's primary role is to provide an object-oriented interface that abstracts the underlying data sources. This allows client applications to access all External Systems through a single uniform interface while avoiding logic specific to each external system. For example, the runtime object model allows you to call a method on a Siebel application in the same way that you would execute a query on a Microsoft SQL Server database. BDC delegates the call to the appropriate ADO.NET provider for databases, Web services proxy for Web services, WCF proxy for WCF services, and .NET Framework assembly for .NET Assembly Connectors. The runtime object model allows applications to read and write External Data.

A secondary role for the runtime OM is that of reading metadata objects from the Metadata Store database and executing the business logic described there. Clients that just need to query the metadata database for metadata information should use the runtime object model.

The administration object model is used to create, read, update, and delete metadata objects in the BDC Metadata Store. Metadata Models are validated during import and changes are then pushed to an in-memory metadata cache to optimize performance. This can result in relatively high latency for metadata changes and a delay of up to one minute before BDC updates this cache, which exists on all front-end web servers and application servers in the SharePoint farm. The administration OM exists both on server deployments of BCS and on Office clients.

Programming against the BDC object model is covered in detail in Chapter 5.

INTEGRATING BCS DATA WITH SHAREPOINT

Now that you understand the different BDC components on the server and how to manage them, let's take a look at the SharePoint features that allow users to interact with External Data.

Using External Lists

External Lists are the easiest and most powerful means of displaying External Data to SharePoint users. Similar in look, feel, and functionality to regular SharePoint lists, External Lists do not store their data in a SharePoint content database, nor do they cache it; they use the Business Data Connectivity layer to fetch real-time data from the external system when a user browses to a list or interacts with an item.

You create an External List the same way you create a document library or other SharePoint list: click the Site Actions menu ⇨ More Options ⇨ External List from the available list templates. Two properties must be specified for the External List: a title and a data source. The latter is simply the name of an External Content Type — it can be typed in or selected from a list of ECTs available in the BDC Service Application that the current SharePoint site is associated with.

The ECT must meet basic criteria in order to be used to provide data for an External List. At a minimum it must include a `SpecificFinder` method and at least one `Finder` method. The set of fields returned by the `Finder` must be the same as or a subset of those returned by the `SpecificFinder`. If the ECT provides `Create`, `Update`, or `Delete` methods, the corresponding create, update, or delete actions will be enabled on the list. If any of those methods are missing, the equivalent actions will not be available on the list.

When an External List is created, a column is generated for each field defined in the ECT, with the display name of the field used as the name of the column. If multiple localized display names are available, SharePoint will use the location of the site to find a match and fall back to the default if the location is not available.

Where possible, data types are mapped directly — a string in the ECT is mapped to a `String` column in the list. One common exception to this rule is `DateTime` fields — a `String` column will be created in the list. Although the data from the external system will be presented to the user in the same format, sorting for these columns will not be the same as for `DateTime` fields on regular lists. (For example, 10/2/2011 will appear before 2/2/2011.)

External Lists support all the standard SharePoint data types, plus they add support for Decimal columns. These are similar to Double columns on regular lists, but allow for greater precision: 28 decimal places instead of 15.

The BDC runtime supports a wider range of data types than SharePoint, and thus direct mapping is not possible for INT64 or any custom type not supported by the .NET Framework.

In addition, any complex fields (nested structures such as `Address`, which contains `Number`, `Street`, `City`, and `State` sub-fields) will not be mapped to columns at list creation time. You can flatten complex fields by using complex formatting in your BDC Metadata Model, but this has the downside of preventing write-back to the external system.

To overcome these limitations, you can define custom field types in the ECT and in custom code deployed to SharePoint. Chapter 5 discusses custom field types in detail and provides an example that allows INT64 fields to be rendered in an External List and its forms, as well as enabling write-back to the external system for those fields.

Permissions

To create an External List, a user must have certain permissions. He or she must have the Manage Lists right on the SharePoint site, and two rights configurable through the BDC Service administration pages: the Execute and Selectable in Clients rights for the ECT that will act as the list's data source.

By default the External List inherits security from the parent site. As with any other list, inheritance can be broken and security managed directly on the list itself. In order to access the list, edit items, or create new views, users must have the corresponding SharePoint permissions. CRUDQ operations have additional layers of security — users must have BDC rights as well as rights on the external system itself.

View Settings

When the list is first created, one view is generated for each Finder method on the ECT. These views can be customized or deleted and new views can be created. The default view corresponds to the default Finder method. View settings generally operate the same as regular lists, with two key exceptions: data source filters and paging.

Data source filters are a setting unique to External Lists and enable you to control the parameters that are sent to the external system at runtime when you are retrieving data for the selected view. If the ECT for an External List contains filter parameters, they will automatically be converted to data source filters along with their default values. The well-known Filters capability found on regular lists also exists for ELs, but acts on the data only once it is in memory on the front-end SharePoint server. Data source filters are critical to building and maintaining scalable BCS solutions that minimize the load on External Systems. Figure 2-12 shows the path a user request travels to retrieve content from an external system and render data in an External List.

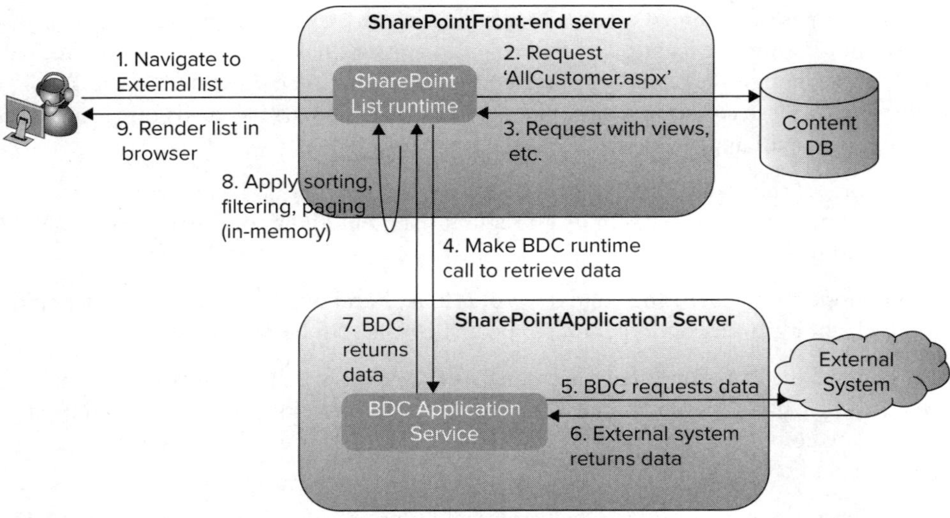

FIGURE 2-12

Paging works differently on External Lists than it does on other SharePoint lists. Standard lists store content in the SharePoint content database, which supports the ability to retrieve a fixed number of records (commonly referred to as a *page*) at a time. This is useful, as it minimizes load on the database — the only items retrieved are those displayed to the user. BDC supports connecting to any external system, which may or may not support this ability to retrieve a page. Thus External Lists will call the `Finder` method for the current view, passing along the appropriate data source filters, and then extract a subset of rows to display in the list. To illustrate how data source filters, standard filters, and paging settings defined on an External List view work together, let's look at the following example.

Building on the AdventureWorks scenario introduced in Chapter 1, imagine we have enhanced the Customers ECT by adding two filter parameters for the default `Finder` method. These are a limit filter with a default value of `50` that we've named `MaxCustomers`, and a wildcard filter defined for the `SalesRegion` field that we've named `SalesRegion`. We've also created a new External List whose data source is the recently enhanced Customers ECT. This list contains a single view (which corresponds to the ECT's only `Finder` method) that has two data source filters: `MaxCustomers` (default `50`) and `SalesRegion` (default `NULL`). When a user browses to our new External List, 50 customers will be retrieved from the database and the first 30 will be displayed in the default list view. The full 50 customers aren't displayed because we didn't change the item limit for the view — by default SharePoint displays 30 items at a time. If we reduce `MaxCustomers` from `50` to `20` in the view settings page, the External List will retrieve 20 customers from the database and show all 20 in the view. To see the full 50 customers in a single page we would set the `MaxCustomers` data source filter and the item limit to `50`. To be even more efficient in retrieving data we could specify `North` as the value for our `SalesRegion` filter. It's a wildcard filter, so it will be interpreted by our external system (SQL Server database) as a `LIKE` operator. Thus our data set will return only items whose `SalesRegion` field contains the string `North`. If we wanted to exclude regions such as Northeast and Northwest and show data only from our North region, we could open SharePoint Designer and change the filter type from `Wildcard` to `Comparison`, and set the operator for the new comparison filter to `Equals`.

DateTime Fields

As noted previously, `DateTime` fields in an ECT are mapped to `String` columns in External Lists. As SharePoint does not support date-only fields, both a date and time must be specified, or a custom field type supplied. (The latter allows you to control how the field should be formatted and presented to the user in both list views and auto-generated SharePoint list forms, avoiding the need to rewrite the entire view/form.)

External Systems commonly use Coordinated Universal Time (UTC) as the time zone in which to store data. While this works well for data storage, end users prefer to work with their local time zones. External Lists and the External Data web parts tackle this problem by converting time zones before presenting `DateTime` fields to end users, as well as before submitting `DateTime` values to the external system.

After retrieving a `DateTime` field from an external system, the BDC runtime examines the `DateTime.Kind` property to determine its time zone. If it is `UTC` or `Unspecified`, no action is taken. If it is marked as `Local`, BDC converts it to UTC by applying an offset based on the SharePoint front-end web server's time zone, as specified by its Windows settings.

Now that the time zone has been standardized to UTC, the External List examines the user profile settings for the current user; if a time zone has been specified, the time is converted from UTC to the user's time zone. If a time zone has not been specified (which is the default state), the time zone of the site on which the External List is hosted is used to convert the External Data. The converted times are then presented to the user in the UI (in some format such as dd/mm/yyyy hh:mm:ss) according to the site locale.

Forms

Two forms technologies can be used with External Lists: autogenerated SharePoint forms and InfoPath forms. Autogenerated SharePoint forms are the default option, available in both SharePoint Foundation and SharePoint Server. They provide a simple, clean user experience and can be extended with custom field types. They can also be connected to the XSLT ListView web part (which is used to render list views for both regular and External Lists) or other ASP.Net parts to enable master-detail scenarios. If the External List contains complex fields or fields not supported by SharePoint, update and create forms will not be generated unless custom field types have been defined for each field. These forms also cannot be customized with different colors, layout, or business logic.

InfoPath forms are available only in SharePoint Server with Enterprise CAL, but offer rich customization as well as consistent client-server functionality. Users can interact with the same customized External List form in the browser and in SharePoint Workspace. InfoPath forms are hosted inside the Browser Form web part, which does not support part-to-part connections. Custom field types that have been registered with BDC and SharePoint will not work with InfoPath forms, but InfoPath does offer broader support for data types as well as support for complex fields. Chapter 4 provides more detail about InfoPath form creation and customization.

The following table compares the two out-of-the-box form technologies for External Lists.

TABLE 2-2: External List Forms Comparison

CAPABILITY	SHAREPOINT FORMS	INFOPATH FORMS
One-click form creation	Yes	Yes
Custom field support	Custom field type	Custom control (client-only)
Complex field support	Custom field type	Yes
Part-to-part communication	Yes	No
Basic customization (layout, colors, declarative business logic)	No	Yes
Advanced customization (code-based business logic)	No	Yes
Server form also works in Office client	No	Yes

Differences from Regular Lists

As noted earlier, one of the goals in creating External Lists is to achieve the same look, feel, and functionality as regular lists. Broadly speaking this has been achieved, but there are differences that you need to be aware of. Consider firing programmatic events that are useful for triggering workflows and custom code to act on data that has just changed. Without a server-side cache of External Data (which itself introduces new technical challenges) or a channel with which External Systems can push changes to SharePoint lists, with External Lists there's no straightforward way to fire an event when data changes.

Another difference relates to modifying External List schema — for example, adding to the Customers External List a column that is useful to a particular sales rep but not the entire sales department. Because the structure of the list is hard-coded to be that of its backing External Content Type, it is not possible to add, delete, or edit columns through the UI or OM. It is possible, however, to enable the reverse scenario — to start with a regular SharePoint list and add External Data columns that map to fields of an ECT. This is discussed later in this chapter.

The following SharePoint capabilities — some out-of-the-box capabilities and some extensibility points — are not available with External Lists:

- Data access with REST
- RSS feeds
- Datasheet view
- Eventing
  - Triggering workflow directly
  - Custom event receivers
- Adding, editing, or deleting columns
- Adding content types (one hardcoded `Item` content type is created per list)
- Versioning of items
- Check-in and checkout of items
- Folders
- Search (not available at the list scope, but available at broader scopes where ECTs rather than lists are crawled — see Chapter 9)
- Attachments (`Byte[]` fields in an ECT can be combined with a custom field type to render content, but `StreamAccessor` methods are not supported for External List views or forms. Consider using External Data web parts, which do support this scenario.)

Other list features are available with External Lists but act differently or gain additional capabilities. As discussed earlier in the "Managing Actions" section, External Data actions are converted automatically to user custom actions when an External List is created. These actions enable a wider set of runtime variables to be passed to the target URL, and can be customized with SharePoint Designer or the SharePoint OM. It is still possible to define additional user custom actions to navigate to a form, start a workflow, or open a URL. External Lists can also be connected to Office client applications — Outlook and SharePoint Workspace. This functionality is similar to what regular lists offer for SharePoint Workspace, but External Lists offer much broader customization options in the case of Outlook. Chapter 6 discusses this in more detail.

The last significant difference involves *lookup fields*, or associations between the current list and another data source. Users can leverage lookup fields to add a column to a current list that points to a different SharePoint list. External content types support a similar concept, *associations*. When an External List is created, an extra column will be provided for each association that exists between its backing ECT and other ECTs. For example, if we create a Product Subcategories list and there is a foreign key–based relationship between the Product Category and Product Subcategories ECTs, a Product Category column would be created on our Product Subcategories list. Each row in the Product Subcategories list would show a hyperlink that users can click to execute the default action of the Product Category ECT. Typically this will be the View Profile action and will take the user to the profile page of the selected Product Category. Users can also expand the item menu to view all the actions associated with the Product Category.

Alternatively, users can select a particular subcategory and open it to view or edit details. An External Item Picker control will be shown on the subcategory form, allowing the user to see the display name of the related parent category (if one exists) in view mode. The user can also edit an existing subcategory or create a new one and pick a category to associate it with. The External Item Picker control is similar to the people picker control: users click a button to launch a dialog in which they can sort the list by clicking a column, or filter by entering search terms.

Figure 2-13 shows how associations are rendered in a list view; Figure 2-14 shows how associations can be viewed, created, and edited at the item level with the External Item Picker.

ProductSubcategoryKey	ProductSubcategoryName	Product Category
1	MP4&MP3	Product Category
2	Recorder	Product Category
3	Radio	Product Category
4	Recording Pen	View Profile
5	Headphones	View Sales Data
6	Bluetooth Headphones	Product Category
7	Speakers	Product Category
8	Audio Accessories	Product Category
9	Televisions	Product Category
10	VCD & DVD	Product Category

FIGURE 2-13

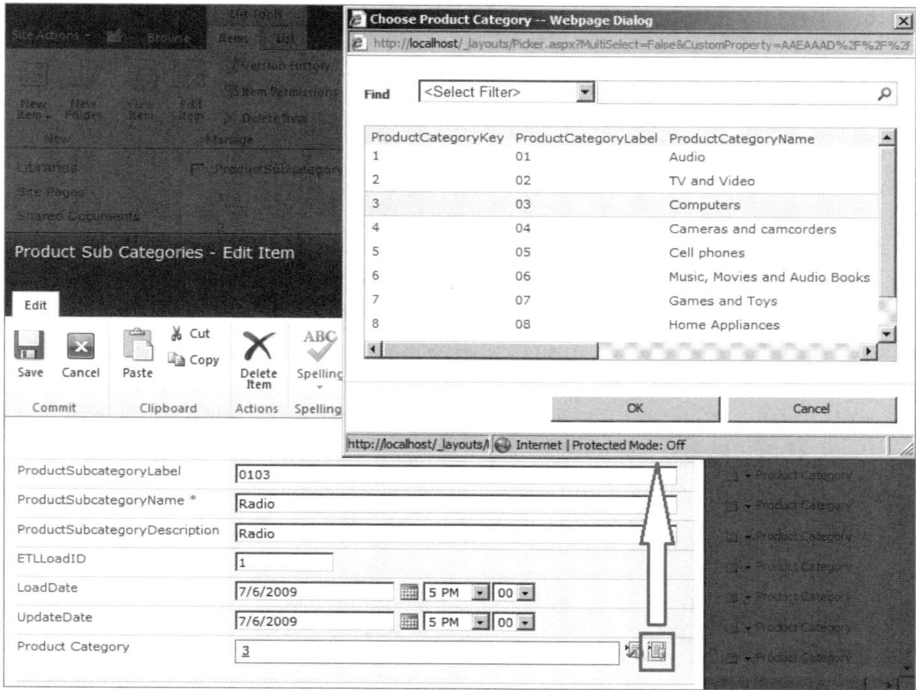

FIGURE 2-14

Finally, when programming against External Lists, there are several things to keep in mind:

- Don't assume that every item has an unsigned int32 ID that is unique. Instead of a simple `ID` field, a `BDCIdentity` field is used to uniquely identify each item.
- Create, update, and delete operations may not be supported by the backing ECT.
- The five fields that exist for every regular list — Title, Created, Created By, Modified, Modified By — are not added to ELs.

Life Cycle and Portability

When an External List is created, the structure of the ECT is used to create list columns, forms, and views, and to configure those elements as needed — for example, by marking fields as required and setting default data source filter values. What happens if the ECT is modified after External Lists have been created — how do the lists respond to these changes? The answer depends on the type of change that has occurred.

- **Changes to filters (adding/editing/removing a filter):** These changes will automatically be reflected on the list. If a default filter value has changed, it will be applied only if an explicit value has not been specified for the corresponding data source filter on the External List.

For example, I have a field on my ECT named `Position` with a default value of `5`. I create an External List and change the value to `6`. If I go back to my ECT and modify the default value to `0`, my External List's value for that field is still `6`. If I had not modified that field on my list (i.e., if I had left the value at `5`), the value would automatically be changed to `0` after my ECT was modified and saved.

- **Adding a new field:** This will not automatically be reflected on the list. The new field will show up on the Edit View page, where you can manually add it. Auto-generated SharePoint forms cannot be customized to include the additional field; in these cases you will want to switch to InfoPath forms or re-create the list. If the new field is marked as required, users will not be able to create or edit items until forms for the list have been updated.
- **Editing properties of a field:** Changes to the display name and to required and read-only properties will automatically be reflected in the view and in auto-generated SharePoint forms. InfoPath forms will need to be manually updated. Changing the data type of a field will cause the list to stop working and require a new one to be created.
- **Removing a field:** This change will automatically be reflected on the list. The field will no longer be displayed in views, and will be removed from auto-generated SharePoint forms. InfoPath forms will need to be manually updated.
- **Adding an association method:** This change will not automatically be reflected on the list. The new field will show up on the Edit View page, where you can manually add it. Auto-generated SharePoint forms cannot be customized to include the additional field; in these cases you will want to switch to InfoPath forms or re-create the list. On a form, the field will be represented by an External Item Picker control.
- **Removing an association:** This change will automatically be reflected on the list. The field will no longer be displayed in views, and will be removed from auto-generated SharePoint forms. InfoPath forms will need to be manually updated.

External Lists and their forms are designed to be portable across SharePoint 2010 site collections and farms. The ECT that the list was originally configured to use must be available on the destination farm. If you are moving External Lists and the old location will no longer be available, you will want to identify users who connected the old External List to Outlook or SharePoint Workspace. These users will continue to be able to work with their data, but will no longer be able to check for updates to the External List. These users should uninstall their existing solutions and connect the new External List to Outlook or SharePoint Workspace.

Saving an External List as a template for reuse by other users is not supported; this option is hidden from the list settings page.

Using External Data Web Parts

BCS provides five web parts in SharePoint Server 2010 that can be connected to an External Content Type to surface data to end users. Largely unchanged from Microsoft Office SharePoint Server 2007, the parts still fill a valuable gap in the overall presentation story for External Data.

These web parts are used to display External Data on the profile page for an ECT, rendering read-only data from the corresponding external system. These web parts may also be used to build line-of-business applications. Most of the parts are capable of displaying External Data actions, which can be used to enable users to navigate to a different page or website, passing in the context of the item that the user was acting on. Table 2-3 lists the different web parts and their primary purposes.

TABLE 2-3: External Data Web Part Capabilities

NAME	PURPOSE	SUPPORTS ACTIONS?
Business Data Item	Shows details for a single external item	Yes
Business Data List	Shows a list of external items	Yes
Business Data Related List	Shows a list of external items related to an item passed as input (typically selected in the Item or List web part)	Yes
Business Data Actions	Shows a list of actions for the selected external item	Yes
Business Data Item Builder	Retrieves input parameters from the URL/query string and passes them to parts on the page. Hidden when the page renders at runtime.	No

To add an External Data web part to a SharePoint page, ensure you have Design permissions for the site and in the Site Actions menu ➪ edit Page. On the Insert tab of the ribbon ➪ web part. From the gallery of available web parts select the Business Data category, and click `Add` to insert the selected part on the page. You can configure the web part by clicking the "Open the tool pane" link in the body of the part, or by clicking the part's drop-down menu and selecting Edit web part. Configuration options vary slightly based on the part, but typically involve selecting a data source (ECT) and a view (`Finder` or `SpecificFinder` method). The Item web part can be hard-coded to display a specific external item or, as is more commonly the case, you can leverage the Item Builder web part to dynamically retrieve the item from the parameters specified in the URL of the page. The List web part is typically configured to show data for a particular ECT, while Related List web parts always require an input item to fetch and render their data.

Many aspects of how the web parts render data can be customized from within the browser. When editing a page that hosts a List or Related List web part, click the Edit View link to specify basic view properties — which columns to show, sort/filter/paging settings, and user profile data filters. You can open the web part tool pane to adjust basic settings such as the title of the part, height and width, fields to display, and the behavior of the part while the page is loading. Figure 2-15 shows the web part tool pane and the default settings for the Item web part hosted on a profile page.

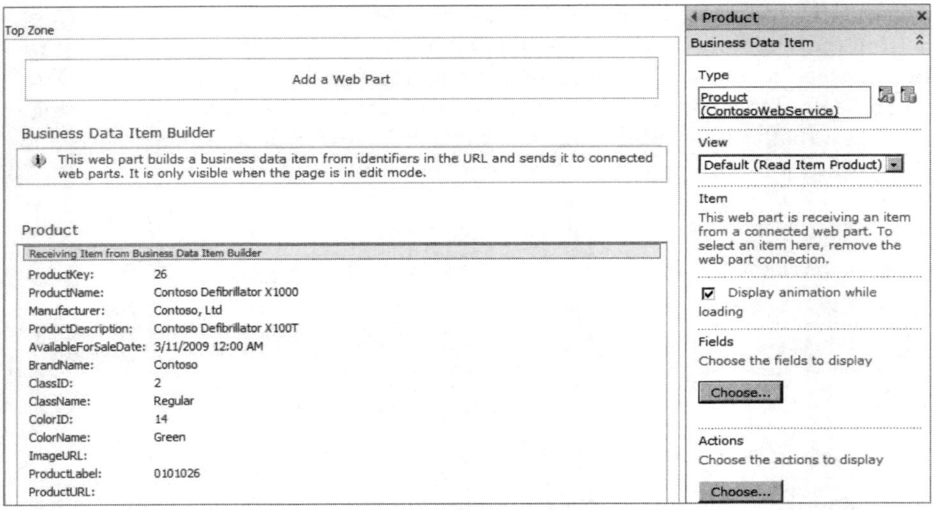

FIGURE 2-15

SharePoint Designer can also be useful for customizing how the data is presented to your users. You can apply conditional formatting to the data — such as specifying that the font is to be displayed in red if a particular product has low inventory — or use aggregate functions to display the average value for a list of orders.

The web parts apply an XSL Transform (XSLT) to convert the raw External Data into a form that can be presented in the web part. The default XSLT is generated at runtime, but you can customize or completely override it with your own XML. To do this, open the web part tool pane menu and click the XSL Editor button. This will open a dialog in which you can paste in your XSL content. Alternatively, you can specify the URL of your XSL file in the XSL Link property under the Miscellaneous header. For more details on XSLT customizations, see Chapter 5.

External Data web parts can be connected to each other to pass information about a selected item. You can define and modify part-to-part connections when editing the web part page in the browser or SharePoint Designer. Note that the protocol used to pass data between External Data web parts is different from the standard ASP.Net part-to-part connection model used by other SharePoint web parts. This means it is not possible to connect a Business Data Item web part to an XSLT List View web part, which is used to render an External List.

Connecting two External Data web parts is a simple process, as shown in Figure 2-16. On the part that will provide data, expand the web part menu and select Edit web part. This shows the web part tool pane, and also exposes the Connections entry in the web part menu. Expand the Connections entry and select the appropriate External Data part(s) to send the item to. This configures the part to send the item that the user has selected to each recipient part when the page is loaded at runtime. If the user selects a new item, the page is refreshed and the new value is sent to the recipient parts.

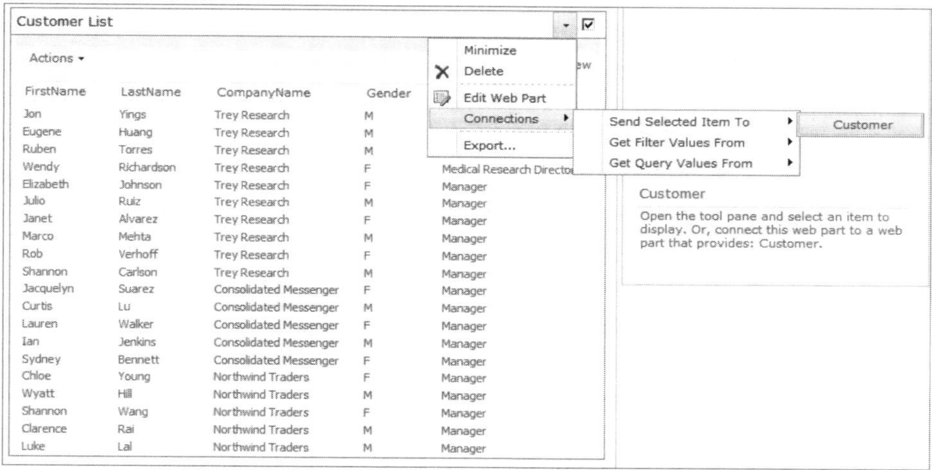

FIGURE 2-16

External Data web parts support the concept of stream or BLOB (Binary Large Object) fields, commonly used by External Systems to store binary file content. The web parts are able to display these file attachments as hyperlinks, allowing users to click the link and open the file using the appropriate application. For example, a Product ECT defines a series of fields (`ProductID`, `Name`, `Weight`, `Cost`, `MSRP`) and standard methods (read list, read item, create, update, delete) as well as a `StreamAccessor` method that returns the user manual (a PDF document) for the product. When a user navigates to the Product profile page he or she sees the standard fields defined in the Product ECT, plus an additional hyperlink with the text "Click here to download." Clicking the link redirects the user to an ASPX page that makes a BDC call to the appropriate `StreamAccessor` method. Data is retrieved in 4 KB chunks. (You can configure the maximum file size by setting properties in the BDC Metadata Model file.) Additional metadata is retrieved from the ECT to determine the MIME type of the file. This information is compared with the MIME types registered on the SharePoint server to determine the appropriate application to launch to view the content. The user then sees a File Open/Save dialog in his or her browser and can view the file. Creating a new file or editing the contents of an existing file and saving it back to the external system is not supported.

See Chapter 7 for specifics about defining and configuring a `StreamAccessor` method.

`Byte[]` *fields are not shown by default in the External Data web parts. If defined in an ECT,* `Byte[]` *fields will be deselected in the default view or form structure of the web parts. Manually editing the configuration properties to show this type of field will result in the web part's printing the string* `System.Byte[]` *at runtime. To display these fields, either define a* `StreamAccessor` *method (which will render a hyperlink, as described earlier) or define a custom formatter (which enables you to render the content in-line and is particularly useful for small images).*

Using the Chart Web Part

SharePoint Foundation 2010 provides a powerful new web part for visualizing data from SharePoint or External Data sources. The Chart web part can be configured to connect to data that is passed to it from another web part at runtime, from a SharePoint list, from an external system (using BCS), or from an Excel Services spreadsheet. While the part-to-part connection option will work with standard SharePoint web parts, it does not use the same protocol as the External Data web parts and thus cannot consume data from them.

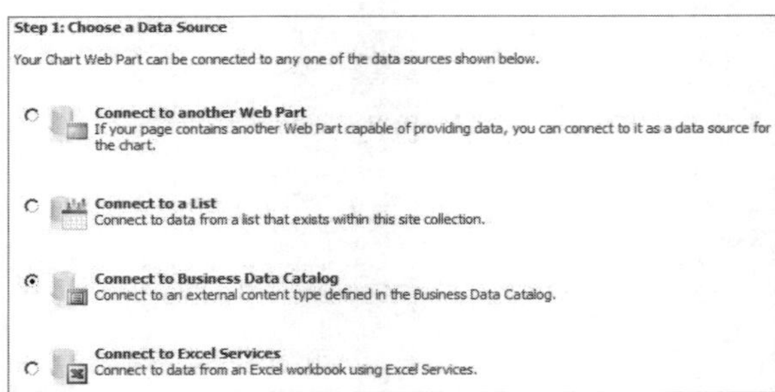

FIGURE 2-17

To configure a Chart web part, first add it to your page (it's under the Business Data category in the web part Gallery) and then click the Data and Appearance link in the body of the part to begin. On the next screen choose Connect Chart to Data to see the four data source types shown in Figure 2-17.

This begins a four-step process to configure your chart. To present External Data in the Chart web part choose either Connect to a List (and select an External List) or Connect to Business Data Catalog (and select an ECT). Regardless of the option you choose, BDC will retrieve the data from the external system using the default `Finder` method — it is not possible to choose a different External List view or `Finder` method on the ECT. To work around this limitation, consider publishing an additional ECT with the appropriate `Finder` method marked as the default.

After selecting a specific data source you will see a preview of the first 100 rows of the data in tabular format, which is similar to what you would see in an External List. The final step involves binding the chart to the data by selecting your x- and y-axes, groupings, labels, and other details. There are numerous advanced settings, and a completely separate wizard walks you through the process of customizing your chart. Even a basic chart that hasn't been customized looks pretty polished, as shown in Figure 2-18.

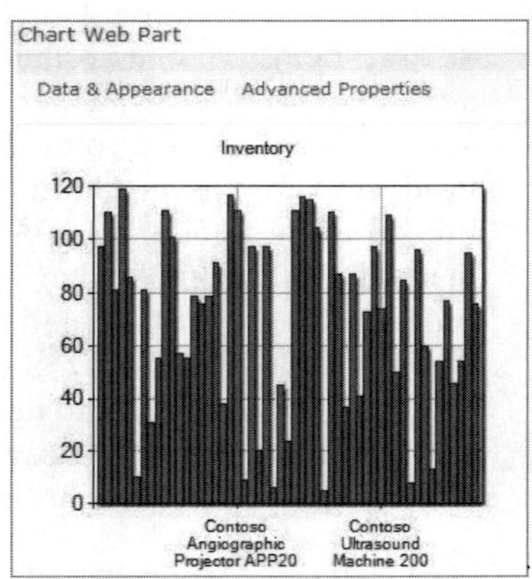

FIGURE 2-18

Creating External Data Columns

An External Data column is a custom SharePoint list column that can be added to any document library or standard list. This feature is powerful as it enables you to bring External Data into SharePoint and store it there. This means that events can be fired off of changes in the data, and that features such as workflow, versioning, custom event handlers, and check-in/checkout are available.

Common scenarios in which External Data columns are used include associating a document such as a request for proposal with the customer for whom it's being prepared, and selecting a value from a list of reference data such as a list of subsidiary branches of a large company.

When you add a column of type External Data to a list, you can choose any number of fields to be brought back from the external system and displayed in the list. For example, when you add a `Customer` column you can display multiple fields such as the company name and address in the list. Figure 2-19 shows a `Customer` External Data column being added to a list with the primary field `CompanyName` and secondary fields called `AddressLine1`, `AddressLine2`, and `BirthDate`.

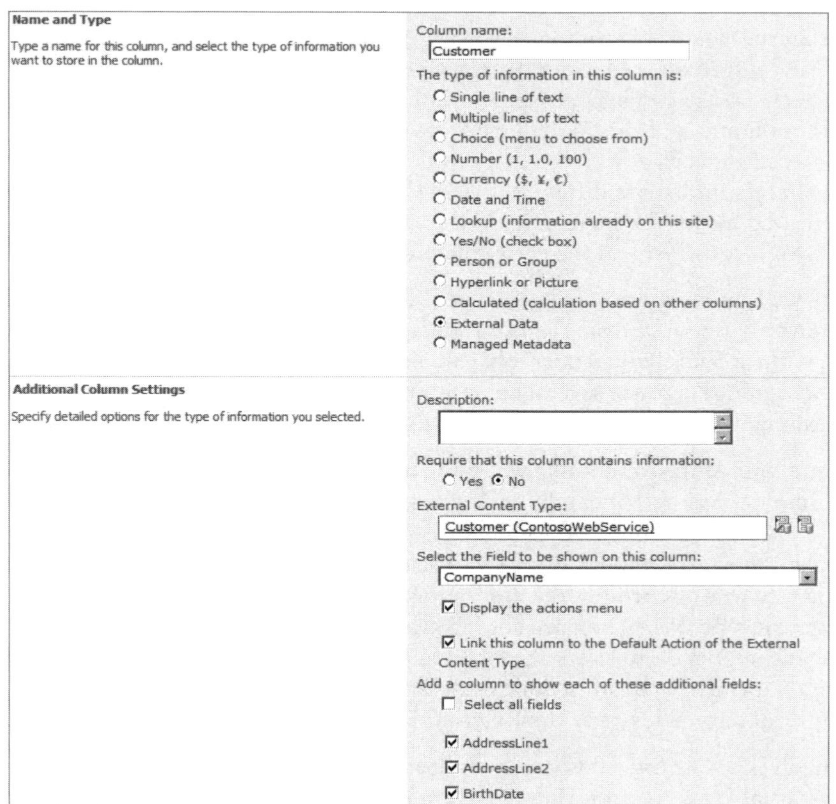

FIGURE 2-19

Lookup Columns

Attempting to add a `Lookup` *column to a SharePoint list and selecting an External List as its target will result in SharePoint's provisioning an External Data column — traditional lookup columns do not natively support External Lists as a data source.*

External Data actions are also available on External Data columns. Users can drill down into a customer's details and perform actions associated with the customer without leaving the document library or list. The primary field of an External Data column is rendered as a hyperlink and executes the default action for that ECT. Other actions are surfaced in a drop-down menu that is shown when you hover over the primary field.

If data changes in the external system, SharePoint is not automatically updated. Creating a new list item or document and picking a value for an External Data column will show the new value, but existing items will continue to show the old value. Editing any field of an existing item and trying to save it will result in your being prompted to pick a new value for the External Data column since the old value no longer exists in the external system.

To refresh values in an External Data column for all rows in the list or document library, users click the Refresh Data button on the header of the primary column. This redirects to the `BusinessDataSynchronizer.aspx` page, passing in the following parameters: the ID of the list, the name of the column, and the URL to navigate to when finished. This page makes a `SpecificFinder` call for each row in the list; if it determines that the values in the external system and the SharePoint list are different, the SharePoint item is updated and its version number is incremented by one. If the item no longer exists in the external system, an `ObjectNotFoundException` is returned and the entire operation is canceled.

While this process works well for most use cases, when you're dealing with large volumes of changed items, or if items are commonly removed from the external system, a custom solution may be useful. Custom code, typically a SharePoint Timer job, can also be used to update External Data columns according to a schedule. There are several community-sourced guides to implementing this functionality; one such example is at `http://tinyurl.com/ExternalDataColumnRefresh`.

External Data columns are limited in two notable ways; the first is site column support. A site column is a reusable column definition that can be consumed by multiple lists across multiple SharePoint sites. Site columns are typically used to establish consistent settings across lists and libraries. When you are defining a site column you cannot select an External Data column as one of the column types. One way to work around this limitation is to add the columns to a list-level (rather than site-level) content type. When you are adding an External Data column to a content type on a particular list, it is important to select the "Add to all content types" checkbox. Selecting this box will enable both the primary and secondary fields to be saved; not selecting this box will prevent you from adding secondary fields after the External Data column has been created.

The second limitation involves `DateTime` fields that are selected for use as either primary or secondary fields of an External Data column. Unlike External Lists, these fields always show `DateTime` values converted to Universal Coordinated Time (UTC), not local time. This can be slightly confusing for users if they use an External List and External Data column showing the same information.

Like External Data web parts, External Data columns are a feature carried over from MOSS 2007 and remain largely unchanged. The major enhancement is their ability to be connected to a Word document in a much richer fashion than in Office 2007. Previously these columns only appeared in the document information panel, and were read-only — users could not pick values for the column in Word. With Word 2010 you can customize a document template by adding Quick Parts bound to External Data columns in a SharePoint document library. For example, a sales rep creating a quote for a customer can now select the customer and the product(s), and have additional information about those items filled in automatically on the document. These capabilities are discussed in more detail in Chapter 3.

Mobile Device Support

The Business Data Item and Item Builder web parts are mobile-enabled and can be used to render an external item on a SharePoint page viewed on a mobile device. Web part connections are also supported for SharePoint pages rendered in mobile mode, enabling the two parts to communicate.

Any web parts that are not mobile-enabled are ignored at runtime when the page is rendered. You can mobile-enable web parts by implementing and deploying a mobile adapter class for each part; this process is beyond the scope of this book but a detailed step-by-step guide is available in the SharePoint Foundation developer documentation at `http://msdn.microsoft.com/en-us/library/ee539079.aspx`.

External Data columns can be rendered in a mobile view of a list or document library, but the data is read-only, as the External Item Picker is not available to select a new item.

Time Zone Support

As noted earlier in the External Lists section, after retrieving a `DateTime` field from an external system, the BDC runtime examines the `DateTime.Kind` property to determine its time zone. If it is marked as `UTC` or `Unspecified`, no action is taken. If it is `Local`, BDC converts the time to UTC by applying an offset based on the SharePoint front-end web server's time zone, as specified by the server's Windows settings. If an Office client application is presenting External Data, the Windows regional settings on that client computer are used to convert from local time to UTC.

This logic ensures that all clients of the BDC runtime receive `DateTime` fields in a single time zone: UTC. Not all clients present that raw value to users, however; most convert it to a form that will be easier for users to understand: their local time zone. The behavior is straightforward when the user, site, and SharePoint server are all located in the same time zone. Complexity increases as these variables change — for example, when users travel frequently (and change their Windows or SharePoint settings) or when a single farm hosts sites that serve users spread across time zones.

For example, let's look at the following scenario:

- `DateTime` value in external system: 07/31/2011, 12:00 a.m.
- User's location: English (US)
- User's time zone: PST (UTC minus eight hours)

Table 2-4 shows the logic applied to external `DateTime` values by out-of-the-box BCS components.

TABLE 2-4: How Time Zones are Handled

COMPONENT	TIME ZONE VALUE	TIME ZONE FORMAT	ACTUAL TIME DISPLAYED
External Data Column			
`DateTime` field (shown in list views or on forms); External Item Picker (shown on forms and dialogs to choose an item)	UTC	UTC	2011-07-31 00:00:00z
External Data List			
`DateTime` field (List view or on forms)	User locale	User locale	30.07. 2011 17:00
External Item Picker (on forms and dialogs to choose an item)	UTC	UTC	2011-07-31 00:00:00z
External Data Web Parts			
Item, List, Related List web parts	UTC	User locale	31.07.2011 0:00
Word			
Content control, External Item Picker (shown on dialogs to choose an item)	UTC	UTC	2011-07-31 00:00:00z
SharePoint Workspace or Outlook			
`DateTime` field (List view or on forms)	User locale	User locale	5:00 PM 7/30/2011
External Item Picker (shown on forms and dialogs to choose an item)	UTC	UTC	2011-07-31 00:00:00z

Several components can be customized to override the default handling of `DateTime` values. These include External Data lists (customize them by creating a custom field renderer that defines behavior for both columns in a view and fields on a standard SharePoint form), External Data web parts (customize them by customizing their XSLs), and InfoPath forms that show data in both SharePoint and SharePoint Workspace (customize them by adding declarative logic or code behind). Chapter 5 describes these customizations in more detail.

User Profile Enhancements Using ECTs

Much as you can add an External Data column to a list, you can also create Business Data properties in the SharePoint Server user profile database. This means that the user profile can now be a mixture of SharePoint, Active Directory, and External Data.

A common scenario that exercises this functionality is appending human resources information stored in SAP to core employee information stored in Active Directory and skills/expertise information stored in SharePoint. This information is all integrated and displayed as part of the standard user profile. From the user's perspective, it all comes from the same place. This solves a common problem among large organizations: where to store personnel data. By using BCS to add External Data to user profiles, you can store the data anywhere and update it regularly.

When a business data property is added to a user profile, a copy of the data is stored in the user profile database. This information is refreshed periodically, and the refresh interval can be configured through the User Profile Service administration pages. Each time a refresh occurs, a `SpecificFinder` call is made to the external system for each user in the user profile store.

BCS also enables you to take user profile properties and use them as filter values when retrieving data from External Systems. These values are called `UserProfile` filters. Filters are described in more detail in Chapter 5.

Searching External Systems

This book devotes all of Chapter 9 to discussing Search and how it can be leveraged to interact with External Data. What follows is a very brief overview of that content.

SharePoint Server 2010 can crawl, index, and do full-text searches on External Content Types. For example, Search can consume the Customer ECT created in Chapter 1 in order to crawl the data and return customer information in search results. To enable this functionality, create a new content source from the Search Service Application administration page. Select Line of Business Data as the type of content to crawl, select the ECT(s) to crawl, initiate the crawl, and wait for the initial crawl to complete.

After the External Data has been crawled once and added to the search index, incremental crawls can be used to capture changes from the external system and maximize efficiency.

The last step of the process is optional — you can define a search scope to allow users to explicitly select that content source in the search UI. By default two search scopes exist: All Sites and People. The former includes data from the new content source; the latter does not. To set the scope, go to the Manage Search service page, ➪ Scopes ➪ New Scope, and enter **Customers** for the name. Once the scope exists, add a rule to it and select your new content source to be included. Finally, update the search scopes to push the new scope definition across your farm.

If your sites are configured to show the search scope's drop-down menu, users can select your new Customers entry, enter a search term, and see External Data returned in the search results page. Clicking a particular customer will navigate to that customer's profile page (assuming View Profile is the default action for the ECT) and show details about the customer and any related items, such as orders.

Search across External Data is available only through content sources and search scopes targeting one or more ECTs; it is not available at the list level. For example, a user navigating to a SharePoint site that contains a regular list and an External List will see results for items in the regular list but not the External List.

These search capabilities are provided by the enterprise search service, which is available in SharePoint Server 2010. SharePoint Foundation offers limited site-specific search functionality that does not provide a way to expose External Data to users.

Using Workflow to Access External Data

SharePoint 2010 offers a powerful workflow engine that is capable of executing Workflow Foundation (WF) workflows, typically defined in either SPD or Visual Studio. These workflows can be simple approval scenarios that exclusively use out-of-the-box workflow activities to read from and write to any SharePoint list. Alternatively, they can be slightly more complex, leveraging partially trusted code that runs in a Sandboxed Workflow Action. They can also be even more advanced and require that fully trusted assemblies be deployed to the SharePoint farm.

Before we dive into the details of these three classes of workflow, it is important that you understand two key factors that apply to workflows when they interact with an External List.

First, as noted in the Using External Lists section, workflows cannot be associated directly with External Lists. This limitation stems from the data's being stored outside SharePoint; the workflow cannot be notified when items change, as there is no eventing model on External Lists. This leaves you two options: either create a site workflow that is explicitly triggered, or have a list workflow bound to a regular list or document library, and have it read or update from an External List. Chapter 4 shows these alternative approaches in action.

Second, workflow activities accessing BCS will always run as service accounts, even when they are configured to run under an impersonation step. (Impersonation steps enable you to specify certain activities that should run in the context of the workflow author rather than the initiator.) The service account is typically the IIS Application Pool account, which has elevated permissions to certain SharePoint resources. To prevent against malicious users, BCS requires that the ECT backing the External List that your workflow is interacting with use Secure Store Service (SSS) or RevertToSelf (which is turned off by default because of its security implications) as the authentication mode.

This means that your external system(s) will always be accessed by workflow as a single account rather than as individual users, and you cannot track which user is making a change. Although you can configure your workflow to pass the SPUser name of the initiator to a column on the External List or to a custom activity that calls the BDC runtime OM, this measure should be taken only for informational purposes and shouldn't be relied upon as a foolproof security mechanism.

This section describes the capabilities and tradeoffs associated with each level of workflow complexity.

Simple Workflows

Any workflow created in SharePoint Designer interacts with lists using the List Item activities: create, update, and delete. The main difference when using one of these activities to interact with an External List (as opposed to a regular list) is that you will find the item to act on by its identifying column (primary key) rather than the SharePoint `ID` column.

To interact with an External List from your site workflow or a workflow bound to a regular list or document library, simply add the create, update, or delete activity, select the External List to act on, and, in the case of update or delete, choose the field that will be used to look at the item. For example, in a Products list you will select the `ProductID` field. You will then pick the specific value you are looking for when the workflow is being executed. This will typically be a field from the current item; in the `Data Source` field, select `Current Item`.

The out-of-the-box List Item activities are useful for a wide variety of scenarios in which ease of creation is paramount and you are working with a small number of columns in an External List. Scenarios that require you to read multiple values from the same External List item will result in numerous trips to and from the external system, as SharePoint does not cache the external item. Thus the List Item activity will call the Read List method (`Finder`) and then the Read Item method (the `Specific Finder`) for each column retrieved. So if you are reading 10 properties in a list of 1,000 items, this will cause 20 calls to the BDC and result in 10,010 items being requested from the external system.

If you are trying to look for an item (for example, the office number of a particular employee) and `NULL` *is returned, you cannot tell the difference between zero items returned and one item returned. Instead you can determine if a particular field of the item is* `NULL`*. To do this, first confirm the existence of the item — for example, find the employee based on name or ID. If the employee exists, then find the office number; if it is* `NULL`*, you know that the employee has no office number listed.*

After you create a new item in an External List, any changes made to that item from the same workflow must refer to the item by the `BDCIdentity` *returned from the Create List Item activity. Trying to find the item by looking for a value from any other column will fail.*

The converse is true for finding existing items: you will never get a value back for `BDCIdentity` *if you try to read it on an existing item. You must find existing items by looking for columns other than* `BDCIdentity`.

Intermediate Workflows

If you are implementing scenarios that require frequent interaction with External Systems or reading a large number of properties, you will want to look for ways to increase the efficiency of those interactions. One way is to cache the item after retrieval from the external system, and to do so in a way that enables you to reuse that data.

An elegant way to enable this caching is to use SPList OM to read from External Lists within a Sandboxed Workflow Action. These actions are custom code functions that you build and can then publish for reuse in the declarative workflow designer. Sandboxed Workflow Actions are written in Visual Studio and uploaded to a SharePoint Solution Gallery. These actions run in isolation to ensure that the core system process is protected and that errors resulting from a specific solution don't affect other SharePoint solutions.

Sandboxed Workflow Actions are ideal when you do not have permission to deploy full-trust activities (common in hosted environments) and need to read many values from an External List or write a simple, reusable function that will work on both regular and External Lists.

The logic behind a Sandboxed Workflow Action can be quite simple: make an SPList OM call to read an external item and store all its properties. SPD does not support iterative loops, so returning an array of items isn't possible, but an XML string is a viable alternative. Then a second action reads a specific field value out of this XML string and writes it to an SPD variable. From there, any workflow activity can efficiently read and act on the data. Packaging these sandboxed actions into a WSP and deploying it to a SharePoint site will enable the actions to show up for reuse in SPD. Workflow designers can then use the sandboxed actions.

The security restrictions around authentication mode noted earlier in this section also apply to SPList OM calls. This means that SSS and RevertToSelf are the only two authentication modes supported for the External List(s) that your code will interact with. The service that executes sandboxed code (`SPUCWorkerProcessProxy.exe`) runs with a different service account from the IIS Application Pool service (`w3wp.exe`). Ensure that a mapping for the SPUCWorkerProcessProxy account has been set up in the SSS.

If you are storing a local copy of the data read from an External List item and you are executing a long-running workflow, ensure that your data doesn't become stale.

A sandboxed action can cause a workflow to fail if it cannot obtain a sandbox worker process application domain. A fixed number of these app domains can be active at a given time, and they are shared across all sandboxed code, including actions, web parts, and event receivers. Although these situations will be rare for most deployments, be careful when using sandboxed actions in situations that involve any of the following:

- Complex actions that take time to complete
- External Lists that are slow to render
- Environments in which many workflows run at the same time
- Scenarios that cannot handle workflow failures

Advanced Workflows

When you are able to deploy full-trust code, you can create custom workflow activities that directly call BDC runtime OM. This gives you even more control over the calls made to the external system and the ability to operate on External Data without requiring an External List. Custom workflow activities are particularly useful when you need to leverage capabilities supported by the BDC runtime but not the SPList OM. Common examples of these capabilities include complex objects (non-flat data structures where read/write access is required), custom data types, and stream/BLOB fields.

The downside of this approach is that the code becomes specific to External Data and will not work with other SharePoint lists.

Another powerful workflow capability that involves full-trust code is the Pluggable Service functionality. This enables you to "listen" to an external system and deliver events from the external system to a SharePoint workflow. When Pluggable Service is combined with out-of-the-box or custom workflow activities that can interact with SharePoint and write back to the external system via External Lists, you can achieve bidirectional communication.

An example of a scenario that could be implemented using this functionality is interaction between SharePoint and a CRM system to manage a portion of the sales life cycle — review and approval of request for proposal (RFP) documents. For each opportunity in the CRM system, a workflow helps the salesperson track progress toward a confirmed sale. At a particular stage in the workflow an RFP document is created. The CRM system, which "owns" the workflow, can easily create a site for the opportunity and a document for the RFP by calling SharePoint web services. With a SharePoint workflow bound to the RFP document, CRM can communicate with the SharePoint workflow via a Pluggable Service. Based on the status of the opportunity, the CRM system can move the workflow forward to an approval step. When all the tasks have been completed in the SharePoint workflow, it calls a CRM web service to report its final status.

Creating code-based custom activities and Pluggable Services is discussed in more detail in Chapter 5.

UPGRADING FROM MOSS 2007

Using Microsoft Office SharePoint Server 2007 with Enterprise CAL, you can define and use read-only entities, actions, and business data columns in lists. You can build web part pages (including profile pages) that leverage the Business Data web parts, configure search, and add business data properties to user profiles.

There are two ways to upgrade a MOSS 2007 farm to SharePoint 2010. These are:

- **In-place upgrade:** This involves running an SP 2010 setup on each machine in the farm. This installs new binaries and upgrades the configuration database, content databases, and shared service databases in one monolithic operation. It can result in extended downtime for farms with a lot of sites or content.
- **Database attach:** This involves running SP 2010 setup on new machines to install binaries, then attaching SQL databases backed up from your MOSS 2007 farm. The act of attaching a SharePoint content or shared service database from 2007 immediately triggers an upgrade.

Upgrade of BDC content from 2007 to 2010 is supported only for in-place upgrade. If you attach a BDC shared service database to a 2010 farm, upgrade actions will not be run and you will not be able to access any of the Metadata Models, profile pages, etc. If other factors prevent you from doing a full in-place upgrade of your MOSS 2007 farm, consider backing up your BDC content, creating a new MOSS 2007 farm (this could even be a single server farm hosted on a virtual machine), and restoring BDC to that farm. Perform an in-place upgrade on the new farm, then back up the upgraded database(s) and attach them to your permanent SharePoint 2010 farm.

Version-to-version upgrade often occurs over the course of many months for larger organizations, and it may not be desirable or even possible to switch all applications that interact with External Data over to SharePoint 2010 immediately. Because of this, when an in-place upgrade is triggered, a new SharePoint 2010 Application Service is created that enables backward compatibility for BDC

Metadata Models created with MOSS 2007. These models can continue to function, unmodified, in a SharePoint 2010 farm. This service appears as the Application Registry Service in Central Administration.

When you're upgrading to 2010, there are several things to keep in mind. The first is the SKU that you are upgrading to. As discussed in Chapter 1, basic BCS functionality is available in SharePoint Foundation 2010, but features such as profile pages and External Data web parts require SharePoint Server 2010 with Enterprise CAL. Ensure that the SharePoint SKU you are upgrading to supports all the functionality currently deployed in your MOSS 2007 farm.

After upgrade is complete, here is a list of items to check or attend to:

- **BDC Service state:** Ensure the BDC service application instance is started by navigating to the Central Administration site.
- **Upgrade logs:** Check your upgrade logs for errors. In certain cases some complex associations between entities cannot be upgraded automatically; these will be clearly called out as errors in the upgrade logs.
- **Permissions:** Consider granting Edit BDC permissions to users who need to work with ECTs in SPD. You can do this through the Central Administration site.
- **Add CRUD capabilities:** When a BDC 2007 Metadata Model is upgraded, its schema is converted to the new BCS 2010 format. Each entity in the model is converted to an ECT and can now be opened for editing in SharePoint Designer. Where appropriate, consider adding create, update, and delete operations.
- **SharePoint Workspace 2010:** By default upgraded ECTs cannot be connected to SharePoint Workspace. MOSS 2007 was server-only and the reasoning was that it would be safer to require administrators to opt into making data available in rich client environments. (Note that the default for new ECTs in 2010 is still server-only, although this can easily be changed through SPD.) It is very easy to enable these upgraded ECTs to be "offlined" to Office client applications: remove the `ExcludeFromOfflineClient` property that was added to each ECT and set to `True` during upgrade.
- **Outlook 2010**: Not only must you remove the `ExcludeFromOfflineClient` property, connecting External Data to Outlook also requires that you map certain fields in the ECT to Outlook fields so data can be displayed in default Outlook views and forms. The easiest way to do this is by opening the ECT in SharePoint Designer and using the wizards shown in Chapter 4 to map the appropriate required fields.
- **Create External Lists**: These lists are the easiest entry points at which to allow users to view and manipulate data in SharePoint and connect to SharePoint Workspace and Outlook. Before creating one of these lists, consider the security of the list (will the right users have access to the parent site? to the External Content Type? to the external system itself?) and its structure (number and structure of views, including data source filters; out-of-the-box versus InfoPath forms).
- **Profile page host:** Profile pages were hosted in a fixed location within the Shared Service administration site in MOSS 2007; that site is deprecated in 2010 (as Application Services are administered from with the Central Administration site) and thus you will need to

define a new profile host site. If you have customized your profile pages you may want to manually move them to the new host site. If not, you can easily "upgrade" your profile pages to create new pages for upgraded ECTs that display both the Item and Related List web parts. These new pages are automatically created in the new profile host site.

- **Pages with Business Data web parts:** Any web part pages that contain Business Data web parts are not immediately upgraded, as this process would require iteration through every page on every web on every site to build the list of affected parts. Instead, the first time an instance of a Business Data web part is rendered after upgrade it executes an on-demand process to update its configuration. This process takes only a few seconds. The web part then sets an internal flag to indicate that the process was successful. Future attempts to load the web part will check the flag and skip the upgrade process.
- **Search:** Upgraded BDC Metadata Models will continue to work with SharePoint 2010 Search, as will incremental crawl functionality for the upgraded ECTs in those models. If you create a new SharePoint 2010 content source from an upgraded SharePoint 2007 BDC Metadata Model, you will have to export the model and modify the XML to add a `LastModifiedTimeStampField` property to the method instance, as shown in the following code. (In the meantime, incremental crawls will be treated as full crawls for new content sources based on upgraded models.) The value for this new property should be the name of the field in your ECT that stores information about when the item was last changed. Import the updated model through the Central Administration site.

```
<MethodInstances>
       <MethodInstance Type="SpecificFinder"
        ReturnParameterName="GetCustomerById"
        Default="true" Name="GetCustomerById"
        DefaultDisplayName="Read Customer"
        LastModifiedTimeStampField="LastChanged">
           <Properties>
             <Property Name="LastDesignedOfficeItemType"
              Type="System.String">Contact</Property>
           </Properties>
       </MethodInstance>
</MethodInstances>
```

After upgrade is complete and access to SharePoint 2007 entities/models is no longer required, the Application Registry Service can be stopped in the Central Administration site's service management page.

SUMMARY

In this chapter we reviewed core BCS concepts such as Metadata Models, External Content Types, and the BDC Service Application. You learned how to set BDC permissions to grant end users and solution designers access to ECTs, how to import and export Metadata Models, and how to manage actions and profile pages. We also discussed throttling — the default settings, as well as viewing and changing the current settings.

We then looked at the SharePoint UI components that allow you to present External Data to end users. From External Lists to web parts, External Data columns to user profiles and search, you saw what each component is capable of doing, and were introduced to the extensibility points and some scenarios.

Upgrading from SharePoint 2007 can be a sizable and complex undertaking; we reviewed how BDC Metadata Models, web parts, and profile pages are upgraded to 2010 as well as the BCS-specific activities that you'll want to consider after the upgrade is complete.

Now that you understand the various BCS components on the server, Chapter 3 explores the world of the rich client, describing BCS capabilities within Office 2010. Chapter 3 provides an overview of External Data in Outlook and SharePoint Workspace 2010, describes how you can surface SharePoint External Data columns in Word 2010, and describes how scenarios involving External Data can work offline through the BCS client cache. An in-depth review of the BDC client runtime, the packaging and deployment infrastructure, and the synchronization pipeline are also covered.

3

Using BCS Solutions in Office 2010

WHAT'S IN THIS CHAPTER

- Understand client-side components
- Understand ClickOnce deployment
- Understand List Synchronization
- Learn to use BCS with Office 2010

One of the most powerful aspects of Business Connectivity Services is the ability to use data from External Systems in Office clients. The complementary architecture of the client-side Business Data Connectivity (BDC) components makes BCS solutions much more capable than typical Office add-ins. Additionally, the out-of-the-box features provide enough capability that a custom solution is often not required.

This chapter provides an in-depth look at BCS from the client perspective. The client-side BDC components are examined in detail, along with the many ways that data can be presented in various Office clients. Along the way you'll also learn the details of how client-side functionality is packaged and deployed. After completing the chapter you'll have a strong understanding of how to make use of BCS in Office 2010.

UNDERSTANDING BUSINESS DATA CONNECTIVITY

Chapters 1 and 2 both discussed Business Data Connectivity and defined it as a grouping of the infrastructure, runtime, and administrative components. On the client side, BDC consists of the BDC Client runtime and the metadata cache. As discussed in Chapter 1, these components are installed by default with the Professional Plus version of Office 2010 so no separate client installation is required.

Understanding the BDC Client Runtime

The BDC Client runtime contains the main operational functions for BCS on the client. The BDC Client runtime has three main purposes. First, it provides the functionality necessary to load and execute BCS solutions on the client. Second, the BDC runtime maps the elements of the BDC Metadata Model to user interface elements in various Office applications. Third, the BDC runtime ensures that information from External Content Types is displayed in context as users work within Office applications. The BDC Client runtime is made up of several subcomponents, which can be found in the `Office 14` installation folder. Table 3-1 lists these subcomponents and their functions.

TABLE 3-1: BDC Client Runtime Subcomponents

SUBCOMPONENT	DESCRIPTION
`BCSAutogen.dll`	Generates the InfoPath and Outlook forms required for the solution based on the entity definition
`BCSClient.Msg.dll`	Provides performance counters and ULS logging
`BCSClientManifest.man`	WMI Instrumentation file
`BCSEvents.man`	WMI Instrumentation file
`BCSLaunch.dll`	Checks BCS prerequisites, ensures BDC Client runtime is installed, launches VSTO installer
`BCSProxy.dll`	Provides COM marshaling between the LOB Synchronization service and the Office applications
`BCSRuntime.dll`	BDC Client runtime component
`BCSRuntimeUI.dll`	Provides UI elements like the Synchronization Status dialog for Office clients
`BDCMetadata.xsd`	BDC Metadata Model schema
`BDCMetadataResource.xsd`	BDC Metadata Model resource schema

When the BDC Client runtime is first invoked on the client, a set of services is also started, to support communication and deployment. If you look in the Event Viewer you will see the messages informing you that the services have started. Table 3-2 lists the services and their purposes.

TABLE 3-2: BDC Client Services

SERVICE	DESCRIPTION
LOB Synchronization service	Provides synchronization between the External System and the client-side metadata cache
Remoter service	Provides an entry point for other services into the LOB Synchronization service
Solution Activation service	Installs the BCS solution and notifies user to close Office applications when required
Solution Verification service	Checks for dependent solutions that require updating as a result of the installation of an updated solution
Throttling service	Implements throttling for returned results

Along with the services, you will also notice that two additional related processes start on the client. These processes can be seen in the Windows Task Manager and support synchronization of data and documents with SharePoint and External Systems. Table 3-3 lists these processes and describes them.

TABLE 3-3: BDC Client Processes

SERVICE	DESCRIPTION
`BCSSync.exe`	Synchronizes client BCS data with External Systems
`MSOSync.exe`	Synchronizes the Office Document Cache with SharePoint

The BCS Client runtime loads every time an Office host application is started. Once loaded, the BCS Client runtime can raise and receive events in the Office application, which supports the presentation of the External Data within the hosting Office application. In order to present the data, the BCS Client runtime relies on artifacts contained within the solution package that is installed from the SharePoint server. The solution package itself is covered in detail in the Understanding Solution Deployment section later in the chapter.

Understanding the Metadata Cache

The metadata cache (also called the client cache) is a client-side, per-user, in-memory Microsoft SQL Server Compact database that maintains the metadata associated with External Systems and BDC Metadata Models. The purpose of the metadata cache is to provide faster data access on the client and allow the data to be taken offline. The metadata cache supports these functions by storing the BDC Metadata Model, storing subscription information, storing local copies of the External Data, and maintaining an operations queue. The metadata cache for a given user is located in the `\Users\{UserName}\AppData\Local\Microsoft\BCS` folder and is named `BusinessDataCache.sdf`. While the metadata cache is not encrypted, accessing the database directly is unsupported and can destroy the BCS installation.

The BDC Metadata Model stored by the cache is the same model used on the server by SharePoint with the exception that the `LobSystemInstance` reflects the connection information to be used by the client as specified in SPD. This connection information is almost always different from the server's information because the client has no access to the accounts running the SharePoint application pool or stored in the Secure Store Service (SSS). As a result the client will almost always connect to the External System using his own credentials.

Understanding Subscriptions in the Metadata Cache

Subscriptions determine what data is stored in the metadata cache. Subscriptions are created automatically by the BCS deployment components during the solution deployment process, but may also be created manually for a custom solution. Subscriptions are simple XML files that are read and used to populate the metadata cache with the information required to retrieve the desired entities. The following code shows the schema for a subscription file:

```
<Subscription
  DefaultDisplayName="String"
  IsCached="Boolean"
  Enabled="Boolean"
  EntityName="String"
  EntityNamespace="String"
  LobSystemInstanceName="String"
  Name="String"
  RefreshIntervalInMinutes="Long"
  View="String">
  <Associations>
    <Association
      DefaultDisplayName="String"
      Enabled="Boolean"
      IsCached="Boolean"
LobSystemInstanceName="String"
      MethodInstanceName="String"
      Name="String"
      RefreshIntervalInMinutes="Long"
      TargetSubscriptionName="String"
      TargetView="String">
      <FilterValues>
        <FilterValue
          FilterDescriptorName="String"
          FilterIndex="Integer"
          Type="String">
        </FilterValue>
      </FilterValues>
```

```
        <LocalizedDisplayNames>
        </LocalizedDisplayNames>
        <Properties>
        </Properties>
      </Association>
    </Associations>
    <Identities>
      <Identity>
      </Identity>
    </Identities>
    <LocalizedDisplayNames>
      <LocalizedDisplayName
        LCID="Integer">
      </LocalizedDisplayName>
    </LocalizedDisplayNames>
    <Properties>
      <Property
        Name="String"
        Type="String">
      </Property>
    </Properties>
    <Queries>
      <Query
        DefaultDisplayName="String"
        Enabled="Boolean"
        IsCached="Boolean"
        MethodInstanceName="String"
        Name="String"
        RefreshIntervalInMinutes="Long">
        <FilterValues>
          <FilterValue
            FilterIndex="Integer"
            FilterDescriptorName="String"
            Type="String">
          </FilterValue>
        </FilterValues>
        <LocalizedDisplayNames>
        </LocalizedDisplayNames>
        <Properties>
        </Properties>
      </Query>
    </Queries>
  </Subscription>
```

Most of the elements in the subscription file schema are optional. A functional subscription requires only a `Subscription` element and a `Query` element. The following code shows an example of a subscription file:

```
<?xml version="1.0" encoding="utf-16" standalone="yes"?>
<Subscription Name="Product Subscription"
  LobSystemInstanceName="ExternalProductSystem"
  EntityNamespace="ExternalProducts"
  EntityName="Product" View="ReadProduct"
```

```
    RefreshIntervalInMinutes="10"
    xmlns="http://schemas.microsoft.com/office/2006/03/BusinessDataCatalog"
  >
    <Queries>
      <Query Name="ProductsQuery" IsCached="true"
        RefreshIntervalInMinutes="10"
        MethodInstanceName="ReadAllProducts" Enabled="true">
      </Query>
    </Queries>
  </Subscription>
```

A subscription begins with a `Subscription` element. The attributes of the `Subscription` element specify the information about the External Content Type to be retrieved. The `Name` attribute is the name of the subscription. The `LobSystemInstanceName` is the value of the `LobSystemInstance` in the BDC Metadata Model. The `EntityNamespace` and `EntityName` specify the ECT to be retrieved and are the values that were used when the ECT was created. The `RefreshInterval` specifies the time period after which the cached data should be refreshed from the External System.

The `Queries` element is a child of the `Subscription` element and contains one or more `Query` elements. The attributes of the `Query` element specify the `Finder` method to execute when refreshing the cache. The name of the `Finder` method is specified in the `MethodInstanceName` attribute. In addition to specifying queries, a subscription may also specify specific entity identities to return. This allows you to supplement the subscription with specific entities that are not part of the query.

For the entities returned, the query may also specify associations to return. This allows you to say, for example, that all related orders should be returned with each customer. Although they are supported, you should be careful about using associations because they can have a significant impact on synchronization. This is because every entity will have multiple items returned through an association. This will bloat the number of items that must be synchronized.

Most subscription files are automatically created by BCS. Subscriptions can be subsequently accessed and modified using the metadata cache object model. However, subscriptions can't be created or deleted using the API. Manually creating subscription files is most often done during the creation of a declarative or data-only solution. These solutions are used when you are targeting Microsoft Outlook or are creating a fully customized solution. Additional coverage of subscriptions, the metadata cache object model, declarative solutions, and custom solutions can be found in Chapter 6.

Understanding Cache Population

The metadata cache stores the identifiers for entity instances and the synchronized data in separate locations within the metadata cache. For each query defined within a subscription, BCS will create a new table in the metadata cache to hold the entity instances. These tables are named using the name of the `SpecificFinder` method, prefixed with `Table1`, `Table2`, `Table3`, and so on to ensure uniqueness.

Synchronization is performed by the `BCSSync.exe` process, which makes calls directly to the External System defined by the `LobSystemInstanceName` specified in the subscription. The synchronization process starts by making a `Finder` call to the method specified in the `MethodInstanceName` of the query. If the `Finder` method returns all the fields defined for the External Content Type, then no additional calls are made. If, however, the `Finder` method does not return all the needed fields, a separate call is made to the `SpecificFinder` method specified by the `View` attribute until the cache is populated. After the cache is populated from the `Finder` and `SpecificFinder` methods, calls are made to return the additional specific identities specified.

The last phase of cache population operates on any associations specified in the subscription. The `Associate()` method returns the `Id` of any associated entity instances. Then a `SpecificFinder` call is made for each returned `Id` to populate the cache. This process shows why associations can be very expensive when populating the cache; it simply takes a lot of time to execute all of the required operations to populate the cache.

Each `Subscription`, `Query`, `Identity`, and `Association` has a `RefreshInterval` attribute (called the `ExpireAfter` property in the metadata cache object model) that specifies when the cache should be refreshed from the External System. When the subscription expires, a refresh is scheduled; however, there is no way to know the exact time when the refresh will run. Refresh operations on the External System can be affected by the availability of the External System and the state of pending operations. Pending operations always receive the highest priority, so the synchronization process will delay refresh operations in order to complete updates to the External System. When the synchronization process has time to perform refresh operations, it always executes the refresh for the oldest expired subscription first.

Because end users cannot delete subscriptions or data from the cache, it will grow over time. However, invalid data is automatically garbage-collected by BCS so that the cache does not become unnecessarily large. Because the process is automatic, end users are freed from worrying about cache management.

The garbage collection process begins after the successful execution of all queries within a subscription. At this point any data in the cache that was not included in the refresh is marked as a candidate for deletion. The next time the same subscription runs, any data marked as a candidate for deletion is *tombstoned*. This means that the data still exists in the cache, but will not be used by BCS. Finally, the garbage collector runs and permanently deletes any tombstoned data.

Understanding Cache Operations

When performing operations on the client, solutions may specify whether they want to read the data directly from the External System or use the metadata cache. If data is read from the External System the cache will typically be updated as part of the operation. If the cache is read directly the solution may optionally provide a *freshness interval* — using an `OperationMode` object — that specifies the maximum acceptable age of the cached data. Before providing any data from the cache, the BDC Client runtime checks the status of the entity instance to determine the data quality. The status of the instance may be `Fresh`, `Invalid`, `Obsolete`, or `Stale`.

An entity instance status of `Fresh` means that the `RefreshInterval` has not passed. In this case the data is assumed to be valid. The BDC Client runtime will simply return the data.

An entity instance status of `Invalid` means that the BDC Client runtime cannot determine if the data in the cache is valid. This can happen when BCS cannot determine if the data in the External System has changed since the last refresh. In this case the data can't be used. The BDC Client runtime calls the `SpecificFinder` method for the entity instance, refreshes the cache data, and returns the new value.

An entity instance status of `Obsolete` means that the BDC Client runtime knows that the data in the External System has changed since the last refresh. In this case the data can't be used. The BDC Client runtime will refresh the data and return the new value.

An entity instance status of `Stale` means that the `RefreshInterval` has passed, but the synchronization process does not think the data in the External System has changed since the last refresh. An entity instance may become stale because the refresh has been delayed while the synchronization service performs higher-priority tasks or because the solution specified a freshness interval smaller than the refresh interval. In this case the BDC Client runtime will return the stale data only if it meets the freshness criteria specified by the solution. Otherwise the BDC Client runtime retrieves the data from the External System, updates the cache, and returns the new value. Figure 3-1 shows the process for reading entity instances.

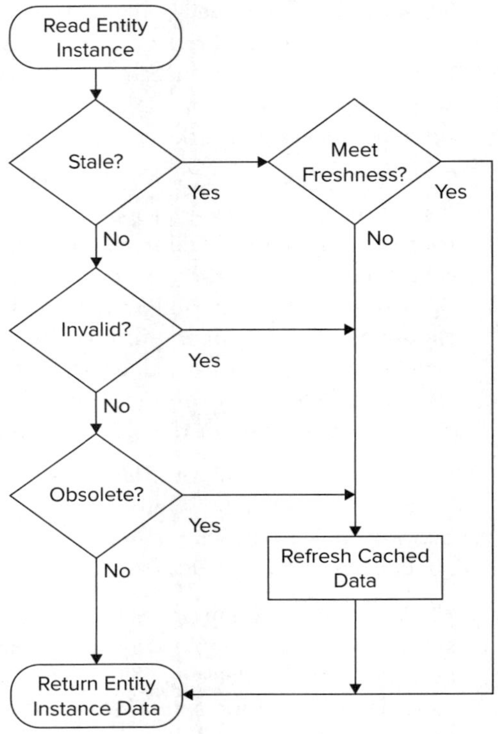

FIGURE 3-1

When the solution executes a create, update, or delete operation on data in the metadata cache, the operations are queued in the `OperationQueue` table in the metadata cache. The queued operations are executed on the External System during the synchronization process, but the exact timing of the operations cannot be predicted.

When a new entity instance is created, a new Create operation is queued and a new entity instance is created in the metadata cache. The `Identity` of the new entity instance is assigned a temporary value in the form of a `GUID` until the External System can be updated. After the synchronization process completes, the metadata cache is updated with the `Identity` assigned by the External System. At this point the entity instance is scheduled for refresh to ensure that any calculated fields are properly updated. If the operation fails, the entity instance's synchronization status is marked as `InError`. Figure 3-2 shows the process for creating new entity instances.

When an existing entity instance is updated, the cache data is updated and an update operation is queued. When the update operation is performed, the synchronization process first calls the `SpecificFinder` method for the entity instance and retrieves the latest values from the External System. The current values in the External System are then compared to the original values of the entity instance. If no conflicts are detected, the update operation is performed and the entity instance is scheduled for refresh. If a conflict is detected, the entity instance synchronization status is marked as `InError` and a `ConflictDetectedException` is thrown. If the first call to the `SpecificFinder` method results in an `ObjectNotFoundException` or an `ObjectDeletedException`, the synchronization process knows that the item has been deleted from the External System. In this case the update operation fails. Figure 3-3 shows the process for updating entity instances.

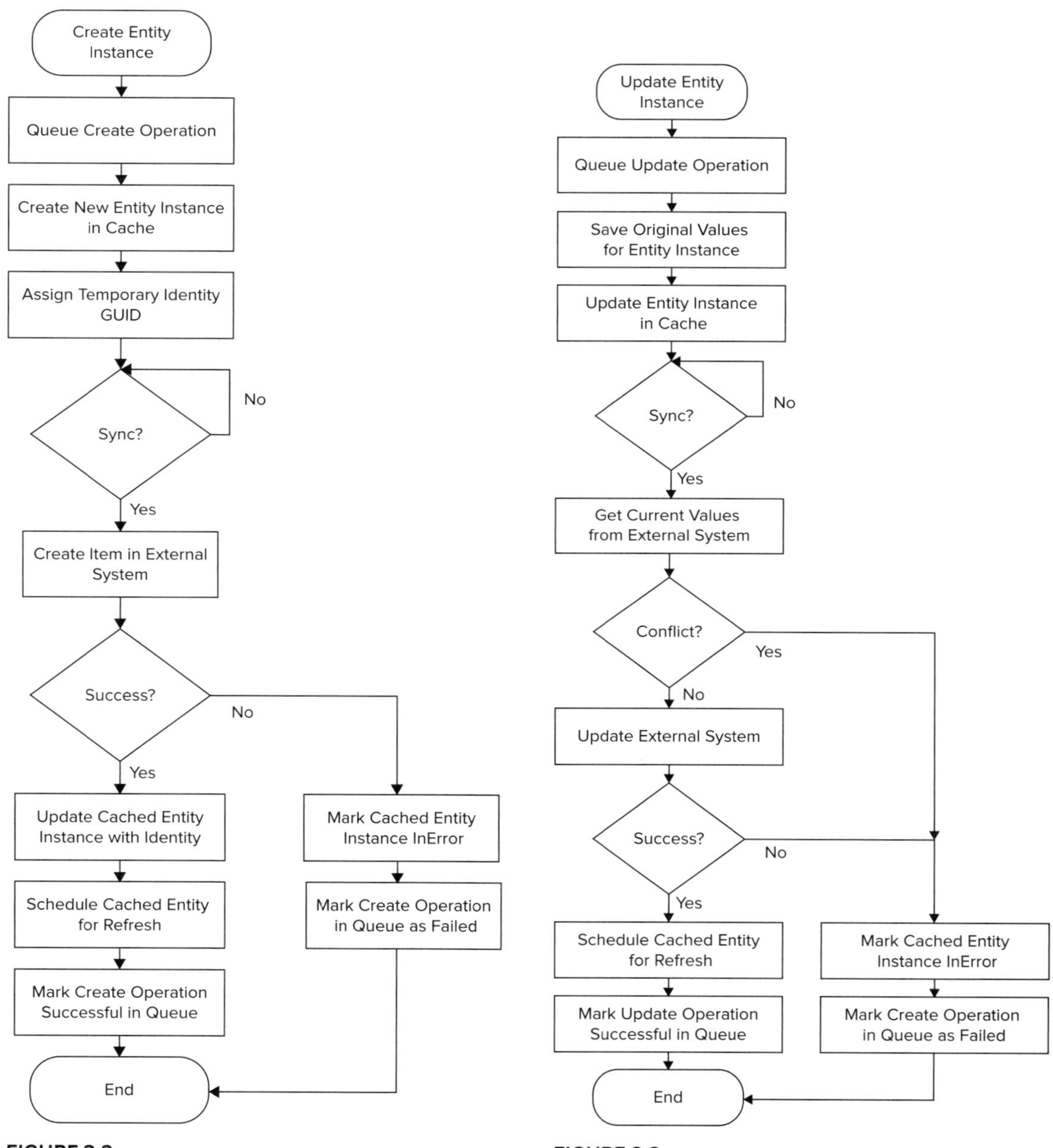

FIGURE 3-2

FIGURE 3-3

When an existing entity instance is deleted, a delete operation is queued. When the delete operation is performed, the synchronization process first calls the `SpecificFinder` method for the entity instance and retrieves the latest values from the External System. The current values in the External System are then compared to the original values of the entity instance. If no conflicts are detected, the delete operation is performed and the entity instance is deleted. If a conflict is detected, the entity instance status is marked as `InError` and a `ConflictDetectedException` is thrown. If the call to the `SpecificFinder` method results in an `ObjectNotFoundException` or `ObjectDeletedException`, the synchronization process knows that the item has been deleted from the External System. In this case the delete operation succeeds and the entity instance is deleted from the cache. Figure 3-4 shows the process for deleting entity instances.

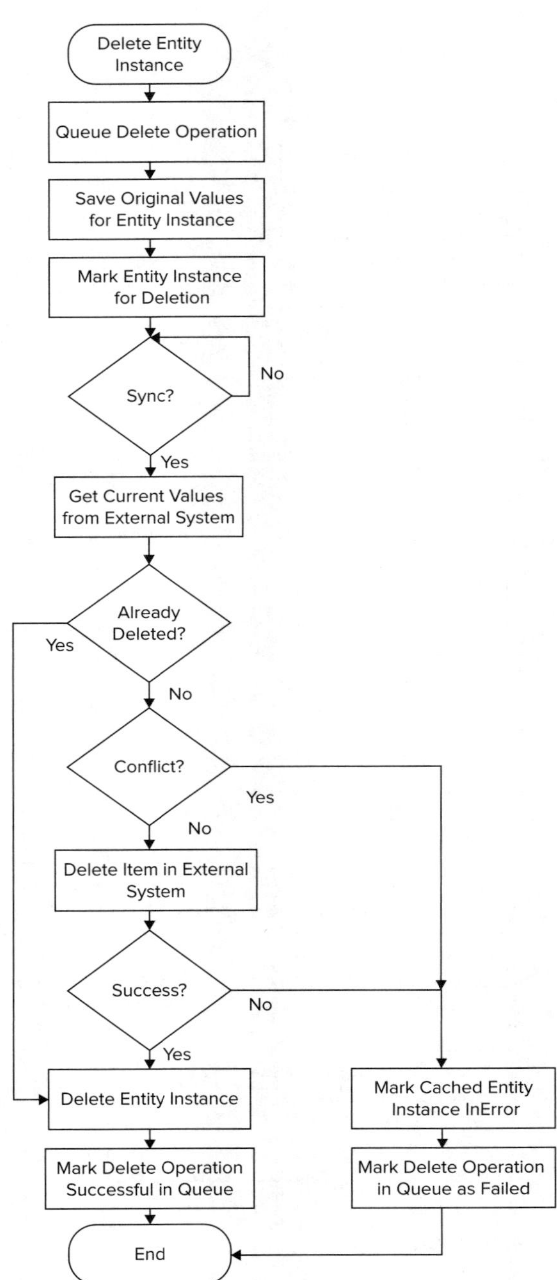

FIGURE 3-4

UNDERSTANDING SOLUTION DEPLOYMENT

As discussed in Chapter 1, BCS creates a ClickOnce deployment package on the SharePoint 2010 server to facilitate accessing External List data on the client. When you click either the Connect to Outlook or Sync to SharePoint Workspace buttons, the BCS deployment component creates a ClickOnce package and saves it into the `ClientSolution` folder underneath the related External List. Once the package is created, BCS launches the Visual Studio Tools for Office (VSTO) installer, which installs the customization on the client. While this process is conceptually simple, there are many factors and limitations to consider when planning to use ClickOnce deployment.

Understanding ClickOnce Deployment

ClickOnce deployment is an alternative to the Windows Installer for deploying client applications. The advantages of ClickOnce deployment include a significantly easier experience for end users and a web-based deployment capability. These features fit in perfectly with the BCS experience when end users need a simple way to install customizations directly from a SharePoint 2010 web page. While a BCS ClickOnce deployment package can consist of several different files, the primary files are the *deployment manifest* and the *application manifest*.

The deployment manifest is an XML file that describes the deployment configuration and can be found in the `ClientSolution` folder as the file with a VSTO extension. For simple solutions BCS uses a `GUID` for the name of the deployment manifest.

The application manifest is an XML file that describes the application being deployed. The application manifest includes information about assemblies, dependencies files, permissions, and update locations. For simple solutions BCS names the application manifest with the same `GUID` as the deployment manifest, but uses a `MANIFEST` extension at the end.

Along with the deployment manifest and application manifest, the BCS deployment component also copies the application files into the `ClientSolution` folder. For a simple solution, the application files consist of the BDC Metadata Model, the External List manifest, and a file with information about the view and a query necessary to create a subscription.

The BDC Metadata Model can be found under the `ClientSolution` folder in a file named `metadata.xml.deploy`. This is the same metadata model used on the server, with the exception that the connection information for the `LobSystemInstance` reflects the options for the client instead of for the server. During ClickOnce installation, the metadata model is stored in the metadata cache.

The External List manifest can be found under the `ClientSolution` folder in a file named `ExternalListManifest.mxl.deploy`. This file contains information about the list and the view to be rendered on the client. The following code shows a typical External List manifest:

```
<?xml version="1.0" encoding="utf-8"?>
<List
  Title="Customers"
  SiteId="579d3abe-acd6-4937-a9b7-caac2d3c4e33"
  SiteTitle="BCS"
xmlns="http://schemas.microsoft.com/office/2006/03/OfficeBusinessApplication">
  <Entity
    LobSystemInstance="MiniCRM"
    EntityNamespace="http://wingtipserver/bcs"
    EntityName="Customer"
    SpecificFinder="Read Item"
    DefaultViewId="88daa82c-6981-4f30-a2bc-d16094af12f1" />
  <Views>
    <View
      Id="88daa82c-6981-4f30-a2bc-d16094af12f1"
      DisplayName="Customer Read List" />
  </Views>
  <Form CreateView="" DisplayView="" EditView="" />
</List>
```

The view and query information can be found under the `ClientSolution` folder in a file named with a GUID and having a `XML.DEPLOY` extension. This file contains information about the list view and the Collaborative Application Markup Language (CAML) query necessary to create it. The following code shows a typical file:

```
<View Name="{88DAA82C-6981-4F30-A2BC-D16094AF12F1}"
  DefaultView="TRUE"
  MobileView="TRUE" MobileDefaultView="TRUE"
  Type="HTML"
  DisplayName="Customer Read List"
  Url="/bcs/Lists/Customers/Read List.aspx" Level="1" BaseViewID="1"
  ContentTypeID="0x"
  ImageUrl="/_layouts/images/generic.png">
  <Method Name="Read List"/>
  <Query>
    <OrderBy><FieldRef Name="ID"/></OrderBy>
  </Query>
  <ViewFields>
    <FieldRef Name="ID" ListItemMenu="TRUE" LinkToItem="TRUE"/>
    <FieldRef Name="Title"/>
    <FieldRef Name="FirstName"/>
    <FieldRef Name="MiddleName"/>
    <FieldRef Name="LastName"/>
    <FieldRef Name="Suffix"/>
    <FieldRef Name="EmailAddress"/>
    <FieldRef Name="Phone"/>
  </ViewFields>
  <RowLimit Paged="TRUE">30</RowLimit>
  <Aggregations Value="Off"/>
</View>
```

The files associated with a simple BCS solution contain enough information to support full CRUD operations on the External List. Additionally, the information in the solution can be used after deployment to create subscriptions, InfoPath forms, and required Outlook UI elements. As you begin to create more advanced solutions, you will have to create your own ClickOnce packages. The good news, however, is that the SDK and Visual Studio 2010 provide tools to help.

Understanding ClickOnce Security

ClickOnce security centers on a trusted publisher model, in which the deployment manifests are signed with a certificate. If a ClickOnce deployment manifest is signed by a trusted publisher, the application automatically installs without prompting the user. If, however, the application is not signed by a trusted publisher, the user is prompted to decide whether or not to install the application. Figure 3-5 shows a typical security dialog for BCS.

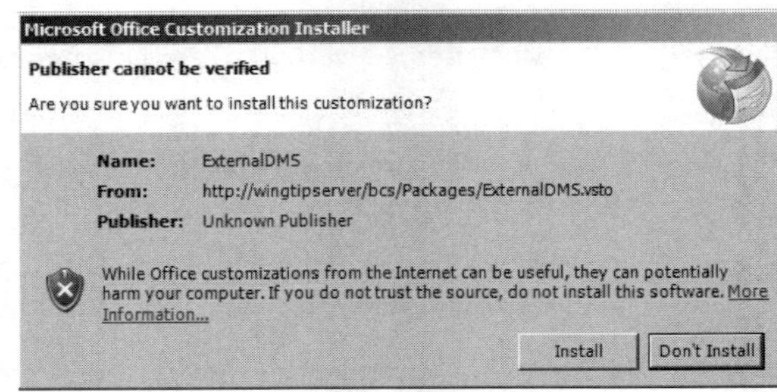

FIGURE 3-5

In the out-of-the-box configuration, BCS does not have a certificate that can be used to sign the ClickOnce packages. Instead, SharePoint generates a self-signed certificate and signs the package. These self-signed certificates are not trusted by the client because they are not issued by a trusted publisher known to the client. This means that a user will generally be prompted to confirm the ClickOnce deployment, but this may not always be the case. Whether or not a user is prompted is determined by the zone in which the package is located.

If the ClickOnce package is deployed from the My Computer, Local Intranet, or Trusted Sites zone, users will be prompted to allow installation. If the ClickOnce package is installed from the Internet or Untrusted Sites zone, installation will not be allowed. In this case, the only way to get the package installed is to have it signed by a trusted publisher.

In order to seamlessly install the ClickOnce application you must provide a trusted certificate to SharePoint that can be used for package signing. Ideally, this certificate should be a Verisign Authenticode certificate suitable for signing code. However, it could also be a certificate issued by Certificate Server, as long as the clients trust your certificates.

Once you have an appropriate certificate you need to create a certificate store named BusinessConnectivityServices on each web front-end server in the SharePoint farm. This is the store in which SharePoint will look for a certificate to sign the ClickOnce packages. You create the certificate store by adding the key `BusinessConnectivityServices` under `HKEY_LOCAL_MACHINE\SOFTWARE\Microsoft\SystemCertificates`. Figure 3-6 shows the key.

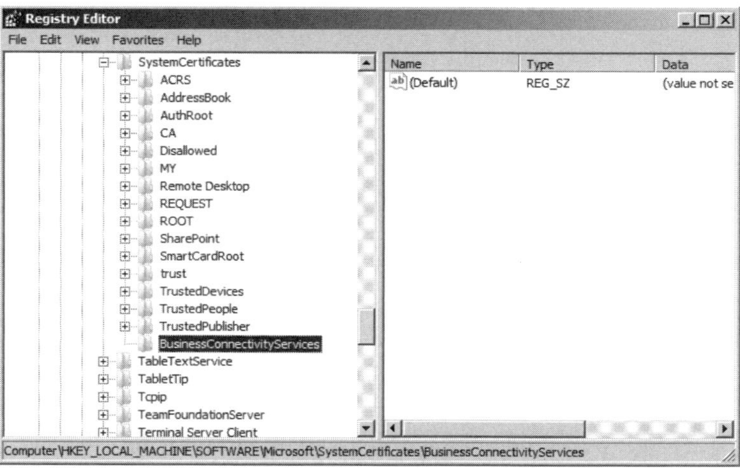

FIGURE 3-6

After the new certificate store is added, the certificate can be imported. The easiest way to do this is to use the Certificates snap-in for the local computer. From the command line type MMC to open a new console. Next select File ⇨ Add/Remove Snap-In from the menu. In the Add or

Remove Snap-Ins dialog select the Certificates snap-in. When prompted, select the local computer as the account. You should now see a BusinessConnectivityServices certificate store into which you can import your certificate. Note that SharePoint expects to find only one certificate in this store; otherwise the package-signing process will fail. Figure 3-7 shows an imported certificate.

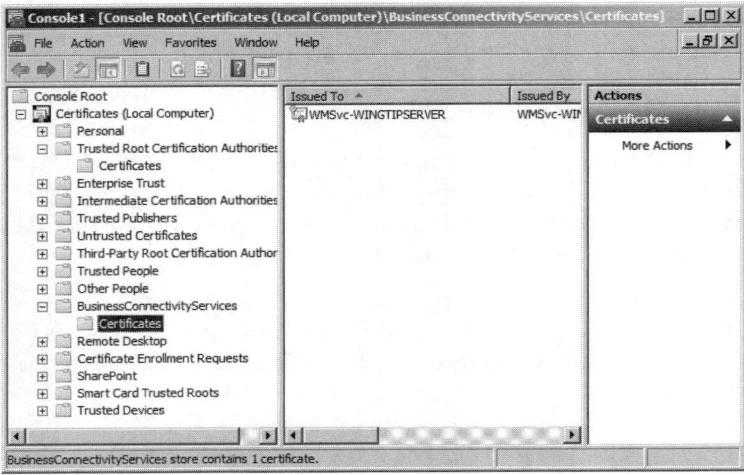

FIGURE 3-7

Finally, you will need to make sure that the account running the SharePoint Application Pool has rights to access the certificate. If this account does not have access, the ClickOnce package will not be signed. The simplest way to ensure the proper rights is to use the Windows HTTP Services Certificate Configuration Tool. This tool is available for download at `http://www.microsoft.com/downloads/details.aspx?familyid=c42e27ac-3409-40e9-8667-c748e422833f&displaylang=en`. Once you have downloaded the tool you can run the following command to determine whether the Application Pool account has access to the certificate:

```
WinHttpCertCfg.exe -l -c
  LOCAL_MACHINE\BusinessConnectivityServices
  -s {Certificate Name}
```

If the account does not have access you can run the following command to grant it access:

```
winhttpcertcfg.exe -g -c
  LOCAL_MACHINE\BusinessConnectivityServices
  -s {Certificate Name}
  -a {Account Name}
```

CONNECTING EXTERNAL LISTS TO OUTLOOK

When a user clicks the Connect to Outlook button in the SharePoint ribbon and installs the required customization, Outlook uses a managed folder named `BCSStorage.PST` to facilitate display of the data in a folder. The customization and PST folder can be found in the `\Users\{UserName}\AppData\Local\Microsoft\BCS` folder, along with the metadata cache database. Once the data and customization are downloaded, end users may interact with the data through an Outlook folder.

Understanding BCS Folder Limitations

Just as External List functionality is a subset of standard SharePoint list functionality, BCS folders in Outlook also have some limitations that are important to consider. These limitations involve the display of data in Outlook along with the availability of the data for use within Outlook.

Understanding Form Limitations

When defining an ECT you can specify that the data should be displayed in Outlook as a Contact item, Task item, Appointment, or Post, depending on the mapping selections made during the creation of the External Content Type. Each of the different Outlook types requires at least one field to be mapped to the ECT. Contact types require a `LastName` or `FullName` field; Task types require a `Subject` field; Appointment types require `Start`, `End`, and `Subject` fields; Post types require a `Subject` field.

In addition to the required fields, ECTs are likely to have many that do not map to particular Outlook fields. These additional fields are displayed in Outlook using a form region in the Outlook inspector. If the additional fields number five or fewer they are displayed in an adjoining Outlook form region, which means they are simply appended to the existing form. If the additional fields number more than five they are placed in a separate Outlook form region. You can access the additional fields in a separate Outlook form region by clicking the appropriate details button in the Outlook ribbon. Figure 3-8 shows additional Reseller details available through the Show Reseller Details button.

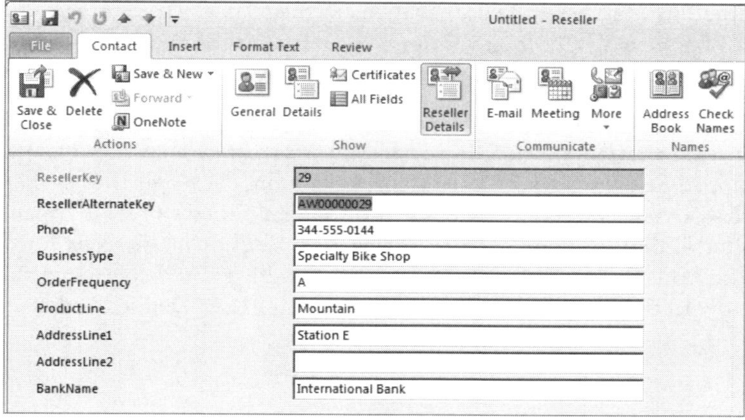

FIGURE 3-8

Unlike standard form regions, the form regions installed with the out-of-the-box customization are not editable. Opening a BCS item will display the item in the appropriate inspector, along with any additional form regions. Clicking the Show button associated with an adjoining region will display the adjoining region containing any additional fields. Subsequently clicking the Developer tab will allow you to click the button entitled Design This Form. Normally this action will expose the Outlook form region for customization. In the case of the out-of-the-box BCS solution, however, the form region is not available. (Note that the Developer tab is normally not visible and that you must activate it from the Options dialog by clicking Customize Ribbon.) Because the adjoining form region is not available you may find that the information display is less than desirable. The additional BCS fields are simply stacked vertically and the label for each field shows the name as defined in the ECT. There is no way after the fact to modify the Outlook region or to hide BCS columns. Therefore, you should plan the definition of your ECT to support the fields you really want to display in Outlook, or create custom form regions as described in Chapter 6.

When the inspector is open for a BCS item, you will also notice that the standard Outlook fields are visible as well. If, for example, an ECT is mapped to a Contact item, that item will have e-mail, phone number, and address fields visible even if there are no ECT fields mapped to them. This means that end users can enter additional data into these fields, but that data will never be synchronized back to the External List. This additional data will survive synchronization — as it is stored in the PST file — but it will be visible only to the end user who entered it. This behavior may be confusing to end users.

Beyond confusion about the data fields themselves, this behavior can lead to confusion regarding the functionality of the items. For example, imagine that you have created an External List that maps to the Task type. As required, you map a field to the task subject field. An end user can then synchronize the list with Outlook and see the items as tasks. However, marking the task as complete has no meaning outside the list in Outlook because no fields in the External List are mapped to the completion field. Such situations are easy to create unless you design your External Lists carefully.

The normal approach to these challenges is to create a custom form and publish it for use in the Outlook folder. Although it is possible to place the BCS form in design mode using the Developer tab, you cannot publish a modified form for use with other items in the folder. Attempting to publish a modified version of a BCS form in Outlook results in an error. All of this means that you are largely stuck with the presentation of the BCS fields and the presence of the additional Outlook fields.

Although the default BCS form region cannot be edited, it is possible to create a view that includes both the mapped and the unmapped fields. On the Home tab of the ribbon, clicking More in the Current View group will reveal a Manage Views link. Clicking the Manage Views link will open the Manage All Views dialog. In this dialog you may create a new view by clicking the New button. If a new table view is created, the fields for the External List can all be added and displayed in the same view. The fields associated with the External List are available under User-Defined Fields in the Folder group.

Understanding Functional Limitations

In addition to the limitations placed on the display of data, there are also several limitations placed on its use. While much of the Outlook functionality is preserved, end users should be aware of limitations and the available workarounds. The following sections discuss the limitations for each of the Outlook types.

External Content Types designed as Outlook contact types generally cannot participate in operations that would require the form to be used. For example, items in a BCS folder designated as a contact type cannot be attached to an e-mail directly. Instead, they must be inserted into the body of an e-mail as text. Additionally, contact types cannot be forwarded or participate in mail merges. Finally, the BCS folder itself does not support the creation of new contact groups.

External Content Types designed as Outlook appointment types do not support inviting attendees, recurrence, or forwarding. Additionally, appointment items cannot be attached to an e-mail directly; instead they must be added to the body of an e-mail as text. Appointments also do not support attachments.

External Content Types designed as Outlook task types do not support recurrence or being forwarded to others. You also cannot assign a task to another user from within Outlook. Additionally, task items may not be attached to e-mails directly. They may, however, be inserted into the body of the e-mail as text.

External Content Types designed as Outlook post types may not be forwarded or attached to e-mails directly. They may be inserted into e-mails as text. Users can reply to posts and those replies will be added to the External System. However, the External List in SharePoint is not capable of showing a threaded discussion, so the items appear simply as a flat list.

Understanding SharePoint Security Limitations

When accessing External Lists through the browser, SharePoint permissions are respected. This means that you can restrict the ability of end users to see lists or edit items based on their SharePoint rights. For example, a user with View permissions will not be able to edit items in an External List through the browser, but will be able to view the list and items.

If end users have at least View permissions for an External List, they can click the Connect to Outlook button and install the solution. Once the solution is installed in Outlook, the list permissions in SharePoint cease to have meaning. The ability to perform operations on the items in an Outlook folder is determined solely by the permissions in the BDC Metadata Model. Therefore, you should give consideration to security within the BDC Metadata Model first, and not rely on SharePoint permissions to secure data in the External System.

Synchronizing Outlook Data

When an External List is connected to Outlook, a default subscription is downloaded that will refresh the cached data every six hours. Although the subscription will automatically refresh the data, you can force synchronization by right-clicking the External List folder in Outlook and selecting Sync Now from the context menu. You can check the synchronization status by right-clicking the folder for the External List and selecting Synchronization Status. A dialog will open, displaying the current synchronization status and available views for the External List. Additionally, a checkbox is available to disable synchronization for the list. Figure 3-9 shows a typical synchronization status dialog.

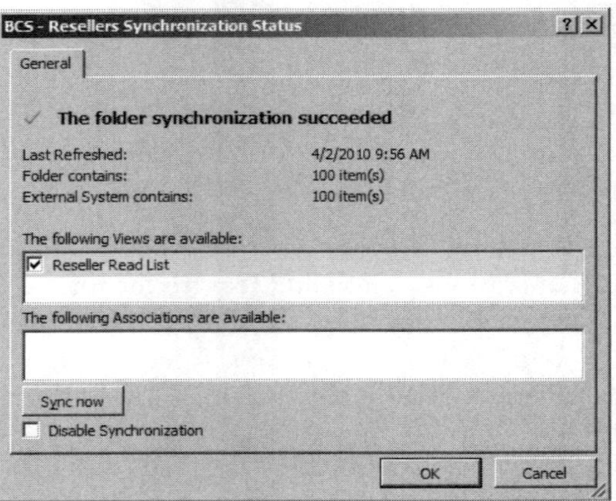

FIGURE 3-9

If errors occur during synchronization, the affected items will appear in the `Sync Issues` folder. Errors occur when the data in the External System has changed since the last synchronization, as described earlier in the chapter. In order to resolve the synchronization errors the end user must open the item and click the File tab. Clicking the File tab opens the backstage view for the item. Here the end user will see a notification that conflicts have occurred. Clicking the button in the Backstage View will open a dialog that allows for resolution. The user may then select to either keep the value in the External System or force the value in Outlook to be saved.

Selecting to force the value in Outlook into the External System will overwrite the changes made previously by other users. However, keeping the value in the External System loses the changes made by the current user. If the current user has made many changes, the data loss may be significant. Users can often avoid data conflicts by simply performing a manual synchronization prior to making any large-scale changes in data. Figure 3-10 shows the backstage view with the Resolve Conflict dialog open.

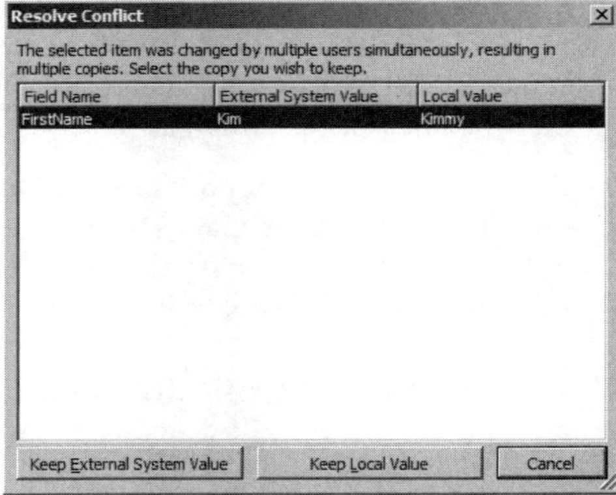

FIGURE 3-10

Managing Client Credentials

While Chapter 8 covers authentication and authorization scenarios in detail, this chapter presents credential management from the end-user perspective. When folders in Outlook are synchronized with External Systems they use the authentication method that was defined for the ECT model. Often the client will simply be accessing the External System using his or her own credentials, but that will not always be the case. When the External System does not use Windows or claims credentials, it may be necessary to use a separate account. In these cases the credentials will be stored in the Credential Manager.

Credential Manager is not part of the BCS infrastructure. It is a utility that is part of the operating system. BCS simply takes advantage of this utility to manage credentials for the end user. If credentials other than the user's are required, BCS will prompt the end user to enter credentials and then store them in Credential Manager.

End users can see and manage their credentials by opening the Credential Manager. They can access it by clicking Control Panel ➪ User Accounts ➪ Manage Your Credentials. BCS credentials will be listed under the Generic Credentials section. Figure 3-11 shows the Credential Manager with BCS credentials stored.

FIGURE 3-11

End users are free to delete the credentials stored in the Credential Manager. In this case they will simply be prompted to enter them again during the next synchronization. If the credentials for the External System change, BCS will prompt the user to enter new credentials and simply overwrite the existing credentials.

Updating Outlook Solutions

Even after an External List is synchronized with Outlook, changes may be made to the schema, views, and operations. In these cases end users can get the latest version of the solution in two ways: through either SharePoint or Outlook. Clicking the Connect to Outlook button in SharePoint will always download the latest solution. Alternately, the end user may right-click the folder in Outlook and select Check for Updates from the context menu. If the solution has not changed, the end user will see a message indicating that no update was installed. Otherwise the latest solution will be installed. Microsoft Outlook itself has no automatic means to update BCS solutions.

When an updated solution is installed, the end user might not immediately see the new data and functionality. This is because Office clients must often be closed in order for the installation to complete. If closing the Office clients is required, the end user will receive a notification that the solution installation is pending.

In addition to updating solutions, end users may also remove them. Right-clicking a folder in Outlook and selecting Delete will remove the solution. Deleting the folder has no impact on the External Data; the solution is simply removed. In order to reinstall the solution the user must return to SharePoint and click the Connect to Outlook button.

Generally, changes that are made to the External List in SharePoint have no effect on the solution once it is deployed to Outlook. For example, if an External List is deleted from SharePoint, the Outlook solution will continue to synchronize the data based on the subscription. This is because the Outlook solution always synchronizes with the External System directly.

If an External List has multiple views, those views are available to the solution in Outlook. The Synchronization Status dialog shows all the available views and allows the end user to select the views that will be synchronized. Changing the selected views and performing synchronization will immediately affect the data in Outlook. Items in any new selected views will appear in the folder, while items in unselected views will be removed from the folder.

If an External List has a view that uses a filter, Outlook will make that view available using the filter value that was in place when the list was first synchronized. Subsequent changes to the filter value in the External List will have no effect on the items appearing in the Outlook folder. Attempting to update the solution either directly in Outlook or by clicking the Connect to Outlook button in SharePoint will also have no effect on the filter value used. This fact means that you should be careful in your use of filter settings with External Lists because you obviously cannot predict when a user will connect an External List to Outlook.

CONNECTING LISTS TO THE SHAREPOINT WORKSPACE

The SharePoint Workspace (SPW) is a new client application that allows end users to create local copies of SharePoint sites for working offline. The SharePoint Workspace, like Microsoft Outlook, provides support for standard lists and libraries as well as External Lists. You can take lists, libraries, and External Lists offline by clicking the Sync to SharePoint Workspace button located on the List tab of the ribbon in SharePoint 2010.

Understanding SPW Architecture

The role of SPW is to create client-side copies of SharePoint data and provide for the two-way synchronization of that data. SPW makes use of three repositories on the client to store offline data: the SharePoint Workspace itself, the Office Document Cache (ODC), and the BCS metadata cache. Standard lists, InfoPath forms, non-Office documents, list schemas, and list views are stored in the SharePoint Workspace. Office documents from libraries are stored in the ODC. External Lists are stored in the BCS metadata cache.

When the client is online, any changes made to standard lists are immediately synchronized with SharePoint. If the client is offline, those changes are kept in the repository until they can be synchronized. SPW also engages in periodic synchronization operations to refresh any data that may have changed in SharePoint.

Understanding the Office Document Cache

The ODC is used by all Office products to manage documents and synchronize changes with SharePoint. The ODC is located at `\Users\{UserName}\AppData\Local\Microsoft\Office\14\OfficeFileCache`. Although ODC is not part of BCS, documents are often a significant part of a SharePoint solution, so understanding how they are handled is important. You can access the ODC through an icon in the system tray, which opens the Upload Center. In the Upload Center you can view items in the cache and manage settings. Figure 3-12 shows the Upload Center with several documents cached pending reconnection to the server.

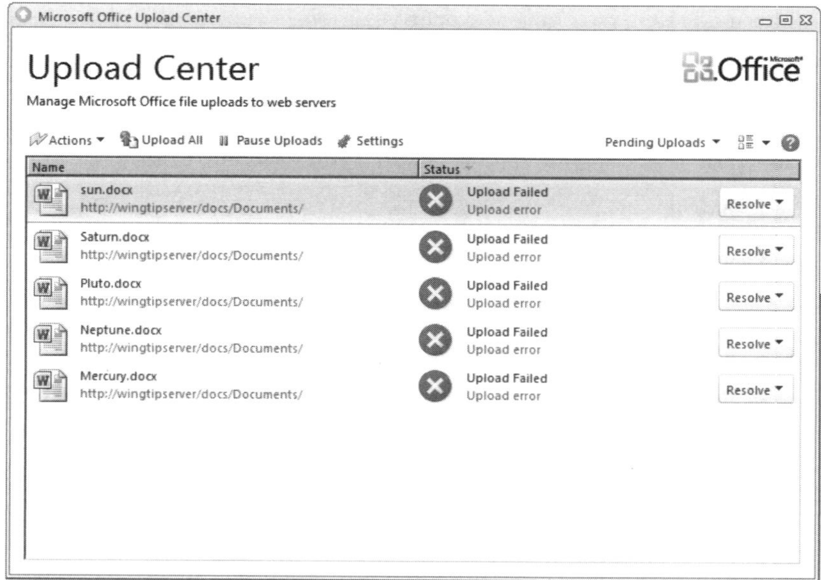

FIGURE 3-12

Synchronization of documents with SharePoint is done through a web service. This web service uses a special document synchronization protocol known as File Sync via SOAP over HTTP (FSSHTTP). After the initial synchronization process, only changes are transferred between SharePoint and SPW. This keeps sync time as short as possible.

In much the same way that External Lists can create conflicts when two or more users edit the same items in a disconnected environment, other users can edit documents that you have taken offline in SPW. Whenever possible, ODC and SharePoint will attempt to merge the changes made by multiple users into the same document. When you open the document again, any differences will appear highlighted in green.

SPW also supports working collaboratively with multiple people on the same document. You are notified by SPW anytime you open a document that is being edited by another user. This notification provides contact information for the other user. As the other user works, portions of the document are locked. When they have finished, you will receive notification and can sync the changes into your copy of the document.

Synchronizing External Lists

When an External List is synchronized to SPW, a VSTO ClickOnce package is created and installed. SPW makes use of the BCS metadata cache to manage data from External Lists, so it needs the customization installed. However, SPW is fundamentally different from BCS because it wants to synchronize with the SharePoint Server, whereas BCS communicates directly with the External System. What this means is that SPW will not synchronize External List data if it cannot communicate with the SharePoint Server. This is true even though BCS only requires communication with the External System to complete synchronization.

In most cases, if SPW cannot communicate with SharePoint, BCS probably cannot communicate with the External System, because the client is disconnected from the network. However, if the SharePoint Server goes down, but the External System is still online, BCS solutions in Outlook will still continue to function correctly, but SPW solutions will exhibit some odd behavior.

When a change is made to an External List in SPW, that change is written to the BCS metadata cache and a queued update operation is created. If SharePoint is offline and the External System is online, the queued operation will execute during the next BCS synchronization. However, if changes are made to the External System from some other source, those changes will not be reflected in SPW because SPW is relying solely on the metadata cache when SharePoint is offline. The same External List in Outlook will reflect the data change because the BCS synchronization will be directly against the External System. SPW will reflect the change only when SharePoint is back online and the next synchronization occurs.

Writing Scripts and Macros

The SharePoint Workspace has extremely limited programmability. Unlike other Office applications, it does not have a Visual Basic for Applications (VBA) environment. You also cannot create custom add-ins for SPW using Visual Studio 2010. The only available option for programming SPW involves creating JavaScript files that manipulate the client-side COM components.

The most useful COM component for use with scripts is the `Groove.SiteClientActiveX` object. This component will allow you to programmatically take sites and lists offline. Invoking this object performs the same function as clicking the Sync to SharePoint Workspace button. The following code shows a sample script for taking a site offline:

```
<script type='text/javascript'>
  function syncSiteSPW(siteUrl)
  {
    var OfflineClientScope_Site = 1;
```

```
    var OfflineClientScope_ListOrLibrary = 2;
    var OfflineClientScope_Folder = 3;
    var a = new ActiveXObject('Groove.SiteClientActiveX');
    if(a.IsOfflineAllowed(
                    OfflineClientScope_Site,
                    100,
                    100,
                    100))
      a.TakeOffline(
        OfflineClientScope_Site,
        1,
        siteUrl,
        1,
        1,
        '',
        '');
    else
      alert('Site cannot be taken offline.');
  }
</script>
```

The two methods available with the `Groove.SiteClientActiveX` object are the `IsOfflineAllowed()` and `TakeOffline()` methods. The `IsOfflineAllowed()` method takes a scope argument that specifies whether to take a site, list, or folder offline. The remaining values specify the site template, `SPBaseType`, and `SPListTemplate` type. The method returns a `Boolean` indicating whether or not the target can be taken offline. If the target can be taken offline, the `TakeOffline()` method can be used to start the synchronization process. The `TakeOffline()` method requires a scope argument, site template, site URL, list ID, and folder ID. The list ID and folder ID are `GUIDs` that are required only for taking a list offline. If the folder ID is not supplied, the root folder is taken offline. The following code shows how to write a script to take a list offline:

```
<script type='text/javascript'>
  function syncListSPW(siteUrl, listId)
  {
    var OfflineClientScope_Site = 1;
    var OfflineClientScope_ListOrLibrary = 2;
    var OfflineClientScope_Folder = 3;
    var a = new ActiveXObject('Groove.SiteClientActiveX');
    if(a.IsOfflineAllowed(
                    OfflineClientScope_ListOrLibrary,
                    100,
                    100,
                    100))
      a.TakeOffline(
        OfflineClientScope_ListOrLibrary,
        1,
        siteUrl,
        1,
        1,
        listId,
```

```
            '');
        else
          alert(List cannot be taken offline.');
      }
    </script>
```

While SPW has limited programmability, the ODC has no programming interface at all. This is unfortunate because BCS does not store `stream` data in the metadata cache; accessing `stream` data always requires a direct connection to the External System. Although using the ODC to manage documents as part of a custom BCS solution would be ideal, it is not possible. As a result, the only way to make use of the ODC programmatically is to invoke file operations through the object models of Office clients in a macro or custom add-in. The following code shows a simple macro that saves a file to SharePoint, thus invoking the ODC.

```
Sub SaveToSharePoint()

  Dim FileName As String
  FileName = "http://adventureworksserver/Documents/ODCTest.docx"

  Application.ActiveDocument.SaveAs2
     FileName:=FileName,
     FileFormat:=docOpenXmlDocument

End Sub
```

USING EXTERNAL DATA IN WORD

Chapter 2 discussed External Data columns, which allow data from External Systems to appear as columns in a list. Along with External Data Columns, you can also create a Lookup column based on the data from an External List. Both of these approaches provide simple ways to make External Data available in SharePoint. Both External Data Columns and Lookup columns based on External Lists get special treatment in Microsoft Word 2010. When creating a document template you may embed a *content control* inside the document that acts as an entity picker for the External Data. This allows users to insert External Data into a Word document while they are writing it. Figure 3-13 shows an invoice being created in Word, where the company name is selected from an External Data Column.

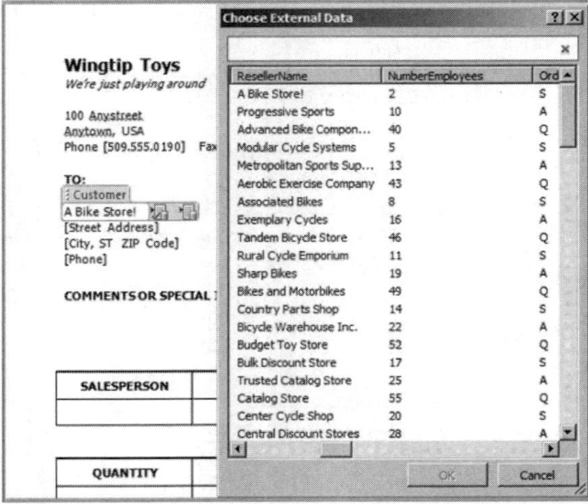

FIGURE 3-13

Using External Data Columns

Adding External Data columns directly to any list or library in SharePoint is a fully supported scenario. When you add an External Data column to a document library, it will appear in the Document Information Panel (DIP) when new documents are created or existing documents are edited. You can go further by embedding the External Data in the Word document through the use of *Quick Parts*.

Quick Parts are available inside Microsoft Word on the Insert tab in the Text group. You can create an enhanced document template by editing the existing template, inserting quick parts, and saving the result as the new template. While editing the template you can select the place in the document where the External Data should be inserted. Once you have selected the appropriate place in the document you can select Insert ⇨ Quick Parts ⇨ Document Property and pick the desired field. Once the field is inserted in the document, the picker becomes active and you may select a value from the External System as in Figure 3-13.

When you are creating an ECT specifically for use in Word documents, there are a few things to keep in mind. The first is that the picker will use cached data first. This means that the available data may not always be complete, depending upon the subscription in place and the frequency with which the data changes. The picker has a button labeled More Results that will force the cache to be refreshed with the latest data.

The second area of concern is the ECT design. The picker executes the default `Finder` method to display the initial set of items. This means that you should give consideration to what items you want returned and to the associated fields. Also be sure to use the Show in Picker setting for any fields that you want to see in the picker control. If no fields are selected for the picker, then all fields are shown by default. Finally, make sure that you set one field as the `Title` field in SPD. This is the field that will actually be inserted into the Word document.

The third issue concerns list size. As with any ECT, you should define filters for the operations to prevent large amounts of data from returning. If no filters are defined, the picker will limit itself to 200 items and warn you. If filters are available beyond that, you'll have the opportunity to narrow your query.

The picker is a read-only solution so you cannot use it to write back to the External System. If you need to write back to the External System you can create a custom add-in or use a workflow that will run when the document is uploaded.

Creating Reusable Site Content Types

The preferred approach for exposing metadata in a Word document is to create site columns and site content types in SharePoint that will then be used as the basis for a document template in a library. Site columns and site content types are the best choice because they allow you to reuse the definitions you create across many libraries while managing them in a single location. Unfortunately, the External Data column can only be created in a list content type. The workaround is to create a Lookup column; however, this is not an officially supported use of ECTs — if you run into trouble with this approach, you can't call Microsoft for help.

When you're creating a SharePoint farm the taxonomy is a critical part of the overall design. *Taxonomy* refers to the *controlled vocabularies* that are used as items in Lookup lists. Controlled vocabularies are sets of terms that are centrally defined and managed. For example, a controlled vocabulary may be built around a set of terms for geography that includes the words *country, region, province, state, town,* and so on. The advantage of a controlled vocabulary is that end users pick terms from a predefined set; they cannot misspell terms or make up their own. Controlled vocabularies support a strong document classification system that significantly improves search results.

When External Data is in an External Data column or Lookup list, it can be thought of as a controlled vocabulary. The values in the field are set in the External System and not easily changed. Therefore, we would ideally like to be able to create and manage these fields centrally.

Because the External Data column can be created only in a list content type, it is not a good candidate for implementing a controlled vocabulary. Instead you can create an External List at the site collection level and use it as the basis for a site column Lookup field. The site column Lookup field can be added to any number of site content types, which in turn can be used as the basis for a document library.

As an example walkthrough, consider an organization that needs to create both invoices and purchase orders. The invoices and purchase orders are created in Microsoft Word using a template and require the contact information for the customer or vendor to be entered. The organization has CRM and ERP systems that contain customer and vendor information, respectively.

As a starting point, ECTs need to be created for vendors and customers. This process can be as simple as opening SPD and defining `Customer` and `Vendor` ECTs based on the data in the CRM and ERP systems. Once these are defined, two External Lists named Customers and Vendors can be created.

Once the External Lists are created, site columns based on them can be created. This process involves going to the site column gallery and creating two new site columns: `Customer` and `Vendor`. The key is to create columns of type `Lookup` and base them on the previously created External Lists. After that, any additional required metadata columns can be created. Figure 3-14 shows several columns created to support the invoice and purchase orders, with the `Customer` and `Vendor` columns being based on External Data.

Site Column	Type
Financial Columns	
Amount	Currency
Customer	External Data
Invoice Number	Single line of text
P.O. Number	Single line of text
Purchasing Department	Choice
Vendor	External Data

FIGURE 3-14

Once the site columns are created they may be used to build a content type hierarchy. In this example a hierarchy based on the `Document` content type was created. This makes sense because invoices and purchase orders will be Word documents. Using the `Document` content type as a starting point, a `Financial Document` content type was created that inherits from `Document`. Then an `Invoice` content type and a `Purchase Order` content type that both inherit from the `Financial Document` content type were created. The content types contain the various fields, including the Lookup fields that are based on the ECTs created earlier. Table 3-4 shows the complete content type hierarchy for the scenario.

TABLE 3-4: Sample Content Type Hierarchy

CONTENT TYPE	COLUMN	TYPE	SOURCE
Document	Title	Text	Item
	Name	File	
Financial Document	Title	Text	Item
	Name	File	Document
	Amount	Currency	
Invoice	Title	Text	Item
	Name	File	Document
	Amount	Currency	Financial Document
	Invoice Number	Text	
	Customer	External Data	
Purchase Order	Title	Text	Item
	Name	File	Document
	Amount	Currency	Financial Document
	P. O. Number	Text	
	Purchasing Department	Choice	
	Vendor	External Data	

After defining the metadata for all three content types, Word templates were added for the `Invoice` and `Purchase Order` content types. These templates were simply based on ones downloaded from the Office Template Gallery, but any templates will work. A template was not created for the `Financial Document` content type because it exists solely to define the common `Amount` field; it will never be used directly to create a document. Once the content types were created, a document library named Financial Documents was created. Finally, the `Invoice` and `Purchase Order` content types were added to the library.

At this point in the walkthrough a new invoice or purchase order can be created from the document library. When a new document is created the metadata fields are visible in the Document Information Panel (DIP) at the top of the document. However, the fields are not yet available in the body of the document. The document template used for the `Invoice` and `Purchase Order` content types must be edited so that the picker for the External Data is embedded into the document.

You can create an enhanced invoice and purchase order template by creating a new document, inserting Quick Parts, and saving the result as the new template. Selecting Insert ➪ Quick Parts ➪ Document Property and the `Vendor` field, for example, will insert the picker into the template for that field. Figure 3-15 shows the list of available Quick Parts for the scenario.

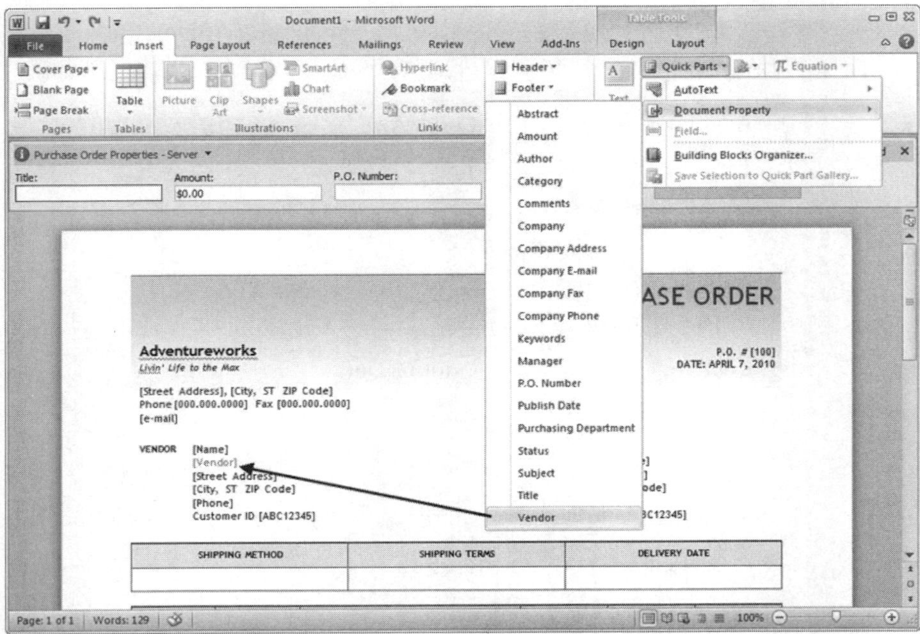

FIGURE 3-15

It's important to note that Quick Parts work for all fields, not just External Data. When a template is completed it can be saved to a temporary location pending uploading as the new template. The only thing left to complete the solution is to substitute the enhanced template for the existing one. This can be done in the Site Content Type Gallery, where you can upload new templates for the `Invoice` and `Purchase Order` content types. Now when new invoices and purchase orders are created, they will automatically have the External Data available and integrated with the document creation process. Of course, the entire solution can be packaged as a feature and deployed using a WSP file.

Understanding External Data Limitations in Word

There are several limitations associated with External Data fields used in Word documents. First, you must have NET Framework 3.5 installed to use the picker in Word documents. If .NET Framework 3.5 is not installed, the end user will see an error message when he or she tries to activate the content control. Second, taking documents out of the document library can have strange effects on the picker control. Generally, documents should not be e-mailed directly to a user. Instead, e-mail a link that refers back to the document library. Third, when you use an External List as the basis for a site column, editing the Document Information Panel containing the column may cause the picker to fail. Finally, if the end user has a version of Office other than 2010, his or her experience will be different. In Word 2007 the picker will not be shown, but the data can be edited. In previous versions of Word, the External Data is read-only.

WORKING WITH EXTERNAL DATA IN MICROSOFT ACCESS

Microsoft Access has some limited capability to use BCS models for data access. In short, you can use BCS models to import data into an Access table. However, this data will be read-only and will not be supported in SharePoint 2010 through Access Services.

In order to use Access with BCS data you must export the BCS model from the SharePoint Designer and save it with an XML extension. By default SPD wants to use a BDCM extension, but you should change it to XML. Once the model is exported you can start Microsoft Access and create a new database.

With a new database created, you can select the External Data tab and choose More ➪ Data Services from the Import & Link group. The Create Link to Data Services dialog opens, enabling you to install a new connection. The new connection refers to a BCS model. Browsing to the exported XML file and opening it will display the available ECTs. You can then select an ECT and create a read-only linked table. Figure 3-16 shows the Create Link to Data Services dialog.

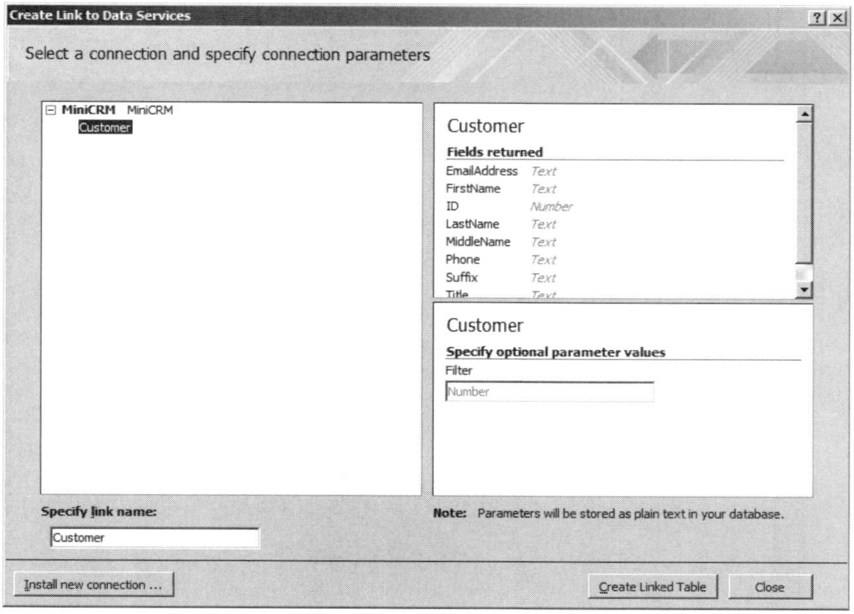

FIGURE 3-16

SUMMARY

One of the significant values of BCS is its support for client-side and disconnected access to data. The BCS client architecture complements the server architecture, which makes it easy to use your knowledge of the server to create client-side solutions. The metadata cache supports offline scenarios that weren't possible with previous versions of SharePoint, which creates additional value for end users. In this chapter you examined these capabilities from the client perspective. As you move ahead you'll create increasingly more complex solutions that will grow naturally from the foundation laid here.

Creating BCS Solutions with the SharePoint Designer

WHAT'S IN THIS CHAPTER?

- Learn the BDC Metadata Model schema
- Learn to create BCS solutions with SharePoint Designer
- Learn to write code against External Lists
- Learn to deploy BCS solutions

SharePoint Designer 2010 (SPD) is the primary application for creating BCS solutions in SharePoint 2010. While Visual Studio 2010 offers a project type and the tooling for BCS, both of which are covered in Chapter 7, SPD is capable of creating External Content Types (ECTs) for all but the most advanced solutions. Furthermore, the SPD toolset is easier to learn than the Visual Studio toolset. As a result, SPD should be considered first for any BCS solution.

Chapter 1 presented a walkthrough of a simple no-code solution using SPD. This chapter will go further to present detailed information about data sources, ECT development, user interaction, and solution management. After completing this chapter you will have a strong understanding of the SPD toolset and be able to create a wide range of BCS solutions.

WORKING WITH THE BDC METADATA MODEL

Chapter 2 introduced the BDC Metadata Model as an XML file that completely defines the ECT, its connection to the External System, and its operations. When creating BCS solutions using the SPD tooling, you are simply building up the XML contained in the BDC Metadata Model. This model is then stored in the Metadata Store.

Although it is possible to create BCS solutions without ever looking at the XML contained in the BDC Metadata Model, professional solutions require a strong understanding of the elements in the model. When you are creating more advanced solutions in BCS, the BDC Metadata Model is often exported from SPD, modified, and imported when a desired feature is not directly supported by the SPD tooling. Furthermore, it is educational to export the BDC Metadata Model and examine it as changes are made.

You can export a BDC Metadata Model from the list of External Content Types in SharePoint Designer. After selecting an ECT you can click the Export BDC Model button, which will bring up the Export BDC Model dialog. In this dialog you can export the Default model or the Client model. The Default model is the one used on the server and the Client model is the one stored in the client cache following the list synchronization. The two models will reflect any differences you made in the connection properties, but will have the same ECT definitions. The models are exported with a BDCM extension, which is the file extension for all BDC Metadata Models. Figure 4-1 shows the Export BDC Model dialog.

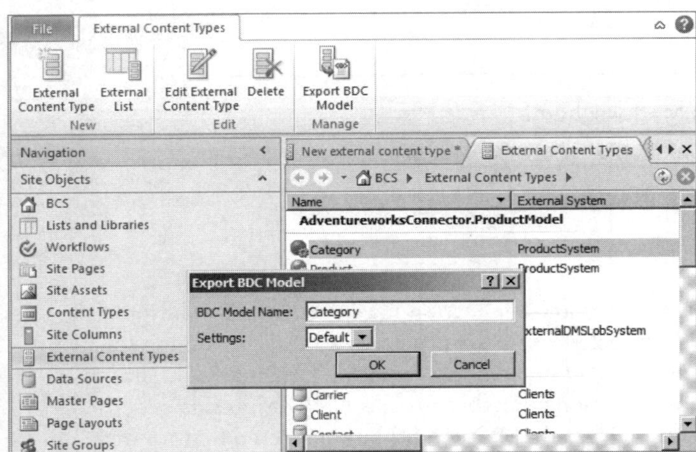

FIGURE 4-1

Once it is exported, the simplest way to work with the BDC Metadata Model is to change the file extension from BDCM to XML and open it in Visual Studio 2010 or a text editor. Although Visual Studio can open files with a BDCM extension, doing so will result in Visual Studio's using its BCS designers instead of showing the XML directly. While the BCS designers are certainly useful tools, they are best suited for working with the .NET Assembly Connectors discussed in Chapter 7.

The schema file for the BDC Metadata Model is named `BDCMetadata.xsd` and can be found in the `/Program Files/Common Files/Microsoft Shared/web server extensions/14/Template/XML` directory. When working with exported models you should copy the schema file into the directory into which you exported the model. If you do this you will get Intellisense support in Visual Studio when you open the file for editing.

You can import a BDC Metadata Model through the BDC Service Application in Central Administration, which was covered in Chapter 2. When importing an edited model back into the BDC Service Application, you should be sure to update the ECT `Version` attribute. As an alternative you can simply delete the existing model before importing the edited model.

Examining the BDC Metadata Model XML directly is an excellent way to learn the intricacies of the schema. Throughout the chapter, both the SPD tooling and the resulting XML will be presented, so that you can see exactly how the tools affect the model. As a starting point, the following code shows some of the basic elements used in the model:

```
<Model xmlns:xsi="http://www.w3.org/2001/XMLSchema-instance"
       xsi:schemaLocation="http://schemas.microsoft.com/.../BDCMetadata.xsd"
       xmlns="http://schemas.microsoft.com/windows/2007/BusinessDataCatalog"
       Name="My Model">
  <LobSystems>
    <LobSystem>
      <LobSystemInstances>
        <LobSystemInstance/>
      </LobSystemInstances>
      <Entities>
        <Entity Name="MyEntity"
                DefaultDisplayName="My Entity"
                Namespace="http://mynamespace"
                Version="1.0.0.0"
                EstimatedInstanceCount="10000" >
          <Methods>
          </Methods>
        </Entity>
      </Entities>
    </LobSystem>
  </LobSystems>
</Model>
```

The `Model` element is the root of the XML and contains the schema reference. This element also contains the `Name` attribute, which is displayed in the BDC Service Application. The `LobSystem` element is a container for the model associated with a particular External System. Notice that it is possible to have multiple External Systems defined in the same model. The `LobSystemInstance` element provides connection information for a particular External System.

The `Entity` element begins the definition of an ECT for a particular External System. The `Name` attribute is the programmatic name of the ECT and the `DefaultDisplayName` attribute is the display name that will appear in the SharePoint UI. The `Namespace` attribute is used for disambiguation between ECTs that have the same programmatic name. The `Version` attribute is used to indicate the latest version of the ECT. You enter all these attributes in SPD when creating a new ECT.

The `EstimatedInstanceCount` attribute is used as a hint to BCS solutions as to how many entity instances can be expected from the External System. The `EstimatedInstanceCount` attribute cannot be edited through SPD, and its use is solely determined by the application consuming the model. You could use this attribute, for example, when creating a custom web part to determine whether to load all the data immediately or on demand. This is a good, albeit simple, example of why you might need to export a model, modify it by hand, and import it.

WORKING WITH EXTERNAL DATA SOURCES

External Data Sources contain the data from External Systems and are the starting point for any BCS solution. Chapter 1 showed that an ECT must be associated with an External Data Source through one of four connector types: SQL Server, WCF Service, .NET Assembly, or Custom. When creating BCS solutions in SPD you will primarily make use of either the SQL Server or WCF Service connectors. The .NET Assembly and Custom connector types are typically part of a solution created in Visual Studio.

When creating a new ECT you can associate an External Data Source by clicking the link entitled Click Here to Discover External Data Sources. Clicking the link takes you to the Operation Designer, where you can see all the available External Data Sources. This view allows additional External Data Sources to be added and existing ones to be removed. The Operation Designer also allows the structure of External Data Sources to be searched with a keyword. This facility helps locate tables, views, and web methods by name, which is helpful if there are many External Data Sources available. Figure 4-2 shows the Operation Designer with the results of a keyword search.

FIGURE 4-2

When you're working with an existing ECT you can open the Operation Designer by clicking the Operations Design View button in the ribbon. You can open the Connection Properties dialog by either clicking the External System link in the ECT Information panel or by clicking the Edit Connection Properties button in the ribbon. You can change the External Data Source associated with an ECT by clicking the Switch Connected System button in the ribbon. Figure 4-3 shows the available buttons in the ribbon.

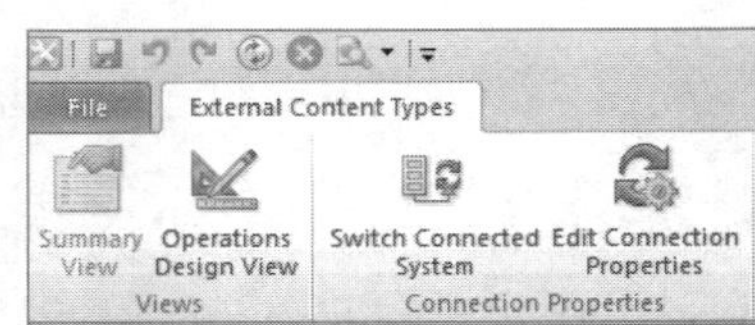

FIGURE 4-3

AUTHENTICATION AND AUTHORIZATION

When you are creating BCS solutions, authentication and authorization against External Systems is a critical area of planning, design, and implementation. The solution must determine what credentials will be used to access the External System and how data will be presented to various users. While some basic security principles are presented in this chapter, Chapter 8 is dedicated to security considerations, including authentication modes and the Secure Store Service. You must have a strong understanding of BCS security before deploying any solution to production.

Connecting with the SQL Server Connector

The SQL Server Connector provides connections to Microsoft SQL Server, Oracle, OLE DB, and ODBC databases. Because databases represent the bulk of available External Data, the SQL Server Connector is used frequently in BCS solutions. SharePoint Designer provides tooling to support connections with Microsoft SQL Server, but connections to Oracle, OLE DB, and ODBC sources require hand-editing of the BDC Metadata Model.

Connecting to Microsoft SQL Server Databases

When adding a new SQL Server Connection in the Operation Designer, you must fill out the SQL Server Connection properties dialog with the required information to connect to the External System. For Microsoft SQL Server databases, this process is straightforward and was presented in Chapter 1. The following code shows the `LobSystemInstance` element for a typical connection to Microsoft SQL Server:

```
<LobSystems>
 <LobSystem Type="Database" Name="MySystem">
  <Properties>
   <Property Name="WildcardCharacter" Type="System.String">%</Property>
  </Properties>
  <LobSystemInstances>
  <LobSystemInstance Name="MySystemInstance">
   <Properties>
    <Property Name="AuthenticationMode" Type="System.String">
      PassThrough
    </Property>
    <Property Name="DatabaseAccessProvider" Type="System.String">
     SqlServer
    </Property>
    <Property Name="RdbConnection Data Source" Type="System.String">
     AWSERVER
    </Property>
    <Property Name="RdbConnection Initial Catalog" Type="System.String">
     Adventureworks
    </Property>
    <Property Name="RdbConnection Integrated Security" Type="System.String">
     SSPI
    </Property>
    <Property Name="RdbConnection Pooling" Type="System.String">
     True
    </Property>
   </Properties>
  </LobSystemInstance>
 </LobSystem>
</LobSystems>
```

For the SQL Server Connector, a series of `Property` elements are used to specify the values that will define the connection to the database. The `AuthenticationMode` property determines how authentication is performed to the External System. The possible values for `AuthenticationMode` are listed in Table 4-1.

TABLE 4-1: Authentication Modes

VALUE	APPLICATION	DESCRIPTION
`PassThrough`	Databases and Web Services	Connects to the External System using credentials of the current user
`RevertToSelf`	Databases and Web Services	Connects to the External System using credentials of the IIS application pool
`WindowsCredentials`	Databases and Web Services	Connects to the External System using Windows Credentials returned from the Secure Store Service
`RdbCredentials`	Databases	Connects to the database using non-Windows credentials returned from the Secure Store Service
`Credentials`	Web Services	Connects to the web service using non-Windows credentials returned from the Secure Store Service

The `DatabaseAccessProvider` property specifies what type of database is targeted. This value may be set to `SqlServer`, `Oracle`, `OleDb`, or `Odbc`. Depending upon the value selected for this property, other properties may be required as children of the `LobSystemInstance` element. In the case of the `SqlServer` example, the `RdbConnection Data Source`, `RdbConnection Initial Catalog`, `RdbConnection Integrated Security`, and `RdbConnection Pooling` properties are required. You'll recognize each of these properties as a component of a standard connection string.

Connecting to Oracle Databases

Because there is no tooling support in SPD for connecting to Oracle data sources, creating models for Oracle databases can be difficult. One approach is simply to start from scratch with a blank XML file, create the required model by hand, and then import the model into the BDC Service Application. Another approach is to model the ECT against a SQL Server database, export the model, edit the model connection properties, and import the changed model. Neither approach is ideal. If you start from scratch you are much more likely to commit typographical errors. On the other hand, modifying a SQL Server model is also an error-prone process because the query syntax differs between SQL Server and Oracle. In any case, you must eventually end up with something that looks like the following code:

```
<LobSystems>
 <LobSystem Type="Database" Name="MySystem">
  <Properties>
   <Property Name="WildcardCharacter" Type="System.String">%</Property>
  </Properties>
  <LobSystemInstances>
   <LobSystemInstance Name="MySystem Instance">
    <Properties>
     <Property Name="AuthenticationMode" Type="System.String">
      RdbCredentials
     </Property>
     <Property Name="DatabaseAccessProvider" Type="System.String">
      Oracle
     </Property>
     <Property Name="RdbConnection Data Source" Type="System.String">
      MY_NET_SERVICE_NAME
     </Property>
     <Property Name="SsoApplicationId" Type="System.String">
      MY_SECURE_STORE_APP_ID
     </Property>
     <Property Name="SsoProviderImplementation" Type="System.String">
      Microsoft.Office.SecureStoreService.Server.SecureStoreProvider,
      Microsoft.Office.SecureStoreService, Version=14.0.0.0,
      Culture=neutral, PublicKeyToken=71e9bce111e9429c
     </Property>
    </Properties>
   </LobSystemInstance>
  </LobSystemInstances>
 </LobSystem>
</LobSystems>
```

BCS META MAN

Because the tooling in SPD does not support all the data sources and operations, a third-party market has emerged for tools that create BCS models. Our favorite third-party tool for creating BCS solutions is BCS Meta Man. BCS Meta Man supports connections to Oracle and ODBC data sources along with other operations not supported by SPD. BCS Meta Man installs as an extension to Visual Studio 2010. Learn more at `http://www.lightningtools.com`.

The `AuthenticationMode` property is set to `RdbCredentials` for connections to Oracle. This means that non-Windows credentials supplied by the Secure Store Service are used to access the Oracle database. The `DatabaseAccessProvider` property is set to `Oracle` to indicate that Oracle is the target system. The `RdbConnection Data Source` property is set to the value of the Net Service Name, which is the alias for the database found in the `tnsnames.ora` file. The `SsoApplicationId` property is set to the name of the application in the Secure Store Service that is providing the credentials. (Chapter 8 covers setting up the Secure Store Service in detail.) The `SsoProviderImplementation` property refers to the implementation of the Secure Store Service. In the sample code, the property references the server-side Secure Store Service. If the model is used on the client, the following code should be substituted:

```
<Property Name="SsoProviderImplementation" Type="System.String">
 Microsoft.Office.BusinessData.Infrastructure.
 SecureStore.LocalSecureStoreProvider,
 Microsoft.Office.BusinessData, Version=14.0.0.0, Culture=neutral,
 PublicKeyToken=71e9bce111e9429c
</Property>
```

Connecting to ODBC Data Sources

Creating models for ODBC Data Sources is also not supported directly in SPD. Just like connections to Oracle databases, you must create the model from scratch or modify an existing model. The following code shows what an ODBC connection looks like in the model XML:

```
<LobSystems>
 <LobSystem Name="ODBC" Type="Database">
  <LobSystemInstances>
   <LobSystemInstance Name="ODBCInstance">
    <Properties>
     <Property Name="AuthenticationMode" Type="System.String">
      PassThrough
    </Property>
     <Property Name="DatabaseAccessProvider" Type="System.String">
      Odbc
     </Property>
     <Property Name="RdbConnection Dsn" Type="System.String">
      MY_DSN_NAME
     </Property>
     <Property Name="RdbConnection uid" Type="System.String">
      MY_USERNAME
     </Property>
     <Property Name="RdbConnection pwd" Type="System.String">
       MY_PASSWORD
     </Property>
     <Property Name="RdbConnection Trusted_Connection" Type="System.String">
      yes
     </Property>
     <Property Name="RdbConnection integrated security" Type="System.String">
      true
     </Property>
    </Properties>
   </LobSystemInstance>
  </LobSystemInstances>
 </LobSystem>
</LobSystems>
```

The `AuthenticationMode` property is set to `Passthrough`, but note that the credentials used to access the data source are provided in the `RdbConnection uid` and `RdbConnection pwd` properties. You can see how these properties build an ODBC connection string. This is the same approach used to build connection strings for Microsoft SQL Server using the SPD tooling.

Connecting to OLE DB Data Sources

Creating models for OLE DB Data Sources, just like creating models for Oracle and ODBC, is not supported by the SPD tooling. The BDC Metadata Model must be created from scratch or saved as a modification of an existing model. The following code shows what an OLE DB connection looks like for a Microsoft Access database:

```
<LobSystems>
 <LobSystem Type="Database" Name="MySystem">
  <LobSystemInstances>
  <LobSystemInstance Name="MySystemInstance">
   <Properties>
    <Property Name="AuthenticationMode" Type="System.String">
      PassThrough
    </Property>
    <Property Name="DatabaseAccessProvider" Type="System.String">
     OleDb
    </Property>
    <Property Name="RdbConnection Data Source" Type="System.String">
     C:\Mydatabase.mdb
    </Property>
    <Property Name="RdbConnection Persist Security Info"
     Type="System.String">
     false
    </Property>
    <Property Name="RdbConnection Connection Provider" Type="System.String">
     Microsoft.ACE.OLEDB.12.0
    </Property>
   </Properties>
  </LobSystemInstance>
 </LobSystem>
</LobSystems>
```

The `AuthenticationMode` property is set to `Passthrough`. `RdbConnection Data Source` refers to the location of the MS Access file. `RdbConnection Connection Provider` specifies the OLE DB provider to use for the connection. Once again, the properties essentially build up a connection string to the database.

Connecting with the WCF Service Connector

The WCF Connector provides connections to web services including Windows Communication Foundation (WCF) and ASP.NET web services. The SharePoint Designer provides tooling for connecting with web services and their associated metadata so that operations may be defined against the services. The key to using a web service as an External Data Source is for SPD to be able to access the metadata of the web service that describes the available operations. SPD supports accessing service metadata through both Web Service Description Language (WSDL) and metadata exchange (MEX).

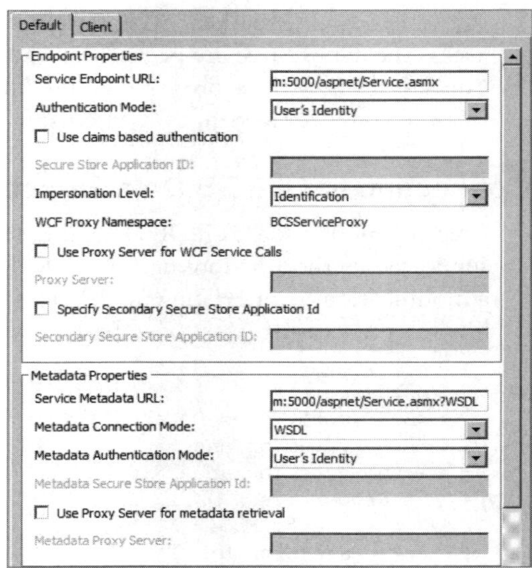

FIGURE 4-4

Connecting to ASP.NET Web Services

ASP.NET web services typically expose WSDL documents to describe the available operations. You access WSDL documents using the endpoint of the service appended with the query string `?WSDL`. Figure 4-4 shows the Connection Properties dialog with settings for an ASP.NET web service. Table 4-2 describes the settings in the dialog.

TABLE 4-2: Web Service Connection Settings

SETTING	DESCRIPTION
Service Endpoint URL	The base address of the web service
Authentication Mode	Used to select a value from Table 4-1
Use Claims Based Authentication	Selected if the web service supports claims authentication
Impersonation Level	Sets the Windows impersonation level as follows: None: No impersonation Anonymous: The server cannot impersonate or identify the client Identification: The server can identify the client, but cannot impersonate the client Impersonation: The server can impersonate the client on the server only Delegation: The server can impersonate the client locally and during requests to remote resources
WCF Proxy Namespace	The programmatic namespace used for the generated proxy class
Use Proxy Server for WCF Service Calls	Specifies a proxy server to use for calling the web service

SETTING	DESCRIPTION
Secure Store Application ID	The name of the Secure Store Service application that will provide credentials for accessing the web service. See Chapter 8 for more details.
Specify Secondary Secure Store Application ID	A secondary Secure Store Service application that will supply additional credentials. These credentials are used when a web service expects credentials to be passed as parameters in the method call. See Chapter 8 for more details.
Service Metadata URL	The address of the metadata document
Metadata Connection Mode	Specifies whether to obtain metadata as WSDL or through a metadata exchange (MEX) endpoint
Metadata Authentication Mode	Used to select an Authentication Mode from the values in Table 4-1 that will be used for accessing service metadata
Use Proxy Server for Metadata Retrieval	Specifies a proxy server to use for returning service metadata

The settings in the Connection Properties dialog are used to generate the properties for the `LobSystem` and `LobSystemInstance` elements of the model. The exact properties presented in the model will vary according to the selections made in the dialog. The following code shows how the settings in Figure 4-4 are translated into the BDC Metadata Model:

```
<LobSystems>
 <LobSystem Type="Wcf" Name="ASP.Net Web Service">
  <Properties>
   <Property Name="ReferenceKnownTypes" Type="System.Boolean">
    True
   </Property>
   <Property Name="WcfMexDiscoMode" Type="System.String">
    Disco
   </Property>
   <Property Name="WcfMexDocumentUrl" Type="System.String">
    http://webserver.aw.com:5000/aspnet/Service.asmx?WSDL
   </Property>
   <Property Name="WcfProxyNamespace" Type="System.String">
    BCSServiceProxy
   </Property>
   <Property Name="WildcardCharacter" Type="System.String">*</Property>
   <Property Name="WsdlFetchAuthenticationMode" Type="System.String">
    PassThrough
   </Property>
  </Properties>
  <Proxy>EABvmrlbJFsHTQdvYZp1cdN6TVqQAAMA...AAAAAA</Proxy>
  <LobSystemInstances>
   <LobSystemInstance Name="Item Service">
    <Properties>
```

```
        <Property Name="UseStsIdentityFederation" Type="System.Boolean">
         False
        </Property>
        <Property Name="WcfAuthenticationMode" Type="System.String">
         PassThrough
        </Property>
        <Property Name="WcfEndpointAddress" Type="System.String">
         http://webserver.aw.com:5000/aspnet/Service.asmx
        </Property>
        <Property Name="WcfImpersonationLevel" Type="System.String">
         Identification
        </Property>
       </Properties>
      </LobSystemInstance>
     </LobSystemInstances>
    </LobSystem>
   </LobSystems>
```

Along with the properties set in the model, you will also notice a `Proxy` element. This element has been significantly truncated in the code listing, but will normally contain a large text string. This large text string is the serialized proxy class that is generated by the SPD tooling when you connect to the web service. This proxy class is used by BCS to communicate with the web service when you call methods. Serializing the class in the BDC Metadata Model makes the class portable and simplifies deployment to client applications.

Connecting to WCF Web Services

WCF web services expose WSDL just like ASP .NET web services, but can also expose a metadata exchange (MEX) endpoint to describe the available operations. MEX endpoints can be used by SPD to support generating a proxy class against the service. Figure 4-5 shows the Connection Properties dialog with settings for a WCF web service exposing a MEX endpoint.

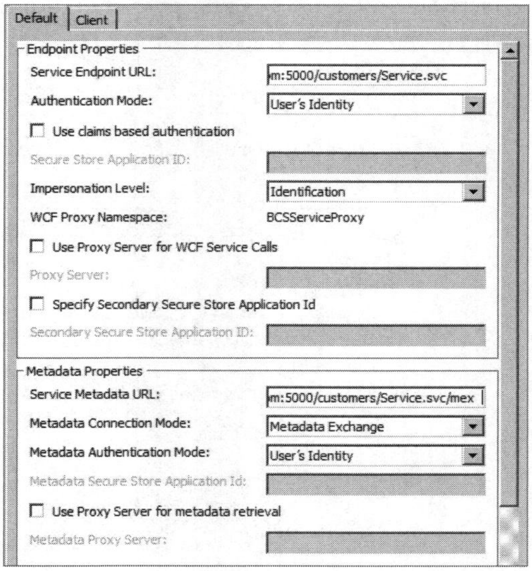

Just as for ASP.NET web services, the values set in the Connection Properties dialog are used to create the `LobSystem` and `LobSystemInstance` elements in the BDC Metadata Model. The properties in the model are the same as for ASP.NET web services, but the values are set up to use a MEX endpoint instead of a WSDL endpoint. The following code shows a sample model connecting to a WCF web service:

FIGURE 4-5

```
<LobSystems>
 <LobSystem Type="Wcf" Name="Web Customers">
  <Properties>
   <Property Name="ReferenceKnownTypes" Type="System.Boolean">
```

```
        true
       </Property>
       <Property Name="WcfMexDiscoMode" Type="System.String">
        WsMetadataExchange
       </Property>
       <Property Name="WcfMexDocumentUrl" Type="System.String">
        http://webserver.aw.com:5000/customers/Service.svc/mex
       </Property>
       <Property Name="WcfProxyNamespace" Type="System.String">
        BCSServiceProxy
       </Property>
       <Property Name="WildcardCharacter" Type="System.String">*</Property>
       <Property Name="WsdlFetchAuthenticationMode" Type="System.String">
        PassThrough
       </Property>
      </Properties>
      <Proxy>EABpFAAA...AAAAAAAAAAAA==</Proxy>
      <LobSystemInstances>
       <LobSystemInstance Name="Web Customers">
        <Properties>
         <Property Name="UseStsIdentityFederation" Type="System.Boolean">
          False
        </Property>
         <Property Name="WcfAuthenticationMode" Type="System.String">
          PassThrough
         </Property>
         <Property Name="WcfEndpointAddress" Type="System.String">
          http://webserver.aw.com:5000/customers/Service.svc
         </Property>
         <Property Name="WcfImpersonationLevel" Type="System.String">
          Identification
         </Property>
        </Properties>
       </LobSystemInstance>
      </LobSystemInstances>
     </LobSystem>
    </LobSystems>
```

CREATING METHODS

BCS method stereotypes define the operations that can be performed against an External System. Chapter 2 introduced the five most common method stereotypes, which are `Finder`, `SpecificFinder`, `Creator`, `Updater`, and `Deleter`. These five method stereotypes are used, respectively, to generate a view of many items, show details for a single item, create a new item, update an existing item, and delete an item. These common method stereotypes, however, are just a few of the method stereotypes supported by BCS.

Table 4-3 shows a complete list of the method stereotypes available for use in BDC Metadata Models. Note that with the exception of the `Finder`, `SpecificFinder`, `Creator`, `Updater`, `Deleter`, and `AssociationNavigator`, the tooling in the SharePoint Designer does not directly support the method stereotypes. In these unsupported cases the model must be exported and edited by hand or a connector project must be created, as described in Chapter 7.

TABLE 4-3: BCS Method Stereotypes

NAME	SPD SUPPORT	DESCRIPTION
`AccessChecker`	No	Returns a value indicating whether or not the current user has rights to a given item
`AssociationNavigator`	Yes	Navigates from one entity to a related entity where a foreign key relationship exists
`Associator`	No	Associates an entity with another entity where no foreign key relationship exists
`BinarySecurityDescriptorAccessor`	No	Returns a security descriptor specifying which users have rights to a given item
`BulkAssociatedIdEnumerator`	No	Returns a set of identifiers representing items associated with an entity
`BulkAssociationNavigator`	No	Supports navigation from one entity to many related entities
`BulkIdEnumerator`	No	Returns all identifiers in a batch to support search indexing
`BulkSpecificFinder`	No	Returns a set of items based on a set of identifiers
`ChangedIdEnumerator`	No	Returns identifiers for items that have changed to support incremental search indexing
`Creator`	Yes	Creates a new item
`DeletedIdEnumerator`	No	Returns identifiers for items that have been deleted to support incremental search indexing
`Deleter`	Yes	Deletes an item
`Disassociator`	No	Disassociates one entity from another
`Finder`	Yes	Returns multiple items based on a wildcard
`GenericInvoker`	No	Performs operations not supported by any of the defined operations
`IdEnumerator`	No	Returns all identifiers to support search indexing
`Scalar`	No	Returns a scalar value

NAME	SPD SUPPORT	DESCRIPTION
SpecificFinder	Yes	Returns a single item based on an identifier
StreamAccessor	No	Returns a document or image based on an identifier
Updater	Yes	Updates an existing item

Implementing Method Stereotypes

When implementing a method stereotype in the BDC Metadata Model, you will use both a `Method` and a `MethodInstance` element. The `Method` element defines the input parameters, output parameters, and filters that will be used with the method stereotype. The `MethodInstance` element defines the type of method stereotype to be implemented. Essentially, the `Method` element is a prototype of the operation while the `MethodInstance` element is a specific implementation of the operation prototype.

BDC Metadata Models will typically consist of many `Method` elements defining operations against the External System. Each `Method` element can consist of one or more `MethodInstance` elements; however, it is typical to have a one-to-one relationship between `Method` and `MethodInstance` elements. This approach simplifies the model and makes developing the solution easier. The following code shows the basic XML schema to implement a method stereotype.

```
<Method Name=[Method Name]>
 <Properties>
  <Property>[Property Value]</Property>
 </Properties>
 <FilterDescriptors>
  <FilterDescriptor Type=["Limit", "PageNumber", "Wildcard", etc]
 </FilterDescriptor>
 <Parameters>
  <Parameter
   Direction=["In", "Out", "InOut", or "Return"]
   Name=[Parameter Name]
   AssociatedFilter=[Name of a FilterDescriptor]>
   <TypeDescriptor
    TypeName=[.NET Framework Type e.g, "System.Int32"] />
  </Parameter>
 </Parameters>
 <MethodInstances>
  <MethodInstance
   Type=["Finder", "SpecificFinder", "Creator", etc]
   Name="MyMethodInstance">
  </MethodInstance>
 </MethodInstances>
</Method>
```

Defining Properties

A `Method` element may contain one or more `Property` elements. These properties are specific to the method definition and will vary depending upon the connector type used to access the External System. Specific values are discussed in detail later in the chapter.

Defining Parameters

A `Method` element may contain one or more `Parameter` elements. Parameters are used as inputs and outputs to methods. Parameters may be defined as `In`, `Out`, `InOut`, or `Return` types. The exact set of parameters required depends on the method stereotype. For example, a `Finder` method generally does not have any `In` or `InOut` parameters and only a single `Return` parameter. A `SpecificFinder` method, on the other hand, may have a single `In` parameter representing the primary key of a record and a single `Return` parameter containing the record.

Parameter elements always contain one or more `TypeDescriptor` elements. `TypeDescriptor` elements are used to map data types in the External System to well-known .NET Framework types that can be used by BCS. The types may be single-value types such as a `System.String` or collections of types. Collections of types are required, for example, when the return value from an External System is a data set.

Defining Filters

A `Method` element may contain zero or more `FilterDescriptor` elements. Filters are used by BCS to provide system or user input to methods. For example, a filter may be set in a view definition for an External List as a way to specify which entity instances to return from an External System. Filters can also be set by the system, such as when a filter is used to limit return data based on the identity of the current user. Filters are always associated with an input parameter. This association is how the filter value is transmitted to or received from the method implementation. Table 4-4 lists the filters supported by BCS.

Understanding Stereotype Requirements

The value of the SPD tooling is that it knows how to create the correct set of properties, parameters, and filters for the supported method stereotypes. In cases where you are implementing method stereotypes by hand, however, you must be aware of the requirements implicit in each method stereotype. It is not enough to simply designate the `Type` attribute of a `MethodInstance` element; the parameters and filters must be defined so that an acceptable method signature results. Table 4-5 lists the parameters required for each method stereotype. Note that filters are generally not required, but may be applied as an option to further refine an operation.

TABLE 4-4: BCS Filters

NAME	SPD SUPPORT	DESCRIPTION

`ActivityId`	`SpecificFinder`
	`Creator`
	`Updater`
	`Deleter`
	`AssociationNavigator`
		Used to pass the `CorrelationId` into an operation

`Batching`	No	Used to keep a persistent bookmark that can be passed into an operation that is returning data in batches
`BatchingTermination`	No	Used to receive a value from an operation indicating whether additional batch operations are required to return all the data
`Comparison`	`Finder`	Used to specify a value that must exactly match a field to return items from a `Finder` operation (e.g., `LastName='Hillier'`)
`Input`	No	Used to pass additional filter data to an operation
`InputOutput`	No	Used to pass additional filter data to an operation and receive a return value

`LastId`	`SpecificFinder`
	`Creator`
	`Updater`
	`Deleter`
	`AssociationNavigator`
		Used to pass the identifier of the last item read to an operation that is returning the data for the item in chunks

`Limit`	`Finder`	Used to specify a maximum limit on the number of items returned from an operation
`Output`	No	Used to receive a return value from an operation
`PageNumber`	`Finder`	Used to specify the zero-based page number that should be returned from a multipage operation

continues

TABLE 4-4 *(continued)*

NAME	SPD SUPPORT	DESCRIPTION

`Password`	`SpecificFinder`
	`Creator`
	`Updater`
	`Deleter`
	`AssociationNavigator`
		Used to pass the password that was provided by the Secure Store Service to the operation for security checks

`SsoTicket`	`SpecificFinder`
	`Creator`
	`Updater`
	`Deleter`
	`AssociationNavigator`
		Used to pass the SSO ticket that was provided by the Secure Store Service to the operation for security checks

`Timestamp`	`Finder`	Used to specify the last time a `Finder` operation was called, so that only changed data is returned

`UserContext`	`SpecificFinder`
	`Creator`
	`Updater`
	`Deleter`
	`AssociationNavigator`
		Used to pass the identity of the caller to an operation

`UserCulture`	No	Used to pass the current culture of the caller to the operation

`Username`	`SpecificFinder`
	`Creator`
	`Updater`
	`Deleter`
	`AssociationNavigator`
		Used to pass the username that was provided by the Secure Store Service to the operation for filtering and security checks

`UserProfile`	`SpecificFinder`
	`Creator`
	`Updater`
	`Deleter`
	`AssociationNavigator`
		Used to pass the profile of the current user to an operation

`Wildcard`	`Finder`	Used to specify a search pattern that can be used to return items from an operation (e.g., `LastName LIKE 'Steve%'`)

TABLE 4-5: Required Parameters and Filters

NAME	INPUT	RETURN
`AccessChecker`	Entity Instance ID	Long Integer (0: Denied, 1:Permitted)
`AssociationNavigator`	Entity Instance ID	Collection of Entity Instances
`Associator`	Entity Instance ID	Collection of Entity Instances
`BinarySecurityDescriptorAccessor`	Entity Instance ID Current User ID	Byte Array (Access Control List)
`BulkAssociatedIdEnumerator`	Collection of Entity Instance IDs	Collection of Entity Instances
`BulkAssociationNavigator`	Collection of Entity Instance IDs	Collection of Entity Instances
`BulkIdEnumerator`	Collection of Entity Instance IDs	Collection of Entity Instance IDs
`BulkSpecificFinder`	Collection of Entity Instance IDs	Collection of Entity Instances
`ChangedIdEnumerator`	Collection of Entity Instance IDs	Collection of Entity Instances
`Creator`	Collection of Fields	None
`DeletedIdEnumerator`	None	Collection of Entity Instance IDs
`Deleter`	Entity Instance ID	None
`Disassociator`	Entity Instance ID	None
`Finder`	None	Collection of Entity Instances
`GenericInvoker`	Anything	None
`IdEnumerator`	None	Collection of Entity Instances
`Scalar`	Entity Instance ID	Single Field
`SpecificFinder`	Entity Instance ID	Single Entity Instance
`StreamAccessor`	Entity Instance ID	Stream
`Updater`	Entity Instance ID Collection of Fields	None

Creating Methods for Databases

Databases are the easiest External Data Source to work with in SPD. Because databases have tables, views, stored procedures, primary keys, and foreign keys, it is easier for the SPD tooling to create valid BDC Metadata Models with little human input. Once an ECT is created and associated with a database as an External System, the Operation Designer will show the available tables, views, and stored procedures with which to work. Any of these objects may be used as the starting point for a method. Figure 4-6 shows a simple database table containing names, and its available tables, views, and procedures.

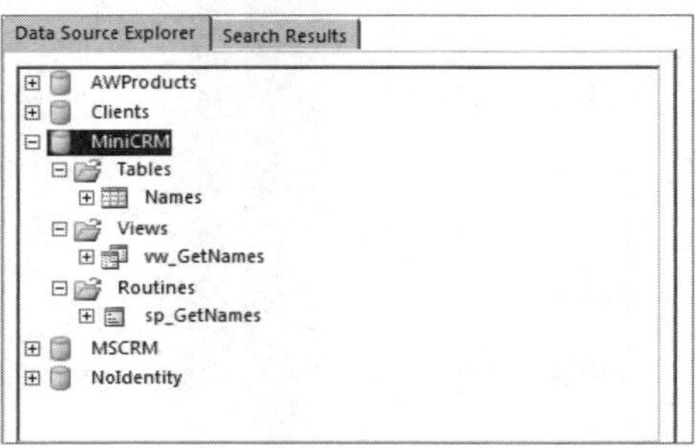

FIGURE 4-6

Creating Finder Methods

`Finder` methods return data views of the External System. These data views can be used as a source for External Lists, External Data web parts, or search. Because of this an ECT can support multiple `Finder` methods. In order to start creating a `Finder` method you can right-click one of the available tables, views, or stored procedures and select New Read List from the context menu. When you create a new `Finder` method, SPD will start the Read List wizard.

The first step of the wizard asks for the name and display name of the `Finder` method. When naming methods you should adopt a standard and use it consistently. The names that you select will appear in several places throughout SharePoint, so it's a good idea to use a naming standard that is readable by end users. Table 4-6 shows a recommended naming standard for the operations supported by SPD tooling.

TABLE 4-6: Recommended Method Naming Standard

METHOD STEREOTYPE	NAME	DISPLAY NAME
`Default Finder`	`AllItems` (`AllCustomers`)	All Items (All Customers)
`Finder`	`ItemsByFilter` (`CustomersByRegion`)	Items By Filter (Customers by Region)
`SpecificFinder`	`GetItem` (`GetCustomer`)	Get Item (Get Customer)
`Creator`	`CreateItem` (`CreateCustomer`)	Create Item (Create Customer)
`Updater`	`UpdateItem` (`UpdateCustomer`)	Update Item (Update Customers)
`Deleter`	`DeleteItem` (`DeleteCustomer`)	Delete Item (Delete Customer)
`AssociationNavigator`	`ChildrenForParent` (`OrdersForCustomer`)	Children for Parent (Orders for Customer)

The next step in the wizard allows you to set up filters for the `Finder` method. Note that when you create the first `Finder` method SPD will automatically mark it as the default `Finder` method. The default `Finder` method is the default view used for External Lists and is the default method called by the crawler during search indexing. This is important because we do not want to filter the default Finder method in any way, so this step in the wizard would be skipped. Because the default `Finder` method is called during search indexing, it is generally not filtered, but this can also cause an error to be thrown in the External List if more than 2,000 items are returned. This problem and its solution are discussed in detail later in the section entitled Understanding the Default Finder.

When you create subsequent `Finder` methods you will want to apply filters. Filters are important because they limit the amount of data that can be returned from the External System, making the solution more efficient. Just as you create views in a standard SharePoint list, you will want to create filtered `Finder` methods in SPD for generating views in the External List.

In the wizard you can add a new filter to a `Finder` method by clicking the Add Filter Parameter button. Clicking this button, however, will result only in the creation of an undefined filter that will generate a warning in the wizard. In order to configure the filter you must click the link entitled Click to Add, which will open the Filter Configuration dialog. Figure 4-7 shows the sequence in the wizard.

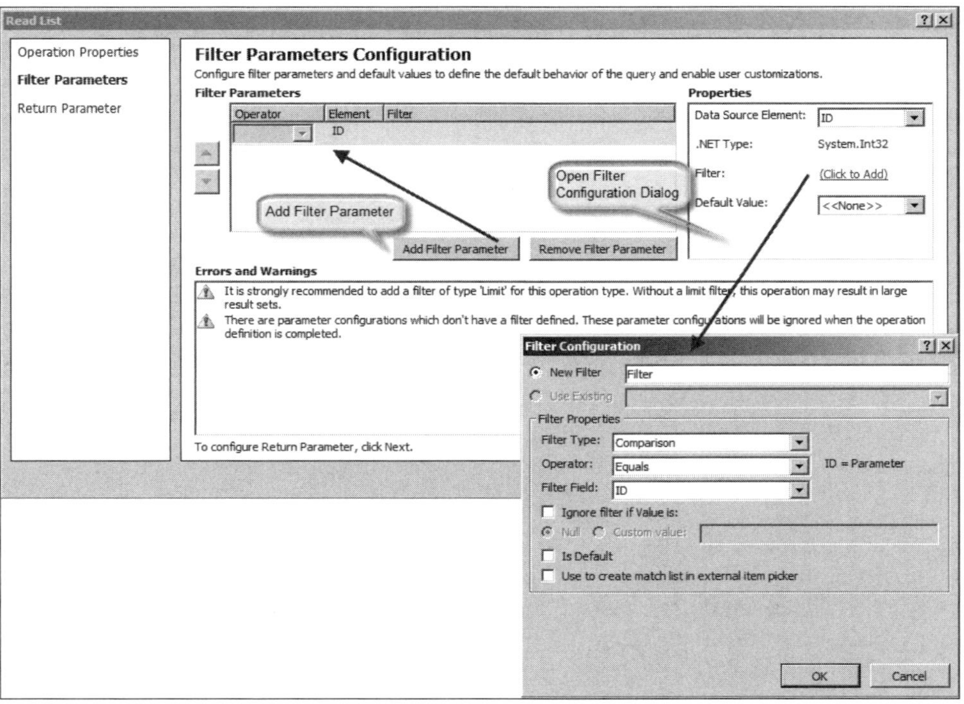

FIGURE 4-7

In the Filter Configuration dialog you can select the type of filter you want and set properties (such as values) to ignore. After you complete the settings in the Filter Configuration dialog you can close it, but the filter definition is still not complete. In the Properties section of the wizard you must select the field to be associated with the filter and provide a default value for the filter. Figure 4-8 shows a complete wildcard filter definition against the `LastName` field of a database table.

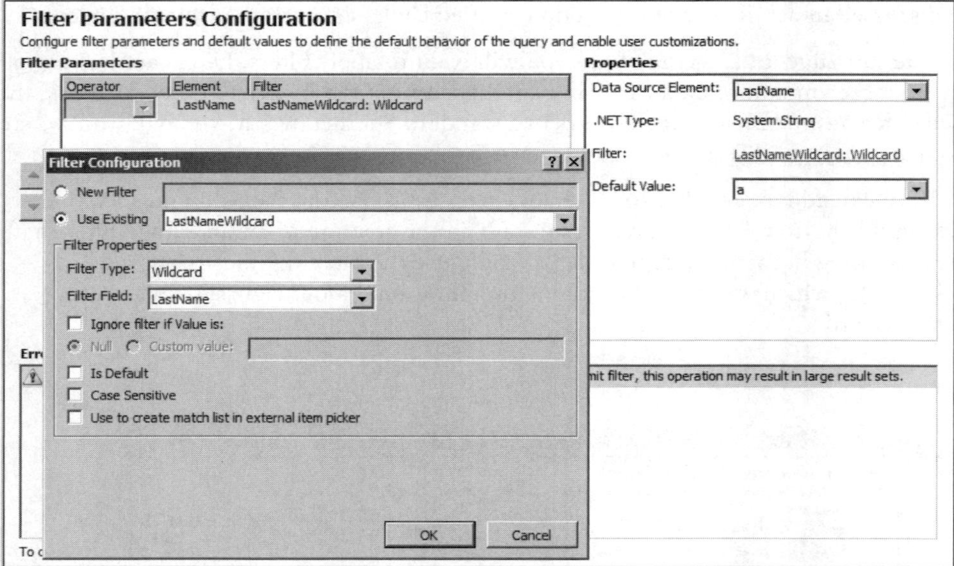

FIGURE 4-8

The next step in the wizard asks you to configure the values returned from the External System. Here you will be asked to specify the `Identifier` for the ECT. The `Identifier` field is the field that has the value that uniquely identifies an entity instance in the External System. For databases this is most often simply the primary key. Simply select this field and check the Map to Identifier Checkbox.

In this step you will also be prompted to specify fields to be displayed in the External Item Picker dialog. This dialog is the picker control that displays entities for selection. The choice of fields is important because the user will see only the fields that you mark, so they should be the fields by which the end user will search. Select each of the fields and click the Show in Picker checkbox.

In this step it's also a good idea to take a close look at the display name for each field. Make sure that these values are readable because they will appear as column headers in External Lists. You can also uncheck any fields that you do not want to display in the view. Finally, if you have a `DateTime` field in the data source that represents the last time the record was edited, mark that field as the `Timestamp` Field. This will allow search to use the field in support of incremental crawls.

Modeling Finder Methods

Using tables, views, or stored procedures as External Data sources will result in the creation of different models. This makes sense, since the syntax to query these sources is different. The following code shows an implementation of the same Finder method using each of the three different sources:

```
<!-- Table -->
<Method IsStatic="false" Name="AllNamesTable">
 <Properties>
  <Property Name="BackEndObject" Type="System.String">
   Names
  </Property>
  <Property Name="BackEndObjectType" Type="System.String">
   SqlServerTable
  </Property>
  <Property Name="RdbCommandText" Type="System.String">
   SELECT [ID] , [Title] , [FirstName] , [MiddleName] , [LastName] ,
   [EmailAddress] , [Phone] FROM [MiniCRM].[Names]
  </Property>
  <Property Name="RdbCommandType"
   Type="System.Data.CommandType, System.Data, Version=2.0.0.0,
   Culture=neutral, PublicKeyToken=b77a5c561934e089">
   Text
  </Property>
  <Property Name="Schema" Type="System.String">
   MiniCRM
  </Property>
 </Properties>
 <Parameters>
  <Parameter Direction="Return" Name="AllNamesTable">
   ...
  </Parameter>
 </Parameters>
 <MethodInstances>
  <MethodInstance Type="Finder" ReturnParameterName="AllNamesTable"
   Name="AllNamesTable" DefaultDisplayName="All Names Table">
 </MethodInstance>
 </MethodInstances>
</Method>

<!-- View -->
<Method IsStatic="false" Name="AllNamesView">
 <Properties>
  <Property Name="BackEndObject" Type="System.String">
   vw_GetNames
  </Property>
  <Property Name="BackEndObjectType" Type="System.String">
   SqlServerView
  </Property>
  <Property Name="RdbCommandText" Type="System.String">
   SELECT [ID] , [Title] , [FirstName] , [MiddleName] , [LastName] ,
   [EmailAddress] , [Phone] FROM [dbo].[vw_GetNames]
  </Property>
  <Property Name="RdbCommandType"
   Type="System.Data.CommandType, System.Data, Version=2.0.0.0,
   Culture=neutral, PublicKeyToken=b77a5c561934e089">
   Text
  </Property>
```

```
      <Property Name="Schema" Type="System.String">
       dbo
      </Property>
     </Properties>
     <Parameters>
      <Parameter Direction="Return" Name="AllNamesView">
       ...
      </Parameter>
     </Parameters>
     <MethodInstances>
      <MethodInstance Type="Finder" ReturnParameterName="AllNamesView"
       Name="AllNamesView" DefaultDisplayName="All Names View">
      </MethodInstance>
     </MethodInstances>
    </Method>

    <!-- Stored Procedure -->
    <Method IsStatic="false" Name="AllNamesProcedure">
     <Properties>
      <Property Name="BackEndObject" Type="System.String">
       sp_GetNames
      </Property>
      <Property Name="BackEndObjectType" Type="System.String">
       SqlServerRoutine
      </Property>
      <Property Name="RdbCommandText" Type="System.String">
       [dbo].[sp_GetNames]
      </Property>
      <Property Name="RdbCommandType"
       Type="System.Data.CommandType, System.Data, Version=2.0.0.0,
       Culture=neutral, PublicKeyToken=b77a5c561934e089">
       StoredProcedure
      </Property>
      <Property Name="Schema" Type="System.String">
       dbo
      </Property>
     </Properties>
     <Parameters>
      <Parameter Direction="Return" Name="AllNamesProcedure">
       ...
      </Parameter>
     </Parameters>
     <MethodInstances>
      <MethodInstance Type="Finder" ReturnParameterName="AllNamesProcedure"
       Name="AllNamesProcedure" DefaultDisplayName="All Names Procedure">
      </MethodInstance>
     </MethodInstances>
    </Method>
```

Notice that the primary difference among the three implementations is the set of `Property` elements used in each. Tables and views, for example, use dynamic SQL statements, while the stored procedure uses a direct call to the procedure. Notice also that none of the methods has any input parameters or filters defined. If parameters were defined, however, a new stored procedure would have to be defined in the database. This is because any input parameters must be reflected in the stored procedure definition, whereas the dynamic SQL statements written against tables and views can simply be changed in the model.

When a stored procedure with input parameters is used, the wizard will present a screen that will allow you to assign filters to the parameters. These filter values can then be set in the view definition of the External List by an end user, or as an input parameter in the External Data web parts. The following code shows a stored procedure that supports a wildcard as an input parameter:

```
<Method IsStatic="false" Name="NamesByWildcardProcedure">
 <Properties>
  <Property Name="BackEndObject" Type="System.String">
   sp_GetNamesWildcard
  </Property>
  <Property Name="BackEndObjectType" Type="System.String">
   SqlServerRoutine
  </Property>
  <Property Name="RdbCommandText" Type="System.String">
   [dbo].[sp_GetNamesWildcard]
  </Property>
  <Property Name="RdbCommandType"
   Type="System.Data.CommandType, System.Data, Version=2.0.0.0,
   Culture=neutral, PublicKeyToken=b77a5c561934e089">
   StoredProcedure
  </Property>
  <Property Name="Schema" Type="System.String">
   dbo
  </Property>
 </Properties>
 <FilterDescriptors>
  <FilterDescriptor Type="Wildcard" FilterField="LastName" Name="Wildcard">
   <Properties>
    <Property Name="CaseSensitive" Type="System.Boolean">
     false
    </Property>
    <Property Name="IsDefault" Type="System.Boolean">
     false
    </Property>
    <Property Name="UsedForDisambiguation" Type="System.Boolean">
     false
    </Property>
   </Properties>
  </FilterDescriptor>
 </FilterDescriptors>
 <Parameters>
  <Parameter Direction="In" Name="@wildcard">
   <TypeDescriptor TypeName="System.String"
    AssociatedFilter="Wildcard" Name="@wildcard">
    <Properties>
     <Property Name="Order" Type="System.Int32">0</Property>
    </Properties>
    <DefaultValues>
     <DefaultValue
```

```
          MethodInstanceName="NamesByWildcardProcedure" Type="System.String">
          A
        </DefaultValue>
        </DefaultValues>
       </TypeDescriptor>
      </Parameter>
      <Parameter Direction="Return" Name="NamesByWildcardProcedure">
       ...
      </Parameter>
     </Parameters>
     <MethodInstances>
      <MethodInstance Type="Finder"
       ReturnParameterName="NamesByWildcardProcedure"
       Name="NamesByWildcardProcedure"
       DefaultDisplayName="Names by Wildcard Procedure">
      </MethodInstance>
     </MethodInstances>
    </Method>
```

In the code, notice that a `FilterDescriptor` of type `Wildcard` has been added to the model. This filter is associated with the `LastName` field and the `@wildcard` input parameter. This passes the value of the filter into the `@wildcard` input parameter. This means that the stored procedure must have a parameter of that exact name available, as shown in the following code:

```
CREATE PROCEDURE [dbo].[sp_GetNamesWildcard]
@wildcard nvarchar(10)
AS
SELECT ID,Title,FirstName,MiddleName,LastName,Suffix,EMailAddress,Phone
FROM MiniCRM.Names
WHERE LastName LIKE @wildcard + '%'
```

When a stored procedure is used as a Creator, you must return the new ID of the new entity instance from the procedure. In The SPD wizard, the ID must be set on the Return parameter (not the In parameter) for the model to work. The following stored procedure uses an identity column, and returns that from the procedure.

```
CREATE PROCEDURE NewEmployee
@Username nvarchar (255),
@FirstName nvarchar (255),
@LastName nvarchar (255),
@SecondLanguage nvarchar (255)
AS
INSERT INTO [dbo].[Employees]([Username] , [FirstName] , [LastName] ,
[SecondLanguage])
VALUES(@Username , @FirstName , @LastName , @SecondLanguage)
SELECT [EmployeeID] FROM [dbo].[Employees] WHERE [EmployeeID] = SCOPE_IDENTITY()
```

Remember that the purpose of filters is to retrieve input from either the end user or the system. In the case of the `Wildcard` filter, the idea is to let the end user set up a view based on a partial string search of the last name. In the SharePoint interface, this search appears as a value that can be set in the view definition of the External List, as shown in Figure 4-9.

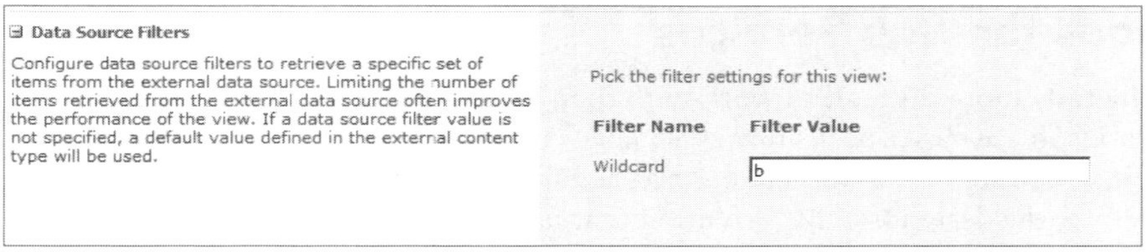

Data Source Filters

Configure data source filters to retrieve a specific set of items from the external data source. Limiting the number of items retrieved from the external data source often improves the performance of the view. If a data source filter value is not specified, a default value defined in the external content type will be used.

Pick the filter settings for this view:

Filter Name	Filter Value
Wildcard	b

FIGURE 4-9

Understanding the Default Finder

The default `Finder` method deserves special consideration in the design of any BCS solution. As stated previously, the first `Finder` method created in SPD will be the default. When you create subsequent `Finder` methods, the wizard will present a checkbox that you can use to change the default `Finder`. If you do nothing, however, it will always be the first one created.

The default `Finder` method serves two important purposes. First, this is the method that will generate the default view for an External List. Second, this method will be used by the search indexer to retrieve records during the crawl process. The method is identified as the default `Finder` through the `Default` attribute of the `MethodInstance` element, and as the target of the crawl through the `RootFinder` property, as shown in the following code:

```
<MethodInstance
 Type="Finder"
 ReturnParameterName="AllNames"
 Default="true"
 Name="AllNames"
 DefaultDisplayName="All Names">
 <Properties>
  <Property Name="RootFinder" Type="System.String"></Property>
 </Properties>
</MethodInstance>
```

When SPD defines a `Finder` as both the default `Finder` and the root `Finder`, this can cause significant problems in your solutions because the default `Finder` should be filtered, but the root `Finder` should not. `Finder` methods should generally have filters on them to limit the number of rows returned. If they do not have filters, BCS will throw an error if they return more than 2,000 rows to an External List. However, root `Finders` should never be filtered because the filtering will exclude items from the search index so that they will never appear in search results. Therefore you must manually edit the BDC Metadata Model to assign the default `Finder` and root `Finder` to different `Finder` methods, unless you know that your data source will never exceed 2,000 rows. Refer to Chapter 9 for complete coverage of search.

Creating Other Methods

Creating `SpecificFinder`, `Creator`, `Updater`, and `Deleter` methods is generally similar to creating `Finder` methods. The wizard will walk you through the steps necessary to define appropriate parameters and filters. In the case of stored procedures, remember that any required input parameters or filters must be explicitly available as parameters in the stored procedure.

Creating Methods for Web Services

Web services are generally more difficult to work with than databases. This is because the form of the exposed methods in a web service can vary widely. There is no standard table or view structure available in a web service, and there are no primary/foreign keys available for inferring relationships. Therefore, the design of a BCS solution that uses web services must be carefully considered.

While it is possible to use an existing web service as an External Data Source, the requirements of the method stereotypes will more often lead to the creation of a custom service for a BCS solution. Custom services should expose methods that correlate closely to BCS method stereotypes. The following code shows the programmatic interface for a simple WCF service.

```
[ServiceContract]
public interface IService
{

    [OperationContract]
    List<Customer> CrawlCustomers();

    [OperationContract]
    List<Customer> GetCustomers(int Limit);

    [OperationContract]
    List<Customer> GetCustomersByRegion(string Region);

    [OperationContract]
    Customer GetCustomer(string Id);

    [OperationContract]
    void CreateCustomer(string FirstName, string LastName);

    [OperationContract]
    void UpdateCustomer(string Id, string FirstName, string LastName);

    [OperationContract]
    void DeleteCustomer(string Id);

}

[DataContract]
public class Customer
{
    [DataMember]
    public string Id { get; set; }
    [DataMember]
    public string FirstName { get; set; }
    [DataMember]
    public string LastName { get; set; }
}
```

Notice how the exposed methods of the web service are designed in accordance with the requirements of Table 4-5. The `Finder` methods return collections of `Customer` entity instances, whereas `SpecificFinder` returns only a single entity instance. The `Creator`, `Updater`, and `Deleter` methods return `void`.

Note also that there are three `Finder` methods exposed. The `CrawlCustomers` method has no filter and is intended for use by the indexer. The `GetCustomers` method accepts a `Limit` filter to prevent errors being caused in the External List if too many results are returned. `GetCustomerByRegion` accepts a filter to limit the return results to customers in a given region. These parameters will all appear in the SPD wizard so that they can be mapped to the appropriate filter types.

Defining Associations

Associations are relationships between ECTs. BCS supports one-to-many, many-to-many, self-referential, and reverse associations. One-to-many associations return many related entity instances from a single parent entity instance. Many-to-many associations return many related entity instances from many different parent entity instances. Self-referential associations return entity instances of the same type as the parent entity instance. Reverse associations return a parent entity instance from a single child entity instance.

Within the SharePoint Designer only one-to-many, self-referential, and reverse associations are supported by the tooling. Like all operations, associations are simply method stereotypes created in the BDC Metadata Model. Associations created in SPD are of type `AssociationNavigator`. The primary reason to create associations is to enable certain user interface elements such as picker controls that allow end users to work with data relationships directly in SharePoint or Outlook.

Creating One-to-Many Associations

The most common type of association in BCS solutions is the one-to-many association, whereby a parent entity instance is related to many child entity instances. This type of association supports such scenarios as a single `Customer` having many `Orders` or a single `Client` having many `Contacts`. Database tables with primary key/foreign key relationships are most often the basis for a one-to-many association.

In order to create a one-to-many association you must first define both External Content Types. The child ECT should be defined so that it contains a foreign key related to the parent ECT. This means that the `Order` ECT contains a `CustomerID` field or the `Contact` ECT contains a `ClientID` field. If the relationship is based on a database table or view, nothing else needs to be done. If the relationship is based on a stored procedure or web service method, you must also create a stored procedure or web method that accepts the parent entity instance identifier and returns the child entity instances.

Once you have the ECTs defined, the new association can be created from the Operation Designer. If the relationship will use tables or views, select the child table or view. If the relationship will use stored procedures or web services, select the procedure or method that will accept the parent entity instance identifier and return the child entity instances. Right-click and select New Association in the context menu, which will start the Association wizard.

In the Association wizard you must map the child ECT to the parent ECT. You do this by clicking the Browse button and selecting the parent ECT from a list. Once the parent ECT is selected you must map the identifier of the parent ECT to the foreign key in the child ECT. Figure 4-10 shows the wizard with a child ECT mapped to a parent ECT through the `ClientID` field.

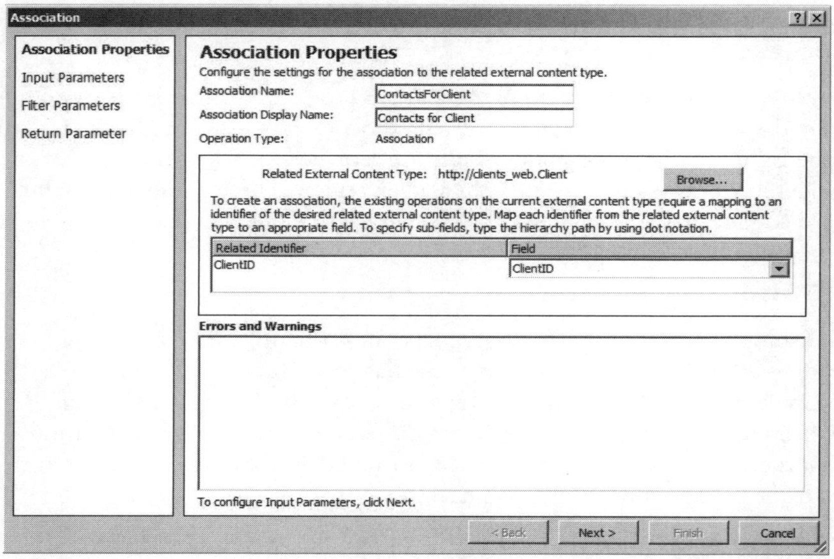

FIGURE 4-10

In the next screen of the wizard you must map the input parameter of the child to the foreign key. Most of the time this field will contain the same name as that of the identifier that was selected in the first screen, but the names may be different. Figure 4-11 shows the wizard and the following code shows the resulting model definition.

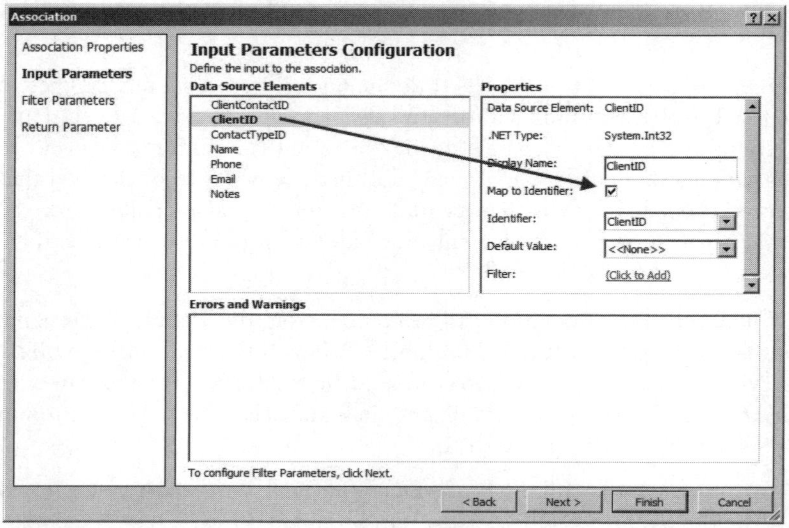

FIGURE 4-11

```
<Method IsStatic="false" Name="ContactsForClient">
 <Properties>
  <Property Name="BackEndObject" Type="System.String">
   ClientContacts
  </Property>
  <Property Name="BackEndObjectType" Type="System.String">
   SqlServerTable
  </Property>
  <Property Name="RdbCommandText" Type="System.String">
   sp_GetAllClientContacts
  </Property>
  <Property Name="RdbCommandType" Type="System.Data.CommandType,
   System.Data, Version=2.0.0.0, Culture=neutral,
   PublicKeyToken=b77a5c561934e089">
   StoredProcedure
  </Property>
  <Property Name="Schema" Type="System.String">dbo</Property>
 </Properties>
 <Parameters>
  <Parameter Direction="In" Name="@ClientID">
   <TypeDescriptor TypeName="System.Int32" IdentifierName="ClientID"
    IdentifierEntityName="Client"
    IdentifierEntityNamespace="http://clients_web"
    ForeignIdentifierAssociationName="ContactsForClient"
    Name="ClientID" />
  </Parameter>
  <Parameter Direction="Return" Name="ContactsForClient">
   ...
  </Parameter>
 </Parameters>
 <MethodInstances>
  <Association Name="ContactsForClient" Type="AssociationNavigator"
   ReturnParameterName="ContactsForClient"
   DefaultDisplayName="Contacts For Client">
   <Properties>
    <Property Name="ForeignFieldMappings" Type="System.String">
     &lt;?xml version="1.0" encoding="utf-16"?&gt;
     &lt;ForeignFieldMappings
     xmlns:xsi="http://www.w3.org/2001/XMLSchema-instance"
     xmlns:xsd="http://www.w3.org/2001/XMLSchema"&gt;
     &lt;ForeignFieldMappingsList&gt;
     &lt;ForeignFieldMapping ForeignIdentifierName="ClientID"
     ForeignIdentifierEntityName="Client"
     ForeignIdentifierEntityNamespace="http://clients_web"
     FieldName="ClientID" /&gt;
     &lt;/ForeignFieldMappingsList&gt;
     &lt;/ForeignFieldMappings&gt;
    </Property>
   </Properties>
   <SourceEntity Namespace="http://clients_web" Name="Client" />
   <DestinationEntity Namespace="http://clients_web" Name="Contact" />
  </Association>
 </MethodInstances>
</Method>
```

One-to-many relationships are used in the SharePoint interface to display entity instances. In an External List of child entity instances, the foreign key for the parent entity instance can be set with the picker, as shown in Figure 4-12. If a profile page is defined for the parent ECT, it will automatically be created to contain a list of related child ECTs.

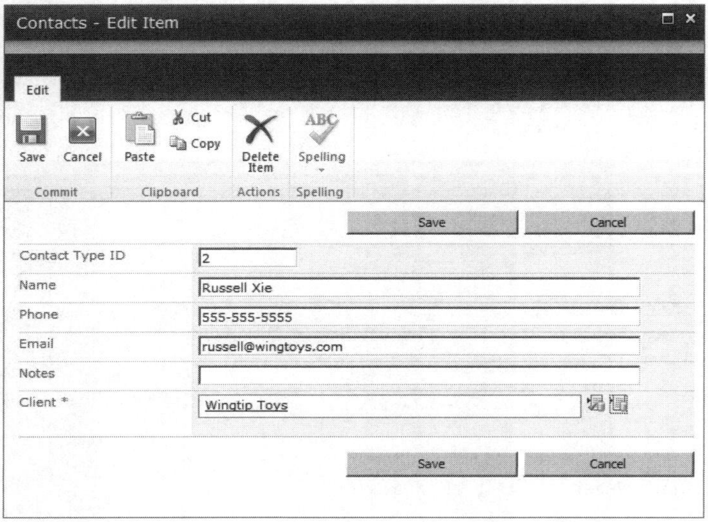

FIGURE 4-12

Creating Self-Referential Associations

Self-referential associations are created just like one-to-many relationships. The difference is that a self-referential relationship uses the same ECT as both the parent and the child. Therefore the ECT must have a separate field defined that acts like the foreign key in a one-to-many relationship, but instead refers to an entity instance of the same type.

As an example, consider creating an organizational chart from a single table of employees. The table contains an `ID` field as the primary key and a `ManagerID` field to relate the current record to another record in the table. Using this information, an association can be created between the `Employee` ECT `ID` and `ManagerID` fields, as shown in the following code:

```
<Method IsStatic="false" Name="EmployeesForManager">
 <Properties>
  <Property Name="BackEndObject" Type="System.String">
   Employees
  </Property>
  <Property Name="BackEndObjectType" Type="System.String">
   SqlServerTable
  </Property>
  <Property Name="RdbCommandText" Type="System.String">
```

```
      SELECT [ID] , [ManagerID] , [Title] , [FirstName] , [MiddleName] ,
      [LastName] , [EmailAddress] , [Phone] FROM [dbo].[Employees]
      WHERE [ManagerID] = @ID
     </Property>
     <Property Name="RdbCommandType"
      Type="System.Data.CommandType, System.Data, Version=2.0.0.0,
      Culture=neutral, PublicKeyToken=b77a5c561934e089">
      Text
     </Property>
     <Property Name="Schema" Type="System.String">
      dbo
     </Property>
    </Properties>
    <Parameters>
     <Parameter Direction="In" Name="@ID">
      <TypeDescriptor TypeName="System.Int32" IdentifierName="ID"
       ForeignIdentifierAssociationName="EmployeesForManager"
       Name="ManagerID" />
     </Parameter>
     <Parameter Direction="Return" Name="EmployeesForManager">
      ...
     </Parameter>
    </Parameters>
    <MethodInstances>
     <Association Name="EmployeesForManager" Type="AssociationNavigator"
      ReturnParameterName="EmployeesForManager"
      DefaultDisplayName="Employees for Manager">
      <Properties>
       <Property Name="ForeignFieldMappings" Type="System.String">
        &lt;?xml version="1.0" encoding="utf-16"?&gt;
        &lt;ForeignFieldMappings
        xmlns:xsi="http://www.w3.org/2001/XMLSchema-instance"
        xmlns:xsd="http://www.w3.org/2001/XMLSchema"&gt;
        &lt;ForeignFieldMappingsList&gt;
        &lt;ForeignFieldMapping ForeignIdentifierName="ID"
        ForeignIdentifierEntityName="Employee"
        ForeignIdentifierEntityNamespace="http://bcs/orgchart"
        FieldName="ManagerID" /&gt;
        &lt;/ForeignFieldMappingsList&gt;
        &lt;/ForeignFieldMappings&gt;</Property>
      </Properties>
      <SourceEntity Namespace="http://bcs/orgchart" Name="Employee" />
      <DestinationEntity Namespace="http://bcs/orgchart" Name="Employee" />
     </Association>
    </MethodInstances>
   </Method>
```

The key to creating the self-referential relationship is the SQL query that returns entity instances where `ManagerID=ID`. Note that SPD does not always create this SQL query correctly when you are creating a new self-referential association in the tooling. Therefore you should be sure to export and examine the query after the method is created. Once it is created correctly you can use the relationships like any others. Figure 4-13 shows a relationship being used in the External Data web parts to display the employees who work for a given manager.

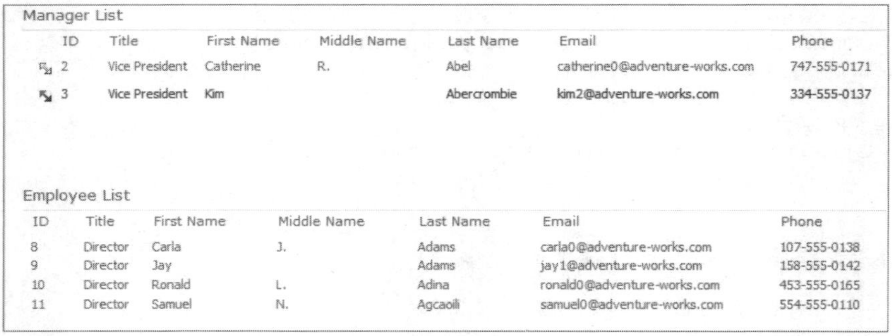

Manager List

ID	Title	First Name	Middle Name	Last Name	Email	Phone
2	Vice President	Catherine	R.	Abel	catherine0@adventure-works.com	747-555-0171
3	Vice President	Kim		Abercrombie	kim2@adventure-works.com	334-555-0137

Employee List

ID	Title	First Name	Middle Name	Last Name	Email	Phone
8	Director	Carla	J.	Adams	carla0@adventure-works.com	107-555-0138
9	Director	Jay		Adams	jay1@adventure-works.com	158-555-0142
10	Director	Ronald	L.	Adina	ronald0@adventure-works.com	453-555-0165
11	Director	Samuel	N.	Agcaoili	samuel0@adventure-works.com	554-555-0110

FIGURE 4-13

Creating Reverse Associations

Reverse associations return a single parent entity instance for a child entity instance. Reverse associations are not supported for tables and views, but are supported for stored procedures and web services. This is because the reverse association is not inherent in the database schema. It must be explicitly programmed through a stored procedure or web service. For example, you could create a stored procedure that takes the identifier for a `Contact` and returns the parent `Client` entity instance, as shown in the following code:

```
CREATE PROCEDURE sp_GetClientByContactID
@ClientContactID int
AS
Select Clients.ClientID, Clients.Name, Clients.Address1, Clients.Address2,
Clients.City, Clients.Province, Clients.PostalCode, Clients.Country,
Clients.Phone, Clients.Fax, Clients.Web
From Clients
Inner Join ClientContacts
On Clients.ClientID = ClientContacts.ClientID
Where ClientContactID = @ClientContactID
```

Once the stored procedure is written, open the Operation Designer for the child ECT. Select the stored procedure, then right-click and select New Reverse Association from the context menu. As with the other associations, you can then browse and select the parent ECT.

Working with Many-to-Many Relationships

As mentioned previously, the SPD tooling does not support creating many-to-many relationships. Remember that the primary reason for defining associations is to enable user interface elements such as the picker control and the External Data web parts. BCS has no special user interface elements to render many-to-many relationships, so creating them in SPD makes no sense. This does not mean, however, that you cannot use these relationships in your BCS solutions.

The simplest way to work with many-to-many relationships is to create a web method or stored procedure that returns one side of the relationship. Then you can create a `Finder` method to display that information. If, for example, you have a many-to-many relationship between a `Resource` ECT and a `Project` ECT, then you can create a `Finder` method that accepts a `Resource` identifier and returns a collection of `Projects`. Similarly, you can create a `Finder` method that accepts a `Project` identifier and returns a collection of `Resources`. If you need more sophisticated support for these relationships, then you will need to create a connector as described in Chapter 7.

WORKING WITH EXTERNAL LISTS

External Lists support many of the same capabilities as standard SharePoint lists, such as custom list actions and custom forms. They do not, however, support all the capabilities of standard lists, such as event handlers and workflows. This section introduces the capabilities of External Lists and how to work around basic limitations. Additional advanced techniques are also presented in Chapter 5.

Creating Custom List Actions

Custom list actions allows you to add a new button to the list item menu, view ribbon, new form ribbon, display form ribbon, or edit form ribbon. The target of the button can be either an existing form or navigation to a URL. For standard lists you can also initiate a workflow from the button, but External Lists do not support this function.

You create new custom list actions from SPD by selecting the list and clicking the Custom Action button in the ribbon. This button will then open the Create Custom Action dialog. Figure 4-14 shows the dialog in the SharePoint Designer.

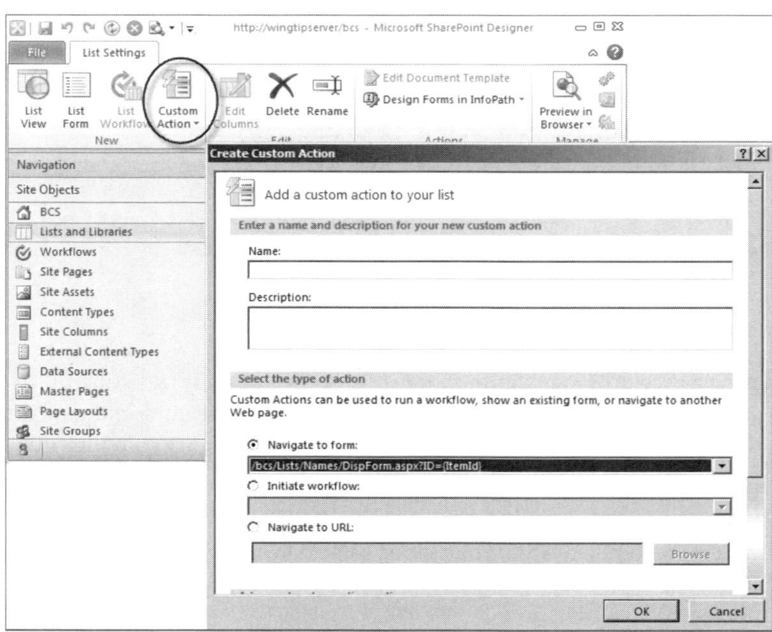

FIGURE 4-14

Creating Custom Forms

For every standard and External List, a set of forms is created to display, edit, and add items. Using SharePoint Designer you can create and customize these forms, either as ASPX pages or as InfoPath forms. This capability helps you enhance data presentation and perform field-level validation on items.

Creating ASPX Forms

When you create an External List, new, edit, and display forms are automatically created as appropriate, based on the operations defined for the associated ECT. Using SPD, you can see these forms by clicking the Lists and Libraries object followed by the list of interest. The existing forms are listed on the summary page, as shown in Figure 4-15.

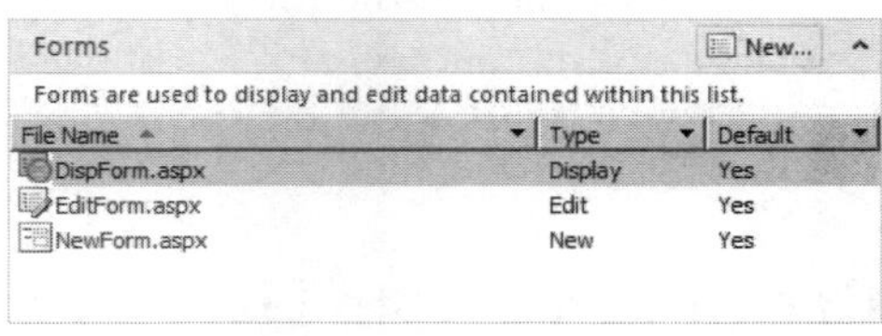

FIGURE 4-15

The default forms created for the External List use the List Form Web Part (LFWP). The LFWP executes Collaborative Application Markup Language (CAML) queries against the External List to display items. Unfortunately, the LFWP does not support modifying its presentation; therefore a new form must be created instead.

Clicking the New button above the form list in the summary page opens the Create New List Form dialog. This dialog is used to create, edit, and display forms that are based on the Data Form Web Part (DFWP). The DFWP uses XSLT to transform list data into a display. Modifying this XSLT can easily change the presentation of list data.

As an example, consider an External List that returns information about SharePoint images. The BCS solution has a column called `Path` that returns the path to the image. In a simple BCS solution, `Path` will appear as a column and the user will simply see the text of the URL. A better experience, however, would be to show the image itself. You can do this by adding a new display form and modifying the XSLT for the field, as shown in the following code:

```
<img>
 <xsl:attribute name="src">
  <xsl:value-of select="@Path"/>
 </xsl:attribute>
</img>
```

Transforming URLs to images or hyperlinks is a common reason for creating a new list form. In addition, you can also make style changes to the form by changing fonts, colors, and images. You can also use JavaScript with the form. Figure 4-16 shows a form displaying an image, hyperlink, and new style.

In addition to using SPD, you can also modify the list forms inside the SharePoint 2010 interface. While viewing the External List, click the List tab in the ribbon. The Modify Form Web Parts button will allow you to select a form to modify. You then use the properties pane to modify the web part rendering the list.

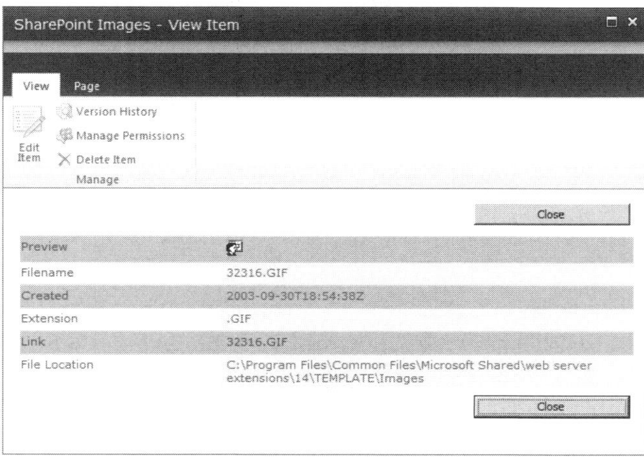

FIGURE 4-16

Creating InfoPath Forms

Instead of ASPX pages, you can choose to create custom InfoPath forms for the External List. InfoPath form creation can be initiated directly from SPD by clicking the Design Forms in InfoPath button from the list summary page. This action will open InfoPath with a default form that you can edit.

InfoPath forms are easier to create, offer simpler styling, and advanced controls. Using InfoPath, you can take advantage of lists and drop-downs as well as styles and themes. When the form is complete, you must save it and then execute a Quick Publish. Quick publishing is available by clicking the File tab in InfoPath. Once published, the form is available for the new, edit, and display forms. Figure 4-17 shows a sample form with a custom style and a drop-down list.

FIGURE 4-17

Accessing External Lists in Code

External Lists may be accessed through code in ways that are familiar to SharePoint developers. Both the server-side and client-side object models can be used. A detailed BCS API is also available to access External Systems, which is discussed in Chapter 5. The code in this section requires that you have an External List created in SharePoint, not just an External System defined in the BDC Service Application.

Using the SPList Object

The standard `SPList` object may be used in code running against the `Microsoft.SharePoint` namespace to access the items in External Lists, but there are a few special requirements. When code accesses the items in an External List, the unique identifier for an item is found in the `BdcIdentity` field and not the standard `ID` of the item. Additionally, in order to access the list items you must enumerate the `SPListItem` collection. Other than those restrictions, accessing the items in the list is straightforward. The following code shows a web part that displays the contents of an External List whose name is provided in a property field:

```
public class ExternalListWebPart : WebPart
{
    private string listName = string.Empty;
    private Label messages;

    [Personalizable(PersonalizationScope.Shared),
    WebBrowsable(true),
    WebDisplayName("Target List"),
    WebDescription("The name of the External List"),
    Category("Configuration")]
    public string ListName
    {
        get { return listName; }
        set { listName = value; }
    }

    protected override void CreateChildControls()
    {
        messages = new Label();
        this.Controls.Add(messages);
    }

    protected override void RenderContents(HtmlTextWriter writer)
    {
        try
        {
            if (listName.Length > 0)
            {
                SPWeb site = SPContext.Current.Web;
                SPList externalList = site.Lists[ListName];

                writer.Write("<table border=\"0\">");
                writer.Write("<tr>");
```

```
                foreach(SPField field in externalList.Fields)
                {
                    if (field.Title != null)
                    {
                        writer.Write("<td align=\"center\">");
                        writer.Write(field.Title);
                        writer.Write("</td>");
                    }
                }
                writer.Write("</tr>");

                foreach (SPListItem item in externalList.Items)
                {
                    writer.Write("<tr>");
                    foreach (SPField field in item.Fields)
                    {
                        if (field.Title != null)
                        {
                            writer.Write("<td>");
                            writer.Write(item[field.Title].ToString());
                            writer.Write("</td>");
                        }
                    }
                    writer.Write("</tr>");
                }

                writer.Write("</table>");

            }
        }
        catch (Exception x)
        {
            messages.Text = x.Message;
        }

        writer.Write("<br/>");
        messages.RenderControl(writer);

    }
}
```

Using the Client Object Model

SharePoint 2010 introduces three new client-side object models: Managed, Silverlight, and JavaScript. Each of the three object models provides an object interface to SharePoint functionality that is based on the objects available in the `Microsoft.SharePoint` namespace, but that uses web service calls behind the scenes. This approach provides a development experience that is easier to program with than the web service model used in previous versions. While none of the models is fully equivalent to the server-side model, they are equivalent to each other, so you can leverage your knowledge of one model into another.

The three client object models are maintained in separate libraries, which are located under the system directory. The managed client object model is contained in the assemblies `Microsoft.SharePoint.Client.dll` and `Microsoft.SharePoint.ClientRuntime.dll`, which can be found in the `ISAPI` folder. The Silverlight client object model is contained in the assemblies `Microsoft.SharePoint.Client.Silverlight.dll` and `Microsoft.SharePoint.Client.Silverlight.Runtime.dll`, which are located in the `LAYOUTS\ClientBin` folder. The JavaScript client object model is contained in the library `SP.js`, which is located in the `LAYOUTS` folder. While each of the models provides a different programming interface, each interacts with SharePoint through a Windows Communication Foundation (WCF) service named `Client.svc`, which is located in the `ISAPI` directory. Figure 4-18 shows a basic architectural diagram for the client object models.

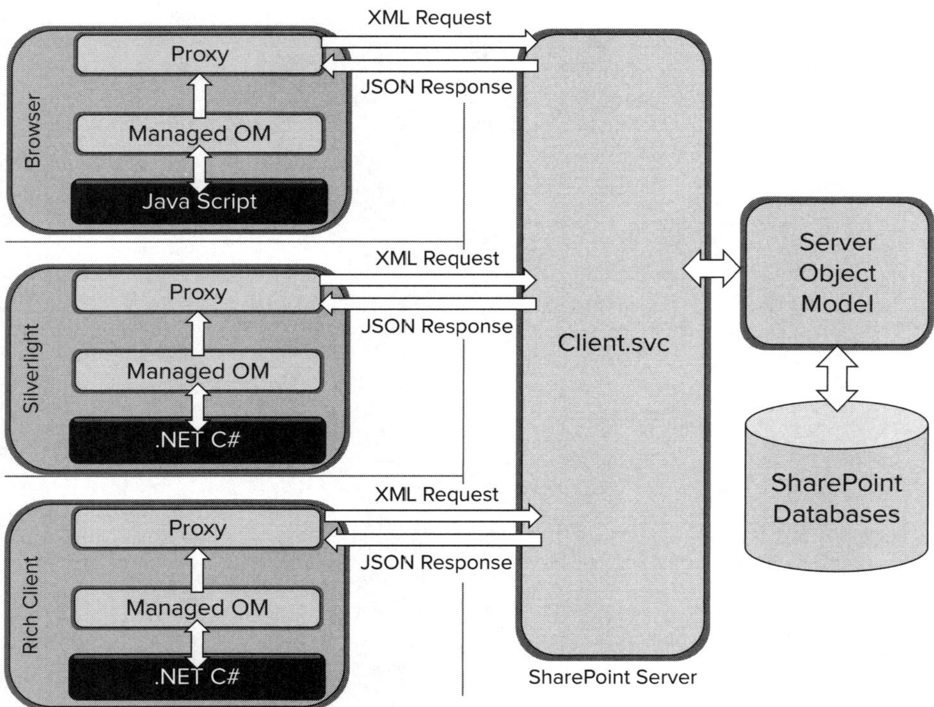

FIGURE 4-18

Each of the three object models presents an object interface in front of a service proxy. Developers write client-side code using the object model, but the operations are batched and sent as a single XML request to the `Client.svc` service. When the XML request is received, the `Client.svc` service makes calls to the server-side object model on behalf of the client. The results of the server-side calls are then sent back to the calling client in the form of a JavaScript Object Notation (JSON) object.

A detailed discussion of all three models is beyond the scope of the chapter. What is important to know is that the client object model allows access to an External List as if it were a standard list following the programming conventions for each of the client object models.

The client object models require a starting point in the form of a context object, which is much like the standard code you write against the server-side object model. The context object provides an entry point into the associated API that can be used to gain access to other objects. The `Load()` method of the context object, and its LINQ variant `LoadQuery()`, are used to batch operations to be sent to the server. The `ExecuteQuery()` and `ExecuteQueryAsync()` methods are used to send the batched operations to the server for execution. The synchronous method is supported by the managed object model, while Silverlight and JavaScript require asynchronous execution.

When you are working with External Lists, there are two special considerations. The first is that CAML queries written using the client object models must explicitly include the names of fields to return in the `ViewFields` element. The second is that the `Load()` method is not supported for External Lists; `LoadQuery()` must be used instead. These principles are shown in the following code, which executes a query against an External List:

```
ClientContext ctx = new ClientContext("http://awserver/sitecollection");

//Load site and list
Web site = ctx.Web;
ctx.Load(site);
List list = site.Lists.GetByTitle("My External List");
ctx.Load(list);

//Create query
//External Lists require the ViewFields explicitly stated in the query
StringBuilder caml = new StringBuilder();
caml.Append("<View><ViewFields><FieldRef Name='");
caml.Append("BdcIdentity");
caml.Append("'/><FieldRef Name='");
caml.Append("Name");
caml.Append("'/></ViewFields><Query><OrderBy><FieldRef Name='");
caml.Append("BdcIdentity");
caml.Append("'/></OrderBy></Query></View>");
CamlQuery query = new CamlQuery();
query.ViewXml = caml.ToString();

listItems = list.GetItems(query);

//LoadQuery is required for External Lists because Load is not supported
returnedItems = ctx.LoadQuery(
  listItems.Include(i => i["BdcIdentity"], i => i["Name"]));

//Execute
ctx.ExecuteQueryAsync(succeedListener, failListener);
```

Initiating Workflows

While you cannot directly associate a workflow with an External List, there are two workarounds that can be used to initiate workflows as part of a BCS solution. The first involves simply writing a site workflow that interacts with an External List. The second involves the use of a standard list to act as the starting point for the workflow. This section covers these techniques. More advanced workflow techniques, such as Sandbox Workflow Actions and Pluggable Services, are covered in Chapter 5.

Site workflows are new to SharePoint 2010. A site workflow is not associated with a SharePoint list. Instead, the site workflow is associated with the site itself. You manage site workflows by navigating to Site Actions ➪ View All Site Content ➪ Site Workflows. On the site workflows page you can add, remove, start, and stop site workflows. Figure 4-19 shows the page.

Start a New Workflow

Assign External List Task
Assigns a task to review an External List item

Workflows

Select a workflow for more details on the current status or history. Show all workflows.

Name	Started	Ended	Status
My Running Workflows			
There are no currently running workflows on this site.			
My Completed Workflows			
Assign External List Task	7/8/2010 11:03 AM	7/8/2010 11:03 AM	Completed
Assign External List Task	7/7/2010 9:40 AM	7/7/2010 9:40 AM	Completed
Assign External List Task (Previous Version:7/7/2010 9:38:05 AM)	7/7/2010 9:38 AM	7/7/2010 9:38 AM	Completed

FIGURE 4-19

You can create site workflows directly in SPD by selecting the `Workflows` object and then clicking the New Site Workflow button. As was pointed out in Chapter 2, any SPD workflow can interact with an External List much as it would with a standard list. The question is simply how to start the workflow, because it cannot be directly associated with the External List. In the case of the site workflow you can use an Initiation Form parameter to allow the user to enter some identifying piece of information about the item in the External List upon which the workflow should run.

Figure 4-20 shows a site workflow with an Initiation Form parameter that accepts the `Product Number` as an input. The `Product Number` is a column in the External List that uniquely identifies an item. Once the user supplies the number, the rest of the workflow can run as if it had been initiated directly from the item in the External List. In this case, the workflow simply assigns a review task to a manager.

In addition to site workflows, External Lists can be used with list workflows when the data is present as an External Column in the list. In this case the approach is to use the projected fields in the workflow directly or to perform a lookup against the External List based on data in the projected fields. Figure 4-21 shows a document library containing sales quotes that are associated with a customer through an External List.

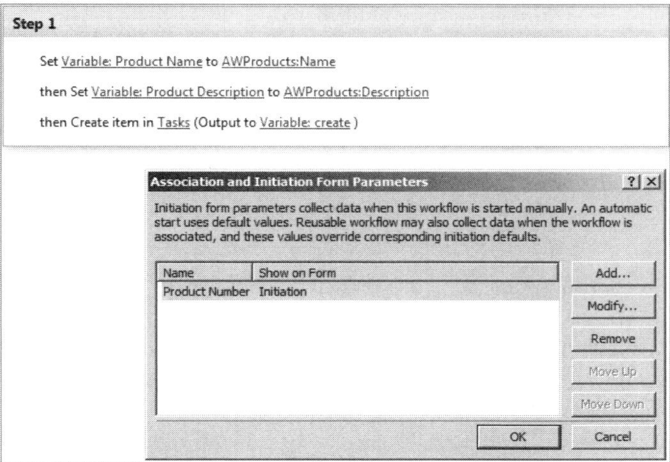

FIGURE 4-20

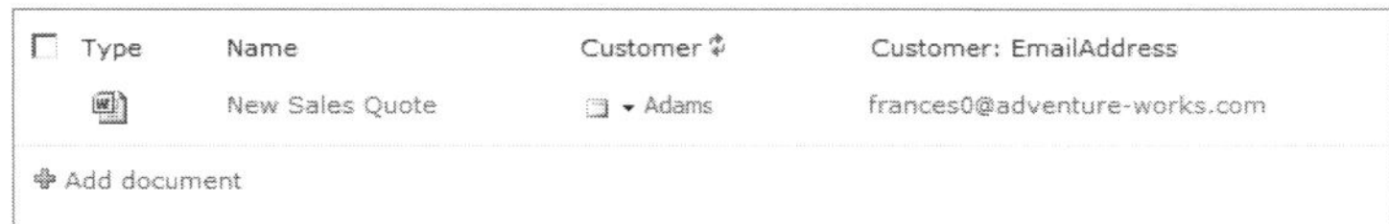

FIGURE 4-21

While the customer data in the library was originally intended for associating customers with documents, it can also be used for workflows. In this example it will be used for an additional workflow on the library that initiates a customer satisfaction survey. The strategy is to have the workflow look up the customer in the External List using the e-mail address. Once the customer is located, all the other fields may be used to build a new task assignment.

When you are working with workflows against External Lists, there are a few things to keep in mind. First, lookups against External Lists that are associated with databases will fail unless the authentication mode is set to `RevertToSelf`. Furthermore, `RevertToSelf` is disabled by default and must be explicitly enabled with the following PowerShell command. See Chapter 8 for a deeper discussion of authentication modes.

```
$bdc = Get-SPServiceApplication
 | where {$_ -match "Business Data Connectivity Service"}
$bdc.RevertToSelfAllowed = $true
$bdc.Update();
```

Second, reading columns from External Lists in a workflow requires separate calls to the `Finder` and `SpecificFinder` methods for each column. This means that reading many columns can easily result in poor performance. Therefore, the number of columns read in a workflow step should be kept as small as possible.

Finally, The `BdcIdentity` field is the only guaranteed unique field in an External List. If you look up items by other fields, only the first matching item is returned. Often this is not an issue, because you can use fields like e-mail address, which are generally unique to one item. If you require a `BdcIdentity`, however, you can only obtain it from the creation of a new item because no other operation will return it.

DEVELOPING SOLUTIONS

When developing professional solutions, you must be concerned with more than simply getting the BCS solution to work. Chief among the additional concerns is that you must be able to move a solution from development to testing to production. You may also need to port an existing application into BCS or to migrate an old BDC solution from SharePoint 2007.

Making Solutions Portable

In previous versions of SharePoint, artifacts created in SPD were bound to the content database and were difficult to reuse. Furthermore, there was no simple way to export artifacts from SPD and move them to another environment. This meant that SPD artifacts could not easily be moved from a development environment to a testing or production environment. Fortunately, the situation has changed significantly. You may now create BCS solutions entirely in SPD and easily move them to other environments.

The most obvious artifacts that should be moved through a development life cycle are the BDC Metadata Models. As previously discussed, these models can be exported from SPD edited and imported through the BDC Service Application. This simple technique makes it possible to build BDC Metadata Models in SPD, export them, modify the connection information as required, and use them in a new environment.

While exporting and importing is straightforward, the ideal approach is to use a feature to install BDC Metadata Models into new environments. The goal of this process is to create a WSP file that contains all the necessary elements for your BCS solution to be installed in another environment. Therefore, you must identify what artifacts you want to move. These can include not only the BDC Metadata Model, but also list instances and customized forms.

If your solution will include list instances, the easiest way to get started is to save the entire site as a template. You can save the site containing your BCS solution as a template from the Site Settings page. Saving the site as a template will result in the creating of a solution package (WSP file) that will be saved into the Solutions Gallery at the root of the site collection. The Solutions Gallery is the location where Sandboxed Solutions are normally deployed and can be accessed from the Site Settings page of the root site in the collection under the Galleries heading.

Once you have saved the site as a template you can open the root site in SPD and examine the Solutions Gallery. In SPD the Solutions Gallery is located at `All Files\_catalogs\solutions`. From here you can select the WSP file that was created when the site was saved as a template and export it to the file system. The purpose of exporting it to the file system is to allow it to be opened in Visual Studio 2010.

Visual Studio 2010 supports a new project type named Import SharePoint Solution Package. The purpose of this project type is to allow you to create a project from a WSP package. In this case the package created by saving the site as a template can be opened. When the new project is created Visual Studio will allow you to select only the artifacts that you want in the project. In this case you would select all the External Lists. After you select the artifacts, Visual Studio will create a feature for deploying the artifacts. These will include the selected list instances and any customized forms. Figure 4-22 shows the dialog for selecting artifacts with three External Lists selected.

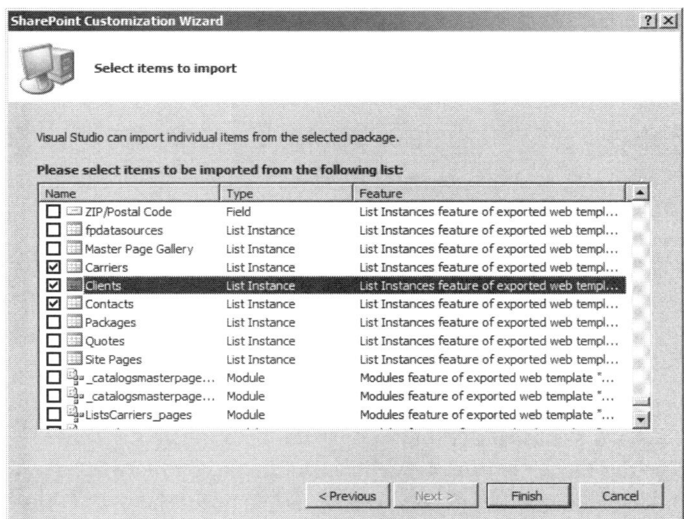

FIGURE 4-22

The final step is to add the BDC Metadata Model to the project. BDC Metadata Models are exported from SPD with a BDCM extension. Visual Studio 2010 understands this extension so that you can simply select to add an existing item to the project and navigate to the BDCM file. When you add the file to the project, a new feature is created for deploying the model. You now have everything you need to create a feature that will deploy the entire BCS solution.

Converting ASP.NET Solutions

When BCS is discussed, the context most often involves the idea of accessing line-of-business systems such as CRM and ERP. There is a strong case to be made, however, that BCS should be the primary technology used for creating web-based applications in SharePoint. Because of this some developers may choose to convert existing ASP.NET applications into BCS applications. In order to understand why this is advantageous, let's take a look at how web-based applications are normally integrated into SharePoint.

The majority of SharePoint developers have an ASP.NET background, which is useful when they're first learning SharePoint. However, a strong ASP.NET development background can also affect the way developers think about designing a SharePoint solution. As an example, consider Figure 4-23, which shows an actual ASP.NET application used to manage contact information.

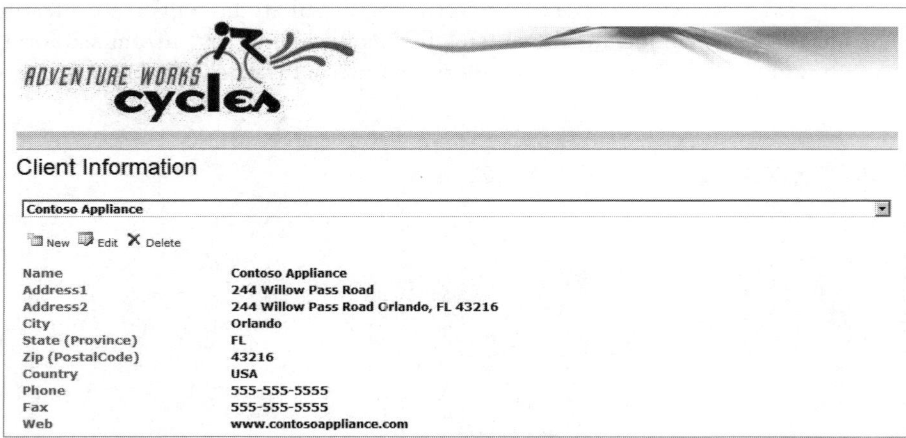

FIGURE 4-23

Many ASP.NET developers have existing applications such as this, and they are told that they must be integrated with SharePoint. Perhaps the most common approach for integrating these applications is to simply deploy them to the `LAYOUTS` directory. Because the `LAYOUTS` directory is a mapped directory in IIS, any web application copied there will run. Furthermore, the application appears to be integrated into SharePoint when viewed in the browser, as shown in Figure 4-24.

Clients ▸ Clients
I Like It
Tags & Notes
Clients
Search this site...
Libraries
Quotes
Packages
Site Pages
Lists
Clients
Carriers
Contacts
Discussions
ASP.NET Apps
Contoso Appliance
New Edit Delete
Name Contoso Appliance
Address1 244 Willow Pass Road
Address2 244 Willow Pass Road Orlando, FL 43216
City Orlando
State (Province) FL
Zip (PostalCode) 43216
Country USA
Phone 555-555-5555
Fax 555-555-5555
Web www.contosoappliance.com

FIGURE 4-24

Initially the idea of copying ASP.NET web applications into the `LAYOUTS` directory is tempting because it is simple and requires little rework. However, the application is not truly integrated into SharePoint. It does not take advantage of the SharePoint security infrastructure and it cannot get access to a SharePoint context. From a BCS perspective, the application data cannot be used as a source for columns, and perhaps most significantly, it cannot be indexed and searched.

The better approach for creating applications that integrate with SharePoint is to use BCS. ECTs can be created against the database and integrated, as discussed throughout the chapter. Much of this work can even be done using only SPD. Figure 4-25 shows the same application created as a BCS solution using no code. The interface is generated through the out-of-the-box External Data web parts. If you wanted a more sophisticated interface, however, you could create your own web parts, as described in Chapter 6.

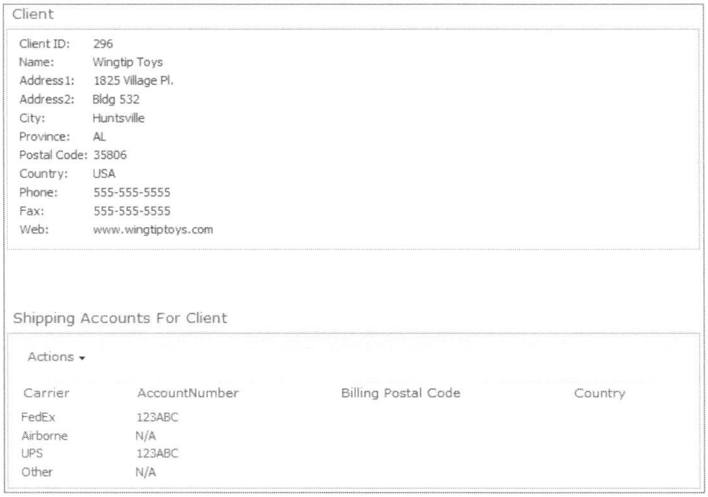

Client

Client ID:	296
Name:	Wingtip Toys
Address1:	1825 Village Pl.
Address2:	Bldg 532
City:	Huntsville
Province:	AL
Postal Code:	35806
Country:	USA
Phone:	555-555-5555
Fax:	555-555-5555
Web:	www.wingtiptoys.com

Shipping Accounts For Client

Actions ▾

Carrier	AccountNumber	Billing Postal Code	Country
FedEx	123ABC		
Airborne	N/A		
UPS	123ABC		
Other	N/A		

FIGURE 4-25

Upgrading BDC 2007 Solutions

If you have worked with the Business Data Catalog in SharePoint 2007, then you may have existing BDC models that you want to upgrade to BCS under SharePoint 2010. SharePoint 2010 supports a service application called the *Application Registry Service*. This service is a backward-compatible service designed to host BDC solutions from MOSS 2007.

Only in-place upgrading is supported for MOSS 2007 BDC solutions. When you perform an upgrade of a MOSS 2007 environment to SharePoint 2010, the upgrade process creates an Application Registry Service and a BDC Service Application. Each model contained in the MOSS 2007 environment is copied into the Application Registry Service. An upgraded version of the model is then copied into the BDC Service Application.

Models in the Application Registry Service have limited value. They cannot be used to create External Lists and the External Data web parts in SharePoint 2010 will not work with them. You can still use the models as content sources for search, and any references to the Single Sign-On Service will be upgraded to refer to the Secure Store Service.

If you want to upgrade your MOSS 2007 solutions without performing an in-place upgrade of the farm, you must upgrade the BDC models by hand. Each model must be exported from the MOSS 2007 BDC repository and edited to meet the requirements of the BDC Service Application.

SUMMARY

When creating BCS solutions for SharePoint 2010, SharePoint Designer should be considered the primary tool. The tooling support in SPD is easier to use than the equivalent tooling in Visual Studio. Additionally, you can export the model and edit it by hand to include capabilities not supported in the SPD tooling. In short, you should be able to use SPD for the majority of your solutions that are based on databases and web services.

5

Programming BCS Solutions in SharePoint 2010

WHAT'S IN THIS CHAPTER?

- Learn the BDC Server Runtime object model
- Learn to use Complex and Unsupported types
- Learn to use BCS in workflow solutions
- Learn the BDC Administration object model

In the first few chapters of the book, significant attention was paid to creating BCS solutions with little coding. However, there are many situations in which the limitations of no-code solutions make it necessary to write custom components. This chapter advances the discussion of custom coding in BCS by presenting several key server-side technologies, including the BDC object models, workflow techniques, and approaches to overcoming data limitations. This information forms the foundation for custom solutions built on External Lists, custom web parts, web services, InfoPath forms, and workflows.

WORKING WITH THE BDC SERVER RUNTIME OBJECT MODEL

The BDC Server Runtime object model is the API used to write custom solutions that run on the SharePoint 2010 server and use BCS artifacts. Using the object model is fairly straightforward and gives you significant control over how and when operations are performed. Additionally, using the object model allows you to create completely custom user interface elements such as console applications and web parts.

The BDC Server Runtime object model is contained in the `Microsoft.SharePoint.dll` and `Microsoft.BusinessData.dll` assemblies. Both of these assemblies are located in the `ISAPI` directory. Any solution you create will need a reference to both of these assemblies, which contain many different namespaces. The following code shows typical `using` statements, and Table 5-1 lists the key namespaces used for working with the BDC Server Runtime object model.

```
//Reference to Microsoft.SharePoint.dll
using Microsoft.SharePoint;
using Microsoft.SharePoint.Administration;
using Microsoft.SharePoint.BusinessData;
using Microsoft.SharePoint.BusinessData.Runtime;
using Microsoft.SharePoint.BusinessData.SharedService;
using Microsoft.SharePoint.BusinessData.MetadataModel;

//Reference to Microsoft.BusinessData.dll
using Microsoft.BusinessData;
using Microsoft.BusinessData.MetadataModel;
using Microsoft.BusinessData.Runtime;
using Microsoft.BusinessData.MetadataModel.Collections;
```

TABLE 5-1: Key Namespaces

NAMESPACE	ASSEMBLY	DESCRIPTION
`Microsoft.SharePoint .Administration`	`Microsoft.SharePoint.dll`	Provides access to the BDC Service application
`Microsoft.SharePoint .BusinessData.MetadataModel`	`Microsoft.SharePoint.dll`	Provides access to the Metadata Catalog
`Microsoft.SharePoint .BusinessData.Runtime`	`Microsoft.SharePoint.dll`	Provides access to filter types
`Microsoft.SharePoint .BusinessData.SharedService`	`Microsoft.SharePoint.dll`	Provides access to the BDC Service Application proxy
`Microsoft.BusinessData .MetadataModel`	`Microsoft.BusinessData.dll`	Provides access to key Metadata elements
`Microsoft.BusinessData .MetadataModel.Collections`	`Microsoft.BusinessData.dll`	Provides access to key Metadata collections
`Microsoft.BusinessData .Runtime`	`Microsoft.BusinessData.dll`	Provides access to key entity instance objects and collections

Connecting to the Metadata Catalog

In order to execute code against BCS solutions using the BDC Server Runtime, you must establish a connection to the Metadata Catalog in which the ECTs are stored. The first step in this process is to make a connection to the BDC Service Application. Establishing this connection is done differently depending upon whether your code is running within a SharePoint context or simply on the SharePoint server. In either case, however, you'll make use of the `Microsoft.SharePoint.SPServiceContext` class.

The `SPServiceContext` class allows your code to communicate with SharePoint service applications. When your code is running inside a SharePoint context (such as a custom web part), you can use the `Current` property to retrieve the current service context. The `GetDefaultProxy()` method may then subsequently be used to get the service proxy for any service. If your code is running outside a SharePoint context (such as in a console application), the context must be explicitly set with a `SPSite` object. In either case you will then make use of the `Microsoft.SharePoint.BusinessData.SharedService.BdcServiceApplicationProxy` class to get a reference to the BDC Service Application proxy. The `GetDefaultProxy()` method of the `SPServiceContext` class will return the default service application proxy for the type specified. The `GetProxies()` method will return all available service application proxies for the type specified. The following code shows how to get the default `BdcServiceApplicationProxy` object, first from within a SharePoint context and then from without:

```
//Within SharePoint Context
BdcServiceApplicationProxy proxy =
  (BdcServiceApplicationProxy)SPServiceContext.Current.
   GetDefaultProxy(typeof(BdcServiceApplicationProxy));

//Outside SharePoint Context
using (SPSite site = new SPSite(siteCollectionUrl))
{
    BdcServiceApplicationProxy proxy =
     (BdcServiceApplicationProxy)SPServiceContext.GetContext(site).
      GetDefaultProxy(typeof(BdcServiceApplicationProxy));
}
```

In addition to using the `BdcServiceApplicationProxy` object to establish context, you may also use the `Microsoft.SharePoint.BusinessData.SharedService.BdcService` class. The `BdcService` class is an abstraction of the BDC Service Application, which is useful for determining whether or not a BDC Service Application is available in the farm. The following code shows how to check the availability of the BDC Service Application in a farm:

```
BdcService service = SPFarm.Local.Services.GetValue<BdcService>();

    if (service == null)
        throw new Exception("No BDC Service Application found.");
```

Once you have established a context you can connect to the Metadata Catalog in the BDC Service Application. The Metadata Catalog on the server is represented by the

`Microsoft.SharePoint.BusinessData.MetadataModel.DatabaseBackedMetadataCatalog` class. Both the `BdcServiceApplicationProxy` object and the `BdcService` object are capable of returning a `DatabaseBackedMetadataCatalog` object. The following code shows both approaches:

```
//Using BdcServiceApplicationProxy
DatabaseBackedMetadataCatalog catalog =
  proxy.GetDatabaseBackedMetadataCatalog();

//Using BdcService
DatabaseBackedMetadataCatalog catalog =
  service.GetDatabaseBackedMetadataCatalog(
  SPServiceContext.GetContext(site));
```

Retrieving Model Elements

Once a connection to the Metadata Catalog is established, elements of the BDC Metadata Models may be retrieved. These include ECTs, systems, and operations. The purpose of retrieving these items is to execute the defined method instances against the defined External System. The `DatabaseBackedMetadataCatalog` class has five methods for retrieving model elements: `GetEntity()`, `GetEntities()`, `GetLobSystem()`, `GetLobSystems()`, and `GetById()`.

Typically your solution will start by retrieving a reference to the ECTs that represent the data you want to use. The simplest way to retrieve an ECT is to use the `GetEntity()` method, passing in the name and namespace for the desired entity. The method returns a `Microsoft.BusinessData.MetadataModel.IEntity` interface representing the ECT, as shown in the following code:

```
IEntity ect = catalog.GetEntity("MyNamespace", "MyEntity");
```

While the code for retrieving an ECT is simple, it is not the most efficient. While the BDC Server Runtime object model generally interacts with cached BDC Metadata Models, the `GetEntity()`, `GetEntities()`, `GetLobSystem()`, and `GetLobSystems()` methods do not. Instead, they call directly to the Metadata Catalog database, which is less efficient. The solution to this problem is to use the `GetById()` method to retrieve the ECTs and LobSystems. The `GetById()` method takes the `Id` and `Type` of the element to return and executes against the cached model. The challenge in using the `GetById()` method is determining the `Id` of the desired element. The best approach is to use the `GetEntity()` method on the first call and save the `Id` of the element for future use. The following code shows the relationship between the `GetEntity()` method and the `GetById()` method.

```
//Get Entity the easy way on first call
IEntity ect = catalog.GetEntity(entityNamespace, entityName);

//Save Entity data
uint ectId = Convert.ToUInt32(ect.Id);
Type ectType = ect.GetType();

//Get Entity the fast way on subsequent calls
ect = (IEntity)catalog.GetById(ectId, ectType);
```

Along with retrieving ECTs and LobSystems from the `DatabaseBackedMetadataCatalog` object, many objects have methods for retrieving related objects. For example, the `GetLobSystem()` method of the `IEntity` interface returns the related LobSystem for the ECT. In this way you can retrieve whatever model elements are required for your application.

Executing Operations

The whole point of connecting to the Metadata Catalog and retrieving the ECT is to allow for the execution of the operations defined as method instances within the BDC Metadata Model. With full access to the operations you can create complete custom applications. These applications can use any of the available method stereotypes, thus overcoming any of the limitations found in the SharePoint Designer and the External Data Web Parts.

The approach used to execute an operation varies slightly from stereotype to stereotype. In the case of `Finder` methods, for example, you must retrieve the method instance before executing. This is because a BDC Metadata Model may define multiple `Finder` methods. In the case of `Creator`, `Updater`, and `Deleter` methods the object model provides a more direct approach, because only a single method instance of these stereotypes may exist in the model for any entity.

Along with specific support for various stereotypes, discussed later in the chapter, the object model also provides generic support to execute any method instance. The following code shows a console application that uses the `Execute()` method of the `IEntity` to execute a `Finder` method and display the results. This code works for any model and any `Finder` method based on the arguments passed to it.

```
static void Main(string[] args)
{
    try
    {

        if (args.Count() != 5)
            throw new Exception("Useage: ExecuteFinder.exe
                                 SiteCollectionUrl,
                                 LobSystemInstance,
                                 EntityName,
                                 EntityNamespace,
                                 FinderMethodInstance");

        string siteCollectionUrl = args[0];
        string lobSystemInstance = args[1];
        string entityName = args[2];
        string entityNamespace = args[3];
        string finderMethodInstance = args[4];

        using (SPSite site = new SPSite(siteCollectionUrl))
        {
            //Connect to the BDC Service Application proxy
            BdcService service =
              SPFarm.Local.Services.GetValue<BdcService>();
```

```
                if (service == null)
                    throw new Exception("No BDC Service Application found.");

                //Connect to metadata catalog
                DatabaseBackedMetadataCatalog catalog =
                  service.GetDatabaseBackedMetadataCatalog(
                  SPServiceContext.GetContext(site));

                //Get Entity
                IEntity ect = catalog.GetEntity(entityNamespace, entityName);

                //Get LobSystem
                ILobSystem lob = ect.GetLobSystem();

                //Get LobSystemInstance
                ILobSystemInstance lobi =
                  lob.GetLobSystemInstances()[lobSystemInstance];

                //Get Method Instance
                IMethodInstance mi =
                  ect.GetMethodInstance(finderMethodInstance,
                                        MethodInstanceType.Finder);

                //Execute
                IEnumerable items = (IEnumerable)ect.Execute(mi, lobi);

                //Display
                foreach (Object item in items)
                {
                    PropertyInfo[] props = item.GetType().GetProperties();

                    foreach (PropertyInfo prop in props)
                    {
                        Console.WriteLine(prop.GetValue(item, null));
                    }
                }

            }
        }
        catch (Exception x)
        {
            Console.WriteLine(x.Message);
        }
    }
```

When executing methods using the generic approach provided by the `Execute()` method, you will often have to pass in parameters, such as when you execute a `SpecificFinder` method. In these cases you must retrieve the required parameters from the method and set them. The following code snippet shows how to do this for a `SpecificFinder` method associated with a BDC Metadata Model that uses the SQL connector.

```
//Get Method Instance
IMethodInstance mi = ect.GetMethodInstance(specificFinderMethodInstance,
  MethodInstanceType.SpecificFinder);

//Get Parameters
IParameterCollection parameters = mi.GetMethod().GetParameters();

//Set Parameters
object[] arguments = new object[parameters.Count];
arguments[0] = entityInstanceIdentifier;

//Execute
ect.Execute(mi, lobi, ref arguments);

//Display
PropertyInfo[] props = arguments[1].GetType().GetProperties();
PropertyInfo prop = props[0];
SqlDataReader reader = (SqlDataReader)(prop.GetValue(arguments[1], null));

if (reader.HasRows)
{
    while (reader.Read())
    {
        Console.WriteLine(reader.GetString(3) + " " + reader.GetString(5));
    }
}
```

Note how the arguments are passed by reference to the `Execute()` method. This is required because the return parameter is placed in the array during execution. You can then read out the return parameter and cast it to an appropriate type for display. In the code sample the return parameter is cast to a `SqlDataReader`, which is the type returned from methods that use the SQL connector.

While CRUD operations are certainly the most common in BCS solutions, accessing documents through streams is often a critical part of any SharePoint solution. Therefore, the `StreamAccessor` stereotype stands out as important. The `Execute()` method can be used to invoke a `StreamAccessor` method and return a stream for downloading. The following code shows a typical `StreamAccessor` method defined in a BDC Metadata Model:

```
<Method Name="ReadContents" DefaultDisplayName="Read Contents">
 <Parameters>
  <Parameter Name="id" Direction="In">
   <TypeDescriptor Name="ID" IdentifierName="ID"
    TypeName="System.Int32" IsCollection="false" />
  </Parameter>
  <Parameter Name="contents" Direction="Return">
   <TypeDescriptor Name="Contents" TypeName="System.IO.Stream" />
  </Parameter>
 </Parameters>
 <MethodInstances>
  <MethodInstance Name="ReadContents" Type="StreamAccessor"
```

```
      ReturnParameterName="contents" ReturnTypeDescriptorPath="Contents"
      DefaultDisplayName="ReadContents">
    </MethodInstance>
  </MethodInstances>
</Method>
```

The method instance returns a `System.IO.Stream` object based on a `System.Int32` value. The `Execute()` method can be used to invoke the `StreamAccessor` if the two values are known. The following code shows how the method instance can be invoked and the stream downloaded to the client based on `QueryString` parameters passed into an ASPX page:

```
//Connect to server-side BCS
BdcServiceApplicationProxy proxy =
  (BdcServiceApplicationProxy)SPServiceContext.
  Current.GetDefaultProxy(typeof(BdcServiceApplicationProxy));

DatabaseBackedMetadataCatalog catalog =
  proxy.GetDatabaseBackedMetadataCatalog();

IEntity ect = catalog.GetEntity("MyNamespace", "DocumentECT");
ILobSystem lob = ect.GetLobSystem();
ILobSystemInstance lobi = lob.GetLobSystemInstances()["MyDMSInstance"];
IMethodInstance mi =
  ect.GetMethodInstance("ReadContents",
                        MethodInstanceType.StreamAccessor);

//Call BCS to get stream
object[] args = { int.Parse(Request.QueryString["DocumentId"]), null };
ect.Execute(mi, lobi, ref args);
byte[] buffer = ((MemoryStream)args[1]).ToArray();

//Download
this.Page.Response.Clear();
this.Page.Response.ClearHeaders();
this.Page.Response.AddHeader("Content-Disposition",
  "attachment; filename=\"" + Request.QueryString["fileName"] + "\"");
this.Page.Response.AddHeader("Content-Length", buffer.Length.ToString());
this.Page.Response.BinaryWrite(buffer);
this.Page.Response.Flush();
this.Page.Response.End();
```

While the `Execute()` method provides good functionality for executing any method instance, most often the application code is tailored for the specific stereotype being invoked. The following sections detail the support provided by the BDC Server Runtime object model for invoking specific method stereotypes.

Executing Finder Methods

`Finder` methods are the backbone of any custom BCS application. To invoke a `Finder` method instance you use the `FindFiltered()` method of the `IEntity`. The `FindFiltered()` method returns entity instances from a `Finder` method using filter criteria. Table 5-2 shows the overloads available for the `FindFiltered()` method.

TABLE 5-2: The FindFiltered() Method

SIGNATURE	DESCRIPTION
`FindFiltered(IFilterCollection, ILobSystemInstance)`	Executes the default `Finder` method using the given filters
`FindFiltered(IFilterCollection, String, ILobSystemInstance)`	Executes a named `Finder` method using the given filters
`FindFiltered(IFilterCollection, String, ILobSystemInstance, OperationMode)`	Executes a named `Finder` method using the given filters and Operation Mode

If the method is the default `Finder` method, its name does not need to be provided. If the `Finder` method to execute is not the default, its name is provided as a `String` value to the `FindFiltered()` method. Be careful to use the name of the method instance as defined in the BDC Metadata Model and not the name of the method.

If the `Finder` method defines filters (such as a limit, wildcard, or page filters), these values must be provided in the call to the `FindFiltered()` method. You can return an `IFilterCollection` by calling the `GetFilters()` method of `IMethodInstance`. The values for the filters may then be set. The following code shows how to get the filter collection and set values:

```
IMethodInstance mi = ect.GetMethodInstance(FinderMethodInstanceName,
                                           MethodInstanceType.Finder);
IFilterCollection filters = mi.GetFilters();
(filters[0] as LimitFilter).Value = 10;
(filters[1] as PageNumberFilter).Value = 2;
(filters[3] as WildcardFilter).Value = "Bike";
(filters[4] as ComparisonFilter).Value = "CN123720";
```

In most applications you will already know what filters the method instance is expecting. In these cases you may set the filters directly, as shown in the preceding code. If, however, you do not know what filters are expected, you can determine this dynamically by iterating through the collection of filters, as shown in the following code:

```
foreach (IFilter filter in filters)
{
    Console.WriteLine("Filter Type:       " +
      filter.FilterDescriptor.FilterType.ToString());
    Console.WriteLine("Filter Field:      " +
      filter.FilterDescriptor.FilterField);
}
```

When executing the `FindFiltered()` method you may optionally specify an `OperationMode` for the call, which allows data to be read from a cache. However, the `OperationMode` has no effect on server-side operations. The purpose of the `OperationMode` is solely to maintain complementary signatures between the BDC Client and BDC Server APIs. Remember that the server never caches data — only model elements. The `OperationMode` has meaning only on the client. If you want to cache data on the server, then you can utilize standard ASP.NET approaches such as the `HttpRuntime.Cache` within a custom web part.

The `FindFiltered()` method returns a `Microsoft.BusinessData.Runtime.IEntityInstanceEnumerator`. The `IEntityInstanceEnumerator` object provides a forward-only collection of entity instances that you can read. After reading the entity instances from the collection, the `Close()` method must be called to release the resources used to access the External System. The following code shows the basic approach:

```
//Connect to BDC Service Application
BdcService service = SPFarm.Local.Services.GetValue<BdcService>();

if (service != null)
{
//Get Metadata elements
  DatabaseBackedMetadataCatalog catalog =
    service.GetDatabaseBackedMetadataCatalog(SPServiceContext.Current);
  IEntity ect = catalog.GetEntity(EntityNamespace, EntityName);
  ILobSystem lob = ect.GetLobSystem();
  ILobSystemInstance lobi =
    lob.GetLobSystemInstances()[LobSystemInstanceName];
}

IMethodInstance mi = ect.GetMethodInstance(FinderMethodInstanceName,
                                           MethodInstanceType.Finder);
IFilterCollection filters = mi.GetFilters();

IEntityInstanceEnumerator items =
  ect.FindFiltered(filters, FinderMethodInstanceName);

while (items.MoveNext())
{
  Console.WriteLine(items.Current[FieldName].ToString());
}

items.Close();
```

In addition to enumerating entity instances, you can also return entity instances in a `System.Data.DataTable`. You do this by calling the `CreateDataTable()` method of the `Microsoft.BusinessData.Runtime.IRuntimeHelper` interface. You can obtain this interface through the `Helper` property of the `DatabaseBackedMetadataCatalog` object. The `CreateDataTable()` method takes an `IEntityInstanceEnumerator` object and builds a `DataTable` from it. The `CreateDataTable()` method can make it easier to work with entity instances because the `DataTable` is a familiar and flexible object. Additionally, the `CreateDataTable()` method supports options that allow for paging through entity instances. The following code shows an example of the `CreateDataTable()` method:

```
//Connect to BDC Service Application
BdcService service = SPFarm.Local.Services.GetValue<BdcService>();

if (service != null)
```

```
{
//Get Metadata elements
  DatabaseBackedMetadataCatalog catalog =
    service.GetDatabaseBackedMetadataCatalog(SPServiceContext.Current);
  IEntity ect = catalog.GetEntity(EntityNamespace, EntityName);
  ILobSystem lob = ect.GetLobSystem();
  ILobSystemInstance lobi =
    lob.GetLobSystemInstances()[LobSystemInstanceName];
}

IMethodInstance mi = ect.GetMethodInstance(FinderMethodInstanceName,
                                           MethodInstanceType.Finder);
IFilterCollection filters = mi.GetFilters();

IEntityInstanceEnumerator items =
  ect.FindFiltered(filters, FinderMethodInstanceName);

DataTable dt = ect.Catalog.Helper.CreateDataTable(items);
```

Executing SpecificFinder Methods

To invoke a `SpecificFinder` method you use the `FindSpecific()` method of the `IEntity` interface. The `FindSpecific()` method returns an `IEntityInstance` entity from a `SpecificFinder` method given an `Identifier`. Table 5-3 shows the overloads available for the `FindSpecific()` method.

TABLE 5-3: The FindSpecific() Method

SIGNATURE	DESCRIPTION
`FindSpecific(Identity, ILobSystemInstance)`	Executes the default SpecificFinder method with an entity instance Identity
`FindSpecific(Identity, ILobSystemInstance, Boolean)`	Executes the default SpecificFinder method with an entity instance Identity with option to execute immediately
`FindSpecific(Identity, String, ILobSystemInstance)`	Executes the named SpecificFinder method with an entity instance Identity
`FindSpecific(Identity, String, ILobSystemInstance, OperationMode)`	Executes the named SpecificFinder method with an entity instance Identity in the specified OperationMode
`FindSpecific(Identity, String, ILobSystemInstance, Boolean)`	Executes the named SpecificFinder method with an entity instance Identity with option to execute immediately
`FindSpecific(Identity, String, ILobSystemInstance, OperationMode, Boolean)`	Executes the named SpecificFinder method with an entity instance Identity in the specified OperationMode with option to execute immediately

If the method is the default `SpecificFinder` method, its name does not need to be provided. If the `SpecificFinder` method to execute is not the default, its name is provided as a `String` value to the `FindSpecific()` method. Be careful to use the name of the method instance as defined in the BDC Metadata Model, and not the name of the method.

When calling the `FindSpecific()` method you will always provide an `Identity` object, which represents the `Identifier` for the desired entity instance. Simply create a new `Identity` object using the appropriate value and pass the object as an argument. `Identity` objects can be created with any data type, but be aware that `String` values are case-sensitive when used as `Identifiers`. The following code shows how to call the `FindSpecific()` method:

```
//Connect to BDC Service Application
BdcService service = SPFarm.Local.Services.GetValue<BdcService>();

if (service != null)
{
//Get Metadata elements
  DatabaseBackedMetadataCatalog catalog =
    service.GetDatabaseBackedMetadataCatalog(SPServiceContext.Current);
  IEntity ect = catalog.GetEntity(EntityNamespace, EntityName);
  ILobSystem lob = ect.GetLobSystem();
  ILobSystemInstance lobi =
    lob.GetLobSystemInstances()[LobSystemInstanceName];
}

//Execute SpecificFinder
int id = 5;
IMethodInstance mi =
  ect.GetMethodInstance(SpecificFinderMethodInstanceName,
                        MethodInstanceType.SpecificFinder);
IEntityInstance item =
   ect.FindSpecific(new Identity(id),
                    SpecificFinderMethodInstanceName,
                    lobi, true);
```

Executing Updater Methods

To invoke an `Updater` method you first use the `FindSpecific()` method to return the entity to update. The field values of the return entity may then be modified and those modifications will be committed through the `Update()` method of the `IEntityInstance` interface. In this scenario two distinct operations are performed against the External System: the initial query to return the item, and the operation that commits the changes. The following code shows how to use the `Update()` method:

```
//Connect to BDC Service Application
BdcService service = SPFarm.Local.Services.GetValue<BdcService>();

if (service != null)
{
```

```
  //Get Metadata elements
    DatabaseBackedMetadataCatalog catalog =
      service.GetDatabaseBackedMetadataCatalog(SPServiceContext.Current);
    IEntity ect = catalog.GetEntity(EntityNamespace, EntityName);
    ILobSystem lob = ect.GetLobSystem();
    ILobSystemInstance lobi =
      lob.GetLobSystemInstances()[LobSystemInstanceName];
  }

  //Execute SpecificFinder
  int id = 5;
  IMethodInstance mi =
    ect.GetMethodInstance(SpecificFinderMethodInstanceName,
                          MethodInstanceType.SpecificFinder);
  IEntityInstance item =
     ect.FindSpecific(new Identity(id),
                      SpecificFinderMethodInstanceName,
                      lobi, true);

  //Update entity instance
  item["Title"] = "My Item";
  item["Description"] = "An updated item";

  item.Update();
```

Executing Creator Methods

To invoke a `Creator` method you use the `Create()` method of the `IEntity` interface. The `Create()` method returns an `Identity` representing the new entity instance. Table 5-4 shows the overloads available for the `Create()` method.

TABLE 5-4: The Create() Method

SIGNATURE	DESCRIPTION
`Create(IFieldValueDictionary, ILobSystemInstance)`	Creates an entity instance
`Create(IFieldValueDictionary, AssociationEntityInstancesDictionary, ILobSystemInstance)`	Creates an entity instance and associates it with other entity instances
`Create(IFieldValueDictionary, Identity, ILobSystemInstance)`	Creates an entity instance with the given Identifier
`Create(IFieldValueDictionary, Identity, AssociationEntityInstancesDictionary, ILobSystemInstance)`	Creates an entity instance with the given Identifier and associates it with other entity instances

When calling the `Create()` method you will pass the values for the new entity instance in a `Microsoft.BusinessData.Runtime.IFieldValueDictionary`. The `IFieldValueDictionary` can be created from a `Microsoft.BusinessData.MetadataModel.IView` interface. This interface represents all the fields that are associated with a given method instance. After obtaining the `IFieldValueDictionary` object you may either set values for the new entity instance or use the default values, as shown in the following code:

```
//Connect to BDC Service Application
BdcService service = SPFarm.Local.Services.GetValue<BdcService>();

if (service != null)
{
//Get Metadata elements
  DatabaseBackedMetadataCatalog catalog =
    service.GetDatabaseBackedMetadataCatalog(SPServiceContext.Current);
  IEntity ect = catalog.GetEntity(EntityNamespace, EntityName);
  ILobSystem lob = ect.GetLobSystem();
  ILobSystemInstance lobi =
    lob.GetLobSystemInstances()[LobSystemInstanceName];
}

//Create new entity instance with default values
IView createView = ect.GetCreatorView(CreatorMethodInstanceName);
IFieldValueDictionary fieldValueDictionary = createView.GetDefaultValues();
ect.Create(fieldValueDictionary, lobi);
```

Executing Deleter Methods

To invoke a `Deleter` method you first use the `FindSpecific()` method to return the entity instance to delete. The entity instance may then be deleted with the `Delete()` method of the `IEntityInstance` interface. The following code shows how to use the `Delete()` method:

```
//Connect to BDC Service Application
BdcService service = SPFarm.Local.Services.GetValue<BdcService>();

if (service != null)
{
//Get Metadata elements
  DatabaseBackedMetadataCatalog catalog =
    service.GetDatabaseBackedMetadataCatalog(SPServiceContext.Current);
  IEntity ect = catalog.GetEntity(EntityNamespace, EntityName);
  ILobSystem lob = ect.GetLobSystem();
  ILobSystemInstance lobi =
    lob.GetLobSystemInstances()[LobSystemInstanceName];
}

//Execute SpecificFinder
int id = 5;
IMethodInstance mi =
  ect.GetMethodInstance(SpecificFinderMethodInstanceName,
                        MethodInstanceType.SpecificFinder);
```

```
IEntityInstance item =
   ect.FindSpecific(new Identity(id),
                    SpecificFinderMethodInstanceName,
                    lobi, true);

//Delete entity instance
item.Delete();
```

Executing AssociationNavigator Methods

To invoke an `AssociationNavigator` method you first use the `FindSpecific()` method to return the source entity in the association. In order to return the entity instances associated with the source entity you call the `FindAssociated()` method of the `IEntity` interface. The `FindAssociatedMethod()` returns the associated entity instances in an `IEntityInstanceEnumerator`, just like a `Finder` method. You may then use any of the techniques discussed previously to access the data contained in the associated entity instances. The following code shows a complete console application that returns associated entity instances:

```
static void Main(string[] args)
{
    try
    {

        if (args.Count() != 8)
            throw new Exception("Useage: ExecuteAssociationNavigators
             SiteCollectionUrl,
             LobSystemInstance,
             SourceEntityName,
             DestinationEntityName, EntityNamespace,
             SpecificFinderMethodInstance,
             AssociationNavigatorMethodInstance,
             EntityInstanceIdentifier");

        string siteCollectionUrl = args[0];
        string lobSystemInstance = args[1];
        string sourceEntityName = args[2];
        string destinationEntityName = args[3];
        string entityNamespace = args[4];
        string specificFinderMethodInstance = args[5];
        string associationNavigatorMethodInstance = args[6];
        string entityInstanceIdentifier = args[7];

        using (SPSite site = new SPSite(siteCollectionUrl))
        {
            //Connect to the BDC Service Application proxy
            BdcService service =
              SPFarm.Local.Services.GetValue<BdcService>();

            if (service == null)
                throw new Exception("No BDC Service Application found.");

            //Connect to metadata catalog
            DatabaseBackedMetadataCatalog catalog =
```

```
  service.GetDatabaseBackedMetadataCatalog(
  SPServiceContext.GetContext(site));

//Get Source ECT and Destination ECT
IEntity sourceEct = catalog.GetEntity(
  entityNamespace, sourceEntityName);
IEntity destinationEct = catalog.GetEntity(
  entityNamespace, destinationEntityName);

//Get LobSystem
ILobSystem lob = sourceEct.GetLobSystem();

//Get LobSystemInstance
ILobSystemInstance lobi =
  lob.GetLobSystemInstances()[lobSystemInstance];

//Get SpecificFinder Method Instance
IMethodInstance mi =
  sourceEct.GetMethodInstance(specificFinderMethodInstance,
  MethodInstanceType.SpecificFinder);

//Get AssociationNavigator method instance
IAssociation association =
  (IAssociation)destinationEct.GetMethodInstance(
  associationNavigatorMethodInstance,
  MethodInstanceType.AssociationNavigator);

//Get Source Entity Instance
IEntityInstance sourceItem = sourceEct.FindSpecific(
  new Identity(int.Parse(entityInstanceIdentifier)), lobi, true);
EntityInstanceCollection sourceInstances =
  new EntityInstanceCollection(1);
sourceInstances.Add(sourceItem);

//Get Associated Entity Instances
IEntityInstanceEnumerator destinationItems =
  destinationEct.FindAssociated(sourceInstances,
  association, lobi, OperationMode.Online);

//Display
IView destinationView =
  destinationEct.GetDefaultSpecificFinderView();
DataTable dt =
  destinationEct.Catalog.Helper.CreateDataTable(
  destinationItems);

foreach (DataRow row in dt.Rows)
{
    for (int i = 0; i < row.ItemArray.Length; i++)
    {
        Console.WriteLine(row.ItemArray[i]);
    }
}
```

```
            }
        }
        catch (Exception x)
        {
            Console.WriteLine(x.Message);
        }
    }
```

WORKING WITH COMPLEX AND UNSUPPORTED TYPES

While BCS often makes it easy to create External Lists for different data sources, some External Systems may expose complex or unsupported types that cannot be rendered by default in External Lists or the External Data Web Parts. *Complex types* are defined as types that contain subtypes as fields. *Unsupported types* are types that cannot be displayed in External Lists. In these cases you may choose to create custom InfoPath forms, define formatting in the BDC Metadata Model, or develop a custom field type to display the data.

The classic example of a complex type is a `Customer` ECT that has an `Address` field that is composed of `Street`, `City`, `State`, and `Zip`. These data types are most often found in web services, where it is easy to define custom classes that encapsulate data. The following code shows the service contract for a simple web service that defines a complex type:

```
[ServiceContract]
public interface IService
{

    [OperationContract]
    List<Customer> GetCustomers();

    [OperationContract]
    Customer GetCustomer(string Id);

    [OperationContract]
    void CreateCustomer(string FirstName, string LastName);

    [OperationContract]
    void UpdateCustomer(string Id, string FirstName, string LastName);

    [OperationContract]
    void DeleteCustomer(string Id);

}

[DataContract]
public class Customer
{
    [DataMember]
    public string CustomerNumber { get; set; }
    [DataMember]
```

```
        public string FirstName { get; set; }
        [DataMember]
        public string LastName { get; set; }
        [DataMember]
        public Address BusinessAddress { get; set; }
    }

    [DataContract]
    public class Address
    {
        [DataMember]
        public string Street { get; set; }
        [DataMember]
        public string City { get; set; }
        [DataMember]
        public string State { get; set; }
        [DataMember]
        public string Zip { get; set; }
    }
```

Notice that the `GetCustomers()` and `GetCustomer()` operations both return `Customer` objects. The `Customer` class defines a `BusinessAddress` field that is itself a class. The `Customer` is therefore said to be a complex type from the BCS perspective. Furthermore, an External List created against this web service will not display the `BusinessAddress` field in either the list or the associated forms. Figure 5-1 shows the associated form with the complex type missing.

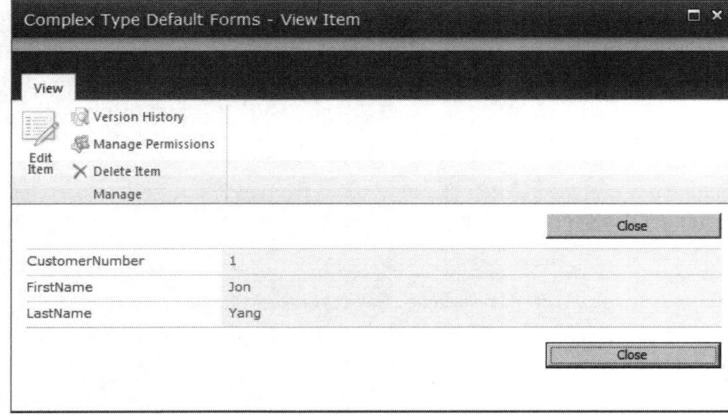

FIGURE 5-1

Unsupported data types are not rendered in External Lists. The unsupported data types are `System.GUID`, `System.Object`, `System.URI`, `System.UInt64`, and `System.Int64`. If you attempt to create a model based on an External System that uses unsupported data types, the SharePoint Designer will issue a warning. Figure 5-2 shows a warning in the SharePoint designer for an External System that contains an `Int64` field.

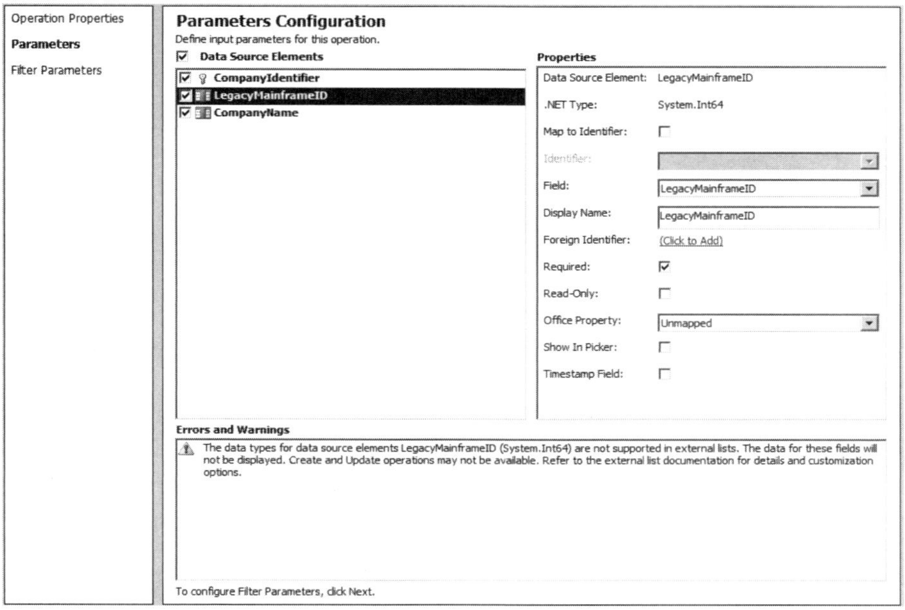

FIGURE 5-2

Using InfoPathForms for Display

The simplest way to handle complex and unsupported types is to use a custom InfoPath form to render them. After creating the External List, click the Design Forms in InfoPath button in the SharePoint Designer, as described in Chapter 4. For complex types InfoPath will open with a blank form, because it does not attempt to create a layout by default for complex types. However, the schema for the complex type will be available, as shown in Figure 5-3.

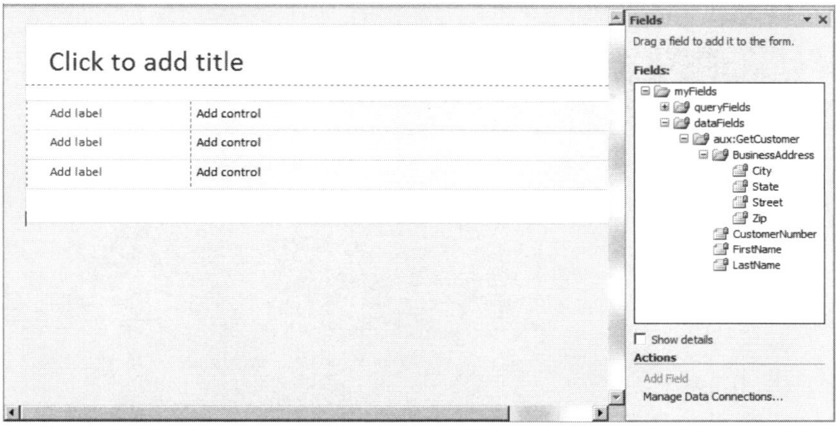

FIGURE 5-3

Using the fields, you can lay out the new form as required. When you are finished, click the Quick Publish button to publish the form. Now the complex type will render as shown in Figure 5-4.

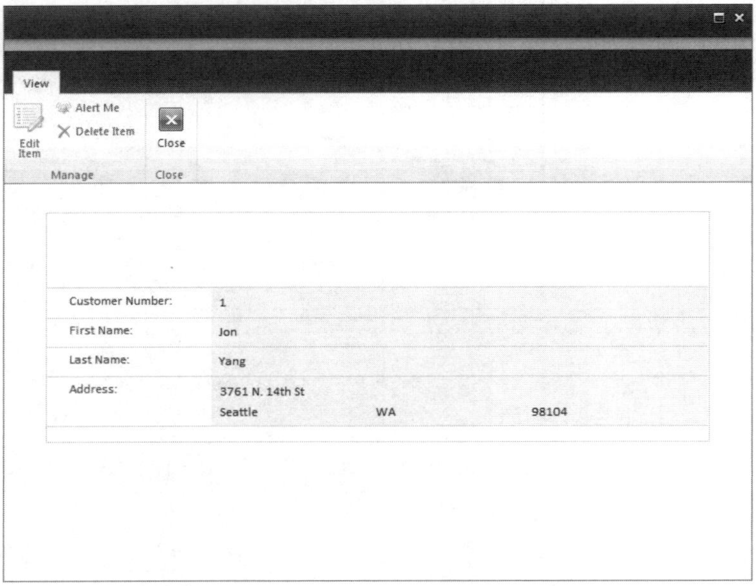

FIGURE 5-4

In the case of unsupported data types, InfoPath will open with a form layout defined and the unsupported data type will be visible in a control. In this case all you have to do is Quick Publish the form and the unsupported type will appear. Figure 5-5 shows an InfoPath form displaying an `Int64` field in an External List.

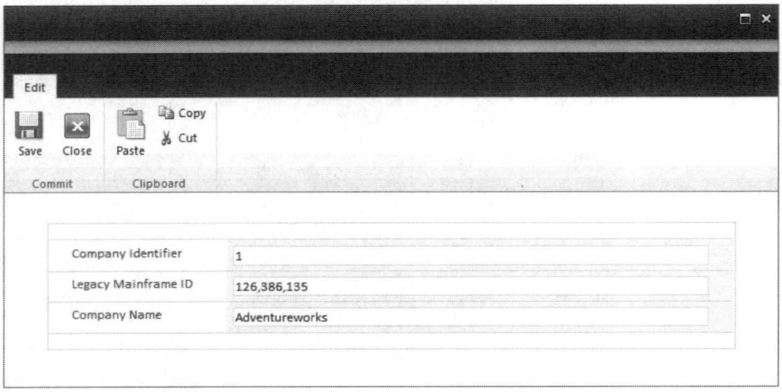

FIGURE 5-5

Using Complex Formatting for Display

Complex formatting is used with complex types to convert them into a form that can be more easily displayed in custom web parts. Complex formatting is defined directly in the BDC Metadata Model and uses either a formatting string directive or a custom rendering method call. Which you use depends on how much control you need over the formatting. The following code shows a `Finder` method definition that uses a formatting string directive against the web service described earlier:

```
<Method Name="ReadList">
 <Parameters>
  <Parameter Name="complexCustomerList" Direction="Return">
   <TypeDescriptor Name="ComplexCustomerList"
    TypeName="System.Collections.Generic.IEnumerable`1[[
    ComplexTypeConnector.ComplexCustomer, ComplexCustomerModel]]"
    IsCollection="true">
    <TypeDescriptors>
     <TypeDescriptor Name="ComplexCustomer"
      TypeName="ComplexTypeConnector.ComplexCustomer, ComplexCustomerModel"
      IsCollection="false">
      <Properties>
       <Property Name="ComplexFormatting" Type="System.String"></Property>
      </Properties>
      <TypeDescriptors>
       <TypeDescriptor Name="CustomerNumber" TypeName="System.String"
        IdentifierName="CustomerNumber" />
       <TypeDescriptor Name="FirstName" TypeName="System.String" />
       <TypeDescriptor Name="LastName" TypeName="System.String" />
       <TypeDescriptor Name="BusinessAddress"
        TypeName="ComplexTypeConnector.Address, ComplexCustomerModel"
        IsCollection="false">
       <Properties>
        <Property Name="FormatString" Type="System.String">
         {0}, {1}, {2} {3}
        </Property>
       </Properties>
       <TypeDescriptors>
        <TypeDescriptor Name="Street" TypeName="System.String" />
        <TypeDescriptor Name="City" TypeName="System.String" />
        <TypeDescriptor Name="State" TypeName="System.String" />
        <TypeDescriptor Name="Zip" TypeName="System.String" />
       </TypeDescriptors>
      </TypeDescriptor>
     </TypeDescriptors>
    </TypeDescriptor>
   </TypeDescriptors>
  </TypeDescriptor>
  </Parameter>
 </Parameters>
```

The `ComplexFormatting` property of the `TypeDescriptor` signals BCS that the `TypeDescriptor` will use complex formatting to format the parameter. The `FormatString` property defines a string that will be constructed of the values of the `TypeDescriptors` in the `BusinessAddress` field.

In this case the `Street`, `City`, `State`, and `Zip` are formatted as a simple comma-delimited line of text. This formatted value may then be retrieved through the `GetFormatted()` method of the `IEntityInstance` interface, as shown in the following code:

```
//Use BCS to call the external system
BdcServiceApplicationProxy proxy =
  (BdcServiceApplicationProxy)SPServiceContext.
  Current.GetDefaultProxy(typeof(BdcServiceApplicationProxy));

DatabaseBackedMetadataCatalog catalog =
   proxy.GetDatabaseBackedMetadataCatalog();

IEntity ect = catalog.GetEntity(
  "ComplexTypeConnector.ComplexCustomerModel", "ComplexCustomer");

ILobSystem lob = ect.GetLobSystem();
ILobSystemInstance lobi =
   lob.GetLobSystemInstances()["ComplexCustomerModel"];

//Retrieve items
IMethodInstance mi = ect.GetMethodInstance("ReadList",
                                            MethodInstanceType.Finder);
IFilterCollection filters = mi.GetFilters();
IEntityInstanceEnumerator items = ect.FindFiltered(filters,
  "ReadList", lobi, OperationMode.Online);

List<ComplexCustomer> customers = new List<ComplexCustomer>();

while (items.MoveNext())
{
    ComplexCustomer customer = new ComplexCustomer();
    customer.CustomerNumber = items.Current["CustomerNumber"].ToString();
    customer.FirstName = items.Current["FirstName"].ToString();
    customer.LastName = items.Current["LastName"].ToString();
    customer.Address =
      items.Current.GetFormatted("BusinessAddress").ToString();
    customers.Add(customer);
}
```

If the formatting string directive does not provide the capability you need, you may take complete control of how the complex type is formatted by using a custom rendering method. A custom rendering method is a `public static` method that takes an array of `Object` and returns a `String`. The array contains the values for all the sub-fields, which you can format and return as text. The following code shows a simple custom rendering method for the `BusinessAddress` field:

```
public static string Render(Object[] values)
{
    string formattedAddress = values[0].ToString() + ", " +
    values[1].ToString() + ", " + values[2].ToString() + " " +
    values[3].ToString();
    return formattedAddress;
}
```

Invoking the custom rendering method is done in the BDC Metadata Model. Just like the formatting string directive, the `ComplexFormatting` property tells BCS that the `TypeDescriptor` has complex formatting. In this case, however, the `RendererDefinition` property is used to reference the custom rendering method. The following code shows a `SpecificFinder` method that uses a custom rendering method:

```
<Method Name="ReadItem">
 <Parameters>
  <Parameter Name="complexCustomer" Direction="Return">
   <TypeDescriptor Name="ComplexCustomer"
    TypeName="ComplexTypeConnector.ComplexCustomer, ComplexCustomerModel"
    IsCollection="false">
    <Properties>
     <Property Name="ComplexFormatting" Type="System.String"></Property>
    </Properties>
    <TypeDescriptors>
     <TypeDescriptor Name="BusinessAddress"
      TypeName="ComplexTypeConnector.Address, ComplexCustomerModel"
      IsCollection="false">
      <Properties>
       <Property Name="RendererDefinition" Type="System.String">
Render!ComplexTypeConnector.ComplexCustomerModel.ComplexCustomerService,
ComplexTypeConnector, Version=1.0.0.0, Culture=neutral,
PublicKeyToken=54683373a69d23a2</Property>
      </Properties>
      <TypeDescriptors>
       <TypeDescriptor Name="Street" TypeName="System.String" />
       <TypeDescriptor Name="City" TypeName="System.String" />
       <TypeDescriptor Name="State" TypeName="System.String" />
       <TypeDescriptor Name="Zip" TypeName="System.String" />
      </TypeDescriptors>
     </TypeDescriptor>
     <TypeDescriptor Name="CustomerNumber" TypeName="System.String"
      IdentifierName="CustomerNumber" />
     <TypeDescriptor Name="FirstName" TypeName="System.String" />
     <TypeDescriptor Name="LastName" TypeName="System.String" />
    </TypeDescriptors>
   </TypeDescriptor>
  </Parameter>
  <Parameter Name="customerNumber" Direction="In">
   <TypeDescriptor Name="CustomerNumber" TypeName="System.String"
    IdentifierEntityName="ComplexCustomer"
    IdentifierEntityNamespace="ComplexTypeConnector.ComplexCustomerModel"
    IdentifierName="CustomerNumber" />
  </Parameter>
 </Parameters>
 <MethodInstances>
  <MethodInstance Name="ReadItem" Type="SpecificFinder"
   ReturnParameterName="complexCustomer"
   ReturnTypeDescriptorPath="ComplexCustomer" />
 </MethodInstances>
</Method>
```

Notice that the value of the `RendererDefinition` property starts with the name of the `static` method followed by a bang (`!`) operator. This operator is followed by the fully qualified type name of the class that contains the method. Finally, the fully qualified name of the assembly containing the class follows. Invocation of the formatting is done through the `GetFormatted()` method, as described earlier. Figure 5-6 shows the formatted field in the custom web part based on the `SPGridView` control.

Complex Type Formatting

Customer Number	First Name	Last Name	Address
1	Jon	Yang	3761 N. 14th St, Seattle, WA 98104
2	Eugene	Huang	2243 W St., Los Angeles, CA 90012
3	Ruben	Torres	5844 Linden Land, Torrance, CA 90505
4	Christy	Zhu	1825 Village Pl., Lebanon, PA 97355
5	Elizabeth	Johnson	7553 Harness Circle, Oregon City, OR 97045

FIGURE 5-6

Using Custom Field Types for Display

Another option for displaying complex or unsupported types is to create a custom field type. A custom field type enables you to specify a new kind of field that can handle unsupported or complex types. Once this field is registered it can be used by BCS to render the types. The following code shows the definition of a `SpecificFinder` method that uses a custom field type to render the normally unsupported `Int64` field named `LegacyMainframeID`. The `SPCustomFieldType` property contains the name of the custom field type to use in the External List.

```
<Method Name="Read Item" DefaultDisplayName="LegacyCompany Read Item">
 <Properties>
  <Property Name="BackEndObject"
   Type="System.String">LegacyCompanyData</Property>
  <Property Name="BackEndObjectType"
   Type="System.String">SqlServerTable</Property>
  <Property Name="RdbCommandText" Type="System.String">
  SELECT [CompanyIdentifier] , [LegacyMainframeID] , [CompanyName]
  FROM [dbo].[LegacyCompanyData] WHERE [CompanyIdentifier] =
  @CompanyIdentifier</Property>
  <Property Name="RdbCommandType" Type="System.Data.CommandType,
   System.Data, Version=2.0.0.0, Culture=neutral,
   PublicKeyToken=b77a5c561934e089">Text</Property>
  <Property Name="Schema" Type="System.String">dbo</Property>
 </Properties>
 <Parameters>
  <Parameter Direction="In" Name="@CompanyIdentifier">
   <TypeDescriptor TypeName="System.Int32"
    IdentifierName="CompanyIdentifier" Name="CompanyIdentifier" />
  </Parameter>
```

```
<Parameter Direction="Return" Name="Read Item">
 <TypeDescriptor TypeName="System.Data.IDataReader, System.Data,
  Version=2.0.0.0, Culture=neutral, PublicKeyToken=b77a5c561934e089"
  IsCollection="true" Name="Read Item">
  <TypeDescriptors>
   <TypeDescriptor TypeName="System.Data.IDataRecord, System.Data,
    Version=2.0.0.0, Culture=neutral, PublicKeyToken=b77a5c561934e089"
    Name="Read ItemElement">
    <TypeDescriptors>
     <TypeDescriptor TypeName="System.Int32" ReadOnly="true"
      IdentifierName="CompanyIdentifier" Name="CompanyIdentifier" />
     <TypeDescriptor TypeName="System.Int64" Name="LegacyMainframeID">
      <Properties>
       <Property Name="SPCustomFieldType" Type="System.String">
        BCSInt64Field
       </Property>
      </Properties>
     </TypeDescriptor>
     <TypeDescriptor TypeName="System.String" Name="CompanyName" />
    </TypeDescriptors>
   </TypeDescriptor>
  </TypeDescriptors>
 </TypeDescriptor>
</Parameter>
</Parameters>
<MethodInstances>
 <MethodInstance Type="SpecificFinder" ReturnParameterName="Read Item"
  ReturnTypeDescriptorPath="Read Item[0]" Default="true" Name="Read Item"
  DefaultDisplayName="LegacyCompany Read Item">
 </MethodInstance>
</MethodInstances>
</Method>
```

Custom field types are not unique to BCS, but are a standard SharePoint feature. Custom field types are used throughout SharePoint to present specialized data such as HTML or rich text. While an entire chapter could easily be written on custom field-type development, this section will detail the basic artifacts that must be created for a custom field type. Custom field types are created as SharePoint features and each is implemented as a class that inherits from one of the several existing field types. In the case of the `BCSInt64Field` defined in the sample, a class was defined that inherits from `Microsoft.SharePoint.SPFieldText`, which represents a text field. The following code shows the definition for the custom field type:

```
public class BCSInt64Field : SPFieldText
{
    public BCSInt64Field(SPFieldCollection fields, string fieldName)
        : base(fields, fieldName)
    { }

    public BCSInt64Field(SPFieldCollection fields,
      string typeName, string displayName)
```

```
            : base(fields, typeName, displayName)
        { }

        public override object GetFieldValue(string value)
        {
            return Convert.ToInt64(value);
        }

        public override string TypeDisplayName
        {
            get
            {
                return "BCSInt64Field";
            }
        }

        public override BaseFieldControl FieldRenderingControl
        {
            get
            {
                BaseFieldControl fc = new BCSInt64FieldControl();
                fc.FieldName = InternalName;
                fc.DisplayTemplateName = "BCSInt64FieldControl";
                return fc;
            }
        }
    }
```

The key part of the code is the `GetFieldValue()` method, which returns the underlying `Int64` value as text. This allows the value to be displayed in the field. Also take note of the override for `FieldRenderingControl`. This method returns a custom field control that supports rendering the field data. The custom field control inherits from `Microsoft.SharePoint.WebControls.BaseFieldControl`. This class is largely responsible for moving data between SharePoint and a user control that displays the data. The following code shows the field control class for the `BCSInt64Field` field:

```
    public class BCSInt64FieldControl : BaseFieldControl
    {
        protected TextBox number = new TextBox();
        protected override string DefaultTemplateName
        {
            get
            {
                return "BCSInt64FieldControl";
            }
        }

        protected override void CreateChildControls()
        {
            if (this.Field != null && this.ControlMode != SPControlMode.Display)
```

```
            {
                base.CreateChildControls();
                this.number = (TextBox)TemplateContainer.FindControl("number");
            }
        }

        public override object Value
        {
            get
            {
                EnsureChildControls();
                String val = number.Text.Trim();
                if (String.IsNullOrEmpty(val))
                {
                    val = "0";
                }
                return Convert.ToInt64(val);
            }
            set
            {
                EnsureChildControls();
                number.Text = Convert.ToString((Int64)this.ItemFieldValue);
            }
        }
    }
```

The custom field control typically displays data through a template defined in a user control. The template is defined inside an ASCX file that is deployed to the `CONTROLTEMPLATES` directory. The following code shows the user control for the `BCSInt64Field` field. Note that the `ID` for the control matches the template name referenced by the field control.

```
<SharePoint:RenderingTemplate ID="Int64FieldControl" runat="server">
    <Template>
        <asp:TextBox ID="number" runat="server" />
    </Template>
</SharePoint:RenderingTemplate>
```

When a new field-type-and-field-control pairing is deployed, an XML file detailing the new field must be deployed to the `14\TEMPLATE\XML` folder. The name of this file must start with `fldtypes_`. When IIS is reset, SharePoint reads all the files that begin with this string and makes them available as fields. The following code shows the field type detail for the `BCSInt64Field` field:

```
<?xml version="1.0" encoding="utf-8" ?>
<FieldTypes>
  <FieldType>
    <Field Name="TypeName">BCSInt64Field</Field>
    <Field Name="ParentType">Text</Field>
    <Field Name="TypeDisplayName">BCS Int64 Field</Field>
    <Field Name="TypeShortDescription">64-bit integer</Field>
    <Field Name="UserCreatable">TRUE</Field>
```

```
      <Field Name="ShowInListCreate">TRUE</Field>
      <Field Name="ShowInSurveyCreate">TRUE</Field>
      <Field Name="ShowInDocumentLibraryCreate">TRUE</Field>
      <Field Name="ShowInColumnTemplateCreate">TRUE</Field>
      <Field Name="Filterable">FALSE</Field>
      <Field Name="Sortable">FALSE</Field>
      <Field Name="FieldTypeClass">Int64FieldType.BCSInt64Field,
       Int64FieldType, Version=1.0.0.0, Culture=neutral,
       PublicKeyToken=920426781bd0a3b7</Field>
    </FieldType>
  </FieldTypes>
```

ADVANCED WORKFLOW SOLUTIONS

Chapter 4 presented techniques for accessing External Lists using SharePoint Designer workflows. Specifically, techniques were presented that used site workflows and External Columns. While these techniques are useful, they suffer from some limitations. This section will examine advanced techniques for accessing External Lists through custom workflows, including custom Visual Studio workflows, pluggable workflow services, and Sandbox workflow actions.

Before beginning a detailed discussion of workflow solutions, it is important that we revisit some security issues that directly affect workflow development. In particular, all workflow solutions suffer from the limitation that the user security token is unavailable. This means that access to External Lists through workflow solutions must be done with a Trusted Subsystem model whereby a single account is used. This is true both in custom Visual Studio workflow solutions and in Sandboxed solutions.

Custom Visual Studio workflow solutions present the biggest challenge because the workflow can execute in a number of different contexts, including the `w3wp.exe` process and the `owstimer.exe` process. A simple solution to this problem is to access the External Lists using `RevertToSelf` as the authentication mode. However, this allows highly privileged accounts to perform operations for end users, so there is some security risk. As an alternative you can map the managed accounts associated with the `w3wp.exe` and `owstimer.exe` processes to an account defined in the Secure Store Service.

Sandboxed Solutions, such as Sandbox workflow actions, run in the `SPUCWorkerProcessProxy.exe` process. In this case you must map the managed account running the `SPUCWorkerProcessProxy.exe` process to an account defined in the Secure Store Service. There is no option to run Sandboxed Solutions as `RevertToSelf`. This is explicitly blocked by BCS because of the security risks involved with untrusted code running under such a privileged account. In fact, BCS blocks access to External Lists for several combinations of connectors and security options in workflow and Sandboxed solutions, as shown in Table 5-5. It's also important to note that hosted environments, such as SharePoint Online, block all combinations except that of the Secure Store Service used with the SQL and WCF connectors.

TABLE 5-5: Blocked Workflow and Sandbox Combinations

AUTHENTICATION MODE	SQL	WCF	.NET ASSEMBLY CONNECTOR	CUSTOM CONNECTOR
Passthrough	Blocked	Blocked	Allowed	Allowed
RevertToSelf	Blocked for Sandbox only	Allowed	Allowed	Allowed
Secure Store	Allowed	Allowed	Allowed	Allowed
Claims	Blocked	Blocked	Blocked	Blocked

Developing Visual Studio Workflows

Development of classic Visual Studio workflows needs only a brief discussion. As long as your solution observes the security restrictions outlined previously, you are free to use the BDC Server Runtime object model within a workflow, either in a code activity or in a custom activity. Additionally, you can use all the other available activities in support.

Developing Pluggable Services

You can use Pluggable Services to send messages out of a workflow and receive a response. Pluggable Services are interesting in BCS solutions because they offer the possibility of two-way communication between SharePoint and External Systems. Chapter 2 hinted at this capability by describing a scenario in which a workflow is running in SharePoint and then sends a message to MSCRM to generate a proposal document. When the proposal document is complete, MSCRM notifies the workflow, which continues. This approach allows BCS solutions not only to access the data available in External Systems, but also to access any functionality offered by an External System.

In order to create a pluggable service you must create a class that inherits from `Microsoft.SharePoint.Workflow.SPWorkflowExternalDataExchangeService`. Additionally, several classes and interfaces must be created to support the service. Finally, you must create a workflow that uses the Call External Method and Handle External Event activities to manage the communication.

When you're building the service, the first step is to create both an interface that defines the method that will send data out of the workflow, and the event that will fire when the External System is finished working. The event will contain custom arguments that must also be defined. The following code shows the interface and event arguments for a Pluggable Service that will generate proposals:

```
[ExternalDataExchange]
public interface IProposalService
{
    event EventHandler<CompletedEventArgs> MessageFromExternalSystem;
    void MessageToExternalSystem(string CustomerName);
}

[Serializable]
public class CompletedEventArgs : ExternalDataEventArgs
```

```
{
    public CompletedEventArgs(Guid id)  : base(id) { }
    public string Message { get; set; }
}
```

Because the operations performed by the External System may be long-running, the Pluggable Service should maintain state information that it can return to the workflow. This will allow the workflow to have context when it resumes. State information is maintained in a simple class like the one shown in the following code:

```
class StateInformation
{
    public SPWeb Web { get; set; }
    public Guid InstanceId { get; set; }

    public StateInformation(Guid instanceId, SPWeb web)
    {
        this.InstanceId = instanceId;
        this.Web = web;
    }
}
```

The service itself is created as a separate class that implements the interface defined previously and inherits from `SPWorkflowExternalDataExchangeService`. In the example, the OpenXML API is used to create a new Word document that simulates the proposal generation. All the work is done through an anonymous method delegate on a separate thread. When the work is complete the event is raised, notifying the workflow that the proposal has been created. The following code shows how the service is implemented:

```
public class ProposalService : SPWorkflowExternalDataExchangeService,
                               IProposalService
{
    public event EventHandler<CompletedEventArgs> MessageFromExternalSystem;

    //Perform long-running work
    public void MessageToExternalSystem(string CustomerName)
    {
        ThreadPool.QueueUserWorkItem(delegate(object state)
        {
            StateInformation stateInfo = state as StateInformation;

            using (WordprocessingDocument package =
                 WordprocessingDocument.Create(
                 "C:\\" + CustomerName + " Proposal.docx",
                 WordprocessingDocumentType.Document))
            {
                //Create content
                Body body = new Body(
                    new Paragraph(
                        new Run(
                            new Text("Proposal for " + CustomerName))));

                //Create package
                package.AddMainDocumentPart();
```

```
                package.MainDocumentPart.Document = new Document(body);
                package.MainDocumentPart.Document.Save();
                package.Close();
            }

            //Notify workflow that long -running work is complete
            RaiseEvent(stateInfo.Web,
                stateInfo.InstanceId,
                typeof(IProposalService),
                "MessageFromExternalSystem",
                new object[] { "Completed Proposal for " + CustomerName });

        }, new StateInformation(WorkflowEnvironment.WorkflowInstanceId,
           this.CurrentWorkflow.ParentWeb));

    }

    public override void CallEventHandler(Type eventType, string eventName,
      object[] eventData, SPWorkflow workflow, string identity, IPendingWork
      workHandler, object workItem)
    {
        var e = new CompletedEventArgs(workflow.InstanceId);
        e.Message = eventData[0].ToString();
        e.WorkHandler = workHandler;
        e.WorkItem = workItem;
        e.Identity = identity;
        this.MessageFromExternalSystem(null, e);
    }
}
```

Once the service is created you may create a workflow that communicates with it. The Call External Method activity is used to send a message out to the Pluggable Service. Figure 5-7 shows the activity configured in the workflow.

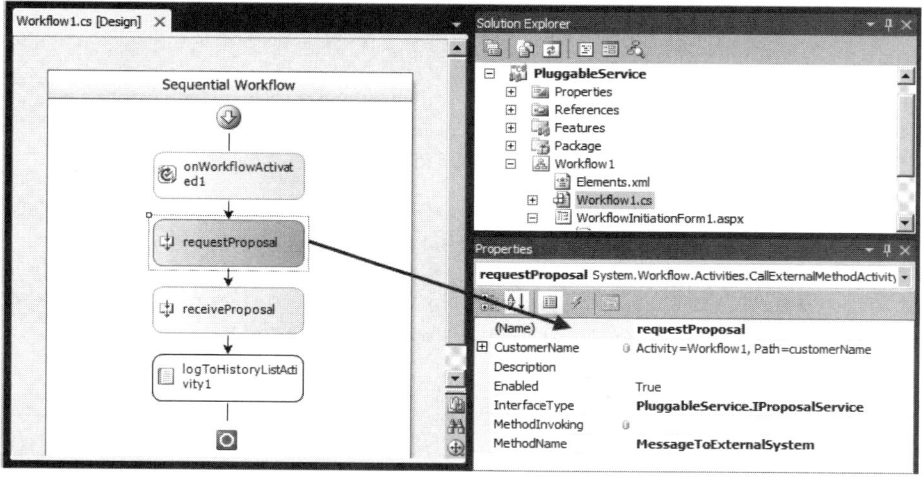

FIGURE 5-7

When the proposal is generated, the External System makes a call back into the workflow. The Handle External Event activity is used to receive the message. Figure 5-8 shows the activity configured in the workflow.

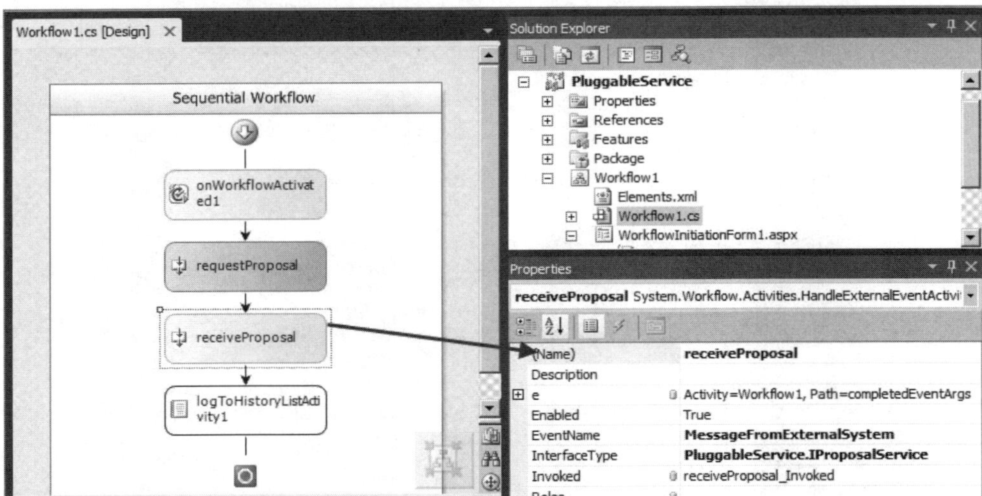

FIGURE 5-8

Once the workflow is developed it may be deployed to SharePoint. However, Pluggable Services must be explicitly listed in the `web.config` file for the Web Application before they can be used. Therefore you must add an entry like the following. Once `web.config` is updated the workflow can be executed and the Pluggable Service invoked.

```
<WorkflowServices>
      <WorkflowService Assembly="PluggableService, Version=1.0.0.0,
       Culture=neutral, PublicKeyToken=722b0ac68bda4fa1"
       Class="PluggableService.ProposalService" />
</WorkflowServices>
```

Working with Sandbox Workflow Actions

Standard workflows and Pluggable Services all require that full-trust code be deployed onto the SharePoint server. In many cases you will not be able to deploy full-trust code and will want to use declarative workflows. Chapter 4 presented some basic declarative workflow approaches for interacting with External Lists, but the actions available in the SharePoint Designer were limited in functionality. As an alternative you can create your own actions for use in SPD. These actions are known as *Sandbox workflow actions*.

The SharePoint SDK ships with two sample Sandbox workflow actions that can be used for reading items from External Lists and reading fields from the items. These samples are a great place to start and provide the basic functionality that would drive you to create a Sandbox workflow action in the first place. In order to understand Sandbox workflow actions better, consider the following code, which retrieves an item from an External List based on the value of a field. You saw something similar in Chapter 4.

```
public class BCSReadActivities
{
    public static Hashtable GetExternalListItemByField(
      SPUserCodeWorkflowContext context,
      String externalListId,
      string fieldName,
      string fieldValue)
    {
        Hashtable returnValues = new Hashtable();
        returnValues["ItemString"] = "";

        using (SPSite site = new SPSite(context.SiteUrl))
        {
            using (SPWeb web = site.OpenWeb(context.WebUrl))
            {
                SPList externalList = web.Lists[new Guid(externalListId)];
                SPField keyField = externalList.Fields[fieldName];
                SPQuery query = new SPQuery();
                query.Query = string.Format(
                  "<Where><Eq><FieldRef Name='{0}'/>
                   <Value Type='{1}'>{2}</Value></Eq></Where>",
                  fieldName, keyField.TypeAsString, fieldValue);

                SPListItemCollection foundItems =
                  externalList.GetItems(query);

                if (foundItems.Count > 0)
                {
                    returnValues["ItemString"] =
                     SerializeItemData(foundItems[0]);
                }
            }
        }
        return returnValues;
    }
}
```

Because SPD workflows do not implement any kind of looping constructs, the preceding activity is designed to return an entire list item, as an XML string, to a variable in the workflow. The other sample Sandbox workflow action in the SDK is designed to read fields from this returned value. Between the two actions you can create SPD workflows that read values from External Lists.

What's important about this code is that it is running against the `SPList` object that represents the External List. The `SPList` is available to the declarative solutions created in SPD when they run as Sandboxed Solutions. Furthermore, the code is more efficient than the out-of-the-box actions for reading list items in SPD. Remember that the out-of-the-box actions must execute both the `Finder` and the `SpecificFinder` on every read. The preceding custom Sandbox workflow action uses a CAML query to return items more efficiently.

In order for you to use the actions in SPD, an Elements file must be created with declarative instructions that describe the action and how to represent it in SPD. These instructions dictate how the sentences and hyperlinks appear when you are designing workflows in SPD. The following code shows the portion of the Elements file that describes the action required to read a list item:

```
<Elements xmlns="http://schemas.microsoft.com/sharepoint/">
  <WorkflowActions>
    <Action Name="Get External List Item by Field (Sandboxed Function)"
     SandboxedFunction="true"
            Assembly="BCSSandboxedActivities, Version=1.0.0.0,
            Culture=neutral, PublicKeyToken=6c20fc6fd829ac73"
            ClassName="Microsoft.SharePoint.Samples.BCSReadActivities"
            FunctionName="GetExternalListItemByField"
            AppliesTo="all" UsesCurrentItem="true"
            Category="User Code Actions">
      <RuleDesigner Sentence="Get List Item from list %1 by using %3
                            for field %2.(Output: %4)">
        <FieldBind Field="externalListId" Text="this list"
         Id="1" DesignerType="ListNames" />
        <FieldBind Field="fieldName" Text="this field"
         Id="2" DesignerType="TextBox" />
        <FieldBind Field="fieldValue" Text="this value"
         Id="3" DesignerType="TextBox" />
        <FieldBind Field="ItemString" Text="ItemString"
         Id="4" DesignerType="ParameterNames" />
      </RuleDesigner>
      <Parameters>
        <Parameter Name="__Context"
         Type="Microsoft.SharePoint.WorkflowActions.WorkflowContext,
         Microsoft.SharePoint.WorkflowActions" Direction="In"
         DesignerType="Hide" />
        <Parameter Name="externalListId" Type="System.String, mscorlib"
         Direction="In" DesignerType="ListNames"
         Description="List to read external list entries from." />
        <Parameter Name="fieldName" Type="System.String, mscorlib"
         Direction="In" DesignerType="TextBox"
         Description="Field name to find the external list item by." />
        <Parameter Name="fieldValue" Type="System.String, mscorlib"
         Direction="In" DesignerType="TextBox"
         Description="Value to find the external list item by." />
        <Parameter Name="ItemString" Type="System.String, mscorlib"
         Direction="Out"
         Description="String the represents the external list item." />
      </Parameters>
    </Action>
```

The `Action` element defines the assembly that contains the action. The `Parameters` element contains a `Parameter` for each of the properties defined for the action. The `Parameter` defines the data type and whether the property is an input or output value. The `RuleDesigner` element contains multiple `FieldBind` elements that map property values in the action to parameters. The `FieldBind` elements also define the `DesignerType` attribute, which specifies the control type that will appear to the user working with the action. The `Sentence` attribute defines the sentence that will appear in the workflow designer and maps the fields using tokens that begin with a percent (`%`) sign.

Once the coding is completed and the Elements file created, the feature may be deployed to SharePoint. The assembly is deployed to the Global Assembly Cache (GAC) while the Elements file is deployed to the feature directory. At this point the action can be used in the SharePoint Designer, as shown in Figure 5-9.

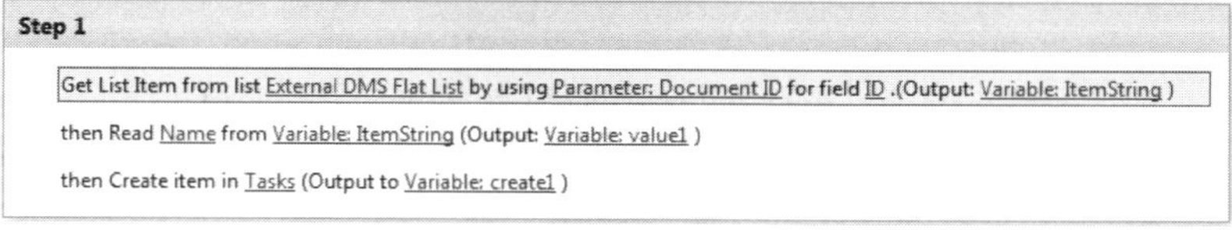
Step 1
Get List Item from list External DMS Flat List by using Parameter: Document ID for field ID .(Output: Variable: ItemString)
then Read Name from Variable: ItemString (Output: Variable: value1)
then Create item in Tasks (Output to Variable: create1)

FIGURE 5-9

When you first create custom actions you may be confused by the fact that the action is deployed to the GAC. After all, the point of creating a Sandbox workflow action is to run the workflow as a Sandboxed Solution. Well, the reality of declarative workflows is that they always run with full trust, even when deployed as Sandboxed Solutions. This is safe, however, because the person using the custom action can create only declarative solutions with it; no one can write custom code that will run fully trusted. So a Sandbox workflow action will require the deployment of code to the GAC and will run as fully trusted, but the declarative workflow itself can be deployed as a Sandboxed Solution.

WORKING WITH THE BDC ADMINISTRATION OBJECT MODEL

Along with the BDC Server Runtime object model, BCS has a BDC Administration object model. The BDC Administration object model enables you to manipulate the metadata for a BDC Metadata Model. In order to work with the Administration object model you must set a reference to the `Microsoft.BusinessData.dll` and `Microsoft.SharePoint.dll` assemblies.

Connecting to the Catalog

As with the BDC Server Runtime object model, you must connect to the appropriate catalog before you can manipulate the data. In the case of the BDC Administration object model you must connect to the `Microsoft.SharePoint.BusinessData.Administration.AdministrationMetadataCatalog` object. You do this through the `GetAdministrationMetadataCatalog()` method, using the same approach as with the BDC Server Runtime object model. The following code shows how to connect with the catalog if your code is running outside a SharePoint context. Inside the context you can use the `SPServiceContext` object, as shown earlier.

```
//Connect to the BDC Service Application proxy
BdcService service = SPFarm.Local.Services.GetValue<BdcService>();

if (service == null)
    throw new Exception("No BDC Service Application found.");
```

```
//Connect to metadata catalog
AdministrationMetadataCatalog catalog =
  service.GetAdministrationMetadataCatalog(
  SPServiceContext.GetContext(siteCollection));
```

Creating BDC Metadata Models in Code

The BDC Administration object model provides a set of objects that allows you to manipulate the Application Model XML. The names of the objects correspond closely to the names of the elements in the Application Model. The following code shows how to create a `Model`, `LobSystem`, and `LoBSystemInstance` that connects to a SQL database using the `Create()` method of the `Model` class:

```
Model model = Model.Create("MiniCRM", true, catalog);
LobSystem lob = model.OwnedReferencedLobSystems.Create(
                "Customer", true, SystemType.Database);
LobSystemInstance lobi = lob.LobSystemInstances.Create("MiniCRM", true);
lobi.Properties.Add("AuthenticationMode", "PassThrough");
lobi.Properties.Add("DatabaseAccessProvider", "SqlServer");
lobi.Properties.Add("RdbConnection Data Source", "AWSERVER");
lobi.Properties.Add("RdbConnection Initial Catalog", "MiniCRM.Names");
lobi.Properties.Add("RdbConnection Integrated Security", "SSPI");
lobi.Properties.Add("RdbConnection Pooling", "true");
```

You create the ECT definition through the `Create()` method of the `Entity` class. You can define the basic information, such as name and namespace. Additionally you can add `Identifiers` for the ECT. The following code shows how to create the ECT:

```
Entity ect = Entity.Create("Customer", "MiniCRM", true,
             new Version("1.0.0.0"), 10000,
             CacheUsage.Default, lob, model, catalog);

ect.Identifiers.Create("CustomerId", true, "System.Int32");
```

Once the ECT is created you can add method definitions. The methods can be any of the supported stereotypes. Each method must have parameters, filters, and method instances defined. The following code shows how to define a `SpecificFinder` and `Finder` method:

```
Method specificFinder = ect.Methods.Create(
  "GetCustomer", true, false, "GetCustomer");

specificFinder.Properties.Add("RdbCommandText",
   "SELECT [CustomerId] ,[FullName] FROM MiniCRM.Names
   WHERE [CustomerId] = @CustomerId");
specificFinder.Properties.Add("RdbCommandType", "Text");

Parameter idParam = specificFinder.Parameters.Create("@CustomerId",
   true, DirectionType.In);
```

```
idParam.CreateRootTypeDescriptor(
    "CustomerId", true, "System.Int32", "CustomerId",
     new IdentifierReference("CustomerId",
        new EntityReference("MiniCRM", "Customer", catalog), catalog),
     null, TypeDescriptorFlags.None, null, catalog);

Parameter custParam = specificFinder.Parameters.Create("Customer",
  true, DirectionType.Return);

TypeDescriptor returnRootCollectionTypeDescriptor =
    custParam.CreateRootTypeDescriptor(
        "Customers", true,
        "System.Data.IDataReader, System.Data, Version=2.0.0.0,
         Culture=neutral, PublicKeyToken=b77a5c561934e089",
        "Customers", null, null, TypeDescriptorFlags.IsCollection,
        null, catalog);

TypeDescriptor returnRootElementTypeDescriptor =
    returnRootCollectionTypeDescriptor.ChildTypeDescriptors.Create(
        "Customer", true,
        "System.Data.IDataRecord, System.Data,
         Version=2.0.0.0, Culture=neutral,
         PublicKeyToken=b77a5c561934e089",
        "Customer", null, null, TypeDescriptorFlags.None, null);

returnRootElementTypeDescriptor.ChildTypeDescriptors.Create(
        "CustomerId", true, "System.Int32", "CustomerId",
        new IdentifierReference("CustomerId",
            new EntityReference("MiniCRM", "Customer", catalog), catalog),
        null, TypeDescriptorFlags.None, null);

returnRootElementTypeDescriptor.ChildTypeDescriptors.Create(
        "FirstName", true, "System.String", "FullName",
        null, null, TypeDescriptorFlags.None, null);


specificFinder.MethodInstances.Create("GetCustomer",
   true, returnRootElementTypeDescriptor,
    MethodInstanceType.SpecificFinder, true);

Method finder = ect.Methods.Create("GetCustomers", true,
   false, "GetCustomers");

finder.Properties.Add("RdbCommandText",
   "SELECT [CustomerId] , [FullName]FROM MiniCRM.Names");
finder.Properties.Add("RdbCommandType", "Text");

Parameter custsParam = finder.Parameters.Create("Customer",
   true, DirectionType.Return);

TypeDescriptor returnRootCollectionTypeDescriptor2 =
    custsParam.CreateRootTypeDescriptor(
```

```
            "Customers", true,
            "System.Data.IDataReader, System.Data,
             Version=2.0.0.0, Culture=neutral,
             PublicKeyToken=b77a5c561934e089",
            "Customers", null, null, TypeDescriptorFlags.IsCollection,
             null, catalog);

    TypeDescriptor returnRootElementTypeDescriptor2 =
        returnRootCollectionTypeDescriptor2.ChildTypeDescriptors.Create(
            "Customer", true,
            "System.Data.IDataRecord, System.Data,
             Version=2.0.0.0, Culture=neutral,
             PublicKeyToken=b77a5c561934e089",
            "Customer", null, null, TypeDescriptorFlags.None, null);

    returnRootElementTypeDescriptor2.ChildTypeDescriptors.Create(
            "CustomerId", true, "System.Int32", "CustomerId",
            new IdentifierReference("CustomerId",
                new EntityReference("MiniCRM", "Customer", catalog), catalog),
            null, TypeDescriptorFlags.None, null);

    returnRootElementTypeDescriptor2.ChildTypeDescriptors.Create(
            "FirstName", true, "System.String", "FullName",
            null, null, TypeDescriptorFlags.None, null);

    finder.MethodInstances.Create("GetCustomers", true,
       returnRootCollectionTypeDescriptor2,
        MethodInstanceType.Finder, true);
```

Once the model is created it may be activated in the BDC Service Application. Activating the ECT makes it available for use. The following code shows how to activate the ECT:

```
ect.Activate();
```

Importing and Exporting Models

In addition to creating models, you can also use the BDC Administration API to perform imports and exports of models. This type of functionality can be useful if you want to create custom tools to use with BCS. Importing and exporting is accomplished with the `Import()` and `Export()` methods, respectively, of the `AdministrationMetadataCatalog` class. The following code shows how to export the permissions from a BDC Metadata Model into a separate resource file using a console application:

```
static void Main(string[] args)
{
    if (args.Count() != 2)
        throw new Exception(
        "Useage: ExportModelResources SiteCollectionUrl, ModelName");

    using (SPSite site = new SPSite(args[0]))
```

```
    {
        //Connect to the BDC Service Application proxy
        BdcService service = SPFarm.Local.Services.GetValue<BdcService>();

        if (service == null)
            throw new Exception("No BDC Service Application found.");

        //Connect to metadata catalog
        AdministrationMetadataCatalog catalog =
            service.GetAdministrationMetadataCatalog(
            SPServiceContext.GetContext(site));

        //Get model
        Model model = catalog.GetModel(args[1]);

        //Export permissions
        FileStream fs = new FileStream("C:\\" + model.Name + ".xml",
          FileMode.CreateNew, FileAccess.ReadWrite);
        catalog.ExportPackage(model.Name, fs, Encoding.Unicode,
          PackageContents.Permissions);
        fs.Close();
    }
}
```

BCS LIMITS

Chapter 2 presented key throttling limits associated with BCS. Throttling limits are critical because they help prevent poor performance in BCS solutions. However, there are a number of additional limits that can affect them. These limitations are important to consider as you create custom BCS solutions. Table 5-6 details all the BCS limits.

TABLE 5-6: BCS Limits

ITEM	LIMIT	CONTEXT	DESCRIPTION
Database Item	Default max: 2,000 Absolute max: 1,000,000	Database request	Number of items per request the database connector can return. The default max is used by the database connector to restrict the number of results that can be returned per page. The application can specify a larger limit via execution context; the absolute max enforces the allowed maximum even for applications that do not respect the default such as indexing.

continues

TABLE 5-6 *(continued)*

ITEM	LIMIT	CONTEXT	DESCRIPTION
External System Connection	Default max: 200 Absolute max: 500	WFE	Number of active/open external system connections at a given time. This limit is enforced at the Web Front End scope, regardless of the type of external system (such as database, WFC, .Net assembly, etc.). The default max is used to restrict the number of connections. An application can specify a larger limit via execution context; the absolute max enforces the allowed maximum even for applications that do not respect the default.
Database Response Latency	Default max: 180 seconds Absolute max: 600 seconds	Database request	Timeout used by the database connector per request. Default value to be used by the database connector. Applications are allowed to specify a larger value programmatically up to the absolute max.
WCF Service Response Latency	Default max: 180 seconds Absolute max: 600 seconds	WCF request	Timeout used by the WCF connector per request. Default max value to be used by the WCF connector. Applications are allowed to specify a larger value programmatically up to the absolute max.
WCF Service Response Size	Default max: 3,000,000 bytes Absolute max: 150,000,000 bytes	WCF response	The upper limit of how much data per request the web service connector can return. Default max value to be used by the WCF connector. Applications are allowed to specify a larger value programmatically up to the absolute max.
ECT Action (in- memory)	5,000	WFE (per tenant)	Total number of actions (across all ECTs) loaded in memory at a given time on a given WFE.

ITEM	LIMIT	CONTEXT	DESCRIPTION
ECT Action Parameter (in-memory)	20,000	WFE (per tenant)	Total number of action parameters loaded in memory at a given time on a given WFE.
ECT Association (in-memory)	30,000	WFE (per tenant)	Total number of ECT associations loaded in memory at a given time on a given WFE.
ECT Association Group (in-memory)	15,000	WFE (per tenant)	Total number of ECT association groups loaded in memory at a given time on a given WFE.
ECT (in-memory)	5,000	WFE (per tenant)	Total number of ECT definitions loaded in memory at a given time on a given WFE.
ECT Filter Descriptor (in-memory)	25,000	WFE (per tenant)	Total number of ECT filter descriptors loaded in memory at a given time on a given WFE.
ECT Identifier (in-memory)	5,000	WFE (per tenant)	Total number of ECT Identifiers loaded in memory at a given point in time on a WFE.
External System (in-memory)	1,000	WFE (per tenant)	Total number of External System (LOBSystem) definitions loaded in memory at a given time on a given WFE.
External System Instance (in-memory)	1,000	WFE (per tenant)	Total number of External System Instance (LOBSystemInstance) definitions loaded in memory at a given time on a given WFE.
ECT Method (in-memory)	25,000	WFE (per tenant)	Total number of ECT methods loaded in memory at a given time on a given WFE.
ECT Method Instance (in-memory)	25,000	WFE (per tenant)	Total number of ECT method instances loaded in memory at a given time on a given WFE.
ECT Method Parameter (in-memory)	100,000	WFE (per tenant)	Total number of ECT method parameters loaded in memory at a given time on a given WFE.

continues

TABLE 5-6 *(continued)*

ITEM	LIMIT	CONTEXT	DESCRIPTION
ECT Type Descriptor	500,000	WFE (per tenant)	Total number of ECT type descriptors loaded in memory at a given time on a given WFE.
ECT Picker Item	200	ECT Picker dialog	Total number of ECTs that can be displayed by the ECT Picker in the UI. Hard non-configurable limit.
ECT Instance Picker Item	200	ECT Instance Picker dialog	Total number of ECT instances that can be displayed by the ECT Picker in the UI. Hard non-configurable limit.
ECT Action (in-store)	50	ECT	Total number of actions per ECT.
ECT Action Parameter (in-store)	20	ECT action	Total number of parameters per ECT action.
ECT Association Group (in-store)	100	ECT	Total number of association groups per ECT.
ECT Association Reference (in-store)	20	ECT association group	Total number of association references per association group.
ECT (in-store)	500	External System (LOBSystem)	Total number of ECTs per External System (LOBSystem).
Source Association ECT (in-store)	10	ECT association	Number of source ECTs per association.
Filter Descriptor (in-store)	200	ECT method	Number of Filter Descriptors per ECT method.
ECT Identifier (in-store)	20	ECT	Number of identifiers per ECT.
External System Instance (LOBSystemInstance; (in-store)	300	External System (LOBSystem)	Number of External System instances (LOBSystemInstances) per External System definition.
Localized Name (in-store)	100	Metadata object	Number of localized names per metadata object.
Custom Property (in-store)	50	Metadata object	Number of custom properties per metadata object.
ECT Method (in-store)	50	ECT	Number of methods per ECT.

ITEM	LIMIT	CONTEXT	DESCRIPTION
Parameter (in-store)	255	ECT method	Number of parameters per ECT method.
TypeDescriptor Nesting Level (in-store)	20	TypeDescriptor	Number of nesting levels per TypeDescriptor.
Default Value (in-store)	15	TypeDescriptor	Number of allowed default values per TypeDescriptor. One default value per method instance.
TypeDescriptor (in-store)	300	TypeDescriptor	Number of child Type Descriptors per root level Type Descriptor.
TypeDescriptor (in-store)	20	Filter descriptor	Number of Type Descriptors per Filter Descriptor.

SUMMARY

While many BCS solutions can be created with no code, much data presentation and functionality requires custom coding. When creating BCS solutions you'll initially be driven to custom code primarily to overcome the UI limitations imposed by External Lists and the Business Data Web Parts. As your solutions become more complex, however, custom code will help to create professional and efficient solutions that can scale along with your SharePoint farm.

Programming BCS Solutions in Office 2010

WHAT'S IN THIS CHAPTER?

- Learn to create Outlook Declarative Solutions
- Learn the BDC Client Runtime object model
- Learn to create custom Office Add-Ins

One of the most attractive attributes of a BCS solution is that it encompasses both client and server functionality. The ability to interact with External Data through Office applications as well as SharePoint sites is significant. Throughout the first half of the book, client-side functionality was presented primarily through no-code solutions. This chapter will examine more advanced client-side solutions, including Outlook declarative solutions, the BDC Client Runtime object model, and custom Office add-ins.

CREATING OUTLOOK DECLARATIVE SOLUTIONS

From the very beginning of the book, we've been using BCS to surface data from External Systems in Microsoft Outlook 2010 using the native Outlook Item Types: Contact, Task, Post, and Appointment. Surfacing data this way is central to BCS and requires no custom code, but Chapter 3 detailed several limitations with the folders, forms, and items created by simple no-code solutions. Developers looking for more control may initially be disappointed because BCS does not expose an API for working with Outlook solutions. However, BCS does support a declarative approach that enables the customization of Outlook solutions.

Outlook declarative solutions (also called intermediate declarative solutions) are add-ins that make use of the existing BCS components to go beyond the capabilities of simple no-code solutions. Outlook declarative solutions can contain multiple ECTs, define new buttons and actions, show custom task panes, define custom views, and present custom form regions. All these enhancements are created declaratively and packaged for click-once deployment.

While it is possible to create all the declarative artifacts and package them by hand, the process is tedious and error-prone. Fortunately, the BCS team at Microsoft has created two tools specifically designed for creating and packaging Outlook declarative solutions. These tools are the BCS Artifact Generator Tool and the BCS Solution Packaging Tool. The BCS Artifact Generator Tool is available at `http://code.msdn.microsoft.com/odcsps14bcsgnrtrtool`, and the BCS Solution Packaging Tool can be found at `http://code.msdn.microsoft.com/odcsps14bcspkgtool`.

Generating Artifacts

Creating an Outlook declarative solution begins with the BCS Artifact Generator Tool. In order to get started with the BCS Artifact Generator Tool, you simply need a model exported from the BDC Service Application. When you run the BCS Artifact Generator Tool, you will be able to import the model into the tool. The tool will validate the model and display the result, as shown in Figure 6-1.

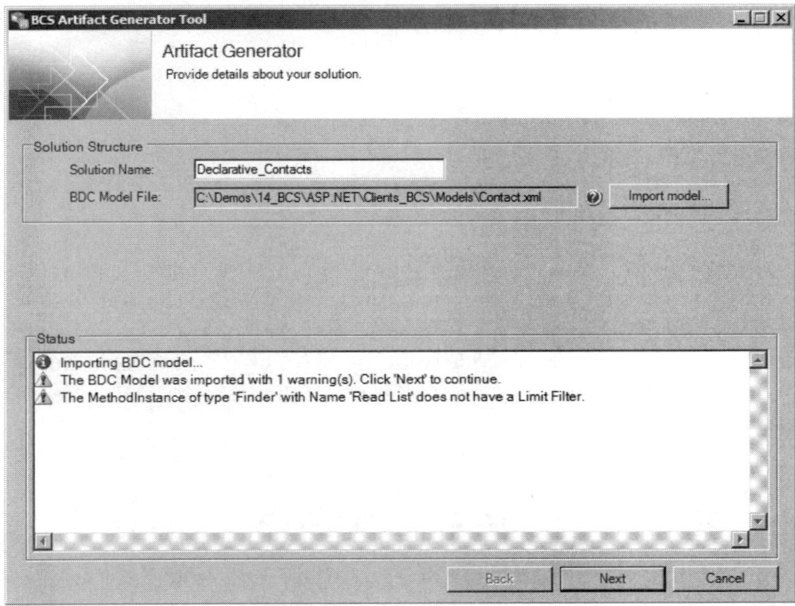

FIGURE 6-1

Once the model is imported you can simply generate the artifacts necessary for a solution. However, taking this approach means that your solution will be little different from the standard no-code solution created in SPD. The point is to customize the solution first. You can customize any of the ECTs present in the model by clicking the Customize button shown next to them in the tool. Clicking the Customize button starts a mini-wizard that walks you through the various customizations. The first customization is to change the display name of the ECT and the icon used in Microsoft Outlook. Figure 6-2 shows the modifications in the tool.

The next screen in the wizard enables you to use a custom form region. Custom form regions are covered in the section Creating Form Regions later in the chapter and enable you to customize how the ECT is displayed. The next step in the wizard enables you to identify any associated ECTs that should be displayed. Associations are also covered later in the chapter in the section entitled Including Associations in Declarative Solutions. Finally, the last screen enables you to add custom actions to the Outlook ribbon. These custom actions are just like actions on the SharePoint server: they use parameterized URLs to perform an operation. Figure 6-3 shows an action to perform a Bing search using the name of the contact.

FIGURE 6-2

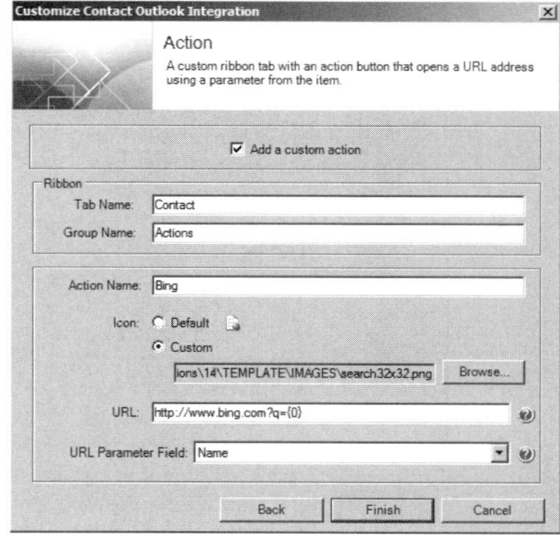

FIGURE 6-3

Once the customizations are completed, the solution is ready. Clicking the Generate Artifacts button will create the required artifacts and open Windows Explorer to the folder where they are located. The artifacts that get created vary according to the options selected. At a minimum, the artifacts include a copy of the BDC Metadata Model, a subscription file, and the solution manifest. Optionally, they may also include a ribbon file for actions, a layouts file for associated ECTs, and image files.

Chapter 1 listed all the required and optional files for Outlook declarative solutions, and Chapter 3 provided more detail on subscription files. The solution manifest (`oir.config`) was mentioned in Chapter 1, but not examined in detail. Understanding the solution manifest structure is important, because some of the solutions covered later in the chapter (such as custom form regions) will require you to edit this file. The following code shows the basic structure of a solution manifest:

```
<?xml version="1.0" encoding="utf-8"?>
<SolutionDefinition
 xmlns:mx="http://schemas.microsoft.com/.../DeclarativeExtensions"
 xmlns="http://schemas.microsoft.com/.../Manifest">
  <SolutionSettings SolutionId="..."
```

```
 SolutionDisplayName="MySolution" SolutionVersion="1.1.1.1" />
<ContextDefinitionGroups>
  <ContextDefinitionGroup ItemType="OutlookContact">
    <ContextDefinition p5:type="mx:DeclarativeContextDefinition"
     ContentType="f9f67f16-e43c-4312-97e0-d9ca6f9e5f7a"
     xmlns:p5="http://www.w3.org/2001/XMLSchema-instance">
      <Entities>
        <Entity Name="MyEntity" EntityTypeName="MyEntity"
         EntityTypeNamespace="http://namespace"
         Description="MyEntity">
          <View Name="PrimaryEntityNameInContext" ViewName="Read Item"
           Description="Read Item" IsPrimary="true">
            <PromotedProperty Name="ID::5" ViewInstancePath="ID"
             OfficeItemPropertyName="ID::5" ReadOnly="true" />
            <PromotedProperty Name="Title" ViewInstancePath="Title"
             OfficeItemPropertyName="Title" ReadOnly="false" />
          </View>
        </Entity>
      </Entities>
      <OfficeItemCustomizations p5:type="OutlookItemCustomizations"
       ItemTypeDisplayName="MyEntity"
       MessageClass="IPM.Contact.91b53a48-d453-4fb0-bd13-296a9e9471b3">
        <OfficeItemProperties>
          <OfficeItemProperty Name="ID::5" PropertyName="ID::5"
           PropertyType="OutlookInteger" />
          <OfficeItemProperty Name="Title" PropertyName="Title"
           PropertyType="OutlookText" />
        </OfficeItemProperties>
        <FormRegions p5:type="mx:DeclarativeFormRegions"
         AutoGenerate="true" />
        <OutlookFolder Description="" Name="Read Item"
         FolderDisplayName="MyEntity" NativeType="FolderContacts"
         SubscriptionName="MyEntity2147483660Subscription"
         FolderName="c23031ef-a1e4-4af6-9a01-e081389b06a9"
         CanCreate="true" CanUpdate="true" CanDelete="true">
          <Picture IconFilePath="personresult.gif" />
        </OutlookFolder>
      </OfficeItemCustomizations>
      <mx:Layouts>
        <mx:Layout LayoutFileName="ShowRelatedItems"
         Name="ShowRelatedItems" />
      </mx:Layouts>
      <mx:Actions>
       <mx:UrlAction Name="Bing"
           Description="" Url="http://www.bing.com?q={0}">
          <mx:Parameters>
            <mx:ExpressionParameter Name="..."
             EntityViewInstanceReference="PrimaryEntityNameInContext"
             Expression="Name" />
          </mx:Parameters>
        </mx:UrlAction>
        <mx:CodeMethodAction Name="Show Related list" Description=""
         MethodType="ShowTaskpaneLayout">
          <mx:Parameters>
            <mx:ConstantParameter Name="LayoutFile"
             Value="ShowRelatedItems" ValueType="System.String" />
```

```
          </mx:Parameters>
        </mx:CodeMethodAction>
      </mx:Actions>
      <mx:ContextEventHandlers>
        <mx:ContextActivated ActionName=" Show Related list" />
      </mx:ContextEventHandlers>
    </ContextDefinition>
  </ContextDefinitionGroup>
```

The `SolutionDefinition` element is the root of the solution manifest. It has the namespace declaration `http://schemas.microsoft.com/office/2009/05/BusinessApplications/Manifest`. This namespace identifies the solution as a BCS solution. The `SolutionSettings` element beneath it defines the basic information about the solution.

The `ContextDefinitionGroup` element contains the definitions for content types associated with the Contact, Task, Post, and Calendar item types in Outlook. This is how the ECT gets mapped to an Outlook type for display. `ContextDefinition` contains the information about the ECT that will be mapped.

The `OfficeItemCustomizations` element defines the user interface to be used for the ECT. The Outlook message type is mapped to the ECT and the fields of the ECT are mapped to data types such as `OutlookInteger` and `OutlookText`. Information about the form region used for the unmapped fields and the Outlook folder is also defined.

The Outlook folder used for the solution can have a custom icon defined. Images can also be defined for Outlook's item and action buttons on the ribbon. The BCS Artifact Generator Tool will enable you to browse for images. Table 6-1 lists the requirements for these images.

TABLE 6-1: Image Requirements

ELEMENT	SIZE	FORMAT
Folder	16x16 px	.jpg, .bmp, .ico, .png
Item	Any size	.ico
Action	Any size	.jpg, .bmp, .ico, .png

The `Layouts` element is used to define a custom layout of controls. Typically layouts are used to display associated entity instances in a separate task pane. Layouts are covered later in the chapter.

The `Actions` element defines buttons that will appear on the ribbon in Microsoft Outlook. Actions can be based on a parameterized URL or on code that runs when the button is clicked. The BCS Artifact Generator Tool supports only parameterized URL actions, but custom code actions can be created and are discussed later in the chapter in the section entitled Creating Custom Actions, Ribbons, and Parts.

The `ContextEventHandlers` element maps actions to events. An action can be automatically fired via either the `ContextActivated` or `ContextDeactivated` element. This allows an action to fire either when it becomes the active item or when it loses the focus. This is often used to display associated entity instances in a task pane, as shown.

Packaging and Deploying Solutions

Once the artifacts are created, they must be packaged for ClickOnce deployment. The BCS Solution Packaging Tool is used to package the artifacts. This is a straightforward operation in which you point the tool to the folder containing the artifacts. The only wrinkle in the process is that the tool requires that the BDC Metadata Model be named `metadata.xml`. Therefore, you must manually rename the BDC Metadata Model created by the BCS Artifact Generator Tool before packaging the solution.

The BCS Solution Packaging Tool can be used to package different types of solutions that are covered throughout the chapter, but for Outlook declarative solutions the Solution Type should be set to Outlook Intermediate Declarative Solution. When packaging the solution, you can also have it signed with a certificate, which will keep the warning dialog from displaying during deployment. When the options are all set, simply click the Package button to create the package files. The BCS Solution Packaging Tool will generate all the required files for an Outlook add-in, as described in Chapter 1. Figure 6-4 shows the BCS Solution Packaging Tool.

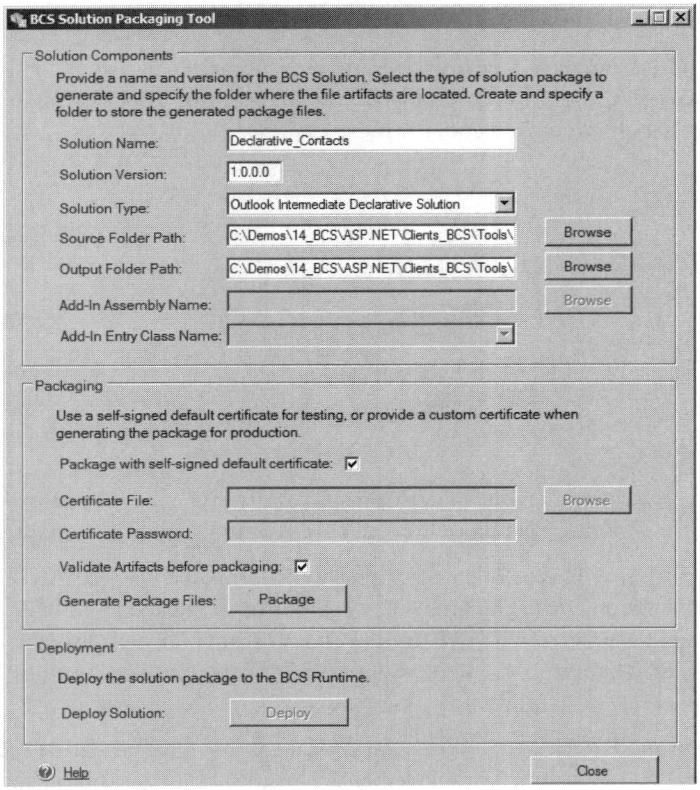

FIGURE 6-4

Once the solution is packaged, you can install it directly from the BCS Solution Packaging Tool by clicking the Deploy button. While this may be useful for testing, for production you will want to put the solution in a document library. This is accomplished by creating a document library in SharePoint with a folder structure that duplicates the structure created by the BCS Solution Packaging Tool.

Create a document library in the site from which you want to deploy the solution. Within the document library, create a folder with the same name as the folder created by the BCS Solution Packaging Tool. Then upload all the files created by the BCS Solution Packaging Tool to the folder. Next, upload the VSTO file to the root of the library, recreating the same package structure as the tool output. Finally, create a link to the VSTO file, which when clicked will install the customization. Users can subsequently uninstall the solution through the Programs and Features applet in the same way that any standard Windows application is uninstalled. Figure 6-5 shows a declarative solution with a ribbon modification to support a Bing search.

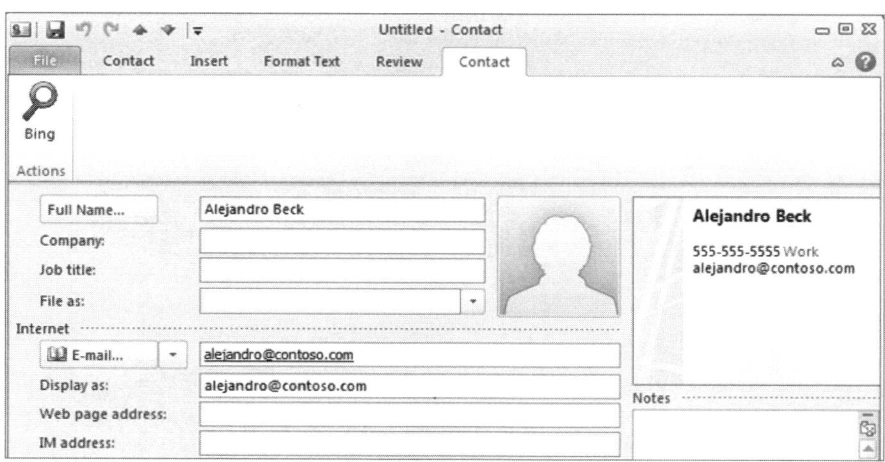

FIGURE 6-5

Creating Custom Form Regions

As shown in Chapter 3, ECT fields that are not mapped to Outlook fields are displayed in a separate form region. An adjoining form region is used if the number of unmapped fields is less than or equal to five. If there are more unmapped fields, a separate form region is used. Using an Outlook declarative solution, you can design a custom form region for displaying the unmapped fields, which will give you the opportunity to improve the user interface.

Form regions are created directly in Microsoft Outlook. In order to create them, you must have the Developer tab available (it is normally hidden). In order to expose it click File ➪ Options ➪ Customize Ribbon and check the Developer checkbox. Figure 6-6 shows the Outlook Options dialog with the Developer tab enabled.

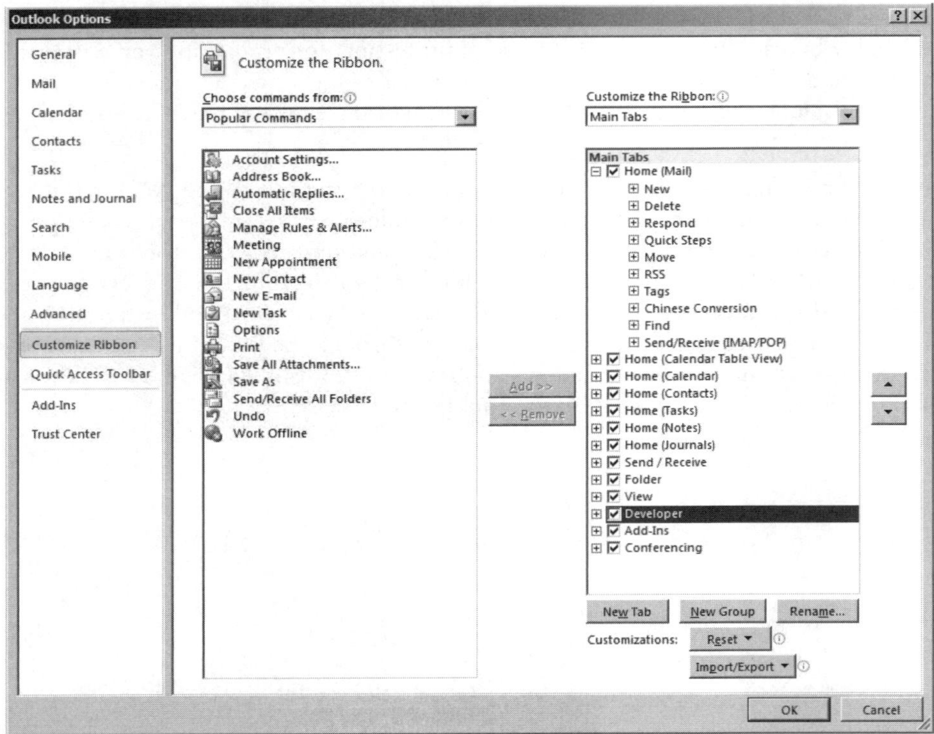

FIGURE 6-6

Once the Developer tab is visible, you may click the Design a Form button and choose to design a form that matches the Outlook type you are using for the ECT. When the new form opens, clicking New Form Region will bring up a blank form region in which you can begin work. Figure 6-7 shows a new form region as part of the Contact form.

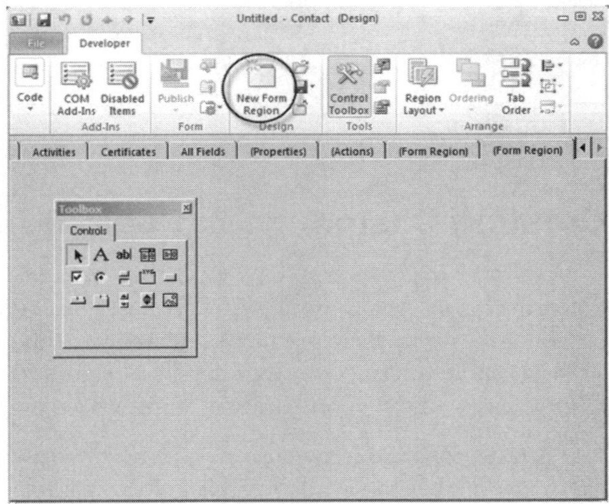

FIGURE 6-7

For each unmapped field you wish to display, drop an appropriate control from the toolbox onto the new form region (for example a TextBox). In the properties of the controls, click the Value tab. Click the New button to define a new field. Name the field using the same name as the field in the ECT that you wish to display. You can also add existing fields, which you do if the goal is to replace the entire default page. Once the design is complete, click the Save Region button and save the file with an `.ofs` extension.

Once the custom form region is created, you can run the BCS Artifact Generator Tool, as described earlier. This time, however, you can elect to use a custom form region and browse to the OFS file you created. When using a custom form region, you may specify that the region should be adjoining, separate, replacement, or replace all. An adjoining region is displayed at the bottom of the standard Outlook inspector window. A separate region is displayed on a separate page. A replacement region replaces the default page of the Outlook inspector window. A replace all form region replaces all the pages so that yours is the only visible page.

After the artifacts are generated, you need to make a few edits by hand. The first thing is to change the name of the BDC Metadata Model to `metadata.xml`, as you did before. Next you have to edit the `oir.config` file to change the `Name` attribute of both the `PromotedProperty` and `OfficeItemProperty` elements to exactly match the names of the new fields you've created. Once these changes are made, you can use the BCS Solution Packaging Tool to package and deploy the customization, as described earlier. Figure 6-8 shows a resulting adjoining form region displaying the URL for the client's SharePoint site.

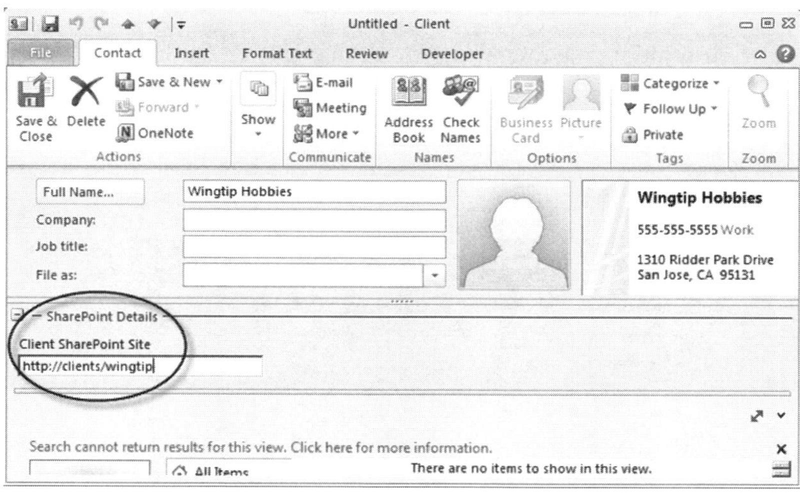

FIGURE 6-8

Creating Custom View Definitions

Along with custom form regions, you can also create custom views for ECTs. In order to create a custom view, first deploy your basic solution using the steps described earlier. Once the solution is deployed, open the folder in Outlook and create a new view. Use the built-in Outlook tools to design the view. Be sure to create a new view for customization, because customizing the default view will affect all folders in Outlook.

Once you have created a new view, right-click the folder and select Export View Definition from the context menu. Save this new view with an `.ovd` extension into the folder containing the generated artifacts for the solution. Next edit the `oir.config` file to add the new view definition to the solution inside the `Views` element, which appears under the `OutlookFolder` element. The following code shows the required edits:

```
<OutlookFolder Description="" Name="Read Item" FolderDisplayName="Client"
 NativeType="FolderContacts" SubscriptionName="Client2147483660Subscription"
 FolderName="182799b1-6355-4ac9-9d31-fca666a004a9" CanCreate="true"
 CanUpdate="true" CanDelete="true" >
  <Views>
    <FolderViewDefinition Name="CustomerView" ViewName="CustomerView"
     ViewType="TableView" IsDefault="true" ViewFileName="ustomerView.ovd" />
  </Views>
</OutlookFolder>
```

Once the `oir.config` file is edited, delete the custom view from Outlook and uninstall the customization from the machine. Use the BCS Solution Packaging Tool to repackage the customization. Install the new customization and confirm that the view is available.

Including Associations in Declarative Solutions

If you have multiple ECTs in your solution that are related, you can create an Outlook declarative solution that shows the associated ECTs in a task pane. Additionally, you can use an InfoPath form to show the details of each related item. Figure 6-9 shows a solution that displays a contact form for a manager and includes a task pane that lists the manager's direct reports.

FIGURE 6-9

In order to create a solution with relationships, you must first merge all the related ECTs into a single model file if they are not merged already. The BCS Artifact Generator Tool needs to have all the ECTs defined in a single file in order to work with the associations. Once you have the model ready, import it into the BCS Artifact Generator Tool. The BCS Artifact Generator Tool will display all the ECTs available in the model and enable you to customize them, as previously shown. Where an association exists, the BCS Artifact Generator Tool will enable you to specify that you want to show the related items in a task pane. Figure 6-10 shows the BCS Artifact Generator Tool when it detects an association between the ECTs.

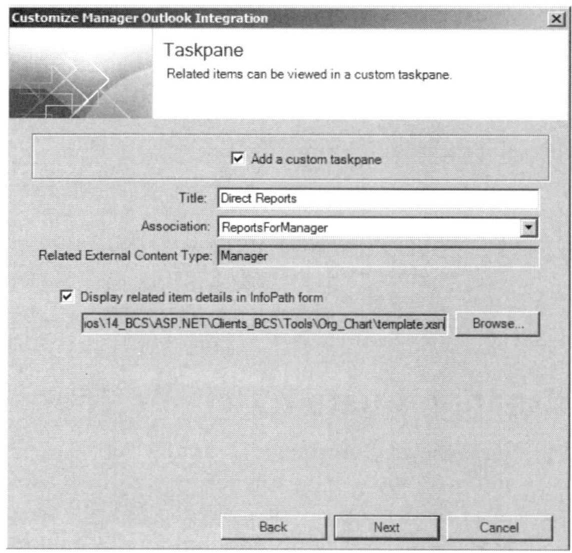

FIGURE 6-10

The BCS Artifact Generator Tool can generate a default user interface for the related entity instances, but you can also make an InfoPath form part of the solution. If you want to use an InfoPath form to show details, you can create an InfoPath form on an External List that uses the associated ECT. Then simply export the XSN file from SPD and reference it in the BCS Artifact Generator Tool. After you have the related item interface defined, you can generate the artifacts for the solution.

Along with the normal artifacts, you'll see that a special layouts file is also created for any associations that will display in a task pane. The layouts file specifies the External Data Parts that will be used in the task pane. The Rich List Part is used to display a grid of related entity instances, and the InfoPath Part is used to display details in the InfoPath form. Additionally, you can modify the layouts file manually to specify exactly what columns should appear in the Rich List Part. The following code shows a typical layouts file. Once the artifacts are all generated and modified, they need to be packaged. The process for packaging is identical to the process for the solutions discussed earlier:

```
<?xml version="1.0" encoding="utf-8"?>
<Container ContainerType="Stack"
  xmlns="http://schemas.microsoft.com/office/2009/05/
       BusinessApplications/Layout">
  <Children>
    <OBPart PartType="List" DataSourceName="PrimaryEntityNameInContext"
     Text="Direct Report" Description="">
      <CustomProperties>
        <CustomProperty Name="DataSourceMode" Value="AssociationList" />
        <CustomProperty Name="DataMemberName" Value="ReportsForManager" />
        <CustomProperty Name="LobSystemInstanceName" Value="Managers" />
        <CustomProperty Name="MaximumVisibleRowCount" Value="12" />
        <CustomProperty Name="ConsumerPartName" Value="IPOBP" />
        <CustomProperty Name="ColumnsXml" Value="&lt;Columns&gt;&lt;Column
         DisplayName=&quot;First Name&quot; Name=&quot;FirstName&quot;
         /&gt;&lt;Column DisplayName=&quot;Last Name&quot;
```

```
          Name=&quot;LastName&quot;/&gt;&lt;/Columns&gt;" />
        </CustomProperties>
      </OBPart>
      <OBPart PartType="InfoPath" Text="Item Details" Description="">
        <CustomProperties>
          <CustomProperty Name="Name" Value="IPOBP" />
          <CustomProperty Name="IsReadOnly" Value="true" />
          <CustomProperty Name="Height" Value="600" />
          <CustomProperty Name="FormLocation" Value="template.xsn" />
        </CustomProperties>
      </OBPart>
    </Children>
  </Container>
```

Creating Custom Actions, Ribbons, and Parts

While the BCS Artifact Generator Tool makes it easy to create basic Outlook declarative solutions, you can go further by creating custom ribbon managers, actions, and External Parts. These elements give you more flexibility when it comes to the appearance and functionality of the solution. A custom ribbon manager enables you to take more control over the ribbon and easily access the underlying Outlook object model. Custom actions enable you to write code that responds to button clicks on the ribbon. Custom External Parts enable you to display custom user interface elements in a task pane.

Extending the basic Outlook declarative solution involves a combination of code and declarative elements. While the coding is reasonably straightforward, the declarative elements require significant hand editing; the BCS Artifact Generator Tool does not support automatically generating the complete artifacts. You can use the BCS Artifact Generator Tool as a starting point, but hand editing is required. All this means that creating this type of solution is error-prone and requires attention to detail. As a simple example, Figure 6-11 shows a Hello, World solution that has a custom ribbon manager, action, and External Part.

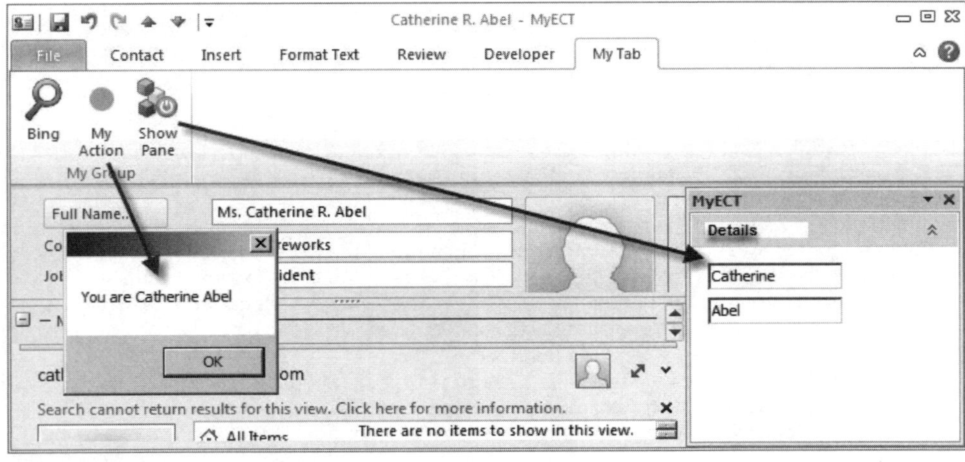

FIGURE 6-11

The custom ribbon manager is the host for the buttons on the ribbon. The custom action simply displays a `MessageBox` with the name of the current entity instance. The custom External Part displays the first name and last name of the current entity instance. This sample exercises the basic functionality of the various extensions.

Coding the Custom Elements

The custom elements are created as part of a class library project that interacts with Microsoft Outlook. Therefore, the project needs to have references to the Office primary interop assemblies (PIA) and the BDC Client Runtime object model. The various assemblies are listed in Table 6-2 and you can add them by browsing to the specified location.

TABLE 6-2: Required References

ASSEMBLY	LOCATION
Microsoft.Office.Interop .Outlook.dll	C:\Program Files (x86) \Microsoft Visual Studio 10.0\Visual Studio Tools for Office\PIA\Office14\
Microsoft.Office. BusinessApplications .Runtime.dll	C:\Windows\assembly\GAC_MSIL\Microsoft .Office.BusinessApplications.Runtime\ 14.0.0.0_71e9bce111e9429c\
Microsoft.Office .BusinessApplications .RuntimeUI.dll	C:\Windows\assembly\GAC_MSIL\Microsoft .Office.BusinessApplications.RuntimeUi\ 14.0.0.0_71e9bce111e9429c\
office.dll	C:\Program Files (x86) \Microsoft Visual Studio 10.0\Visual Studio Tools for Office\PIA\Office14\
Microsoft.BusinessData.dll	C:\Program Files (x86) \Microsoft Office\Office14\

When creating custom extensions, start by creating the custom ribbon manager, because the other components may make use of it. A custom ribbon manager is a class that inherits from `Microsoft.Office.BusinessApplications.Runtime.RibbonManager`. Its main function is to act as an interface to the underlying Outlook object model, which it does in the `GetEnabled()` method. The following code shows how to create a custom ribbon manager:

```
using System;
using System.Runtime.InteropServices;
using System.Windows.Forms;
using Microsoft.Office.Core;
using Microsoft.Office.BusinessApplications.Runtime;
using Outlook = Microsoft.Office.Interop.Outlook;
using Microsoft.BusinessData.Runtime;
```

```
using Microsoft.Office.BusinessData.Offlining;
using Microsoft.BusinessData.MetadataModel;

namespace MyCustomComponents
{
    [ComVisible(true)]
    public class MyRibbonManager :
      Microsoft.Office.BusinessApplications.Runtime.RibbonManager
    {
        public static Outlook.Application currentOutlookApplication;

        public override bool GetEnabled(IRibbonControl control)
        {
            if (currentOutlookApplication == null)
            {
                Outlook.Inspector CurrentInspector =
                 control.Context as Outlook.Inspector;
                currentOutlookApplication =
                 CurrentInspector.Application as Outlook.Application;
            }
            return base.GetEnabled(control);
        }

        public override void OnAction(IRibbonControl control)
        {
            base.OnAction(control);
        }

        public override string GetCustomUI(string ribbonID)
        {
            return base.GetCustomUI(ribbonID);
        }

        public override bool GetVisible(IRibbonControl control)
        {
            return base.GetVisible(control);
        }

        public override void OnLoad(IRibbonUI ribbon)
        {
            base.OnLoad(ribbon);
        }
    }
}
```

Custom actions represent the code to run when a button is clicked on the ribbon. The custom action is a simple class with a single method that accepts an array of arguments. The first argument passed in always represents the current entity instance. The following code shows the custom action for the sample, which just displays the name of the current entity instance:

```
using System;
using Microsoft.BusinessData.Runtime;
using System.Windows.Forms;
using Outlook = Microsoft.Office.Interop.Outlook;

namespace MyCustomComponents
```

```
{
    public class MyAction
    {
        public void MyMethod(params object[] parameters)
        {

            IEntityInstance entityInstance =
              parameters[0] as IEntityInstance;

            try
            {
                string fName = entityInstance["FirstName"].ToString();
                string lName = entityInstance["LastName"].ToString();

                MessageBox.Show("You are " + fName + " " + lName);
            }
            catch (Exception)
            {
                MessageBox.Show("Cannot find Entity Instance");
            }
        }
    }
}
```

In production solutions you will often want to use the ribbon manager and a custom action together. Specifically, you will want to use the ribbon manager to gain access to the underlying Outlook object model for the purpose of creating new items in Outlook or doing something similar. The following code shows how you can create a new task item in Outlook from a custom action with the support of the ribbon manager:

```
IEntityInstance entityInstance = parameters[0] as IEntityInstance;
Outlook.TaskItem newTaskItem =
 (Outlook.TaskItem)MyRibbonManager.currentOutlookApplication.CreateItem(
  Outlook.OlItemType.olTaskItem);
newTaskItem.Subject = "My New Task";
newTaskItem.StartDate = DateTime.Now;
newTaskItem.DueDate = DateTime.Now.AddDays(7);
newTaskItem.Display(false);
```

Custom External Parts are user controls that inherit from `Microsoft.Office.BusinessApplications.Runtime.UI.WinFormsOBPartBase`. In the user control you create the user interface that you want displayed in a task pane. Typically this is data related to the current entity instance, but it can be anything. The implementation should override the `OnDataSourceChanged()` method, which allows access to the current entity instance. The `SaveCore()` method is called when the current entity instance is saved. Using these two methods, your External Part can react to the opening and saving of entity instances in the application. The following code shows a simple example of displaying information from the current entity instance in `TextBox` controls:

```
using System;
using System.ComponentModel;
using System.Windows.Forms;
using Microsoft.Office.BusinessApplications.Runtime.UI;
```

```
using Microsoft.BusinessData.Runtime;
using Microsoft.Office.BusinessData.Offlining;
using Microsoft.BusinessData.Offlining;
using Outlook = Microsoft.Office.Interop.Outlook;
using Microsoft.BusinessData.MetadataModel;

namespace MyCustomComponents
{
    public partial class MyExternalPart : WinFormsOBPartBase
    {
        private IEntityInstance entityInstance;
        bool isDirty = false;

        public MyExternalPart()
        {
            InitializeComponent();
        }

        protected override void OnDataSourceChanged(
 Microsoft.Office.BusinessApplications.Model.DataSourceChangedEventArgs args)
        {
            base.OnDataSourceChanged(args);
            entityInstance = this.DataSource as IEntityInstance;
            fname.Text = entityInstance["FirstName"].ToString();
            lname.Text = entityInstance["LastName"].ToString();
        }

        protected override void SaveCore()
        {
            if (isDirty)
            {
                //Take action, if necessary
            }
            base.SaveCore();
        }

        protected override bool IsDirtyCore
        { get { return isDirty; } }

        private void fname_TextChanged(object sender, EventArgs e)
        { isDirty = true;  }

        private void lname_TextChanged(object sender, EventArgs e)
        { isDirty = true; }
    }
}
```

Packaging the Custom Elements

Once the assembly is created, it can be packaged as part of an Outlook declarative solution. The easiest way to do this is to start with the BCS Artifact Generator Tool and create artifacts based on the BDC Metadata Model for the solution. Once these artifacts are created, you can copy the compiled assembly into the same folder. After you modify the artifacts by hand, they will be packaged along with the assembly.

Start by editing the `oir.config` file. In the `ContextDefinition` element, take note of the `ContentType` attribute because it will be used in the ribbon definition later. If you used the BCS Artifact Generator Tool, this will be a `GUID`. Note that the `ContentType` attribute has no relationship to the name of the ECT used in the solution.

The first modification to make is to the `SolutionDefinition` element, where you need to reference an additional namespace. The additional namespace will allow for the declaration of the custom ribbon manager. The following code shows the complete `SolutionDefinition` element:

```
<SolutionDefinition
xmlsn:mx="http://schemas.microsoft.com/office/2009/05/
          BusinessApplications/Manifest/DeclarativeExtensions"
  xmlns="http://schemas.microsoft.com/office/2009/05/
          BusinessApplications/Manifest"
  xmlns:xsl="http://www.w3.org/2001/XMLSchema-instance">
```

The next modification is to the `SolutionSettings` element. In this element, the custom ribbon manager is declared by means of the fully qualified name of the class and assembly created earlier. The following code shows the complete `SolutionSettings` element:

```
<SolutionSettings SolutionId="MyECT_2824546f-241e-4e35-8d23-a2b99226119e"
    SolutionDisplayName="MyECT" SolutionVersion="1.1.1.3"
    xsl:type="mx:DeclarativeSolutionSettings"
    CustomRibbonManager="MyCustomComponents.MyRibbonManager,
    MyCustomComponents, Version=1.0.0.0, Culture=neutral,
    PublicKeyToken=85f26924cfa9ee60"/>
```

Depending upon the choices you made in the BCS Artifact Generator Tool, you may or may not already have a separate file for the ribbon definition. In any case, `oir.config` must reference this file in the `ContextDefinitionGroup` element. The following code shows a complete `ContextDefinitionGroup` element with the ribbon file referenced:

```
<ContextDefinitionGroup xsl:type="mx:DeclarativeContextDefinitionGroup"
  ItemType="OutlookContact" RibbonFileName="MyRibbon.xml" >
```

When buttons are clicked on the ribbon, they can invoke a parameterized URL, show a task pane, or invoke custom code. The definitions for these behaviors are part of the `Actions` element in the `oir.config` file. The following code shows how to define each of the different types of actions:

```
<mx:Actions>
  <mx:UrlAction Name="Bing" Description="" Url="http://www.bing.com?q={0}">
    <mx:Parameters>
      <mx:ExpressionParameter Name="LastNameParam"
       EntityViewInstanceReference="PrimaryEntityNameInContext"
       Expression="LastName" />
    </mx:Parameters>
  </mx:UrlAction>
```

```
    <mx:CodeMethodAction Name="MyMethod" Description="MyMethod"
      MethodType="Custom" MethodName="MyMethod"
      QualifiedTypeName="MyCustomComponents.MyAction, MyCustomComponents,
      Version=1.0.0.0, Culture=neutral, PublicKeyToken=85f26924cfa9ee60">
    </mx:CodeMethodAction>
    <mx:CodeMethodAction Name="ShowMyExternalPart" Description="Show Pane"
     MethodType="ShowTaskpaneLayout">
      <mx:Parameters>
        <mx:ConstantParameter Name="LayoutFile" Value="MyLayout"
         ValueType="System.String" />
      </mx:Parameters>
    </mx:CodeMethodAction>
  </mx:Actions>
```

The `UrlAction` element defines a parameterized action and is created by the BCS Artifact Generator Tool. The `CodeMethodAction` element can define either a `Custom` action or a `ShowTaskpaneLayout` action. A `Custom` action is mapped to the fully qualified name of the class that contains the action and references the name of the method within the class to call. A `ShowTaskpaneLayout` action is used to display a custom External Part, but the reference to the user control assembly is kept in a separate layout file. The name of the `Layout` element is referenced in the `ShowTaskpaneLayout` action. In turn, the `Layout` element references the name of the layout file, as shown in the following code:

```
  <mx:Layouts>
    <mx:Layout Name="MyLayout" LayoutFileName="MyLayout"></mx:Layout>
  </mx:Layouts>
```

The final modification to the `oir.config` file is the inclusion of a `ContextEventHandler` to execute the `ShowTaskpaneLayout` action when a new item is opened. This way, the task pane will display automatically, just as in the solutions created earlier. The following code shows how to create the `ContextEventHander` for the sample. After this modification the `oir.config` file can be saved.

```
  <mx:ContextEventHandlers>
    <mx:ContextActivated ActionName="ShowMyExternalPart" />
  </mx:ContextEventHandlers>
```

The next file to create or modify is the ribbon file. This is an XML file that has the name referenced in the `oir.config` file. The key to the ribbon file is to get the format correct. You will need the name of the content type noted earlier and the name of the actions. The following code shows the ribbon file for the sample:

```
  <customUI xmlns="http://schemas.microsoft.com/office/2006/01/customui"
    onLoad="OnLoad" loadImage="GetImage">
    <ribbon>
      <tabs>
        <tab id="mytabid" getVisible="GetVisible"
         label="My Tab" tag="Solution">
          <group id="mygroupid" label="My Group"
           tag="Context[MyContentType.groupid]" getVisible="GetVisible">
```

```
            <button id="mybuttonid1" label="Bing" getEnabled="GetEnabled"
             onAction="OnAction" size="large" image="search32x32.png"
             tag="Action[MyContentType.Bing]" />
            <button id="mybuttonid2" label="My Action" getEnabled="GetEnabled"
             onAction="OnAction" size="large" image="placeholder32x32.png"
             tag="Action[MyContentType.MyMethod]" />
            <button id="mybuttonid3" label="Show Pane" getEnabled="GetEnabled"
             onAction="OnAction" size="large" image="parts32x32.png"
             tag="Action[MyContentType.ShowMyExternalPart]" />
          </group>
        </tab>
      </tabs>
    </ribbon>
  </customUI>
```

The final file to create or modify is the layout file. This is an XML file that has the name referenced earlier. The key part of this file is the fully-qualified reference to the custom External Part. The following code shows the layout file for the sample:

```
<?xml version="1.0" encoding="utf-8" ?>
<Container ContainerType="Stack"
  xmlns="http://schemas.microsoft.com/office/2009/05/
  BusinessApplications/Layout"
  xmlns:loc="http://schemas.microsoft.com/office/2009/05/
  BusinessApplications/Localization">
  <CustomProperties />
  <Children>
    <OBPart DataSourceName="PrimaryEntityNameInContext"
     PartType="Custom" Text="Details" FillParent="true"
     QualifiedTypeName="MyCustomComponents.MyExternalPart,
     MyCustomComponents, Version=1.0.0.0, Culture=neutral,
    PublicKeyToken=85f26924cfa9ee60">
      <CustomProperties />
    </OBPart>
  </Children>
</Container>
```

After you complete the custom modifications, all the artifacts can be packaged with the BCS Solution Packaging Tool. There are no special considerations for the packaging. The tool will package all the artifacts, including files, images, and assemblies. Once these are all packaged, you can deploy the solution to a document library, as discussed previously.

WORKING WITH THE BDC CLIENT RUNTIME OBJECT MODEL

The BDC Client Runtime object model is the API used to write custom solutions that run in Office clients and use BCS artifacts. The BDC Client Runtime object model is designed to complement the BDC Server Runtime object model and contains many of the same classes, methods, and properties. Therefore, you can leverage your knowledge of the BDC Server Runtime object model to get started quickly.

The BDC Client Runtime object model is contained in the `Microsoft.BusinessData.dll` and `Microsoft.Office.BusinessData.dll` assemblies. Both of these assemblies are located in the `Office 14` directory, which is the installation directory for Office 2010. The `Microsoft.BusinessData.dll` assembly provides classes that parallel the server-side objects contained in the BDC Server Runtime object model. The `Microsoft.Office.BusinessData.dll` assembly contains classes that specifically support Office clients.

Any solution you create will need a reference to both BDC Client Runtime assemblies as well as `Microsoft.Office.BusinessApplications.Runtime.dll` and `Microsoft.Office.BusinessApplications.RuntimeUi.dll`, which were mentioned earlier in the chapter. Furthermore, if you are using the 32-bit version of Office 2010, you must explicitly set the build target for your solution to `x86` in the Visual Studio project properties. Table 6-3 lists the key namespaces you use when working with the BDC Client Runtime object model, and the following code shows typical `using` statements:

```
//Reference to Microsoft.BusinessData.dll
using Microsoft.BusinessData;
using Microsoft.BusinessData.Runtime;
using Microsoft.BusinessData.Offlining;
using Microsoft.BusinessData.MetadataModel;
using Microsoft.BusinessData.MetadataModel.Collections;

//Reference to Microsoft.Office.BusinessData.dll
using Microsoft.Office.BusinessData;
using Microsoft.Office.BusinessData.Runtime;
using Microsoft.Office.BusinessData.Offlining;
using Microsoft.Office.BusinessData.MetadataModel;
```

TABLE 6-3: Key Namespaces

NAMESPACE	DESCRIPTION
`Microsoft.BusinessData.MetadataModel` `Microsoft.Office.BusinessData.MetadataModel`	Provides access to key Metadata elements
`Microsoft.BusinessData.MetadataModel.Collections` `Microsoft.Office.BusinessData.MetadataModel.Collections`	Provides access to key Metadata collections
`Microsoft.BusinessData.Offlining` `Microsoft.Office.BusinessData.Offlining`	Provides access to the client-side cache
`Microsoft.BusinessData.Runtime` `Microsoft.Office.BusinessData.Runtime`	Provides access to key entity instance objects and collections

Connecting to the Metadata Catalog

Just like server-side solutions, client-side solutions require a connection to the BDC Metadata catalog. The difference between client and server solutions is that the client will never access the BDC Service Application. Instead, the client must access either the BCS client cache or a special file-based catalog. Most production solutions will use the BCS client cache, which is updated with BDC Metadata Models and data as specified by an associated subscription file. However, solutions do have the option to use a file-based catalog into which BDC Metadata Models are loaded when the application starts.

A connection to the BCS client cache is made through the `Microsoft.Office.BusinessData.RemoteSharedFileBackedMetadataCatalog` class and may only be established from within an Office client. This means you cannot use the `RemoteSharedFileBackedMetadataCatalog` class to access the BCS client cache from projects such as console or Windows applications. The BCS client cache is intended for use only with Office clients, so the BDC Client Runtime object model protects it from access by other types of applications. For the most part, this means that you will use the following code as part of an Office add-in to connect with the BCS client cache:

```
RemoteSharedFileBackedMetadataCatalog catalog =
  new RemoteSharedFileBackedMetadataCatalog();
```

If you want to create BCS solutions using projects other than Office add-ins, you can create a catalog for them through the `Microsoft.Office.BusinessData.MetadataModel.FileBackedMetadataCatalog` class. The `FileBackedMetadataCatalog` class enables you to create complete client-side solutions that do not require Office clients, but does not allow access to the BCS client cache. Instead, this class creates a catalog in memory must have models imported into it for use. The catalog is specific to the application and is destroyed when the application closes. The following code shows how to create a `FileBackedMetadataCatalog` and load it with a model from an XML file:

```
FileBackedMetadataCatalog catalog = new FileBackedMetadataCatalog();
FileStream fs = new FileStream("MyModel.xml",
                                FileMode.Open, FileAccess.Read);
catalog.ImportPackage(fs, new ParseContext(), PackageContents.All);
fs.Close();
```

Once a connection to one of the two catalogs is established, elements of the BDC Metadata Models may be retrieved. Because the client-side catalogs function differently from the server-side catalog, not all of the same operations are supported. Both the `RemoteSharedFileBackedMetadataCatalog` class and the `FileBackedMetadataCatalog` class support the `GetEntity()`, `GetEntities()`, `GetLobSystem()`, and `GetLobSystems()` methods. Because these catalogs do not cache models like the BDC Service Application, the `GetById()` method is not available. Just like server solutions, client solutions will generally start by retrieving a reference to the needed ECTs using the `GetEntity()` method and passing in the name and namespace for the desired entity.

When creating client-side solutions, you may elect to receive events for two important scenarios. First, you can receive a notification whenever your application gains or loses a connection to the hosting BCS process. Second, you can receive a notification when your client application needs to create a web service proxy.

Office solutions can perform operations only when they have a valid connection to the underlying BCS host process. Your application can receive notification of changes in the connection status through the `ConnectionAcquired`, `ConnectionLost`, and `PreConnectionLost` events. These events are supported on the `RemoteSharedFileBackedMetadataCatalog` class.

When using the `FileBackedMetadataCatalog` class against a web service source, you can either have BCS generate a client proxy for you, or you can create your own. You can receive notification when the solution needs a proxy through the `SubscribeOnPostGenerateProxyAssemblyBytes()` and the `SubscribeOnPreGenerateProxyAssemblyBytes()` methods. Using these methods, you can set up event handlers that will return a custom proxy that you generate yourself. The following code shows how to structure the events:

```
FileBackedMetadataCatalog catalog = new FileBackedMetadataCatalog();
catalog.SubscribeOnPostGenerateProxyAssemblyBytes(ProxyGeneratedHandler);
catalog.SubscribeOnPreGenerateProxyAssemblyBytes(ProxyGeneratingHandler);

public void ProxyGeneratedHandler(byte[] proxyAssemblyBytesGenerated,
                                  ILobSystemStruct lobSystemStruct)
{

}

public byte[] ProxyGeneratingHandler(ILobSystemStruct lobSystemStruct)
{

}
```

Understanding the Execution Context

Whenever operations are performed on an External System, you have the option to create an *execution context* that can track the operations performed and pass information between the consuming application and a custom connector. All three of the catalog classes (`DatabaseBackedMetadataCatalog`, `RemoteSharedFileBackedMetadataCatalog`, and `FileBackedMetadataCatalog`) support the creation of a context, but it can be particularly useful with client-side solutions to track additional information.

You create an execution context with the `CreateExecutionContext()` method of the catalog. This method returns an `IExecutionContext` interface. The `IExecutionContext` interface enables you to handle the `MethodExecuting` and `MethodExecuted` events. These events notify your application that a method is about to be executed on an External System or that it has just completed.

The `IExecutionContext` interface contains a collection of `ExecutedMethods` that provide information about the methods executed on the External System. This information includes errors that occurred in the connector. Using this approach, you can elegantly handle connector-level errors in your solutions.

In addition to tracking method execution, the `IExecutionContext` interface also supports a property bag that allows direct communication between the client solution and the connector. Using the property bag, the client and connector can exchange data directly, which allows them an additional line of communication. Note that the property bag is meaningful only when used with a .NET Assembly or custom connector. The standard connectors do not look for these properties, and their behaviors cannot be altered through them. The following code shows snippets from a data class that shows how to use the execution context:

```
//Members
FileBackedMetadataCatalog catalog;
IExecutionContext ctx;

//Properties
public bool HasError { get; set; }
public string ConnectorErrorMessage { get; set; }

//This code would be in constructor
catalog = new FileBackedMetadataCatalog();
ctx = catalog.CreateExecutionContext();
ctx.MethodExecuted += new ExecutionEventHandler(ctx_MethodExecuted);
ctx["CatalogType"] = catalog.GetType().ToString();
ctx.ManageProperty("CatalogType");

//Event handler
void ctx_MethodExecuted(IExecutionContext context,
                        IExecutionInfo executingMethod)
{
    foreach (IExecutionInfo info in ctx.ExecutedMethods)
    {
        if (info.Exception != null)
        {
            HasError = true;
            ConnectorErrorMessage = info.Exception.Message;
        }
    }
}

//Dispose
public void Dispose()
{
    ctx.Dispose();
}
```

The `IExecutionContext` is created by the catalog and associated with the thread running the application. Therefore, using the execution context costs additional processing overhead. For this reason, the execution context should be used only when necessary. Additionally, the execution context should be disposed of when the catalog is destroyed to avoid holding on to resources when they are no longer needed.

You create the properties in the property bag simply by setting a value to a newly named property. The properties may be designated as either managed or unmanaged. Managed properties are disposed of when the execution context is disposed of, but unmanaged properties are not disposed of. On the connector side, properties may be accessed directly from the property bag, because the execution context is exposed to the connector. Chapter 7 covers connectors in detail.

Executing Cache Operations

Executing operations against a client-side catalog is very similar to executing them against a server-side catalog. The biggest difference between the server and client is the fact that the `RemoteSharedFileBackedMetadataCatalog` can interact with the client cache. This allows for offline scenarios that are not supported by the other catalogs. Where cache operations are not a factor, however, the code is nearly identical, and you can use the samples in Chapter 5 as a guide. Consider the following console application code, which executes a `Finder` method on the client against any BDC Metadata Model that uses the SQL connector. Note the similarities between this listing and the related one in Chapter 5.

```
static void Main(string[] args)
{
    string modelFile = args[0];
    string lobSystemInstance = args[1];
    string entityName = args[2];
    string entityNamespace = args[3];
    string finderMethodInstance = args[4];

    FileBackedMetadataCatalog catalog = new FileBackedMetadataCatalog();
    FileStream fs = new FileStream(modelFile, FileMode.Open,
                                   FileAccess.Read);
    catalog.ImportPackage(fs, new ParseContext(), PackageContents.All);
    fs.Close();

    //Get entity
    IEntity ect = catalog.GetEntity(entityNamespace, entityName);

    //Get LobSystem
    ILobSystem lob = ect.GetLobSystem();

    //Get LobSystemInstance
    ILobSystemInstance lobi = lob.GetLobSystemInstances()[lobSystemInstance];

    //Get Method Instance
    IMethodInstance mi = ect.GetMethodInstance(finderMethodInstance,
                                               MethodInstanceType.Finder);

    //Get Parameters
    IParameterCollection parameters = mi.GetMethod().GetParameters();

    //Execute
    object[] arguments = new object[parameters.Count];
    ect.Execute(mi, lobi, ref arguments);

    //Display
    PropertyInfo[] props = arguments[0].GetType().GetProperties();
```

```
        PropertyInfo prop = props[0];
        SqlDataReader reader = (SqlDataReader)(prop.GetValue(arguments[0],
                                                            null));

        if (reader.HasRows)
        {
            while (reader.Read())
            {
                for (int i = 0; i < reader.VisibleFieldCount; i++)
                {
                    switch (reader.GetDataTypeName(i))
                    {
                        case "nvarchar":
                            Console.Write(reader[i].ToString());
                            Console.Write(" ");
                            break;

                        case "int":
                            Console.Write(reader.GetInt32(i));
                            Console.Write(" ");
                            break;

                        default:
                            Console.Write(" ");
                            break;
                    }
                }

                Console.WriteLine();
            }
        }
    }
```

Cache operations become meaningful when you are executing operations against a `RemoteSharedFileBackedMetadataCatalog` object. In this case, an `OperationMode` object may be passed in either the `FindFiltered()` or `FindSpecificMultiple()` methods of the `IEntity` interface. The `OperationMode` object specifies behaviors for the operation based on the set of properties shown in Table 6-4. For more detailed information on the cache population and synchronization process, see Chapter 3.

TABLE 6-4: OperationMode Properties

PROPERTY	DESCRIPTION
`AllowPartialData`	Allows partial data to be returned from the operation
`CacheUsage`	Specifies how to use cached data during the operation
`DoNotDetectConflicts`	Allows conflicts to be ignored during the operation
`Freshness`	Specifies the required data freshness for the operation

The `AllowPartialData` property may be set to `True` or `False`. When it is set to `True`, partial data may be returned from the cache for an entity instance. This situation can occur when the `Finder` method does not return all the available fields for an entity instance. In this case, the cache is partially populated. In a subsequent call to a `SpecificFinder` method, BCS would normally finish populating the cache with the missing fields. If `AllowPartialData` is set to `True`, the data is returned directly from the cache that has the missing data.

The `CacheUsage` property provides more control over how the data in the client cache is used. This property may be set to `Default`, `Online`, `Offline`, or `Cached`. When it is set to `Default`, the operation behaves normally based on the BDC Metadata Model. When it is set to `Online`, all operations are performed against the External System directly, and the data in the cache will never be updated. When it is set to `Offline`, all read operations will be performed against the cache; data will never be read from the External System. When it is set to `Cached`, `SpecificFinder` operations will read data from the cache unless the data is stale or missing, in which case these operations will read data from the External System. `Finder` operations will return only data from the cache, even if the data is stale or missing.

The `DoNotDetectConflicts` property may be set to `True` or `False`. When it is set to `True`, conflicts in the cache are ignored. When it is set to `False`, the original values from `SpecificFinder` calls are used to detect conflicts with the cache.

The `Freshness` property is a `System.TimeSpan` type that specifies the freshness requirement for the retrieved data. If the data in the cache is determined to be stale, it will be refreshed from the External System. The following code shows a sample with a `FindSpecificMultiple()` method that will read data from the cache if it is less than 10 minutes old:

```
//Connect to client cache
RemoteSharedFileBackedMetadataCatalog catalog =
  new RemoteSharedFileBackedMetadataCatalog();
IEntity ect = catalog.GetEntity("ExternalDMSConnector", "Document");
ILobSystem lob = ect.GetLobSystem();
ILobSystemInstance lobi = lob.GetLobSystemInstances()["ExternalDMSSystem"];
IMethodInstance mi = ect.GetMethodInstances()["ReadAllItems"];
IFilterCollection filters = mi.GetFilters();

List<Identity> identities = new List<Identity>();
identities.Add(new Identity(103));

OperationMode om = new OperationMode();
om.CacheUsage = CacheUsage.Cached;
om.Freshness = new TimeSpan(0, 10, 0);

IEntityInstance ei = ect.FindSpecificMultiple(identities,
                       bulkSpecificFinderName, lobi, om);
```

Exploring the Client Cache

Because the client cache is such a significant part of BCS solutions, it won't be long before you feel the need to explore the cache and understand the data it contains. The starting point for working with the client cache is the `Microsoft.Office.BusinessData.Offlining.RemoteOfflineRuntime` class. Using this class, you can gain access to the synchronization manager, subscription manager, and Metadata catalog. An instance of the `RemoteOfflineRuntime` class can be created from within the context of an Office add-in; it cannot be created from non-Office applications, because it provides methods for accessing the client cache.

The `GetSynchronizationManager()` method returns an `ISynchronization` object. The `ISynchronizationManager` interface provides methods that allow for synchronization management. Table 6-5 lists the available methods.

TABLE 6-5: ISynchronizationManager Methods

METHOD	DESCRIPTION
`GetAllInstancesInError`	Returns all entity instances in the cache that are in an error state
`GetAllOperationsInError`	Returns all failed operations from the operation queue
`GetOperation`	Gets an operation from the operation queue
`GetOperationExecutionSummary`	Gets the current number of completed, failed, and pending operations from the operation queue
`GetOperations`	Gets all pending operations from the operation queue
`PopulateCache`	Populates the cache with data based on information such as identifiers, filters, and associations.
`ResolveIdentity`	Returns an identity from the cache

Note that while the `ISynchronizationManager` has methods for reading and populating the cache, there is no method for clearing the cache. Data in the cache will be removed only by the garbage collection process discussed in Chapter 3. The following code shows how to use the `ISynchronizationManager` to return a summary of operations:

```
RemoteOfflineRuntime rt = new RemoteOfflineRuntime();
ISynchronizationManager syncMan = rt.GetSynchronizationManager();
IProgressSummary opSummary = syncMan.GetOperationExecutionSummary();
Text1.Text = "Total Operations: " + opSummary.Total.ToString();
Text2.Text = "Failed Operations: " + opSummary.Failed.ToString();
Text3.Text = "Pending Operations: " + opSummary.Pending.ToString();
```

The `GetSubscriptionManager()` method returns an `ISubscriptionManager` object. The `ISubscriptionManager` interface provides the `GetSubscription()` and `GetSubscriptions()` methods for retrieving the subscriptions in the cache. The `ISubscriptionManager` is used to gain access to an `ISubscription` interface that represents a subscription. The `ISubscription` interface can be used to alter a subscription and can be used to cause a subscription to execute through the `RequestRefresh()` method. Just as with the `ISynchronizationManager` interface, there are no methods to remove data or subscriptions from the cache. The following code shows how to gather information about subscriptions:

```
RemoteOfflineRuntime rt = new RemoteOfflineRuntime();
ISubscriptionManager subscriptionManager = rt.GetSubscriptionManager();
ISubscriptionCollection subscriptions =
  subscriptionManager.GetSubscriptions();

foreach (ISubscription subscription in
         subscriptionManager.GetSubscriptions())
{
    NameField.Text = subscription.Name;

    EnabledField.Text = subscription.Enabled.ToString();
    StatusField.Text = subscription.GetStatus().RefreshStatus;
    LastRefresh.text = subscription.LastRefreshed.ToString();
    ExpiresField.text = subscription.ExpireAfter.ToString();

    StringBuilder sb = new StringBuilder();
    foreach (IField f in subscription.View.Fields)
    {
        Sb.Append(f.Name);
    }
}
```

The `GetMetadataCatalog()` method is used to return an `IMetadataCatalog` object. This object may be cast into a `RemoteSharedFileBackedMetadataCatalog` object and used to get information about the BDC Metadata Model and the values of entity instances. The following code shows how to return data from the cache using the catalog:

```
//Systems Information
INamedLobSystemDictionary systems = cache.GetLobSystems("*");

foreach (string k1 in systems.Keys)
{
    ILobSystem lob = systems[k1];
    INamedLobSystemInstanceDictionary lobis = lob.GetLobSystemInstances();

    List<string> s = new List<string>();

    foreach (string k2 in lobis.Keys)
    {
        ILobSystemInstance lobi = lobis[k2];
        s.Add(lobi.Name);
    }
}

//ECT Information
```

```
INamespacedEntityDictionaryDictionary entities = cache.GetEntities("*");

List<string> e = new List<string>();

foreach (IEntity entity in cache.GetEntities("*"))
{

    e.Add(entity.Name);
    List<string> f = new List<string>();
    List<string> m = new List<string>();

    //Property Information
    foreach (IField fld in entity.GetDefaultSpecificFinderView().Fields)
    {
        f.Add(fld.name);
    }

    // Method Information
    foreach (string key in entity.GetMethodInstances().Keys)
    {
        IMethodInstance mi = entity.GetMethodInstances()[key];
        m.Add(mi.Name);
    }

    //Cached Data
    IEntityInstanceEnumerator instanceEnumerator = entity.FindFiltered(
      entity.GetDefaultFinderFilters(),
      entity.GetMethodInstances(MethodInstanceType.Finder)[0].Value.Name,
      entity.GetLobSystem().GetLobSystemInstances()[0].Value,
      OperationMode.CachedWithoutRefresh);

    int c = 0;
    while (instanceEnumerator.MoveNext())
    {
        c++;
        if (c < 11)
        {
            StringBuilder data = new StringBuilder();
            IEntityInstance entityInstance = instanceEnumerator.Current;
            foreach (IField f in
                     entity.GetDefaultSpecificFinderView().Fields)
            {
                try
                {
                    data.Append(entityInstance[f.Name].ToString());
                    data.Append("|");
                }
                catch { }
            }
        }
    }
}
```

Using the `RemoteOfflineRuntime` class, you can easily create a cache explorer solution that displays information about the data in the cache. Just remember that it must be created as an Office add-in to gain access. The code for this chapter has just such a sample add-in, and Figure 6-12 shows a screen shot of it in use.

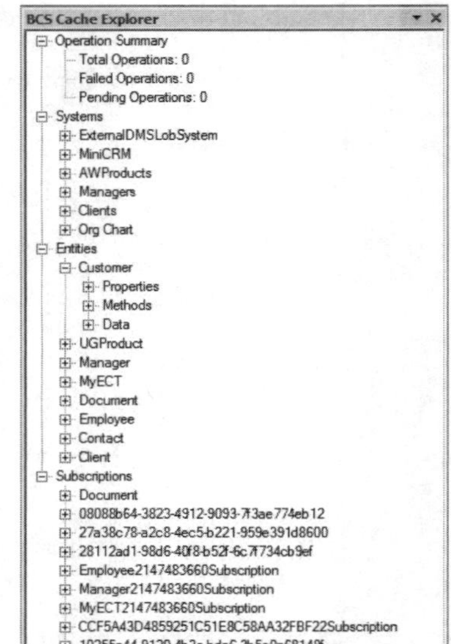

FIGURE 6-12

CREATING OFFICE ADD-INS

Microsoft Office 2010 add-ins are the ultimate client-side BCS solutions. Creating an add-in gives you complete control over the user interface and allows you complete access to the BDC Client Runtime object model. For these reasons, many BCS solutions feature custom add-ins. You can start an add-in project in Visual Studio 2010 from the Visual C# ➪ Office ➪ 2010 project group. Here you can choose to create an add-in for Word, Excel, Outlook, Visio, InfoPath, Project, or PowerPoint.

Adding Ribbon Support

Once a new project is started, you can define custom buttons for the ribbon using the Ribbon Support component. The Ribbon Support component is available from the Add New Item dialog. When you add this component, Visual Studio adds a new class to your project along with an XML file that holds button definitions. The Ribbon Support component has both a visual designer and a straight XML file variant. Both types can achieve the same result, but if you need more control, use the XML version.

When the Ribbon Support component is added, it comes with some code to automatically add the new elements to the target application's ribbon, but this code is commented out. In order to load your new elements, you must uncomment this code and copy it into the `ThisAddin`, `ThisWorkbook`, or `ThisDocument` class, as appropriate. This code overrides the `CreateRibbonExtensibilityObject()` method. This is the method that is called when the Office application loads the Ribbon Support component. The following code shows the uncommented lines along with the startup and shutdown event handlers for a basic Word add-in:

```
namespace WordAddIn1
{
    public partial class ThisAddIn
    {
        private void ThisAddIn_Startup(object sender, System.EventArgs e)
        {
        }

        private void ThisAddIn_Shutdown(object sender, System.EventArgs e)
        {
        }

        protected override Microsoft.Office.Core.IRibbonExtensibility
          CreateRibbonExtensibilityObject()
        {
            return new Ribbon1();
        }
```

```
        #region VSTO generated code

        /// <summary>
        /// Required method for Designer support - do not modify
        /// the contents of this method with the code editor.
        /// </summary>
        private void InternalStartup()
        {
            this.Startup += new System.EventHandler(ThisAddIn_Startup);
            this.Shutdown += new System.EventHandler(ThisAddIn_Shutdown);
        }

        #endregion
    }
}
```

Along with the code file, the Ribbon Support component also provides an XML file that defines what buttons appear in the ribbon. By default, this comes with a tab and group already defined, but no controls. The ribbon supports a variety of controls that you can see by simply using the IntelliSense that appears when you edit the file. Figure 6-13 shows the XML file being edited and the following code shows the XML used for the sample:

```
<?xml version="1.0" encoding="UTF-8"?>
<customUI xmlns="http://schemas.microsoft.com/office/2009/07/customui"
  onLoad="Ribbon_Load">
  <ribbon>
    <tabs>
      <tab idMso="TabInsert">
        <group id="BCSGroup" label="BCS">
          <button id="BCSButton"
                  label="Insert BCS Data"
                  onAction="BCSButton_OnClick"/>
        </group>
      </tab>
    </tabs>
  </ribbon>
</customUI>
```

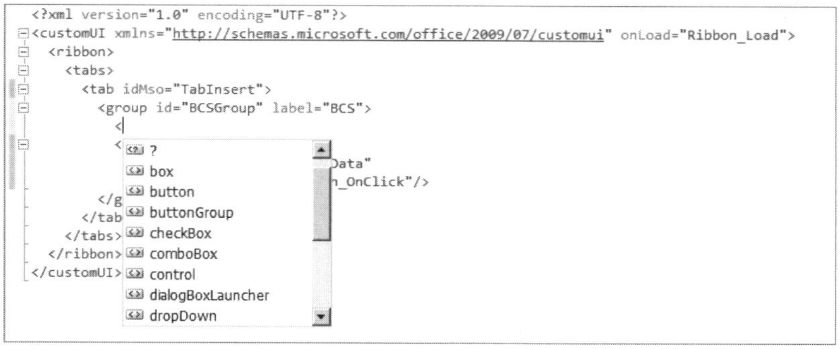

FIGURE 6-13

The customUI element contains the entire definition for the tabs, groups, and controls that will be added to the ribbon. The onLoad attribute references a callback method in the associated code file that runs when the controls are loaded. The ribbon element contains a tabs element with multiple tab elements for adding new tabs or customizing existing tabs. If you are targeting an existing tab, the idMso attribute will contain the identifier for the existing tab. New tabs are identified with an id attribute. The isMso value of an existing tab is always the word Tab followed by the name of the tab as it appears in the application ribbon. The group element is used to create a new group within a tab.

When you define controls within a group, there are various action attributes that enable you to map actions to code. The preceding sample code has a single button with an action of BCSButton_OnClick. This callback method must exist inside the Ribbon Support component. In the Ribbon Support component is a region named Ribbon Callbacks in which you should define the callback methods. The region already contains a callback for the onLoad event. Here you can add your own callback and use the BDC Client Runtime object model as required. Additionally, you can make use of the object model for the application itself. As an example, the following code shows a callback coded to insert data from the client cache into a Word document:

```
public void BCSButton_OnClick(Office.IRibbonControl control)
{
    try
    {
        string lobSystemInstance = "MiniCRM";
        string entityName = "Contact";
        string entityNamespace = "http:///bcs";
        string finderMethodInstance = "Read List";

        RemoteSharedFileBackedMetadataCatalog catalog =
          new RemoteSharedFileBackedMetadataCatalog();

        //Get entity
        IEntity ect = catalog.GetEntity(entityNamespace, entityName);

        //Get LobSystem
        ILobSystem lob = ect.GetLobSystem();

        //Get LobSystemInstance
        ILobSystemInstance lobi =
          lob.GetLobSystemInstances()[lobSystemInstance];

        //Get Method Instance
        IMethodInstance mi = ect.GetMethodInstance(
          finderMethodInstance, MethodInstanceType.Finder);
        IEntityInstanceEnumerator items = ect.FindFiltered(
         mi.GetFilters(), finderMethodInstance, lobi,
         new OperationMode(CacheUsage.Cached, false));

        //Print them out
        while (items.MoveNext())
        {
            Microsoft.Office.Interop.Word.Range currentRange =
```

```
                    Globals.ThisAddIn.Application.Selection.Range;
                currentRange.Text = items.Current["FirstName"].ToString()
                    + " " + items.Current["LastName"].ToString() + ", ";
            }

            items.Close();
        }
        catch (Exception x)
        {
            MessageBox.Show(x.Message);
        }
    }
```

Creating a Custom Task Pane

In addition to customizing the ribbon, you can also add custom task panes to the Office application. Custom task panes enable you to create an interface with whatever controls you need and are an excellent means of integrating External System data with Office 2010 applications. Once again, you'll be able to use the BDC Client Runtime object model to perform operations.

Custom task panes are designed and built through user controls. You simply add a user control to your project and design whatever interface you need using available controls from the toolbox. As an example, Figure 6-14 shows a simple user control with a `ListBox` and a `Button`. Using these controls, the sample will display a list of entity instances and allow them to be inserted into a Word document.

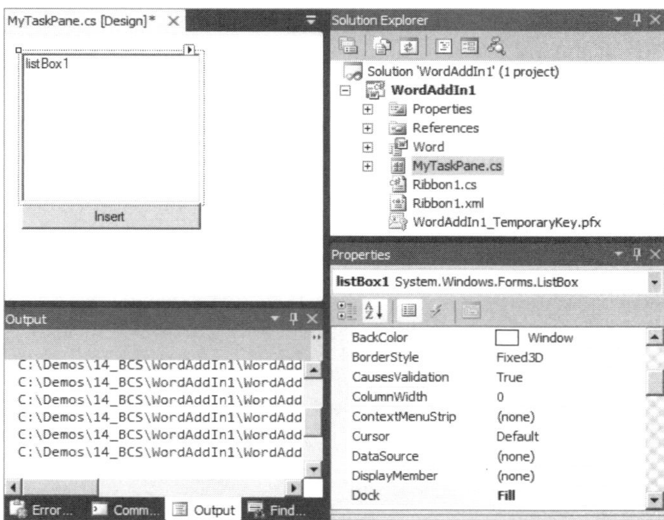

FIGURE 6-14

Writing the code for the add-in is straightforward. When the user control loads, the entity instances from the External System are loaded into the `ListBox`. The user can select an item from the list and insert it into the document by clicking the `Button`. In the click event, the code uses the Word object model to insert the selected text. The following is the code for the custom task pane:

```
private void MyTaskPane_Load(object sender, EventArgs e)
{

    try
    {
        string lobSystemInstance = "MiniCRM";
        string entityName = "Contact";
        string entityNamespace = "http:///bcs";
        string finderMethodInstance = "Read List";

        RemoteSharedFileBackedMetadataCatalog catalog =
          new RemoteSharedFileBackedMetadataCatalog();

        //Get entity
        IEntity ect = catalog.GetEntity(entityNamespace, entityName);

        //Get LobSystem
        ILobSystem lob = ect.GetLobSystem();

        //Get LobSystemInstance
        ILobSystemInstance lobi =
          lob.GetLobSystemInstances()[lobSystemInstance];

        //Get Method Instance
        IMethodInstance mi = ect.GetMethodInstance(
          finderMethodInstance, MethodInstanceType.Finder);
        IEntityInstanceEnumerator items = ect.FindFiltered(
         mi.GetFilters(), finderMethodInstance, lobi,
         new OperationMode(CacheUsage.Cached, false));

        //Add to list
        while (items.MoveNext())
        {
            listBox1.Items.Add(items.Current["FirstName"].ToString()
              + " " + items.Current["LastName"].ToString());
        }

        items.Close();
    }
    catch (Exception x)
    {
        MessageBox.Show(x.Message);
    }
}

private void insertButton_Click(object sender, EventArgs e)
{
    if (listBox1.SelectedIndex > -1)
    {
        Microsoft.Office.Interop.Word.Range currentRange =
          Globals.ThisAddIn.Application.Selection.Range;
```

```
            currentRange.Text = listBox1.SelectedItem.ToString();
        }
    }
```

Once the user control is designed and coded, you must write the code to display the custom task pane at runtime. You do this in the startup event of the add-in. In the `ThisAddIn_Startup` event, you create a `CustomTaskPane` object and add the user control. The following shows the code for loading the task pane at startup:

```
private MyTaskPane myTaskPane;

private void ThisAddIn_Startup(object sender, System.EventArgs e)
{
    myTaskPane = new MyTaskPane();
    Microsoft.Office.Tools.CustomTaskPane newTaskPane =
        this.CustomTaskPanes.Add(myTaskPane, "BCS");
    newTaskPane.Visible = true;
}
```

Packaging Data-Only Solutions

Because your BCS add-ins will be accessing the client cache, they will need to ensure that data gets synchronized between the External System and the cache. When you are working with simple no-code solutions, a subscription file is created and downloaded when the user clicks the Connect to Outlook button on the ribbon in SharePoint. When you create your own add-in, however, you need to create a subscription file to include with the solution. This type of package that includes a subscription file and an add-in is referred to as a *data-only solution* because no BCS add-in components are used.

Once the add-in is complete, create a subscription file as an XML file. There are two ways to create a subscription file. First, you can simply make it by hand, as discussed in Chapter 3. Second, you can use the BCS Artifact Generator Tool to generate a solution for the External System and simply copy the subscription file out of the artifact set. The following shows a sample subscription file for the solution:

```
<?xml version="1.0" encoding="utf-8"?>
<Subscription LobSystemInstanceName="MiniCRM"
 EntityNamespace="http://wingtipserver/bcs" EntityName="Contact"
 Name="ContactSubscription" View="Read Item" IsCached="true"
 RefreshIntervalInMinutes="360"
 xmlns="http://schemas.microsoft.com/office/2006/03/BusinessDataCatalog">
  <Queries>
    <Query Name="Read List" MethodInstanceName="Read List"
     DefaultDisplayName="Read List" RefreshIntervalInMinutes="180"
     IsCached="true" Enabled="true" />
  </Queries>
</Subscription>
```

You package the add-in solution with the BCS Solution Packaging Tool. You will need three files copied into a folder together. First export the BDC Metadata Model and rename it `metadata.xml`, as discussed earlier in the chapter. Second, copy the subscription file into the folder. Third, copy the compiled assembly for the add-in into the folder. Now start the BCS Solution Packaging Tool and select the option to make a "Data Solution for Office Add-in" from the Solution Type drop-down. All the artifacts will be packaged together in a ClickOnce package, which you can deploy to a document library, as discussed previously.

When you are deploying data-only solutions to Office clients, you will want to make sure that the related External Data is available in the cache before your add-in starts operating. You can check the status of the dependent data-only solution with the `Microsoft.Office.BusinessApplications.Runtime.Deployment.SolutionRegistry` class. This class has a `GetCurrentSolutionVersion()` method for retrieving information about the solution and a `GetPendingSolutionDeploymentStatus()` method for determining status. Both methods take the name of the solution as the argument.

In your add-in, you should create a function for checking the status of the data-only solution. This way, your add-in will know if the External Data is available. You may then choose how to respond based on the status. The following code shows a simple function that displays a `MessageBox` if the data-only solution is not yet deployed when the add-in starts:

```
public bool ValidateDataOnlySolution()
{

    //Validate the the correct version of the solution is installed
    string currentVersion =
     SolutionRegistry.GetCurrentSolutionVersion("MySolution");

    bool retVal = true;

    if (currentVersion != "2.5.0.0")
    {

        SolutionDeploymentStatus status =
         SolutionRegistry.GetPendingSolutionDeploymentStatus("MySolution");

        switch (status)
        {
            case SolutionDeploymentStatus.None:
                MessageBox.Show("Dependent BCS Data missing.");
                retVal = false;
                break;

            case SolutionDeploymentStatus.InstallationStarted:
                MessageBox.Show("Dependent BCS Data installing.");
                break;

            case SolutionDeploymentStatus.PendingActivation:
                SolutionRegistry.StartSolutionActivation("ExternalDMS");
                MessageBox.Show("Dependent BCS Data pending.");
                retVal = false;
                break;

            case SolutionDeploymentStatus.PendingDeactivation:
                MessageBox.Show("Dependent BCS Data missing.");
```

```
                retVal = false;
                break;

            case SolutionDeploymentStatus.InError:
                MessageBox.Show("Dependent BCS Data failed.");
                retVal = false;
                break;
        }

    }

    return retVal;
}
```

SUMMARY

While server-side solutions such as External Lists are powerful means of incorporating data into SharePoint, client-side solutions in BCS can significantly ease the work burden for information workers. Because information workers spend so much time copying data from External Systems and pasting it into documents, Outlook declarative solutions and custom add-ins can really save them time by incorporating data directly into documents and task panes.

In this chapter, you saw that Outlook declarative solutions enable you to create more sophisticated solutions for Microsoft Outlook. You also saw that custom Office add-ins can give you the complete power of the .NET Framework and the BDC Client Runtime object model. Both of these solutions are excellent means of helping end users get more from their business data.

7

Developing and Using Connectors

WHAT'S IN THIS CHAPTER?

- Learn to create .NET Assembly Connectors
- Learn to create Custom Connectors

Connectors are obviously a critical part of the BCS infrastructure because they allow operations to be performed on External Systems. The two connectors that ship with BCS — SQL and WCF — have been used in samples throughout the book. There are many situations, however, in which External Systems do not support access through the SQL or WCF connectors, such as when an External System is only accessible through a proprietary API. In other scenarios, you may wish to implement stereotypes that are not supported by the SharePoint Designer, custom business rules, error handling, or transactions. In these cases a connector must be developed using Visual Studio 2010.

DEVELOPING CONNECTORS

BCS supports the creation of two different types of connectors: a *Custom connector* and a *.NET Assembly Connector*. The term *Custom connector* is somewhat unfortunate because it sounds like a generic term but is actually a specific term referring to a connector that targets a given type of system. The .NET Assembly Connector, on the other hand, is a connector that targets a specific instance of a system. As a concrete example, you would create a custom connector to allow BCS to access Microsoft Exchange, but you would create a .NET Assembly Connector to allow BCS to access your particular instance of Microsoft Exchange. The difference is that the custom connector works against generic Microsoft Exchange servers, whereas the .NET Assembly Connector can handle the specific modifications made to a particular installation of Microsoft Exchange. Another way to think about the differences is that custom connectors are not bound to any particular ECT, whereas .NET Assembly Connectors are tightly bound to one.

Because a .NET Assembly Connector is bound to an ECT, you should create them only when the External System schema is fixed. If the schema is subsequently changed, the ECT and associated .NET Assembly Connector have to be modified, recompiled, and deployed to support the new schema. Because custom connectors are not tied to an ECT, they can handle schema changes in the External System without recompiling. The ECTs that use the custom connector obviously still need to be updated, but this can happen in SharePoint Designer with no recompilation.

While both the custom connector and the .NET Assembly Connector are well integrated into BCS, the .NET Assembly Connector generally has more support than the custom connector. .NET Assembly Connectors have their own project type in Visual Studio 2010, along with design tools and a complete deployment/debugging experience. Synchronization of External Lists based on .NET Assembly Connectors is fully supported in the same way as for any other External List. For these reasons, developers are likely to make many more .NET Assembly Connectors than custom connectors. Custom connectors are much more likely to be developed by third-party vendors that want to support BCS access to their systems.

CREATING .NET ASSEMBLY CONNECTORS

A .NET Assembly Connector associates a custom assembly with an ECT so that you can precisely control how information is accessed, processed, and returned from External Systems. You create a .NET Assembly Connector in Visual Studio 2010 using the Business Data Connectivity Model project type. Figure 7-1 shows the New Project dialog in Visual Studio 2010.

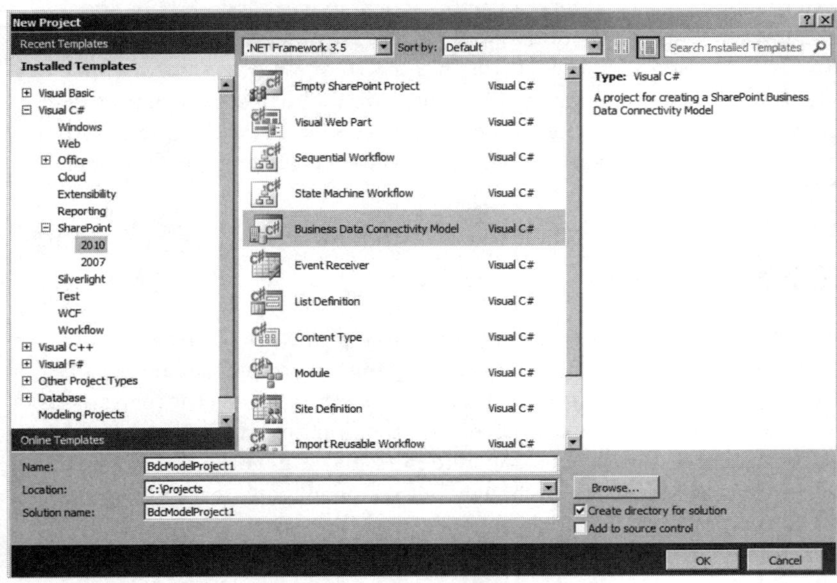

FIGURE 7-1

The Visual Studio Business Data Connectivity Model project template is a complete working sample project. Immediately after it is created you may hit F5 and make External Lists in SharePoint. This is a good start because the tooling can be somewhat confusing when you first use it; a complete working sample helps guide you to success. The detailed examination of the project template in the next section will help you understand.

Understanding the Project Tooling

When you're working with the Business Data Connectivity Model project template there are three explorers and designers available: the BDC Model Explorer, the Entity Design Surface, and the Method Details pane. The BDC Model Explorer is used to navigate the nodes of the BDC Metadata Model. The Entity Design Surface is used to design the ECT that will be associated with the .NET Assembly Connector. The Method Details pane is used to create the function signatures for ECT operations. Along with these three new elements, the Business Data Connectivity Model project template also gives you the standard windows such as the Solution Explorer and the Properties pane. Figure 7-2 shows the new tooling in Visual Studio 2010.

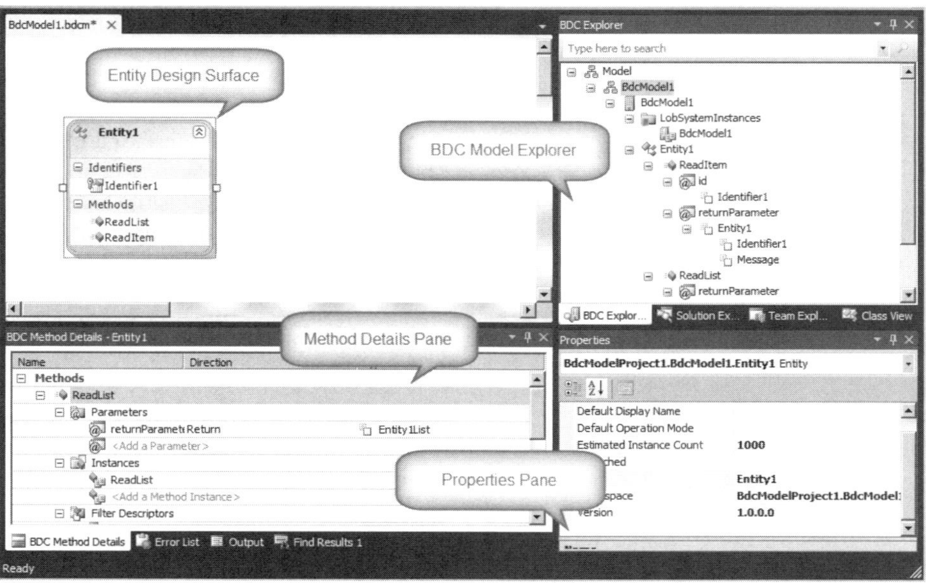

FIGURE 7-2

While the Visual Studio tooling is helpful, there are times when you must access the underlying BDC Metadata Model as XML, either for direct editing or simply to verify the work you have done using the tools. The BDC Metadata Model can be found in the Solution Explorer as the file with the `.bdcm` extension. You can open this file as XML by right-clicking it and selecting Open With from the context menu. In the Open With dialog you may then choose to open the file with the XML (Text) Editor.

In order to be successful with the tooling, you must understand how the various explorers and designers relate to the underlying model XML. Furthermore, you must understand what elements of the project are affected as you make changes. In particular, the BDC Model Explorer and the Method Details pane can be confusing if their relationships to the underlying XML are not well understood. Figure 7-3 shows the BDC Model Explorer labeled with the related XML elements.

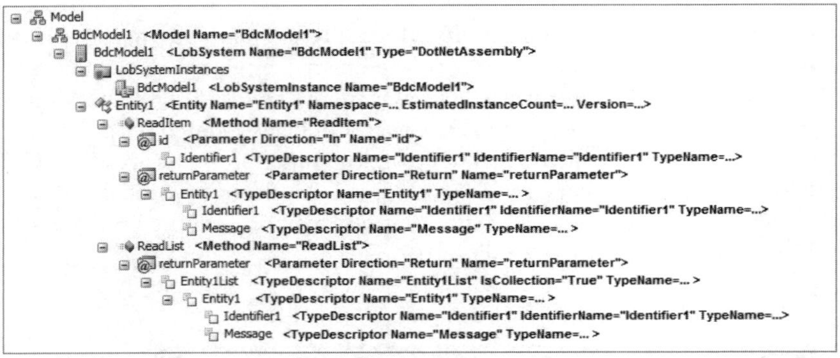

Model
BdcModel1 <Model Name="BdcModel1">
BdcModel1 <LobSystem Name="BdcModel1" Type="DotNetAssembly">
LobSystemInstances
BdcModel1 <LobSystemInstance Name="BdcModel1">
Entity1 <Entity Name="Entity1" Namespace=... EstimatedInstanceCount=... Version=...>
ReadItem <Method Name="ReadItem">
id <Parameter Direction="In" Name="id">
Identifier1 <TypeDescriptor Name="Identifier1" IdentifierName="Identifier1" TypeName=...>
returnParameter <Parameter Direction="Return" Name="returnParameter">
Entity1 <TypeDescriptor Name="Entity1" TypeName=... >
Identifier1 <TypeDescriptor Name="Identifier1" IdentifierName="Identifier1" TypeName=...>
Message <TypeDescriptor Name="Message" TypeName=... >
ReadList <Method Name="ReadList">
returnParameter <Parameter Direction="Return" Name="returnParameter">
Entity1List <TypeDescriptor Name="Entity1List" IsCollection="True" TypeName=... >
Entity1 <TypeDescriptor Name="Entity1" TypeName=... >
Identifier1 <TypeDescriptor Name="Identifier1" IdentifierName="Identifier1" TypeName=...>
Message <TypeDescriptor Name="Message" TypeName=... >

FIGURE 7-3

Figure 7-3 shows that not all of the underlying BDC Metadata Model can be represented in the BDC Model Explorer. In particular, the BDC Model Explorer shows methods but not method instances. The Method Details pane provides the interface necessary to define the method instances. Figure 7-4 shows the relationship between the items in the Method Details pane and the underlying XML.

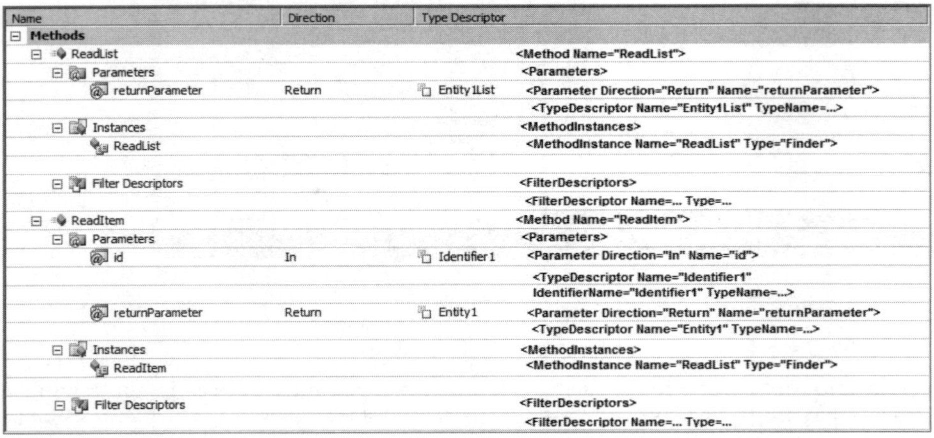

Name
Direction
Type Descriptor
Methods
ReadList <Method Name="ReadList">
Parameters <Parameters>
returnParameter Return Entity1List <Parameter Direction="Return" Name="returnParameter">
<TypeDescriptor Name="Entity1List" TypeName=...>
Instances <MethodInstances>
ReadList <MethodInstance Name="ReadList" Type="Finder">
Filter Descriptors <FilterDescriptors>
<FilterDescriptor Name=... Type=...
ReadItem <Method Name="ReadItem">
Parameters <Parameters>
id In Identifier1 <Parameter Direction="In" Name="id">
<TypeDescriptor Name="Identifier1" IdentifierName="Identifier1" TypeName=...>
returnParameter Return Entity1 <Parameter Direction="Return" Name="returnParameter">
<TypeDescriptor Name="Entity1" TypeName=...>
Instances <MethodInstances>
ReadItem <MethodInstance Name="ReadList" Type="Finder">
Filter Descriptors <FilterDescriptors>
<FilterDescriptor Name=... Type=...

FIGURE 7-4

The Entity Design Surface is also used to edit the underlying BDC Metadata Model. However, it is focused on the creation of entities. Using this tool, you can create new entities, assign the `Identifier`, and create new methods. Figure 7-5 shows how the Entity Design Surface maps to the underlying model.

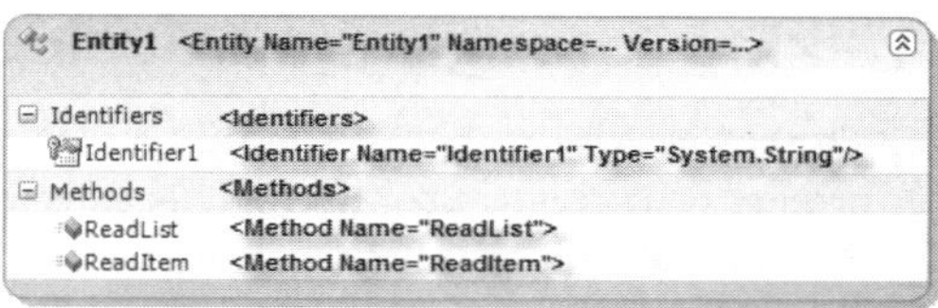

FIGURE 7-5

Regardless of which tool you are using, the Properties pane can be used to edit the selected node. The Properties pane lists the type of the node and its attributes. Although the nodes have many attributes, most of them are not required. It is not always clear, however, which attributes are required to implement any given node. The better you understand the model, the more likely you are to successfully create the one you need.

For the most part, the tooling is designed to edit the underlying BDC Metadata Model, with one exception. A class module is used to implement the method instances that you define in the model. This class module is created automatically and is always given the name of the entity followed by the word `Service`. This class is known as the *service class*. If you change the name of the entity in your model, the service class name will be updated automatically. If you delete the service class from the project, it will be recreated the next time you make any changes to the method definitions.

The methods implemented in the service class have types defined by the input and return parameters in the BDC Metadata Model. These types can be simple types or classes. Typically, however, the `Finder` and `SpecificFinder` methods will return classes that represent the ECT associated with the .NET Assembly Connector. In the Business Connectivity Model project template, a class named `Entity1.cs` is created by default and is returned from the `Finder` and `SpecificFinder` methods. These methods are also created by default when you create a project with the Business Connectivity Model project template.

Even though the project template includes a class that has the same name as the entity, there is actually no connection between the entity definition and the entity class. Changing the name of the entity in the model does not change the name of the class, and the class is never automatically generated. The class is really just a payload returned from the .NET Assembly Connector. Its name is meaningless, but it is a best practice to keep the name of the class synchronized with the name of the entity it represents. The methods in the service class return instances of the entity class, which are passed on to External Lists for display. In more advanced scenarios, you may choose to implement the entity classes in a separate project so that they can be easily referenced by custom web parts that will display the data.

The tooling is largely focused on defining and implementing methods as opposed to defining the data returned by the entity class. In the default project template, the entity has a data field named `Message`, which is defined as a `TypeDescriptor` with a `TypeName` of `System.String`. The entity class has a corresponding property whose value is set during the execution of the `Finder` or `SpecificFinder` methods. In order to add or modify data fields for the ECT, you must make changes to the model in the BDC Model Explorer and add new properties to the entity class. This is a manual process — the tooling will never automatically generate members for the entity class.

Walking through the Development Process

The easiest way to become familiar with the Visual Studio Business Data Connectivity Model project is to create a solution. This example will present and walk you through the complete development process for building a .NET Assembly Connector. It will make use of a subset of product and category data from the AdventureWorks database to create a connector that will allow full CRUD operations. As a starting point, an object relational model (ORM) was created over the database using the Entity Framework so that the .NET Assembly Connector can simply access the database through LINQ. Readers interested in learning more about the Entity Framework can find complete coverage on MSDN at `http://msdn.microsoft.com/en-us/library/bb399572.aspx`.

Creating a New Project

The first step in developing the connector is to create a new Business Data Connectivity Model project. While the default model created by the project template is valuable for learning about the tooling, it provides little help in developing a connector. For this reason, it is best to simply delete the default `Entity1` entity from the Entity Design Surface. Along with the entity, you should also delete the entity service class and the entity class from the Solution Explorer. This will leave you with a simple BDC Metadata Model that looks like the following XML, which you can view as text directly in Visual Studio:

```
<?xml version="1.0" encoding="utf-8"?>
<Model xmlns:xsi="http://www.w3.org/2001/XMLSchema-instance"
       xmlns:xsd="http://www.w3.org/2001/XMLSchema"
       xmlns="http://schemas.microsoft.com/windows/2007/BusinessDataCatalog"
       Name="ProductModel">
  <LobSystems>
    <LobSystem Name="ProductSystem" Type="DotNetAssembly">
      <LobSystemInstances>
        <LobSystemInstance Name="ProductSystemInstance" />
      </LobSystemInstances>
    </LobSystem>
  </LobSystems>
</Model>
```

The `LobSystem` element is a critical part of the model. Note how the element indicates that the system will be implemented through an assembly. This syntax differs significantly from that of the examples in previous chapters, which used databases and web services. This element is also used by both SPD and Visual Studio 2010 to determine whether or not to provide tooling support for a model. SPD does not provide tooling support for .NET Assembly Connectors, and Visual Studio provides tooling support only for .NET Assembly Connectors.

Also notice in the preceding XML that careful attention has been paid to naming the elements. The `Model`, `LobSystem`, and `LobSystemInstance` nodes have all been named appropriately. When you are creating connectors, naming is critical for maintaining clarity as the BDC Metadata Model becomes more complex. Remember to name elements correctly early in the development process. Renaming elements later can cause problems as described in the section entitled Packaging Considerations later in the chapter.

Creating a New Entity

Because the default entity was deleted, the next step is to add a new entity to the project. Entities can be added to the project from the toolbox, which has an Entity object that can be dragged onto the Entity Design Surface. When you add a new entity, you'll notice that a new service class is automatically created. Additionally, the Properties pane will present several properties that can be set. Here you will at least set the `Name` property for the entity. In this case, the entity is named `Product`.

The next step is to add the `Identifier` for the entity. The `Identifier` is the primary key by which a unique entity instance can be identified. You can create a new `Identifier` by right-clicking the entity and selecting Add ➪ Identifier. Using the Properties pane, you can set the name and data type for the `Identifier`. For the walkthrough, an `Identifier` named `ProductID` was created, with a data type of `System.Int32`. The following code shows the BDC Metadata Model for the entity:

```
<Entities>
  <Entity Name="Product" Namespace="AdventureworksConnector.ProductModel"
   Version="1.0.0.133" DefaultDisplayName="Adventureworks Product"
   DefaultOperationMode="Online" EstimatedInstanceCount="1000"
   IsCached="false">
    <Properties>
      <Property Name="Class" Type="System.String">
       AdventureworksConnector.ProductModel.ProductService,
       ProductSystem</Property>
    </Properties>
    <Identifiers>
      <Identifier Name="ProductID" TypeName="System.Int32" />
    </Identifiers>
  </Entity>
</Entities>
```

The next step is to create the entity class that will contain the data from the External System. Remember that Visual Studio does not automatically create an entity class, so you must add a new class manually. Within the class, you must add properties for each of the data fields you want to return. The following code shows the entity class created for the walkthrough:

```
namespace AdventureworksConnector
{
    public class Product
    {
        public int ProductID { get; set; }
        public string Name { get; set; }
        public string Number { get; set; }
        public string Color { get; set; }
        public decimal Price { get; set; }
        public string Description { get; set; }
    }
}
```

While the preceding entity class is fairly simple, there are a couple of things to point out. First, each of the properties in the class will correspond to a column in an External List. Second, the data is strongly typed; the types defined in the class are what are returned from the connector.

Creating a Finder Method

The next step is to create the methods for the entity. Returning to the Entity Design Surface, you may create new methods by right-clicking the entity and selecting Add ➪ Method. You may also create a new method in the Method Details pane, which is a better idea because Visual Studio defines the model for the stereotype when you start here. Remember that a method is just a stereotype and that you must create a method instance in order to implement the method. You can create a new method instance by clicking the Add Method Instance link in the Method Details pane. Once you have created the method instance you can specify the `Type` of the method instance in the Properties pane. Typically, your first method will be a `Finder` method. For the walkthrough, a `Finder` method named `ReadProducts` was created.

Once the method instance is defined, you must define its parameters. In the case of the default `Finder` method you will typically define a return parameter only. Other method instances may require input parameters as well as filters. You can create a new parameter by clicking the Add a Parameter message in the Method Details pane. Using the Properties pane, you can then change the parameter name and direction. For the walkthrough, a `Return` parameter named `ProductList` was created.

When a parameter is defined, Visual Studio automatically creates a `TypeDescriptor` for the parameter. The `TypeDescriptor` acts as a mapping between the data types found in the External System and the data types returned by the .NET Assembly Connector. Clicking the `TypeDescriptor` in the Method Details pane will enable you to define the `TypeName` for the `TypeDescriptor`. In the case of a `Finder` method, the `TypeDescriptor` is typically a collection of entity instances. Therefore, the `IsCollection` property should be set to `True` before you select the `TypeName`. Once the `TypeDescriptor` is designated as a collection, you can open the `TypeName` picker, click the Current Project tab, and select the `Product` class. Visual Studio automatically sets the return type to be a collection. Figure 7-6 shows the Type Name picker in Visual Studio.

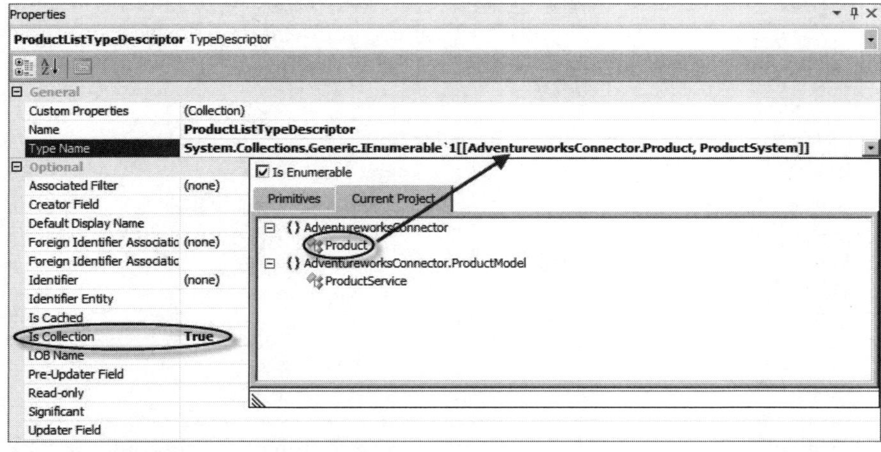

FIGURE 7-6

At this point you can open the code for the service class and see that Visual Studio has created a method whose signature is based on the method, parameter, and `TypeDescriptor` settings. However, our work is not yet done because the return `TypeDescriptor` was designated as a collection. Therefore a new `TypeDescriptor` must be added to represent the member of the collection. Additionally, each field in the collection member must be defined.

In order to create the additional `TypeDescriptors`, you will work in the BDC Model Explorer. In the Explorer, you can see the `TypeDescriptor` defining the collection. You may define a collection member by right-clicking the collection `TypeDescriptor` and selecting Add Type Descriptor from the context menu. This `TypeDescriptor` will have a `TypeName` of `Product`, but will not be a collection. Finally, you must add a `TypeDescriptor` for every property of the entity you want to return. Take care to set the `Identifier` property for the `TypeDescriptor` that represents the `Identifier` of the entity in order to designate this property as the one containing the `Identifier` value. Figure 7-7 shows the complete `Finder` method in the BDC Model Explorer.

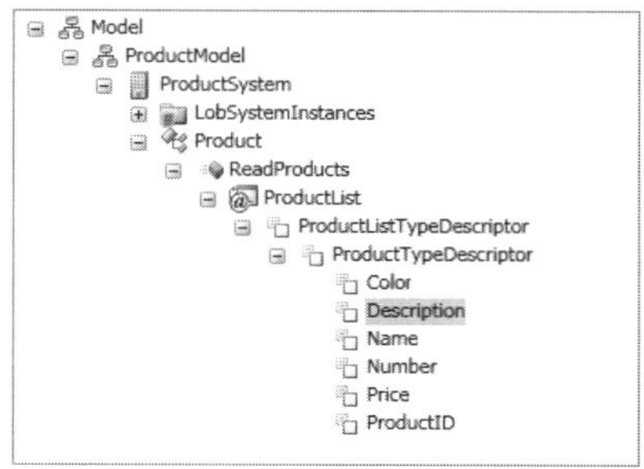

FIGURE 7-7

Finally, return to the Method Details pane and select the method instance for the `Finder`. In the Properties pane, set `Return Parameter Name` and `Return TypeDescriptor` to reference the items already created. This completes the definition of the `Finder`. The following code shows the completed `Finder` method definition in the BDC Metadata Model:

```
<Method Name="ReadProducts">
 <Parameters>
  <Parameter Name="ProductList" Direction="Return">
   <TypeDescriptor Name="ProductListTypeDescriptor"
    TypeName="System.Collections.Generic.IEnumerable`1[
    [AdventureworksConnector.ProductModel.Product, ProductSystem]]"
    IsCollection="true">
     <TypeDescriptors>
      <TypeDescriptor Name="ProductTypeDescriptor"
       TypeName="AdventureworksConnector.ProductModel.Product, ProductSystem"
       IsCollection="false">
        <TypeDescriptors>
         <TypeDescriptor Name="Name" TypeName="System.String" />
         <TypeDescriptor Name="Number" TypeName="System.String" />
         <TypeDescriptor Name="Color" TypeName="System.String" />
         <TypeDescriptor Name="Price" TypeName="System.Decimal"
          IsCollection="false" />
         <TypeDescriptor Name="Description" TypeName="System.String" />
        <TypeDescriptor Name="ProductID" TypeName="System.Int32"
         IsCollection="false" IdentifierName="ProductID" ReadOnly="true" />
       </TypeDescriptors>
      </TypeDescriptor>
     </TypeDescriptors>
    </TypeDescriptor>
```

```
      </Parameter>
    </Parameters>
    <MethodInstances>
     <MethodInstance Name="ReadProductsInstance" Type="Finder"
      ReturnParameterName="ProductList"
      ReturnTypeDescriptorPath="ProductListTypeDescriptor" />
    </MethodInstances>
   </Method>
```

Creating a SpecificFinder Method

Because the minimum requirements for an External List include a `Finder` and `SpecificFinder` method, the next step is to create the `SpecificFinder` method. You use the same procedure as for the `Finder` method, with two exceptions. First, the return type is a single entity instance as opposed to a collection. Second, `SpecificFinder` requires an input parameter that contains the `Identifier` of the entity instance to return. You must explicitly designate this input parameter as accepting an `Identifier` by setting the `Identifier` property.

As with the `Finder` method, you must also add a `TypeDescriptor` for every property of the entity you want to return and set the `Identifier` property for the `TypeDescriptor` that contains the `Identifier` value. In this case, however, you can simply copy the `TypeDescriptors` from the `Finder` method in the BDC Model Explorer and paste them under the `SpecificFinder` method. Figure 7-8 shows the complete `SpecificFinder` method in the BDC Model Explorer.

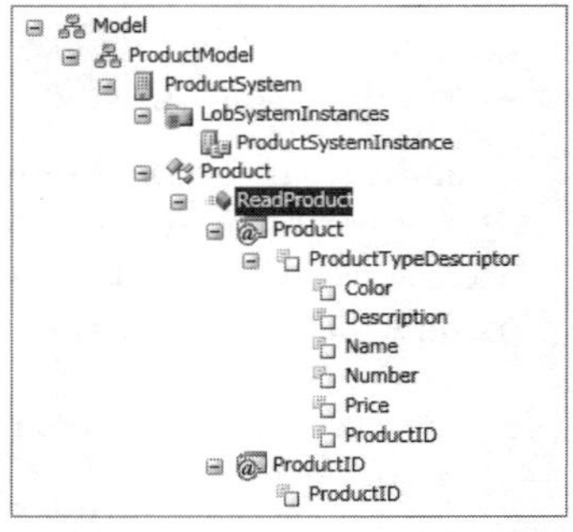

FIGURE 7-8

One last thing you must do is set the `Read-Only` property to `True` for the `TypeDescriptor` that represents the `Identifier`. You must do this because the `ProductID` is handled as an identity column in the database. The user cannot update the value for this field. Setting the `Read-Only` property ensures that the auto-generated forms in SharePoint will reflect the fact that the field cannot be changed. The following code shows the completed `SpecificFinder` method definition in the model:

```
<Method Name="ReadProduct">
 <Parameters>
  <Parameter Name="ProductID" Direction="In">
   <TypeDescriptor Name="ProductID" TypeName="System.Int32"
    IsCollection="false" IdentifierName="ProductID" />
  </Parameter>
  <Parameter Name="Product" Direction="Return">
   <TypeDescriptor Name="ProductTypeDescriptor"
    TypeName="AdventureworksConnector.Product, ProductSystem"
    IsCollection="false">
    <TypeDescriptors>
     <TypeDescriptor Name="Color" TypeName="System.String" />
     <TypeDescriptor Name="Description" TypeName="System.String" />
```

```
        <TypeDescriptor Name="Name" TypeName="System.String" />
        <TypeDescriptor Name="Number" TypeName="System.String" />
        <TypeDescriptor Name="Price" TypeName="System.Decimal"
         IsCollection="false" />
        <TypeDescriptor Name="ProductID" TypeName="System.Int32"
         IsCollection="false" IdentifierName="ProductID"
         ReadOnly="true" />
      </TypeDescriptors>
     </TypeDescriptor>
    </Parameter>
    </Parameters>
    <MethodInstances>
     <MethodInstance Name="ReadProductInstance" Type="SpecificFinder"
      ReturnParameterName="Product"
      ReturnTypeDescriptorPath="ProductTypeDescriptor" />
    </MethodInstances>
  </Method>
```

Handling Connection Information

At this point, the minimum required methods are defined, and you can turn your attention to implementing them in code. As a first order of business, you must consider how to handle connection information for the External System. The simplest way to store connection information is as a property in the BDC Metadata Model. You may add custom properties to any node in the BDC Metadata Model, and connection information is typically attached to the `LobSystemInstance` node.

In the BDC Explorer, you can select the `LobSystemInstance` node and then click the Custom Properties ellipsis in the Properties pane. This will open the Property editor dialog, where you can add a new custom property to hold the connection string. Figure 7-9 shows the custom property for the walkthrough and the BDC Metadata Model follows.

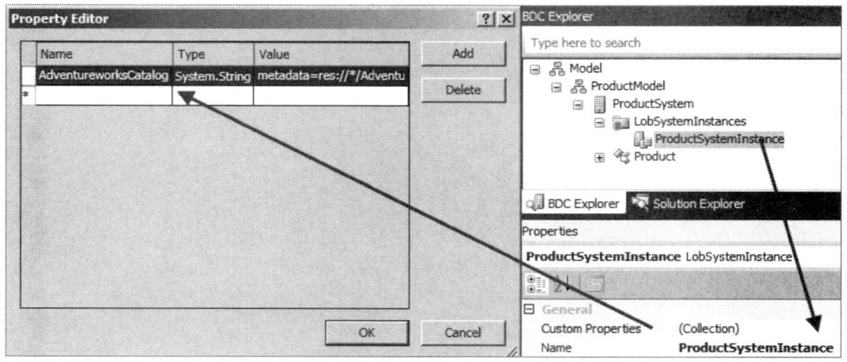

FIGURE 7-9

```
<LobSystemInstance Name="ProductSystemInstance">
 <Properties>
  <Property Name="AdventureworksCatalog" Type="System.String">
   Connection string goes here
  </Property>
 </Properties>
</LobSystemInstance>
```

Once the custom property is created, the service class can be modified to support reading the connection information. You start this process by setting a reference to the `Microsoft.BusinessData.dll` assembly located in the `ISAPI` folder beneath the SharePoint system directory. Once the reference is made, the service class must be updated to implement the `Microsoft.BusinessData.SystemSpecific.IContextProperty` interface.

You don't need to write any code in order to implement the interface, because the BDC Server Runtime takes care of managing the properties that must be set. You can, however, now use the interface to retrieve the property previously stored in the model. The following is the interface and connection information retrieval code:

```
internal string GetConnectionInfo()
{
    INamedPropertyDictionary props =
      this.LobSystemInstance.GetProperties();

    if (props.ContainsKey("AdventureworksCatalog"))
        return props["AdventureworksCatalog"].ToString();
    else
        return string.Empty;
}

public Microsoft.BusinessData.Runtime.IExecutionContext
       ExecutionContext
{
    get;
    set;
}

public Microsoft.BusinessData.MetadataModel.ILobSystemInstance
       LobSystemInstance
{
    get;
    set;
}

public Microsoft.BusinessData.MetadataModel.IMethodInstance
       MethodInstance
{
    get;
    set;
}
```

Implementing the Methods

Now that the connection information can be stored and retrieved, you can turn your attention to implementing the methods. This is a matter of writing the necessary code to return the data from the External System, but there are two changes that must be made to the service class first.

If you examine the code that Visual Studio generates in the project, you will notice that all the methods are `static`. This is because the .NET Assembly Connector will perform slightly better with `static` methods. However, once the `IContextProperty` interface is implemented, the class can no longer use the `static` methods. Therefore, the `static` keyword must be removed. The code generated by Visual Studio also uses `IEnumerable<T>` as the return type for the `Finder` method. If you want to be able to open the ECT in the SharePoint Designer, however, this must be changed to `IList<T>`.

Once the changes are made, the code for the methods can finally be added to the connector. After you finish and compile the code, the .NET Assembly Connector may be deployed. At this point, a new External List can be created. The following code shows the complete implementation for the methods, which uses LINQ queries against the Entity Framework layer discussed previously:

```
namespace AdventureworksConnector.ProductModel
{
    public partial class ProductService : IContextProperty
    {
        public IList<Product> ReadProducts()
        {
            AdventureworksCatalog catalog =
              new AdventureworksCatalog(GetConnectionInfo());

            var q = from p in catalog.Products
                    orderby p.ProductName
                    select p;

            List<Product> products = new List<Product>();

            foreach (var i in q)
            {
                products.Add(
                    new Product()
                    {
                        ProductID = i.ProductID,
                        Name = i.ProductName,
                        Number = i.ProductNumber,
                        Description = i.ProductDescription,
                        Color = i.ProductColor,
                        Price = i.ProductPrice
                    });
            }

            return products;
        }

        public Product ReadProduct(int ProductID)
        {
```

```
            AdventureworksCatalog catalog =
              new AdventureworksCatalog(GetConnectionInfo());

            var q = from p in catalog.Products
                    where p.ProductID == ProductID
                    select p;

            if (q.Count() == 1)
            {
                return new Product()
                {
                    ProductID = q.First().ProductID,
                    Name = q.First().ProductName,
                    Number = q.First().ProductNumber,
                    Description = q.First().ProductDescription,
                    Color = q.First().ProductColor,
                    Price = q.First().ProductPrice
                };
            }
            else
                return null;
        }
    }
}
```

Adding Creator, Updater, and Deleter Methods

In order for the .NET Assembly Connector to be fully functional, it must have methods to create, update, and delete items. You can create new methods by clicking the Add a Method link in the Method Details pane. As stated previously, when you start from the Method Details pane, Visual Studio generates model elements appropriate for the method.

The `Creator` method takes an entity instance as an input and returns a new entity instance. The input entity instance is simply a container for the new values, with the exception of the `Identifier`, because that value is created in the External System. Each field that contains information necessary for the creation of the new item has a `CreatorField` property set to `True`. The following code shows the `Creator` method model definition:

```
<Method Name="CreateProduct">
 <Parameters>
  <Parameter Name="ProductOut" Direction="Return">
   <TypeDescriptor Name="ProductOutTypeDescriptor"
    IsCollection="false"
    TypeName="AdventureworksConnector.ProductModel.Product, ProductSystem">
    <TypeDescriptors>
     <TypeDescriptor Name="Color" TypeName="System.String" />
     <TypeDescriptor Name="Description" TypeName="System.String" />
     <TypeDescriptor Name="Name" TypeName="System.String" />
     <TypeDescriptor Name="Number" TypeName="System.String" />
     <TypeDescriptor Name="Price"
      IsCollection="false" TypeName="System.Decimal" />
```

```
        <TypeDescriptor Name="ProductID" IdentifierName="ProductID"
         IsCollection="false" TypeName="System.Int32" />
      </TypeDescriptors>
    </TypeDescriptor>
  </Parameter>
  <Parameter Name="ProductIn" Direction="In">
    <TypeDescriptor Name="ProductTypeDescriptor"
     IsCollection="false"
     TypeName="AdventureworksConnector.Product, ProductSystem">
      <TypeDescriptors>
        <TypeDescriptor Name="Color" TypeName="System.String"
         CreatorField="true" />
        <TypeDescriptor Name="Description" TypeName="System.String"
         CreatorField="true" />
        <TypeDescriptor Name="Name" TypeName="System.String"
         CreatorField="true" />
        <TypeDescriptor Name="Number" TypeName="System.String"
         CreatorField="true" />
        <TypeDescriptor Name="Price" IsCollection="false"
         TypeName="System.Decimal" CreatorField="true" />
      </TypeDescriptors>
    </TypeDescriptor>
  </Parameter>
 </Parameters>
 <MethodInstances>
  <MethodInstance Name="CreateProductInstance" Type="Creator"
   ReturnParameterName="ProductOut"
   ReturnTypeDescriptorPath="ProductOutTypeDescriptor" />
 </MethodInstances>
</Method>
```

The `Updater` method takes an entity instance as an input. The input entity instance is the entity to update. Each field that contains information necessary to update the item in the External System has an `UpdaterField` property set to `True`. The following code shows the `Updater` method model definition:

```
<Method Name="UpdateProduct">
 <Parameters>
  <Parameter Name="ProductIn" Direction="In">
   <TypeDescriptor Name="ProductTypeDescriptor" IsCollection="false"
    TypeName="AdventureworksConnector.ProductModel.Product, ProductSystem">
    <TypeDescriptors>
     <TypeDescriptor Name="Color" TypeName="System.String"
      UpdaterField="true" />
     <TypeDescriptor Name="Description" TypeName="System.String"
      UpdaterField="true" />
     <TypeDescriptor Name="Name" TypeName="System.String"
      UpdaterField="true" />
     <TypeDescriptor Name="Number" TypeName="System.String"
      UpdaterField="true" />
     <TypeDescriptor Name="Price" IsCollection="false"
      TypeName="System.Decimal" UpdaterField="true" />
     <TypeDescriptor Name="ProductID" TypeName="System.Int32"
```

```
        IsCollection="false" ReadOnly="false" UpdaterField="true" />
      </TypeDescriptors>
    </TypeDescriptor>
   </Parameter>
  </Parameters>
  <MethodInstances>
   <MethodInstance Name="UpdateProductInstance" Type="Updater" />
  </MethodInstances>
</Method>
```

Although it is less likely that you will want to allow end users to edit the `Identifier` of an entity instance, you can do this in the `Updater` method. In order for the `Identifier` to be updated, the `Updater` method must accept a separate parameter containing the new value for the `Identifier`. This parameter must have the `PreUpdaterField` property set to `True`. The following code shows the BDC Metadata Model for the parameter and the resulting function signature:

```
<Parameter Name="NewProductID" Direction="In">
 <TypeDescriptor Name="ProductID" TypeName="System.Int32"
  IsCollection="false" PreUpdaterField="true"
  IdentifierName="ProductID" />
</Parameter>


public void UpdateProduct(Product ProductIn, int NewProductID){}
```

The `Deleter` method takes an `Identifier` as an input. The `Identifier` is the entity to delete. The following code shows the `Deleter` method model definition:

```
<Method Name="DeleteProduct">
 <Parameters>
  <Parameter Name="ProductID" Direction="In">
   <TypeDescriptor Name="ProductID" TypeName="System.Int32"
    IdentifierEntityName="Product"
    IdentifierEntityNamespace="AdventureworksConnector.ProductModel"
    IdentifierName="ProductID" />
  </Parameter>
 </Parameters>
 <MethodInstances>
  <MethodInstance Name="DeleteProduct" Type="Deleter" />
 </MethodInstances>
</Method>
```

Visual Studio offers you a list of several methods to create and will even build out the correct function signature for you. The only modification you must make is to remove the `static` keyword from the signatures. Then the methods can be implemented with the following code:

```
public Product CreateProduct(Product ProductIn)
{
    AdventureworksCatalog catalog =
     new AdventureworksCatalog(GetConnectionInfo());
    AdventureworksData.Product newProduct = new AdventureworksData.Product()
```

```
        {
            ProductName = ProductIn.Name,
            ProductNumber = ProductIn.Number,
            ProductColor = ProductIn.Color,
            ProductPrice = ProductIn.Price,
            ProductDescription = ProductIn.Description
        };

        catalog.AddToProducts(newProduct);
        catalog.SaveChanges();

        ProductIn.ProductID = newProduct.ProductID;
        return ProductIn;
    }

    public void UpdateProduct(Product ProductIn)
    {
        AdventureworksCatalog catalog =
         new AdventureworksCatalog(GetConnectionInfo());

        AdventureworksData.Product product =
         catalog.Products.First(p => p.ProductID == ProductIn.ProductID);

        product.ProductName = ProductIn.Name;
        product.ProductNumber = ProductIn.Number;
        product.ProductColor = ProductIn.Color;
        product.ProductDescription = ProductIn.Description;
        product.ProductPrice = ProductIn.Price;

        catalog.SaveChanges();
    }

    public void DeleteProduct(int ProductID)
    {
        AdventureworksCatalog catalog =
         new AdventureworksCatalog(GetConnectionInfo());
        AdventureworksData.Product product =
         catalog.Products.First(p => p.ProductID == ProductID);
        catalog.DeleteObject(product);
        catalog.SaveChanges();
    }
```

Adding a StreamAccessor Method

The .NET Assembly Connector supports any of the available method stereotypes listed in Chapter 4, in addition to the basic CRUD methods. Because of this support, .NET Assembly Connectors are often written solely to implement stereotypes not available in SPD. A good example of one of these additional methods is the `StreamAccessor`. The `StreamAccessor` method is used to return a `Stream` from the .NET Assembly Connector typically associated with a file. In the walkthrough, the External System contained a photo for each product. A `StreamAccessor` can be used to return the photo. The input parameter is the `Identifier`, and the output parameter is the `Stream`. The following code shows the BDC Metadata Model for the `StreamAccessor` method definition:

```
<Method Name="ReadPhoto">
 <Parameters>
  <Parameter Name="ProductID" Direction="In">
   <TypeDescriptor Name="ProductID" TypeName="System.Int32"
    IdentifierName="ProductID" IsCollection="false" />
  </Parameter>
  <Parameter Name="Photo" Direction="Return">
   <TypeDescriptor Name="PhotoTypeDescriptor" TypeName="System.Stream" />
  </Parameter>
 </Parameters>
 <MethodInstances>
  <MethodInstance Name="ReadPhotoInstance" Type="StreamAccessor"
   ReturnParameterName="Photo"
   ReturnTypeDescriptorPath="PhotoTypeDescriptor" />
  </MethodInstances>
</Method>
```

Implementing a `StreamAccessor` is a matter of reading the file contents and returning them as a `Stream`. In this case, the file is kept as a BLOB in the database. The following code shows how the method was implemented in the walkthrough:

```
public Stream ReadPhoto(int ProductID)
{
    AdventureworksCatalog catalog =
     new AdventureworksCatalog(GetConnectionInfo());

    var q = from p in catalog.Products
            where p.ProductID == ProductID
            select p;

    if (q.Count() == 1)
    {
        byte[] buffer = q.First().ProductPhoto;
        return new MemoryStream(buffer);
    }
    else
        return null;
}
```

As discussed in Chapter 2, `StreamAccessor` methods are not supported in External Lists, but they are supported in the External Data web parts. Of course, you can also use the BDC Runtime API to call the method in your own custom code as well. Entities that expose a `StreamAccessor` will show a hyperlink in the External Data web part that will allow a download of the file. This hyperlink opens the `DownloadExternalData.aspx` page, sending in a set of query string parameters to invoke the `StreamAccessor` method for the correct entity instance. The `MIMETypeField` and `MIMEType` properties of the `MethodInstance` element can be used to specify the MIME type of the ECT, which determines the application that will be used to open the document.

Creating Associations between Entities

In production systems, you will undoubtedly define multiple ECTs, and these ECTs will have relationships among themselves. In the walkthrough, each product was assigned to a category, so it makes sense that there should be a new ECT to represent the category and that it should be related to the `Product`. To get started, a new entity named `Category` was created, along with the `Finder` and `SpecificFinder` methods. The process of creating the new ECT is identical to the process of creating the `Product` entity.

In addition to the new `Category` entity's being created, the `Product` entity must be updated to contain the `CategoryID` of the associated category. The model, entity class, and service class will all require changes to support the new `CategoryID` field. The changes, however, are straightforward and similar to those required by the other fields defined in the entity.

Once the entities are defined, you can define an association using the Association item in the toolbox. This item works a little differently from most toolbox items. Instead of dragging and dropping the shape, you must click the shape in the toolbox. Then you can click the one (parent) entity and drag an association to the many (child) entity.

When you create the association, Visual Studio will present the Association Editor dialog. In this dialog, you must map each `TypeDescriptor` that represents the foreign key from the many (child) entity to the one (parent) entity. In the walkthrough, each of the `TypeDescriptors` representing the `CategoryID` in the `Product` entity was mapped to the `CategoryID` `Identifier` in the `Category` entity.

The Association Editor creates a one-to-many and a reverse association by default. The one-to-many association returns all child entity instances for a given parent, and the reverse association returns the parent entity instance for a given child. In the case of the walkthrough, only the one-to-many association was retained; the reverse association was deleted. Figure 7-10 shows the Association Editor dialog for this example.

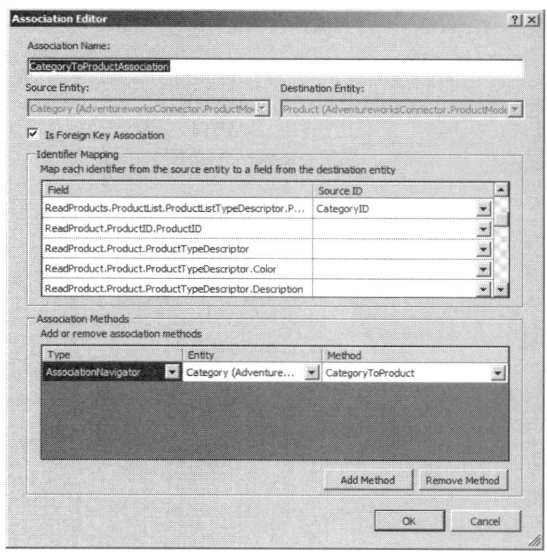

FIGURE 7-10

When the Association Editor dialog is closed, the underlying model will be updated with `AssociationNavigator` methods. These methods pass in an `Identifier` and return associated entities. In the walkthrough, a `Category Identifier` was passed in and multiple `Product` entity instances were returned. The following code shows the resulting model XML:

```
<Method Name="CategoryToProduct">
 <Parameters>
  <Parameter Name="categoryID" Direction="In">
   <TypeDescriptor Name="CategoryID" TypeName="System.Int32"
    IdentifierEntityName="Category"
```

```
    IdentifierEntityNamespace="AdventureworksConnector.ProductModel"
    IdentifierName="CategoryID"
    ForeignIdentifierAssociationEntityName="Category"
    ForeignIdentifierAssociationEntityNamespace=
      "AdventureworksConnector.ProductModel"
    ForeignIdentifierAssociationName=
      "CategoryToProductAssociationNavigator" />
  </Parameter>
  <Parameter Name="productList" Direction="Return">
   <TypeDescriptor Name="ProductList"
   TypeName="System.Collections.Generic.IEnumerable`1[
   [AdventureworksConnector.ProductModel.Product, ProductSystem]]"
   IsCollection="true">
    <TypeDescriptors>
     <TypeDescriptor Name="Product" IsCollection="false"
      TypeName="AdventureworksConnector.ProductModel.Product, ProductSystem">
       <TypeDescriptors>
        <TypeDescriptor Name="Color" TypeName="System.String" />
        <TypeDescriptor Name="Description" TypeName="System.String" />
        <TypeDescriptor Name="Name" TypeName="System.String" />
        <TypeDescriptor Name="Number" TypeName="System.String" />
        <TypeDescriptor Name="Price" IsCollection="false"
         TypeName="System.Decimal" />
        <TypeDescriptor Name="ProductID" IsCollection="false"
         ReadOnly="true" TypeName="System.Int32"
         IdentifierEntityName="Product"
         IdentifierEntityNamespace="AdventureworksConnector.ProductModel"
         IdentifierName="ProductID" />
        <TypeDescriptor Name="CategoryID"
         IdentifierEntityNamespace="AdventureworksConnector.ProductModel"
         IdentifierEntityName="Category" IdentifierName="CategoryID"
         ForeignIdentifierAssociationEntityNamespace=
          "AdventureworksConnector.ProductModel"
         ForeignIdentifierAssociationEntityName="Category"
         ForeignIdentifierAssociationName=
          "CategoryToProductAssociationNavigator"
         IsCollection="false" TypeName="System.Int32" />
       </TypeDescriptors>
      </TypeDescriptor>
     </TypeDescriptors>
    </TypeDescriptor>
   </Parameter>
  </Parameters>
 <MethodInstances>
  <Association Name="CategoryToProductAssociationNavigator"
   Type="AssociationNavigator" ReturnParameterName="productList"
   ReturnTypeDescriptorPath="ProductList">
  <SourceEntity Name="Category"
   Namespace="AdventureworksConnector.ProductModel" />
  <DestinationEntity Name="Product"
   Namespace="AdventureworksConnector.ProductModel" />
  </Association>
 </MethodInstances>
</Method>
```

Function stubs are created in the service class for each of the AssociationNavigator methods. Implementing these methods requires executing the necessary code to return the required entities. The following code shows the implementation for the walkthrough:

```
public IList<Product> CategoryToProduct(int categoryID)
{
    AdventureworksCatalog catalog =
     new AdventureworksCatalog(GetConnectionInfo());

    var q = from p in catalog.Products
            where p.CategoryID == categoryID
            orderby p.ProductName
            select p;

    List<Product> products = new List<Product>();

    foreach (var i in q)
    {
        products.Add(
            new Product()
            {
                ProductID = i.ProductID,
                Name = i.ProductName,
                Number = i.ProductNumber,
                Description = i.ProductDescription,
                Color = i.ProductColor,
                Price = i.ProductPrice,
                CategoryID = i.CategoryID
            });
    }

    return products;
}
```

Understanding Non–Foreign Key Relationships

While it is common to have associations between entities through foreign keys, that is not always the case. The situation in which you're most likely to find a non–foreign key relationship is that of a many-to-many relationship. A database may be designed, for example, to keep the relationships in a separate table so that they are not directly available through a foreign key.

In addition to the AssociationNavigator methods, you may need to include Associator and Disassociator methods. These are intended to modify the data in the External System that manages the relationship. The methods, for example, can be used to modify the table that contains a many-to-many relationship in the database.

As a quick sidebar example, consider an External System that relates people to action items. A table named Resources maintains information about the people, while a table named ActionItems maintains tasks. In the system design, many tasks can be assigned to a single resource and many resources can be assigned to a single task. Your application will want to show the tasks assigned to a given resource and show the resources assigned to a given task. In this case, you will use the

Association Editor but uncheck the Is Foreign Key Association checkbox. Additionally, you will add `Associator` and `Disassociator` methods.

The `Associator` and `Disassociator` methods have two input parameters. These are the `Identifiers` of the entity instances to associate or disassociate. In code, you can use these values to modify the table defining the many-to-many relationship. The following code shows the BDC Metadata Model for the `Associator` method:

```
<Method Name="AssociateResourceToTask">
 <Parameters>
  <Parameter Name="resourceID" Direction="In">
   <TypeDescriptor Name="ResourceID" TypeName="System.Int32"
    IdentifierEntityName="Resource"
    IdentifierEntityNamespace="ActionItems.ActionItemsModel"
    IdentifierName="ResourceID"
    ForeignIdentifierAssociationEntityName="Resource"
    ForeignIdentifierAssociationEntityNamespace="ActionItemsModel"
    ForeignIdentifierAssociationName="AssociateResourceToTaskAssociator" />
  </Parameter>
  <Parameter Name="taskID" Direction="In">
   <TypeDescriptor Name="TaskID" TypeName="System.Int32"
    IdentifierEntityName="Task"
    IdentifierEntityNamespace="ActionItemsModel"
    IdentifierName="TaskID" />
  </Parameter>
 </Parameters>
 <MethodInstances>
  <Association Name="AssociateResourceToTaskAssociator" Type="Associator">
   <SourceEntity Name="Resource" Namespace="ActionItemsModel" />
   <DestinationEntity Name="Task" Namespace="ActionItemsModel" />
  </Association>
 </MethodInstances>
</Method>
```

Testing the Connector

Once the .NET Assembly Connector is complete, it may be deployed and tested. Using the connector developed in the walkthrough, you should be able to create External Lists and use the External Data Web Parts. The associations between the entities should result in appropriate pickers appearing when entity instances are created or edited. As with all features created in Visual Studio 2010, you can easily debug the .NET Assembly Connector by setting breakpoints in the code and pressing F5.

CREATING CUSTOM CONNECTORS

A custom connector is a single assembly that works with multiple ECTs. The purpose of the custom connector is to enable you to simply change the BDC Metadata Model when the schema of the External System changes. Unlike with the .NET Assembly Connector, no code changes are required to the custom connector assembly when schema changes occur. Custom connectors are useful when you want to create a connector for a generic system type and allow others to create the specific BDC Metadata Model.

Understanding Project Elements

Custom connectors are created in Visual Studio 2010, but there are no integrated tools for creating them. However, it is possible to start with a Business Data Connectivity Model project and modify it to become a custom connector. While most of the project tooling will not work with custom connectors, you can gain the benefits of packaging, deployment, and debugging using the Visual Studio Tools for SharePoint.

The process for starting a new custom connector involves first creating a Business Data Connectivity Model project. After the new project is created, you can delete the entity from the Entity Design Surface. You can then open the project XML as text and change the `Type` attribute in the `LobSystem` element to `Custom`. The following code shows a sample of the resulting BDC Metadata Model. In particular, note the `Type` attribute in the `LobSystem` element:

```
<?xml version="1.0" encoding="utf-8"?>
<Model xmlns:xsi="http://www.w3.org/2001/XMLSchema-instance"
 xmlns:xsd="http://www.w3.org/2001/XMLSchema"
 xmlns="http://schemas.microsoft.com/windows/2007/BusinessDataCatalog"
 Name="MyModel">
  <LobSystems>
    <LobSystem Name="MySystem" Type="Custom">
      <LobSystemInstances>
        <LobSystemInstance Name="MySystemInstance" />
      </LobSystemInstances>
    </LobSystem>
  </LobSystems>
</Model>
```

Along with the model, you will also create an assembly to implement the connector and execute methods. The starter code that is created for a .NET Assembly Connector has no use in a custom connector. Therefore, both the entity class and the service class can simply be deleted from the project.

At this point you will have a feature that can be used to deploy the model and associated assembly to SharePoint. Changing the `Type` attribute of the model prevents the Entity Design Surface and Method Details panes from functioning. You will, however, be able to use the BDC Model Explorer. Additionally, you will get model validation when you compile the project. For the most part you will find that you must create the model by hand, so strong knowledge of the BDC Metadata Model schema is critical for success.

Walking through the Development Process

As with the .NET Assembly Connector, the best way to learn to create a custom connector is by walking through a sample project. This sample will create a custom connector that can be used to read elements and attributes from an XML file. The concept is to create a connector that can read a collection of elements from any XML file, regardless of its structure or location. When the custom connector is completed, you will be able to read different files by simply creating a new BDC Metadata Model. For this walkthrough a simple XML file containing product data is used to start. The following code shows the structure of the XML:

```
<?xml version="1.0" encoding="utf-8" ?>
<Products>
  <Product ProductID="1" ProductName="Mountain Bike"/>
  <Product ProductID="2" ProductName="Skateboard" />
</Products>
```

Starting the Project

In order to get started you perform the steps outlined earlier for creating a new .NET Assembly Connector project. This gives you the starting point for the BDC Metadata Model. Next you can add a class to the project that will implement the custom connector functionality. For the walkthrough, a new class named `Connector` is added. Finally, the underlying BDC Metadata Model needs to be updated to associate the connector class with the model using the `SystemUtilityTypeName` property of the `LobSystem` element and the `SystemUtilityInstallDate`. The following XML shows the model with the assembly referenced, although no code has yet been added to the assembly:

```
<?xml version="1.0" encoding="utf-8"?>
<Model xmlns:xsi="http://www.w3.org/2001/XMLSchema-instance"
 xmlns:xsd="http://www.w3.org/2001/XMLSchema"
 xmlns="http://schemas.microsoft.com/windows/2007/BusinessDataCatalog"
 Name="XMLProductModel">
 <LobSystems>
  <LobSystem Name="XMLProduct" Type="Custom">
   <Properties>
    <Property Name="SystemUtilityTypeName"
     Type="System.String">
     XMLConnector.Connector,
     XMLConnector,Version=1.0.0.0,Culture=neutral,
     PublicKeyToken=0d0e9d91635dcb0c
    </Property>
    <Property Name="SystemUtilityInstallDate" Type="System.DateTime">
     2010-05-25 00:00:00Z
   </Property>
   </Properties>
  </LobSystem>
 </LobSystems>
</Model>
```

Handling Connection Information

Just like the .NET Assembly Connector, the custom connector should store its connection information within the BDC Metadata Model. For this example, the connection information is the path to the XML file that you want to read. This value is added as a custom property of the `LobSystemInstance` element. The following code shows the XML definition for the `LobSystemInstance` element:

```
<LobSystemInstances>
 <LobSystemInstance Name="XMLProductInstance" >
  <Properties>
   <Property Name="XMLDataSource" Type="System.String">
    C:\Products.xml
   </Property>
  </Properties>
 </LobSystemInstance>
</LobSystemInstances>
```

The connector will read the `XMLDataSource` property at runtime. You can see already that if you create additional models, they can reference the same custom assembly but different data sources. This shows the flexibility of the custom connector.

Defining the Entity

The next step is to define the entity in the model. The most important part of the entity definition is the `Identifier`. As in any BCS model, the `Identifier` is the primary key to each entity instance. In this example, the connector assumes that the name of the `Identifier` is also the name of an available attribute inside the XML data file. This design restriction makes the development of new Metadata Models slightly easier. For the walkthrough, the `Identifier` is `ProductID`. The following code shows the model definition for the entity:

```
<Entities>
 <Entity Namespace="http://www.aw.com/training" Version="1.0.0.0"
  EstimatedInstanceCount="100" Name="Product"
  DefaultDisplayName="Adventureworks Product">
  <Identifiers>
   <Identifier TypeName="System.String" Name="ProductID" />
  </Identifiers>
 </Entity>
</Entities>
```

Defining the Finder Method

Once the entity is defined, the first method to create is the `Finder` method. Like all methods, the `Finder` method must define a set of parameters and `TypeDescriptors` for the signature. Additionally, a method instance must be defined. The following code shows the `Finder` method definition for the walkthrough:

```
<Method Name="Read Products" DefaultDisplayName="Read Products">
 <Properties>
  <Property Name="EntityElement" Type="System.String">Product</Property>
 </Properties>
 <Parameters>
  <Parameter Direction="Return" Name="Product List">
   <TypeDescriptor
    TypeName="Microsoft.BusinessData.Runtime.DynamicType[]"
    Name="Nodes" IsCollection ="true">
    <TypeDescriptors>
     <TypeDescriptor
```

```
          TypeName="Microsoft.BusinessData.Runtime.DynamicType" Name="Node">
          <TypeDescriptors>
           <TypeDescriptor Name="ProductID" DefaultDisplayName="Product ID"
            TypeName="System.String" IdentifierName="ProductID"
            ReadOnly="true" />
           <TypeDescriptor Name="ProductName"
            DefaultDisplayName="Product Name" TypeName="System.String" />
          </TypeDescriptors>
         </TypeDescriptor>
        </TypeDescriptors>
       </TypeDescriptor>
      </Parameter>
     </Parameters>
     <MethodInstances>
      <MethodInstance Type="Finder" ReturnParameterName="Product List"
       Default="true" Name="Read List" DefaultDisplayName="Read Products" />
     </MethodInstances>
    </Method>
```

The definition of the `Finder` method has several interesting elements that are new. The first is the `EntityElement` property. This property is used to specify the entity within the XML file that will be returned. The custom connector is designed to return a collection of XML elements from the source file, and this property tells the connector which one to get. You could use a different design in your custom connector, but all connectors will use properties such as this to handle configuration information. The connector will read the `EntityElement` property value at runtime.

The next interesting element in the model is the `Return` parameter. The design of the `Finder` method is to have no input parameters and a single return parameter that is the collection of XML elements. Notice, however, that the `Return` parameter has a `TypeName` of `Microsoft.BusinessData.Runtime.DynamicType[]`. The `DynamicType` class has a structure that can be created at runtime. This is critical because the whole point of the custom connector is to handle data sources with different schemas.

Using the `DynamicType` class, you can define the return schema on the fly and support all manner of different data sources. The actual schema will be constructed based on the `TypeDescriptors` defined in the method. The design of the custom connector is such that it expects the names of the `TypeDescriptors` to be the same as the names of the attributes that must be returned from the XML file. Note that the model has `ProductID` and `ProductName TypeDescriptors`, which have the same names as the attributes in the source XML file. Again, your design could be different, but all custom connectors will need to make some assumptions about the relationship of the model to the data source or provide detailed mapping capabilities through custom properties in the Metadata Model.

Implementing the Finder Method

Now that the `Finder` method is modeled, it can be implemented in the connector class. Coding the connector begins with setting a reference to the `Microsoft.BusinessData.dll` assembly. This assembly contains the interfaces that the custom connector will implement.

The only interface that a custom connector must implement is the `Microsoft.BusinessData.Runtime.ISystemUtility` interface. This interface has two members: `ExecuteStatic()` and `CreateEntityInstanceDataEnumerator()`. The `ExecuteStatic()` method takes an `IMethodInstance` object, an `ILobSystemInstance` object, an `Object` array of arguments, and an `IExecutionContext` object. This is the method that the custom connector implements to execute the methods defined in the model. The `CreateEntityInstanceDataEnumerator()` method converts a data stream from the External System into an enumerator.

Implementing the `ExecuteStatic()` method is reasonably straightforward. The custom connector receives information about the system elements defined in the model, along with arguments being passed to the method instance. The implementation code uses these arguments to operate on the data source. The following code shows the implementation of the `ExecuteStatic()` method with only the `Finder` method defined:

```
public void ExecuteStatic(
            IMethodInstance methodInstance,
            ILobSystemInstance lobSystemInstance,
            object[] methodSignatureArgs,
            IExecutionContext context)
  {
    if (methodInstance == null)
        throw (new ArgumentNullException("methodInstance"));
    if (lobSystemInstance == null)
        throw (new ArgumentNullException("lobSystemInstance"));
    if (methodSignatureArgs == null)
        throw (new ArgumentNullException("args"));

    //Get properties
    string xmlDataSource =
      lobSystemInstance.GetProperties()["XMLDataSource"] as string;
    string entityElement =
      methodInstance.GetMethod().GetProperties()["EntityElement"] as string;

    //Implement Methods
    switch (methodInstance.MethodInstanceType)
    {
        case MethodInstanceType.Finder:
            ExecuteFinder(methodInstance,
                          xmlDataSource,
                          entityElement,
                          methodSignatureArgs);
            break;

        default:
            throw new Exception("Method Instance Type not implemented.");
    }
  }
```

Notice that after validating the input arguments, the connector reads the `XMLDataSource` and `EntityElement` properties from the model XML. These are the configuration elements that allow the connector to work with XML files having different schemas and locations. Next the code determines what type of method stereotype was invoked. In this case, all `Finder` methods are handled through a call to `ExecuteFinder()`. Your design could certainly be more complex and have different implementations for different `Finder` methods. The following code shows the `ExecuteFinder()` method:

```
private void ExecuteFinder(IMethodInstance methodInstance,
                           string XMLDataSource,
                           string EntityElement,
                           object[] args)
{
    List<DynamicType> returnValues = new List<DynamicType>();
    XDocument dataSource = XDocument.Load(XMLDataSource);

    var q = from e in dataSource.Descendants(EntityElement)
            select e;

    foreach (var i in q)
    {
        DynamicType dt = new DynamicType();

        foreach (XAttribute a in i.Attributes())
        {
            dt.Add(a.Name.ToString(), a.Value);
        }

        returnValues.Add(dt);
    }

    args[0] = returnValues;
}
```

Note that the `ExecuteFinder()` method does not have a return value. Instead, the return value is saved into the first element in the `Object` array. This is because the `Object` array has a member for each of the parameters defined in the method. The order of the members is the same as the order in which they are defined in the model. In this case there is only one parameter, which is the `Return` parameter.

Next, note that the return parameter is a collection of `DynamicType` objects. Remember that `DynamicType` objects can have their structures defined at runtime. You do this in the code by adding a key/value pair for each attribute in the XML data file. The end result is that a collection is returned based on the targeted entity element and containing all the attributes found in the XML file.

Defining the SpecificFinder Method

Creating the `SpecificFinder` method in the BDC Metadata Model is similar to creating the `Finder` method, except that an `Identifier` parameter must be defined so that exactly one entity instance is returned. Because a single entity instance is returned, only a single `DynamicType` is used as the `Return` parameter, as opposed to an array.

Additionally, this custom connector is going to support editing the `Identifier` value, so we must plan ahead by ensuring that none of the return values are marked as `ReadOnly`. Marking return fields as `ReadOnly` in the `SpecificFinder` method will prevent them from being edited in SharePoint-generated forms. The following code shows the BDC Metadata Model for the `SpecificFinder` method. If you compare it to the `SpecificFinder` created for the .NET Assembly Connector project, you'll see the varying uses of the `ReadOnly` property:

```
<Method Name="Read Product" DefaultDisplayName="Read Product">
 <Properties>
  <Property Name="EntityElement" Type="System.String">Product</Property>
 </Properties>
 <Parameters>
  <Parameter Direction="In" Name="ProductID">
   <TypeDescriptor TypeName="System.String"
    IdentifierName="ProductID" Name="ProductID" />
  </Parameter>
  <Parameter Direction="Return" Name="Product">
   <TypeDescriptor
    TypeName="Microsoft.BusinessData.Runtime.DynamicType"
    Name="Node">
    <TypeDescriptors>
     <TypeDescriptor Name="ProductID" DefaultDisplayName="Product ID"
      TypeName="System.String" IdentifierName="ProductID" ReadOnly="true" />
     <TypeDescriptor Name="ProductName" DefaultDisplayName="Product Name"
      TypeName="System.String" />
    </TypeDescriptors>
   </TypeDescriptor>
  </Parameter>
 </Parameters>
 <MethodInstances>
  <MethodInstance Type="SpecificFinder" ReturnParameterName="Product"
   Default="true" Name="Read Product" DefaultDisplayName="Read Product" />
 </MethodInstances>
</Method>
```

Implementing the SpecificFinder Method

Implementing the `SpecificFinder` method is similar to implementing the `Finder` method with the exception that the connector must use the `Identifier` value passed in to retrieve exactly one entity instance. The biggest challenge in implementing `SpecificFinder` is to determine which attribute in the source XML represents the `Identifier`.

Again, the design of the connector is such that it assumes that the name of the parameter is the same as the name of an attribute. Therefore, the connector must find the parameter in the model that is tagged as the `Identifier` and use that to create a query on the data source. The following code shows how to loop through the `TypeDescriptors` and find the one that is the `Identifier`:

```
private string GetIdentifier(IMethodInstance methodInstance)
{
  string identifier = string.Empty;

  foreach (IParameter param in methodInstance.GetMethod().GetParameters())
```

```
        {
          if (param.GetRootTypeDescriptor().ContainsIdentifier)
          {
              if (param.GetRootTypeDescriptor().IsIdentifierSet)
              {
                identifier = param.GetRootTypeDescriptor().GetIdentifier().Name;
                  break;
              }
              else
              {
                foreach (ITypeDescriptor td in
                         param.GetRootTypeDescriptor().GetChildTypeDescriptors())
                {
                  if (td.IsIdentifierSet)
                    identifier = td.GetIdentifier().Name;
                }
              }
            }
          }
        return identifier;
      }
```

Once the name of the attribute that corresponds to the identifier is returned, it can be used to execute the `SpecficFinder` method. The `ExecuteStatic` method is also updated to call the `GetIdentifier()` method on startup and to call the `ExecuteSpecificFinder()` method if the type of the method instance is `SpecificFinder`. The following code shows the implementation of the `SpecificFinder` method. Note how `args[0]` contains the `Identifier` and `args[1]` contains the return value; this corresponds to the order in which they were defined in the BDC Metadata Model:

```
private void ExecuteSpecificFinder(IMethodInstance methodInstance,
                                   string XMLDataSource,
                                   string EntityElement,
                                   string identifier,
                                   object[] args)
{
    XDocument dataSource = XDocument.Load(XMLDataSource);

    var q = from e in dataSource.Descendants(EntityElement)
            where e.Attribute(identifier).Value == args[0].ToString()
            select e;

      DynamicType dt = new DynamicType();

      foreach (XAttribute a in q.First().Attributes())
      {
          dt.Add(a.Name.ToString(), a.Value);
      }

      args[1] = dt;
}
```

Defining the Creator Method

The `Creator` method defines a set of input parameters for each of the fields in the data source. Each `TypeDescriptor` associated with an input parameter is tagged by means of the `CreatorField` attribute. After the new item is created, it is returned from the `Creator` method. The following code shows the model XML for the `Creator` method. Note that `ProductID` is not tagged as `ReadOnly` because our solution allows it to be edited:

```
<Method Name="Create Product" DefaultDisplayName="Create Product">
 <Properties>
  <Property Name="EntityElement" Type="System.String">Product</Property>
 </Properties>
 <Parameters>
  <Parameter Direction="In" Name="InProductID">
   <TypeDescriptor Name="ProductID" DefaultDisplayName="Product ID"
    TypeName="System.String" CreatorField="true"
    IdentifierName="ProductID"  />
  </Parameter>
  <Parameter Direction="In" Name="InProductName">
   <TypeDescriptor Name="ProductName"
    DefaultDisplayName="Product Name"
    TypeName="System.String" CreatorField="true" />
  </Parameter>
  <Parameter Direction="Return" Name="OutProduct">
   <TypeDescriptor
    TypeName="Microsoft.BusinessData.Runtime.DynamicType" Name="Node">
    <TypeDescriptors>
     <TypeDescriptor Name="ProductID" DefaultDisplayName="Product ID"
      TypeName="System.String" IdentifierName="ProductID" />
     <TypeDescriptor Name="ProductName" DefaultDisplayName="Title"
      TypeName="System.String" />
    </TypeDescriptors>
   </TypeDescriptor>
  </Parameter>
 </Parameters>
 <MethodInstances>
  <MethodInstance Type="Creator" ReturnParameterName="OutProduct"
   Name="Create Product" Default="true"
   DefaultDisplayName="Create Product" />
 </MethodInstances>
</Method>
```

Implementing the Creator Method

Implementing the `Creator` method is moderately complex because the TypeDescriptors in the BDC Metadata Model must determine the schema for the data source. This involves looping through the `TypeDescriptors` for the input parameters and setting values in the data source. The following code shows the implementation. Note how the code checks to see if the proposed `ID` is already in use:

```
private void ExecuteCreator(IMethodInstance methodInstance,
                            string XMLDataSource,
                            string EntityElement,
                            string identifier,
                            object[] args)
{
    //Connect to data source
    XDocument dataSource = XDocument.Load(XMLDataSource);

    //Check to see if new ID is in use
    var q1 = from e in dataSource.Descendants(EntityElement)
             where e.Attribute(identifier).Value == args[0].ToString()
             select e;

    if (q1.Count() > 0)
        throw new Exception("ID already in use.");

    //Get all of the In TypeDescriptors by name
    var tds = from p in methodInstance.GetMethod().GetParameters()
              where p.Direction == DirectionType.In
              select new { p.GetRootTypeDescriptor().Name };

    //Create a new element
    XElement newElement = new XElement(EntityElement);

    //Set the attribute values for the new element
    int i = -1;
    foreach (var td in tds)
    {
        i++;
        newElement.Add(new XAttribute(td.Name, args[i].ToString()));
    }

    //Save new element
    dataSource.Descendants(EntityElement).Ancestors()
              .First().Add(newElement);
    dataSource.Save(XMLDataSource);

    //Get the newly-created element and return it
    var q = from e in dataSource.Descendants(EntityElement)
            where e.Attribute(identifier).Value == args[0].ToString()
            select e;

    if (q.First() != null)
    {
        DynamicType dt = new DynamicType();

        foreach (XAttribute a in q.First().Attributes())
        {
            dt.Add(a.Name.ToString(), a.Value);
        }

        args[args.Count() - 1] = dt;
    }
}
```

As with previous method implementations, the custom connector assumes that the names of the `TypeDescriptors` are the same as the names of the attributes in the data source. Once a query is written to return the name of the `TypeDescriptors` associated with the input parameters, you can create the new element by assigning attributes the values of the input parameters. Once the new element is created in the data source, a query can be written to return it from the method call.

Defining the Updater Method

The `Updater` method defines a set of input parameters for each of the fields in the data source. There is no `Return` parameter for the method because the `Finder` method will be called after the item is updated. The following code shows the BDC Metadata Model for the `Updater` method:

```
<Method Name="Update Product" DefaultDisplayName="Update Product">
 <Properties>
  <Property Name="EntityElement" Type="System.String">Product</Property>
 </Properties>
 <Parameters>
  <Parameter Direction="In" Name="NewProduct">
   <TypeDescriptor
    TypeName="Microsoft.BusinessData.Runtime.DynamicType" Name="Node">
    <TypeDescriptors>
     <TypeDescriptor Name="ProductID" DefaultDisplayName="Product ID"
      TypeName="System.String" IdentifierName="ProductID"
      UpdaterField="true" />
     <TypeDescriptor Name="ProductName" DefaultDisplayName="Title"
      TypeName="System.String" UpdaterField="true" />
    </TypeDescriptors>
   </TypeDescriptor>
  </Parameter>
  <Parameter Direction="In" Name="InProductID">
  <TypeDescriptor Name="ProductID" DefaultDisplayName="Product ID"
   TypeName="System.String" PreUpdaterField="true" />
  </Parameter>
 </Parameters>
 <MethodInstances>
  <MethodInstance Type="Updater" Name="Update Product" Default="true"
   DefaultDisplayName="Update Product" />
 </MethodInstances>
</Method>
```

The `Updater` method is particularly interesting in this walkthrough because the custom connector allows the `Identifier` for the entity to be updated. In most External Systems, the `Identifier` is managed by the system. In the .NET Assembly Connector example, for instance, the `Identifier` was created as an identity field in the database. Therefore the `Identifier` was tagged in the `SpecificFinder` method as `ReadOnly`, which prevented it from being edited in the `Updater` method. There are times, however, when you may need to allow the `Identifier` to be updated.

In order to support updating of the `Identifier`, you must first ensure that neither the `Finder` nor `SpecificFinder` methods has tagged the `Identifier` as `ReadOnly`. This was done earlier in the walkthrough when these methods were defined. The next step is to define an input parameter that supports all the fields for the item, including the `Identifier`. The associated `TypeDescriptors` must be tagged with the `UpdaterField` property set to `True`. At this point, the `Identifier` can be edited.

The challenge with editing the `Identifier` is that you need both its old value and its new value. The old value is used to find the `Identifier` in the data source, and the new value is used to update it. In order to support this function, you must add an additional input parameter to the `Updater` method that is tagged with the `PreUpdaterField` property. This parameter will always contain the current value of the `Identifier`. Note how this is accomplished in the Metadata Model.

Implementing the Updater Method

The key to implementing the `Updater` method is to retrieve both the current and future values of the `Identifier`. The current value is used to retrieve the item from the data source, and the future value is then set. Along the way, you also need to make sure that the future value of the `Identifier` is not in use already and throw an error if it is. The following code shows the implementation for the `Updater` method:

```
private void ExecuteUpdater(IMethodInstance methodInstance,
                            string XMLDataSource,
                            string EntityElement,
                            string identifier,
                            object[] args)
{
    //Get TypeDescriptors for In Parameter
    ITypeDescriptor rootTd =
     (from p in methodInstance.GetMethod().GetParameters()
      where p.Direction == DirectionType.In &&
      p.GetRootTypeDescriptor().GetChildTypeDescriptors().Count > 0
      select p).First().GetRootTypeDescriptor();

    //Retrieve In Parameter values
    DynamicType dt = args[0] as DynamicType;
    string newID = dt[rootTd.GetChildTypeDescriptors().
      Where(td => td.ContainsIdentifier).First().Name].ToString();
    string oldID = args[1] as string;

    //Check to see if new ID is in use
    XDocument dataSource = XDocument.Load(XMLDataSource);

    var q1 = from e in dataSource.Descendants(EntityElement)
             where e.Attribute(identifier).Value == newID
             select e;

    if (q1.Count() > 0)
        throw new Exception("ID already in use.");

    //Get item to update
    var q2 = from e in dataSource.Descendants(EntityElement)
             where e.Attribute(identifier).Value == oldID
             select e;
```

```
        //Update the item
        foreach (var td in rootTd.GetChildTypeDescriptors())
        {
            if (!td.ContainsIdentifier)
               q2.First().Attribute(td.Name).Value = dt[td.Name].ToString();
            else
            {
                q2.First().Attribute(td.Name).Value = newID;
                oldID = newID;
            }
        }

        //Save changes
        dataSource.Save(XMLDataSource);

    }
```

Defining the Deleter Method

The `Deleter` method is straightforward. It uses the `Identifier` to select the item to delete. The following code shows the BDC Metadata Model:

```
<Method Name="Delete Product" DefaultDisplayName="Delete Module">
 <Properties>
  <Property Name="EntityElement" Type="System.String">Product</Property>
 </Properties>
 <Parameters>
  <Parameter Direction="In" Name="ProductID">
   <TypeDescriptor TypeName="System.String"
    IdentifierName="ProductID" Name="ProductID" />
  </Parameter>
 </Parameters>
 <MethodInstances>
  <MethodInstance Type="Deleter" Default="true"
   Name="Delete Product" DefaultDisplayName="Delete Product" />
 </MethodInstances>
</Method>
```

Implementing the Deleter Method

The code implementation of the `Deleter` method is straightforward. The value of the `Identifier` is used to delete the item from the data source. The following code shows the implementation of the `Deleter` method:

```
private void ExecuteDeleter(IMethodInstance methodInstance,
                              string XMLDataSource,
                              string EntityElement,
                              string identifier,
                              object[] args)
{
    //Delete the element
```

```
        //Assumes one In parameter, which is identifier to delete

        XDocument dataSource = XDocument.Load(XMLDataSource);

        var q = from e in dataSource.Descendants(EntityElement)
                where e.Attribute(identifier).Value == args[0].ToString()
                select e;

        q.First().Remove();
        dataSource.Save(XMLDataSource);
    }
```

Creating Configurable Connection Properties

Custom connectors can expose configurable properties that show in the Central Administration site so that they can be edited by administrators. In the walkthrough, two configurable properties have been defined: `SystemUtilityTypeName` and `SystemUtilityInstallDate`. `SystemUtilityTypeName` refers to the type that implements the connector, and `SystemUtilityInstallDate` refers to the date that the model was put online. The custom connector exposes configurable connection properties by implementing the `Microsoft.BusinessData.Runtime.IAdministrableSystem` interface.

Using this interface, you can build a collection of properties to display. Figure 7-11 shows how the properties appear in Central Administration and the implementation code follows.

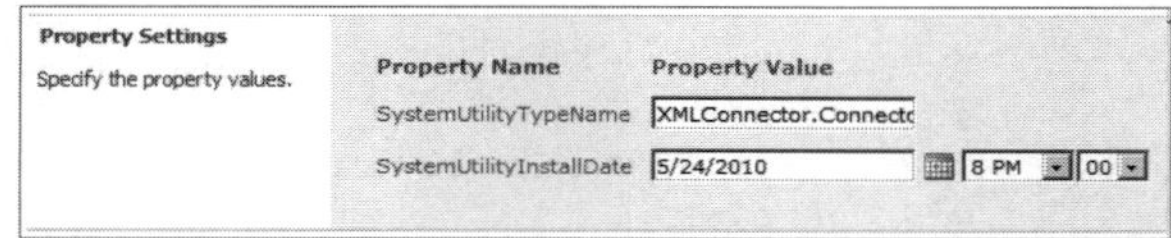

FIGURE 7-11

```
    public IList<AdministrableProperty> AdministrableLobSystemProperties
    {
        get
        {
            return new List<AdministrableProperty>()
            {
                new AdministrableProperty(
                 "SystemUtilityTypeName",
                 "Name of assembly",
                 typeof(string),"SystemUtilityTypeName",
                 typeof(string),true),
                new AdministrableProperty(
                 "SystemUtilityInstallDate",
                 "Date assembly was installed",
                 typeof(DateTime),
                 "SystemUtilityInstallDate", typeof(DateTime),false)
            };
        }
    }
```

Specifying a Connection Manager

The BDC service normally provides a connection manager for every External System instance. The connection manager is used for getting connections to External Systems and maintaining a pool for efficiency. If you want, you can provide your own connection manager by implementing the `Microsoft.BusinessData.Infrastructure.IConnectionManager` interface.

In the walkthrough, the custom connector implements `IConnectionManager` but always returns `NULL` when a connection is requested. This is because the connection to the individual file is accomplished within the method execution code. The connector does not maintain a pool of connections. Your design may be different.

Using the Custom Connector

Once the custom connector is complete, it may be deployed to SharePoint. The custom connector assembly must be installed in the GAC, and the BCS model must be loaded into the BDC service. If you followed the steps to create the custom connector from a Business Data Connectivity Model project, you can deploy directly from Visual Studio 2010. The assembly and model will be deployed correctly. Once the assembly and model are deployed, you may immediately create External Lists based on the ECTs defined in the model. Debugging the connector is a simple matter of connecting to the `w3wp.exe` process and setting breakpoints.

One thing you will notice if you deploy the custom connector in the walkthrough is that the default edit form in SharePoint does not support modifying the `Identifier`. This is certainly strange because the model was carefully designed to support this scenario. Unfortunately the default edit form does not respect the definition of the `Updater` method that allows the `Identifier` to be modified. The workaround is to upgrade the forms to use InfoPath. When you create InfoPath forms for the External Lists, the `Identifier` field will be editable.

The great advantage of the custom connector, of course, is that once it is deployed, you may create new models that use the same custom connector. As an example, consider building an External List based on `Reseller` data in a new XML file, such as the one in the following code:

```
<?xml version="1.0" encoding="utf-8" ?>
<Resellers>
  <Reseller ResellerID="1" ResellerName="A Bike Store"/>
  <Reseller ResellerID="2" ResellerName="Progessive Sports" />
</Resellers>
```

In order to build a model that will work with this new file, you have to define a new entity whose parameters have the names of attributes in the XML. You also need to make changes to the `XMLDataSource` property and the `EntityElement` property. However, you do not need to make any changes to the code in the custom connector. The structure of the `DynamicType` will be created at runtime to match the structure of the source XML file. This idea can now be extended to any element in any XML file. The following code shows the Metadata Model for the new ECT:

```
<Entities>
 <Entity Namespace="http://www.aw.com/training" Version="1.0.0.0"
  EstimatedInstanceCount="100" Name="Reseller"
  DefaultDisplayName="Adventureworks Reseller">
  <Identifiers>
   <Identifier TypeName="System.String" Name="ResellerID" />
  </Identifiers>
  <Methods>
```

```
<Method Name="Read Resellers" DefaultDisplayName="Read Resellers">
 <Properties>
  <Property Name="EntityElement" Type="System.String">Reseller</Property>
 </Properties>
 <Parameters>
  <Parameter Direction="Return" Name="Reseller List">
   <TypeDescriptor TypeName="Microsoft.BusinessData.Runtime.DynamicType[]"
    Name="Nodes" IsCollection ="true">
    <TypeDescriptors>
     <TypeDescriptor TypeName="Microsoft.BusinessData.Runtime.DynamicType"
      Name="Node">
      <TypeDescriptors>
       <TypeDescriptor Name="ResellerID" DefaultDisplayName="Reseller ID"
        TypeName="System.String" IdentifierName="ResellerID"/>
       <TypeDescriptor Name="ResellerName"
        DefaultDisplayName="Reseller Name" TypeName="System.String" />
      </TypeDescriptors>
     </TypeDescriptor>
    </TypeDescriptors>
   </TypeDescriptor>
  </Parameter>
 </Parameters>
 <MethodInstances>
  <MethodInstance Type="Finder" ReturnParameterName="Reseller List"
   Default="true" Name="Read List" DefaultDisplayName="Read Resellers" />
 </MethodInstances>
</Method>
<Method Name="Read Reseller" DefaultDisplayName="Read Reseller">
 <Properties>
  <Property Name="EntityElement" Type="System.String">Reseller</Property>
 </Properties>
 <Parameters>
  <Parameter Direction="In" Name="ResellerID">
  <TypeDescriptor TypeName="System.String" IdentifierName="ResellerID"
   Name="ResellerID" />
 </Parameter>
 <Parameter Direction="Return" Name="Reseller">
  <TypeDescriptor TypeName="Microsoft.BusinessData.Runtime.DynamicType"
   Name="Node">
    <TypeDescriptors>
     <TypeDescriptor Name="ResellerID" DefaultDisplayName="Reseller ID"
      TypeName="System.String" IdentifierName="ResellerID"/>
     <TypeDescriptor Name="ResellerName"
      DefaultDisplayName="Reseller Name"
      TypeName="System.String" />
    </TypeDescriptors>
   </TypeDescriptor>
  </Parameter>
 </Parameters>
 <MethodInstances>
 <MethodInstance Type="SpecificFinder" ReturnParameterName="Reseller"
  Default="true" Name="Read Reseller"
  DefaultDisplayName="Read Reseller" />
 </MethodInstances>
</Method>
```

```
<Method Name="Create Reseller" DefaultDisplayName="Create Reseller">
 <Properties>
  <Property Name="EntityElement" Type="System.String">Reseller</Property>
 </Properties>
 <Parameters>
  <Parameter Direction="In" Name="InResellerID">
   <TypeDescriptor Name="ResellerID" DefaultDisplayName="Reseller ID"
    TypeName="System.String" CreatorField="true"
    IdentifierName="ResellerID"  />
  </Parameter>
  <Parameter Direction="In" Name="InResellerName">
   <TypeDescriptor Name="ResellerName" DefaultDisplayName="Reseller Name"
    TypeName="System.String" CreatorField="true" />
  </Parameter>
  <Parameter Direction="Return" Name="OutReseller">
   <TypeDescriptor TypeName="Microsoft.BusinessData.Runtime.DynamicType"
    Name="Node">
    <TypeDescriptors>
     <TypeDescriptor Name="ResellerID" DefaultDisplayName="Reseller ID"
      TypeName="System.String" IdentifierName="ResellerID" />
     <TypeDescriptor Name="ResellerName" DefaultDisplayName="Title"
      TypeName="System.String" />
    </TypeDescriptors>
   </TypeDescriptor>
  </Parameter>
 </Parameters>
 <MethodInstances>
  <MethodInstance Type="Creator" ReturnParameterName="OutReseller"
   Name="Create Reseller" Default="true"
   DefaultDisplayName="Create Reseller" />
 </MethodInstances>
</Method>
<Method Name="Update Reseller" DefaultDisplayName="Update Reseller">
 <Properties>
  <Property Name="EntityElement" Type="System.String">Reseller</Property>
 </Properties>
 <Parameters>
  <Parameter Direction="In" Name="NewReseller">
   <TypeDescriptor TypeName="Microsoft.BusinessData.Runtime.DynamicType"
    Name="Node">
    <TypeDescriptors>
     <TypeDescriptor Name="ResellerID" DefaultDisplayName="Reseller ID"
      TypeName="System.String" IdentifierName="ResellerID"
      UpdaterField="true" />
     <TypeDescriptor Name="ResellerName" DefaultDisplayName="Title"
      TypeName="System.String" UpdaterField="true" />
    </TypeDescriptors>
   </TypeDescriptor>
  </Parameter>
  <Parameter Direction="In" Name="InResellerID">
   <TypeDescriptor Name="ResellerID" DefaultDisplayName="Reseller ID"
    TypeName="System.String" PreUpdaterField="true" />
  </Parameter>
 </Parameters>
```

```
        <MethodInstances>
         <MethodInstance Type="Updater" Name="Update Reseller" Default="true"
          DefaultDisplayName="Update Reseller" />
         </MethodInstances>
        </Method>
       <Method Name="Delete Reseller" DefaultDisplayName="Delete Moduele">
        <Properties>
         <Property Name="EntityElement" Type="System.String">Reseller</Property>
        </Properties>
        <Parameters>
         <Parameter Direction="In" Name="ResellerID">
          <TypeDescriptor TypeName="System.String" IdentifierName="ResellerID"
           Name="ResellerID" />
         </Parameter>
        </Parameters>
        <MethodInstances>
         <MethodInstance Type="Deleter" Default="true" Name="Delete Reseller"
          DefaultDisplayName="Delete Reseller" />
         </MethodInstances>
        </Method>
       </Methods>
      </Entity>
    </Entities>
```

HANDLING ERRORS IN CONNECTORS

Connectors must deal with several categories of errors that can occur during operations. Specifically, a connector may have a runtime error, such as a failure to connect with the External System. It may also fail data validation in the connector code or External System. Additionally, the connector may fail because of a concurrency conflict between multiple users updating the same entity instance. Fortunately both custom connectors and .NET Assembly Connectors take the same approach to handling these problems.

Handling Runtime and Validation Errors

Handling runtime and validation errors in connectors is straightforward because unhandled errors are simply bubbled back up to the browser and displayed in the External List. The general approach is to handle any errors within the connector code when it makes sense to do so, but if the error needs to be returned to the user, a `Microsoft.BusinessData.Runtime.RuntimeException` should be thrown. The `RuntimeException` class has several derivations that are useful for connectors, but it is easiest to just throw a `LobBusinessErrorException`, which is the most generic derivation.

Handling Concurrency Issues

Whenever an External System is being updated through BCS, there is the possibility that near-simultaneous updates will cause conflicts. You must decide how your connector will respond in such cases. The simplest way to handle update conflicts is to simply allow the last update to proceed. This means that your connector will execute an update regardless of the state of the entity instance in the External System. External Lists in SharePoint are designed to support this type of update.

Whenever an item in an External List is edited, the item is refreshed from the underlying External System before the connector submits the changed fields. The connector refreshes the item by calling the `SpecificFinder` method just before the `Updater` method is called. This approach significantly reduces the chance of a conflict during the update process and also means that you do not have to implement any special conflict resolution code in the connector.

If you want to have more control over conflict resolution in your connector, you must plan on implementing a custom user interface, such as a Web Part, to call your connector. When you implement a custom user interface, you can choose to call the `Updater` method without a prior call to the `SpecificFinder`. This will result in the current entity instance's being passed for update. You may then evaluate the entity instance to see if an error should be thrown.

If you take a more detailed approach to conflict resolution, your ECT will need to provide additional fields to manage the values necessary to assess conflicts. In particular, you should implement fields that contain the original values of the entity instance. These values can then be used during conflict assessment. The following code shows a `SpecificFinder` method modified from the earlier .NET Assembly Connector walkthrough to include original item values:

```
<Method Name="ReadProduct">
 <Parameters>
  <Parameter Name="ProductID" Direction="In">
   <TypeDescriptor Name="ProductID" TypeName="System.Int32"
    IsCollection="false" IdentifierName="ProductID" />
  </Parameter>
  <Parameter Name="Product" Direction="Return">
   <TypeDescriptor Name="ProductTypeDescriptor"
    TypeName="AdventureworksConnector.ProductModel.Product, ProductSystem"
    IsCollection="false">
    <TypeDescriptors>
     <TypeDescriptor Name="Color" TypeName="System.String" />
     <TypeDescriptor Name="Description" TypeName="System.String" />
     <TypeDescriptor Name="Name" TypeName="System.String" />
     <TypeDescriptor Name="Number" TypeName="System.String" />
     <TypeDescriptor Name="Price" TypeName="System.Decimal" />
     <TypeDescriptor Name="ProductID" TypeName="System.Int32"
      IsCollection="false" IdentifierName="ProductID" ReadOnly="true" />
     <TypeDescriptor Name="CategoryID" TypeName="System.Int32"
      IsCollection="false" IdentifierEntityName="Category"
      IdentifierEntityNamespace="AdventureworksConnector.ProductModel"
      IdentifierName="CategoryID"
      ForeignIdentifierAssociationEntityName="Category"
      ForeignIdentifierAssociationEntityNamespace=
      "AdventureworksConnector.ProductModel"
      ForeignIdentifierAssociationName=
      "CategoryToProductAssociationNavigator" />
     <TypeDescriptor Name="OriginalName" TypeName="System.String"
      ReadOnly="true" />
     <TypeDescriptor Name="OriginalNumber" TypeName="System.String"
      ReadOnly="true" />
     <TypeDescriptor Name="OriginalColor" TypeName="System.String"
      ReadOnly="true" />
```

```
      <TypeDescriptor Name="OriginalPrice" TypeName="System.Decimal"
       ReadOnly="true" />
      <TypeDescriptor Name="OriginalDescription" TypeName="System.String"
       ReadOnly="true" />
      <TypeDescriptor Name="OriginalCategoryID" TypeName="System.Int32"
       ReadOnly="true" />
     </TypeDescriptors>
    </TypeDescriptor>
   </Parameter>
  </Parameters>
  <MethodInstances>
   <MethodInstance Name="ReadProductInstance" Type="SpecificFinder"
    ReturnParameterName="Product"
    ReturnTypeDescriptorPath="ProductTypeDescriptor" />
  </MethodInstances>
 </Method>
```

Note that the `TypeDescriptors` containing the original values for each field are marked as `ReadOnly`. This is because the original values are simply going to be used for conflict resolution. There is no intent to display these values to the user for editing. The original values are simply set in the `SpecificFinder`, as shown in the following code:

```
public Product ReadProduct(int ProductID)
{
    AdventureworksCatalog catalog =
    new AdventureworksCatalog(GetConnectionInfo());

    var q = from p in catalog.Products
            where p.ProductID == ProductID
            select p;

    if (q.Count() == 1)
    {
        return new Product()
        {
            ProductID = q.First().ProductID,
            Name = q.First().ProductName,
            Number = q.First().ProductNumber,
            Description = q.First().ProductDescription,
            Color = q.First().ProductColor,
            Price = q.First().ProductPrice,
            CategoryID = q.First().CategoryID,
            OriginalName = q.First().ProductName,
            OriginalNumber = q.First().ProductNumber,
            OriginalDescription = q.First().ProductDescription,
            OriginalColor = q.First().ProductColor,
            OriginalPrice = q.First().ProductPrice,
            OriginalCategoryID = q.First().CategoryID
        };
    }
    else
        return null;
}
```

The `Updater` method must accept all the changed values along with the original values. Even though the original values are not changed, they must be explicitly included in the method or the values will be `NULL` in code. The following code shows the BDC Metadata Model for the `Updater` method:

```
<Method Name="UpdateProduct">
 <Parameters>
  <Parameter Name="ProductIn" Direction="In">
   <TypeDescriptor Name="ProductTypeDescriptor" IsCollection="false"
    TypeName="AdventureworksConnector.ProductModel.Product, ProductSystem">
    <TypeDescriptors>
     <TypeDescriptor Name="Color" TypeName="System.String"
      UpdaterField="true" />
     <TypeDescriptor Name="Description" TypeName="System.String"
      UpdaterField="true" />
     <TypeDescriptor Name="Name" TypeName="System.String"
      UpdaterField="true" />
     <TypeDescriptor Name="Number" TypeName="System.String"
      UpdaterField="true" />
     <TypeDescriptor Name="Price" TypeName="System.Decimal"
      UpdaterField="true" />
     <TypeDescriptor Name="ProductID" TypeName="System.Int32"
      ReadOnly="false" UpdaterField="true" />
     <TypeDescriptor Name="CategoryID" TypeName="System.Int32"
      UpdaterField="true" IdentifierEntityName="Category"
      IdentifierEntityNamespace="AdventureworksConnector.ProductModel"
      IdentifierName="CategoryID"
      ForeignIdentifierAssociationEntityName="Category"
      ForeignIdentifierAssociationEntityNamespace=
      "AdventureworksConnector.ProductModel"
      ForeignIdentifierAssociationName=
      "CategoryToProductAssociationNavigator" />
     <TypeDescriptor Name="OriginalName" TypeName="System.String"
      UpdaterField="true"/>
     <TypeDescriptor Name="OriginalNumber" TypeName="System.String"
      UpdaterField="true"/>
     <TypeDescriptor Name="OriginalColor" TypeName="System.String"
      UpdaterField="true"/>
     <TypeDescriptor Name="OriginalPrice" TypeName="System.Decimal"
      UpdaterField="true"/>
     <TypeDescriptor Name="OriginalDescription" TypeName="System.String"
      UpdaterField="true"/>
     <TypeDescriptor Name="OriginalCategoryID" TypeName="System.Int32"
      UpdaterField="true"/>
    </TypeDescriptors>
   </TypeDescriptor>
  </Parameter>
 </Parameters>
 <MethodInstances>
  <MethodInstance Name="UpdateProductInstance" Type="Updater" />
 </MethodInstances>
</Method>
```

Once the original values and current values are passed into the `Updater` method, conflict checking can be done. The basic approach is to compare the original field value with the value currently in the External System. If the original value is different from the value in the External System, a conflict has occurred. At this point the connector can throw an error, which the user interface can catch. The end user can then be presented with a conflict resolution screen and, the update can be retried. The following code shows the implementation of the `Updater` method:

```
public void UpdateProduct(Product ProductIn)
{
    Product ProductDb = ReadProduct(ProductIn.ProductID);

    if (
        ProductDb.Name == ProductIn.OriginalName &&
        ProductDb.Number == ProductIn.OriginalNumber &&
        ProductDb.Color == ProductIn.OriginalColor &&
        ProductDb.Description == ProductIn.OriginalDescription &&
        ProductDb.Price == ProductIn.OriginalPrice &&
        ProductDb.CategoryID == ProductIn.OriginalCategoryID
        )
    {
        AdventureworksCatalog catalog =
         new AdventureworksCatalog(GetConnectionInfo());
        AdventureworksData.Product product =
         catalog.Products.First(p => p.ProductID == ProductIn.ProductID);

        product.ProductName = ProductIn.Name;
        product.ProductNumber = ProductIn.Number;
        product.ProductColor = ProductIn.Color;
        product.ProductDescription = ProductIn.Description;
        product.ProductPrice = ProductIn.Price;
        product.CategoryID = ProductIn.CategoryID;
        catalog.SaveChanges();
    }
    else
        throw new ConflictDetectedException(
         "The underlying data in the External System has changed.");
}
```

Because the original values returned with the entity instance are simply used for conflict detection and resolution, you will want to ensure that they are hidden from the user interface and search crawls. You can add several properties to the `TypeDescriptor` elements for the fields to help hide them.

The `SuppressCrawl` property may be set to `True` to prevent the fields from being indexed by search. The `HideInListWebPartByDefault` and `HideInItemWebPartByDefault` properties can be set to `True` so that the fields are not displayed in the External Data Web Parts. Unfortunately, there is no property to hide the fields in an External List. Instead, they must be excluded from the list views.

PACKAGING CONSIDERATIONS

As with all SharePoint projects, Business Data Connectivity Model projects are packaged for deployment as cabinet files with a WSP extension. When projects containing BDC Metadata Models are packaged in WSP files, special attention must be given to the values set for the *Feature Properties*. Feature Properties are set within Visual Studio 2010 and appear as Property elements within the Feature.xml file of the project. Business Data Connectivity Model projects have five key Feature Properties as shown in the following code:

```
<?xml version="1.0" encoding="utf-8"?>
<Feature xmlns="http://schemas.microsoft.com/sharepoint/"
 Description="A .NET Assembly Connector"
 Id="bc975901-3142-4fbf-9e3c-1f124b6c890d"
 ReceiverAssembly="..."
 ReceiverClass="..."
 Scope="Farm"
 Title="My Connector">
  <Properties>
    <Property Key="GloballyAvailable" Value="true" />
    <Property Key="MyModel"
     Value="BdcAssemblies\MyConnector.dll" />
    <Property Key="IncrementalUpdate" Value="true" />
    <Property Key="ModelFileName" Value="MyModel\MyModel.bdcm" />
    <Property Key="SiteUrl" Value="http://awserver/bcs/" />
  </Properties>
  <ElementManifests>
    <ElementFile Location="MyModel\MyModel.bdcm" />
    <ElementFile Location="BdcAssemblies\MyConnector.dll" />
  </ElementManifests>
</Feature>
```

Most of the properties in the file are set by Visual Studio and do not require any editing. However, these properties should always be verified before packaging. Renaming elements during development and the particulars of the target SharePoint environment may necessitate changes to the values.

The first property is the GloballyAvailable property. All BDC Metadata Models are available globally in SharePoint. The GloballyAvailable property is set to true as part of the project template and should not be changed.

The second property uses the name of the LobSystem as the Key. The Value references the assembly that implements the operations defined in the model. This property is set by Visual Studio and generally does not need to be changed. In some scenarios, this property may be set incorrectly if you rename the LobSystem after creating operations in the BDC Metadata Model

The third property is the IncrementalUpdate property, which supports modifying parts of the BDC Metadata Model. This property is set by Visual Studio and also does not need to be changed.

The fourth property is the `ModelFileName` property. This property references the BDCM file that contains the model. This property is set by Visual Studio and generally does not need to be changed. In some scenarios, this property may be set incorrectly if you rename the model during development.

The fifth property is the `SiteUrl` property. This property is used to identify the BDC Service Application where the BDC Metadata Model should be deployed. The `SiteUrl` property is not present by default in the Business Data Connectivity Model project. When the property is not present, the deployment assumes a value for the property of `http://localhost:80`. This means that the BDC Metadata Model will be deployed to the BDC Service Application associated with the site located at `http://localhost:80`. If, however, no site exists at `http://localhost:80`, then the deployment will fail. In this case, you must explicitly set the `SiteUrl` value to reference a site associated with the correct BDC Service Application.

You can review and modify the Feature Properties directly in Visual Studio 2010. First, select the BDC Metadata Model project item in the Solution Explorer. Second, select the Feature Properties item from the Properties window, which will open a dialog. Finally, set the property values in the dialog. Figure 7-12 shows how to set the values.

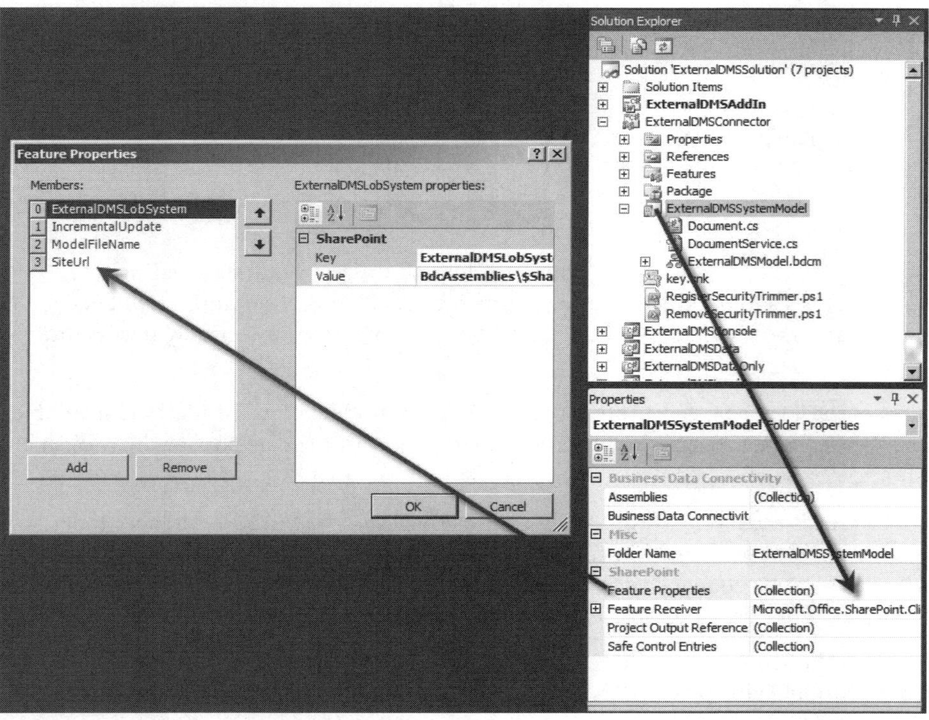

FIGURE 7-12

SUMMARY

The .NET Assembly Connector and custom connector both allow significant control over how External Systems are accessed by SharePoint. The .NET Assembly Connector has better tooling support and will likely be used by developers within organizations where specific systems are deployed. The custom connector is a more generic solution but has less tooling support. It will most likely be used by third parties that want to support access to their product through SharePoint. You should feel free, however, to use the connector type that best fits your needs.

Working with BCS Security

WHAT'S IN THIS CHAPTER?

- Understand server authentication options
- Understand the Secure Store Service
- Understand client authentication options
- Understand claims authentication

Security with regard to authentication and authorization is an integral part of connecting to any system. When you connect to an External System through Business Connectivity Services, security can take on new levels of complexity as user context changes through various security schemes, impersonation, and delegation. Furthermore, the data in External Systems is likely to be valuable or sensitive. BCS developers have a serious responsibility to ensure that appropriate authentication and authorization controls are in place for their solutions. Therefore, a thorough understanding of security scenarios is critical to creating successful BCS solutions.

This chapter presents the different security models and how they affect BCS solutions from Integrated Windows Authentication to claims-based authentication. For each case, some background information is provided, followed by configuration options for BCS. These options will allow you to create BCS solutions that work correctly in your environment.

UNDERSTANDING BDC PERMISSIONS

All the BCS models created in SharePoint Designer or Visual Studio are ultimately stored in the BDC Metadata catalog. Access to the BDC Metadata catalog is managed through the Business Data Connectivity service application. Before examining the various security scenarios surrounding BCS solutions, you must properly configure the permissions for the

BDC service application. If appropriate rights are not granted in the BDC service application for a given model, users will be denied access to the model by the BDC service application even before they attempt to access the External System. In this situation, users will receive the message “Access Denied by Business Connectivity Services.”

The BDC service application is managed starting at the same page as all service applications in the farm. From the Central Administration home page, click the link entitled Manage Service Applications beneath the Application Management group. This link will open the list of all service applications on the farm. Selecting the Business Data Connectivity service and clicking the Administrators button in the ribbon will open a dialog in which administrator rights may be assigned for the service. Users added to this dialog will have full control over the BDC service application and any External Content Types defined within. Figure 8-1 shows the dialog.

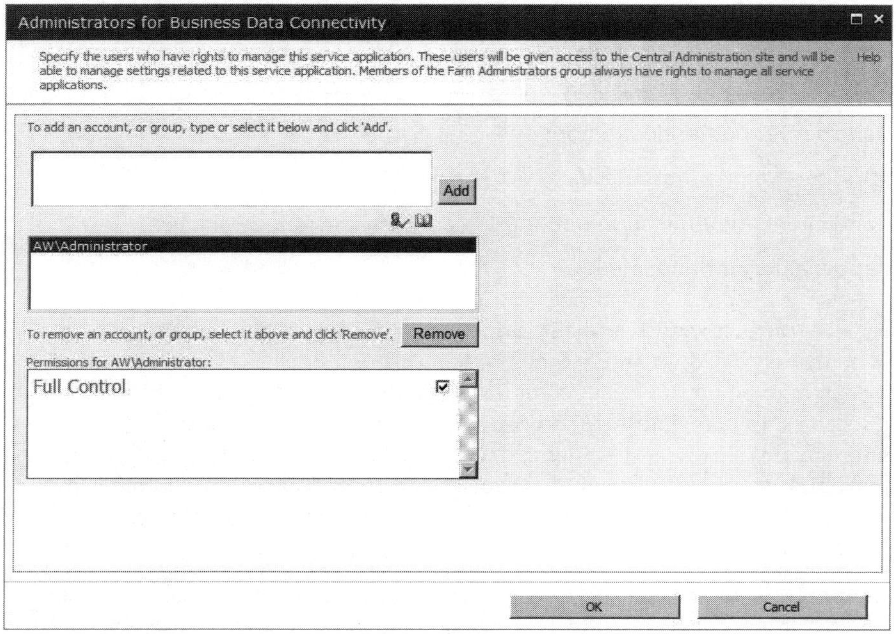

FIGURE 8-1

Clicking the Manage button in the ribbon will open the management page for the service application. In the service application, you can select to see a list of BDC Metadata Models, External Content Types, or External Data Sources. The service application defines a hierarchy of these objects where permissions may be granted. The hierarchy starts with the entire Metadata Catalog, followed by individual BDC Metadata Models, followed by External Content Types and External Data Sources as shown.

```
Metadata Catalog
    BDC Metadata Models
        External Content Types
        External Data Sources
```

A drop-down menu is associated with each BDC Metadata Model, External Content Type, and External Data Source. Dropping the menu and clicking Set Permissions will open a dialog in which you can set permissions for the object. Additionally, you can set permissions at the catalog level by clicking the Set Catalog Permissions button in the ribbon. In all cases you can push permissions down the hierarchy by checking the "Propagate permissions" box. Figure 8-2 shows the dialog.

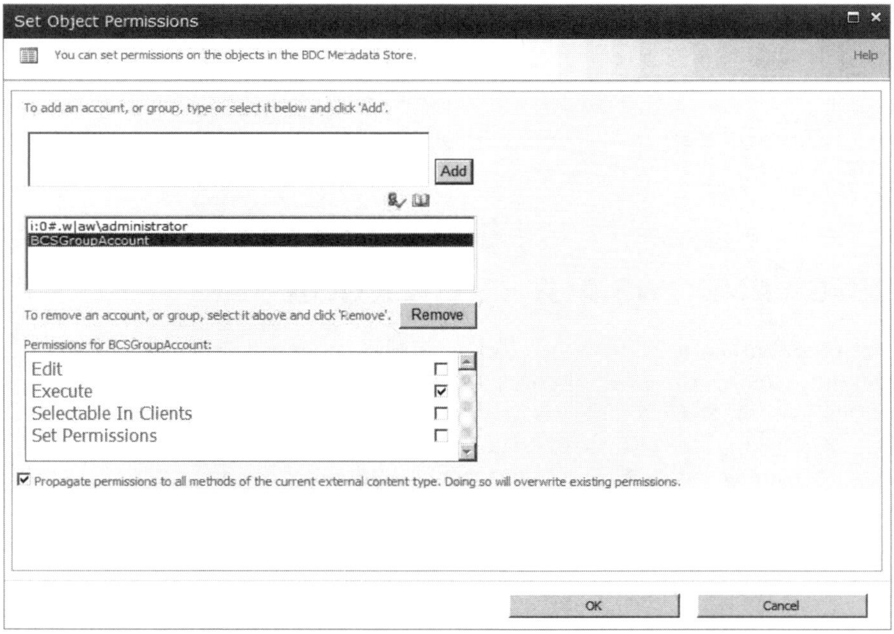

FIGURE 8-2

There are four different rights available in the dialog: Edit, Execute, Selectable In Clients, and Set Permissions. The Edit right grants the ability to edit models, data sources, and External Content Types. The Execute right grants the ability to perform CRUD operations. The Selectable In Clients right grants the ability to create new External Lists, use the External Data web parts, and pick External Content Types from the picker. The Set Permissions right grants the ability to set permissions in the BDC service.

If the External System is capable of performing security checks, the BDC service permissions may be configured with little restriction. If, however, the External System cannot perform per-user security, the BDC service permissions may be used to control access to the External System at the model level. In all cases, the assigned permissions are stored in the BDC Metadata Model at the appropriate level using an `AccessControlList` element. The following code shows an example:

```
<AccessControlList>
  <AccessControlEntry Principal="aw\administrator">
    <Right BdcRight="Edit" />
    <Right BdcRight="Execute" />
    <Right BdcRight="SetPermissions" />
    <Right BdcRight="SelectableInClients" />
  </AccessControlEntry>
  <AccessControlEntry Principal=" aw\brianc">
    <Right BdcRight="Edit" />
    <Right BdcRight="Execute" />
    <Right BdcRight="SelectableInClients" />
  </AccessControlEntry>
  <AccessControlEntry Principal=" aw\spworker">
    <Right BdcRight="Edit" />
    <Right BdcRight="Execute" />
  </AccessControlEntry>
</AccessControlList>
```

UNDERSTANDING WINDOWS AUTHENTICATION

Despite the fact that other authentication mechanisms — such as claims — are available, Windows authentication remains the most common security model for SharePoint. When using Windows authentication, SharePoint users are authenticated by Internet Information Server (IIS) against accounts in Active Directory. If the user is successfully authenticated, the user and role information is sent to SharePoint, where additional steps are taken to create a valid `SPUser`.

The most important aspect of Windows authentication for BCS developers is to correctly identify the account under which a user is accessing a BCS solution. Depending upon the configuration of IIS and SharePoint, the identity of the user can be either a specific user account, a subsystem account, or an anonymous account. Each of these situations has unique impact on the implementation of BCS solutions.

When using Windows authentication in IIS, three different approaches are available: *Basic authentication*, *Digest authentication*, and *Integrated Windows authentication*. Basic authentication transmits user names and passwords as clear text. Digest authentication transmits a secure hash containing the user name and password. Integrated Windows authentication transmits a token that was created when the user originally logged on to the network. When a new web application is created through Central Administration that uses *Classic Mode authentication*, the resulting IIS website is configured to use Integrated Windows authentication. Figure 8-3 shows the authentication process when Integrated Windows authentication is in use.

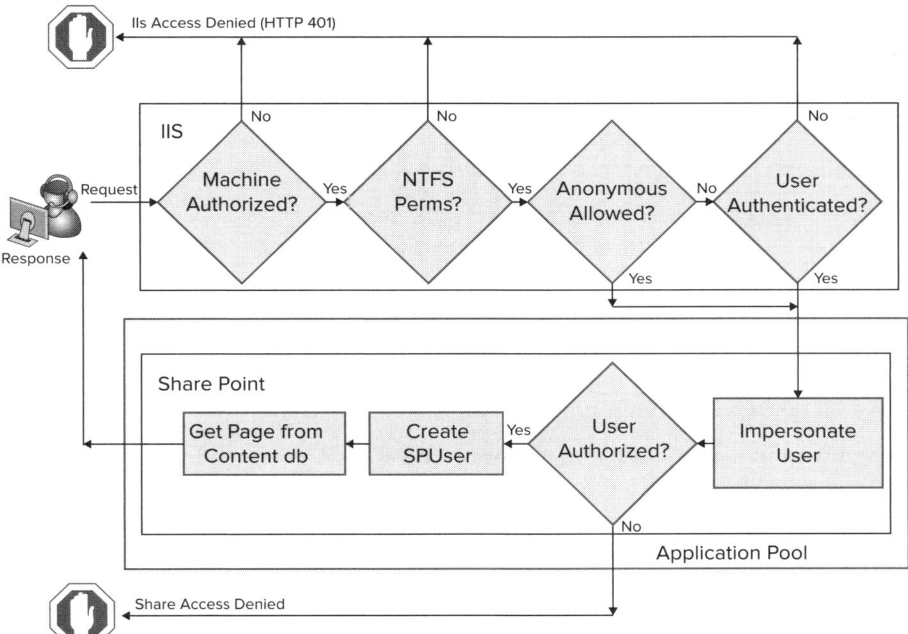

FIGURE 8-3

Integrated Windows authentication requires both the client and the server to be in the same domain or in trusted domains. When the user makes a request through the browser for a SharePoint resource, IIS requests the browser to authenticate. The browser responds by sending a token representing the current Windows user. If IIS cannot authenticate the user, then a 401 Access Denied response is sent. If IIS successfully authenticates the user, the information is passed on to SharePoint.

When SharePoint receives the user information, it must check the permission set for the user as defined in SharePoint. This permission set is a combination of the policies for the web application, group memberships, permission levels, and permissions assigned to the user. If SharePoint cannot authorize the user to access the desired resource, SharePoint returns an Access Denied page. This page is different from the 401 page sent by IIS and typically invites the user to log on with different credentials or send an e-mail to request access to the desired resource. If the user is authorized to access the resource, SharePoint retrieves the resource from the content database and returns it to the user.

Like all ASP.NET applications, SharePoint executes inside an *application pool*. An application pool is an instance of the `w3wp.exe` process running under an assigned identity. In SharePoint this assigned identity is the account used to access the content databases to retrieve requested resources.

Integrated Windows authentication supports two protocols, which you may select when creating a new web application with Classic Mode authentication. These protocols are NTLM and Kerberos. NTLM authenticates clients using a challenge-response mechanism. Kerberos, on the other hand, is a ticket-based authentication mechanism.

A simple analogy that is often used to describe the difference between NTLM and Kerberos involves rides at amusement parks. The challenge-response protocol of NTLM requires that the client be authenticated for access to each individual resource. This is analogous to visiting a carnival where you must pay for each ride. The ticket-based protocol of Kerberos involves a single authentication that is good for all resources. This is analogous to visiting a theme park where you pay once at the gate and then have unlimited access to all the rides.

While both NTLM and Kerberos are secure protocols, Kerberos is the most secure because it authenticates both the client and the server. NTLM authenticates only the client. Additionally, Kerberos is less "chatty" than NTLM, which requires more communication to accomplish authentication. However, Kerberos requires special configuration steps while NTLM just works out of the box. For this reason alone, NTLM is still widely used with SharePoint farms.

Understanding Impersonation

In addition to using Integrated Windows authentication, IIS websites created by Central Administration also have *ASP.NET Impersonation* enabled by way of the <identity impersonate="true"/> element in the web.config file. When ASP.NET Impersonation is enabled in this way — and anonymous access is disabled — the account of the currently authenticated user is used to make all resource requests. Impersonation allows SharePoint to use the rights of the current user to access resources and execute code. Both NTLM and Kerberos support impersonation.

While impersonation is valuable for implementing security in ASP.NET, it is limited to the server on which IIS is running. This means that if the code in a SharePoint page attempts to access a resource — like a database — on a different server, it will not use the account of the current user. Instead, it will use the identity of the application pool. This situation is commonly referred to as the *double-hop issue*.

The limitation imposed on impersonation is there by design. If it were possible to impersonate users across the network with no limitations, a serious security threat would exist. Compromised code could be hijacked to perform all kinds of operations in the name of the current user. Impersonation limitations have a significant impact on how connections are made to External Systems, and BCS solutions must work within these limitations.

Understanding Delegation

While impersonation is limited to the IIS server, *delegation* allows the credentials of the currently authenticated user to be passed along to another server. This means that External Systems can be accessed with the credentials of the user and not the application pool. Because of its superior security, only Kerberos supports delegation. Kerberos may be enabled for a web application through the Authentication Providers dialog as shown in Figure 8-4, but it also requires additional configuration.

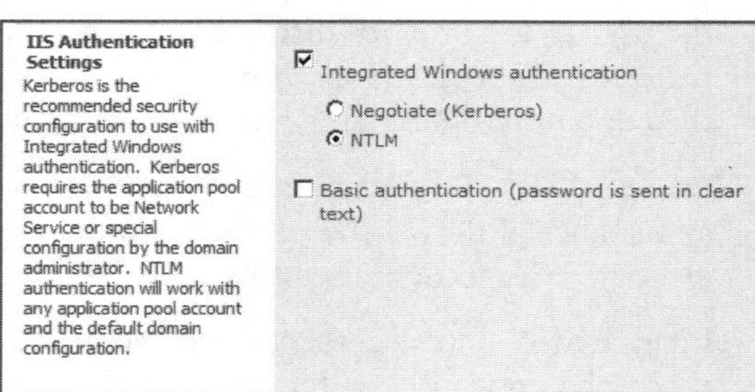

FIGURE 8-4

Because of the security threat mentioned previously, only the domain controller is trusted for delegation without additional configuration. In order to access an External System using the credentials of the current user, the application pool running SharePoint must be configured to support delegation.

The additional steps required to implement Kerberos are beyond the scope of this chapter and are certainly not trivial. Moving to Kerberos is an organizational decision that will involve IT management. Nonetheless, implementing Kerberos is the single easiest way to facilitate proper authentication and authorization against External Systems. The ability to pass the current user's credentials all the way through to the External System eliminates the need for common accounts that must be managed separately.

Understanding Anonymous Access

Along with impersonation and delegation, users may also access IIS anonymously. When an IIS site has enabled anonymous access, all users will initially be authenticated as the anonymous user account, which is specified in IIS. Anonymous access is enabled for a SharePoint site whenever anonymous access is specifically enabled in Central Administration for the web application, or the site is configured to use forms-based authentication.

Anonymous access has a significant impact on BCS solutions because all users share the same identity. As a result there is no way to distinguish among the users accessing External Systems. In many situations such a limitation may be unacceptable. For example, when NTLM authentication is in use and anonymous access is enabled, the anonymous user account will be the one used to access External Systems subject to double hop.

GETTING STARTED WITH SERVER AUTHENTICATION

The most common BCS authentication scenario involves a database or web service as the External System, presented in the browser as an External List. Most often these systems are internal to the organization and use either Integrated Windows authentication or simple username/password authentication. In these scenarios BCS supports two authentication models: *Impersonation and Delegation* and *Trusted Subsystem*. In the Impersonation and Delegation model BCS uses Integrated Windows authentication along with impersonation or delegation, depending upon how the network is configured. In the Trusted Subsystem model, BCS uses a single account to access the External System regardless of the current user identity.

The `AuthenticationMode` element in the Application Model determines how authentication is performed. Possible values for the `AuthenticationMode` element are `Passthrough`, `RevertToSelf`, `WindowsCredentials`, `RdbCredentials`, and `Credentials`. `Passthrough` is used to pass the credentials of the current user to the External System and `RevertToSelf` is used to pass the credentials of the application pool. Together these two options represent the simplest authentication strategies for BCS.

`WindowsCredentials`, `RdbCredentials`, and `Credentials` are used to pass a separate set of credentials from the Secure Store Service (SSS). Before the SSS can be use with BCS, it must be properly configured. Configuration and use of SSS is covered later in the chapter.

Using Passthrough Authentication

`Passthrough` authentication implements the Impersonation and Delegation authentication model. Setting the value of the `AuthenticationMode` element to `Passthrough` causes BCS to attempt a connection to the designated External System based on the current NTLM or Kerberos network configuration. If the network is configured to use Kerberos and delegation, External Systems will be accessed with the credentials of the current user. Under NTLM and impersonation, External Systems will be accessed with the credentials of the application pool or anonymous user. The following code shows a model with the `AuthenticationMode` element set to `Passthrough`.

```
<LobSystemInstances>
  <LobSystemInstance Name="Adventureworks Data Warehouse">
    <Properties>
      <Property Name="AuthenticationMode" Type="System.String">
        PassThrough
      </Property>
      <Property Name="DatabaseAccessProvider" Type="System.String">
        SqlServer
      </Property>
      <Property Name="RdbConnection Data Source" Type="System.String">
        AWSQL
      </Property>
      <Property Name="RdbConnection Initial Catalog"
              Type="System.String">AdventureworksDW</Property>
      <Property Name="RdbConnection Integrated Security" Type="System.String">
        SSPI
      </Property>
      <Property Name="RdbConnection Pooling" Type="System.String">true</Property>
      <Property Name="ShowInSearchUI" Type="System.String"></Property>
    </Properties>
  </LobSystemInstance>
</LobSystemInstances>
```

`Passthrough` is simple to configure: select Connect with User's Identity when setting up the External System connection in SharePoint Designer. This option is available both during the initial definition of the External System connection and later through the Connection Properties dialog accessible from the summary page. Figure 8-5 shows the option in the SharePoint Designer.

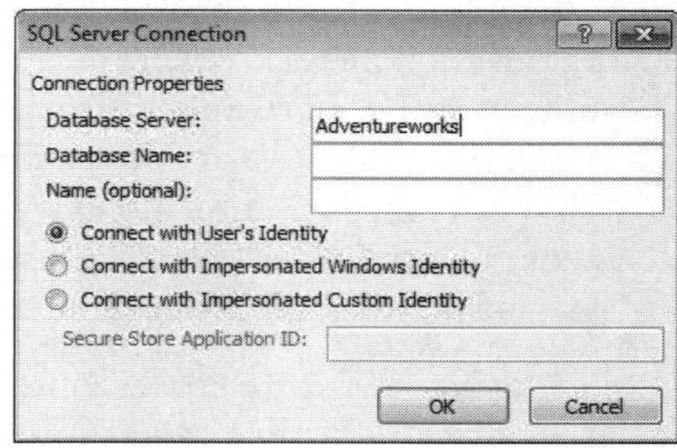

FIGURE 8-5

`Passthrough` authentication is simple to configure and use. However, it requires Kerberos authentication to work across all situations. Once again, Kerberos is the best configuration to use with BCS solutions.

Using RevertToSelf Authentication

`RevertToSelf` falls within the Trusted Subsystem model of authentication because it uses a single account for all users. Setting the value of the `AuthenticationMode` element to `RevertToSelf` causes

BCS to use the credentials of the application pool to access the External System. The following code shows a model with the `AuthenticationMode` element set to `RevertToSelf`.

```
<LobSystemInstances>
  <LobSystemInstance Name="Adventureworks Data Warehouse">
    <Properties>
      <Property Name="AuthenticationMode" Type="System.String">
        RevertToSelf
      </Property>
      <Property Name="DatabaseAccessProvider" Type="System.String">
        SqlServer
      </Property>
      <Property Name="RdbConnection Data Source" Type="System.String">
        AWSQL
      </Property>
      <Property Name="RdbConnection Initial Catalog"
                Type="System.String">AdventureworksDW</Property>
      <Property Name="RdbConnection Integrated Security" Type="System.String">
        SSPI
      </Property>
      <Property Name="RdbConnection Pooling" Type="System.String">true</Property>
      <Property Name="ShowInSearchUI" Type="System.String"></Property>
    </Properties>
  </LobSystemInstance>
</LobSystemInstances>
```

You configure `RevertToSelf` by editing the connection information to the External System after it is defined; the option is not available during the initial connection configuration. In the SharePoint Designer, on the Summary View for the External Content Type, you can edit the connection information by clicking the hyperlink for the External System. Figure 8-6 shows the Connection Properties dialog. Specify `RevertToSelf` by selecting the option BDC Identity from the Authentication Mode drop-down.

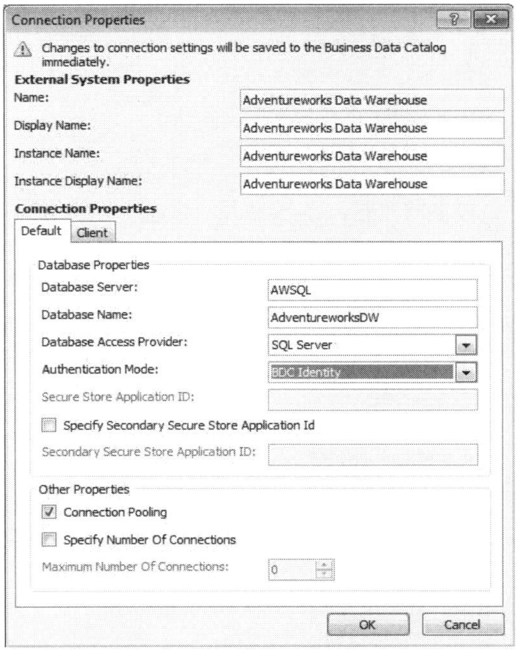

FIGURE 8-6

While using `RevertToSelf` is a simple way to provide access to External Systems regardless of the user's identity, it is important to understand that the application pool identity is a powerful one whose credentials must be protected. Along with being the account under which the web application runs, the application pool identity is also used to access the content database, as mentioned earlier. Furthermore, the application pool identity is the account under which code runs when the `SPSecurity.RunWithElevatedPrivileges` method is called in SharePoint, which essentially allows code to perform any action in a SharePoint farm.

Within SharePoint, the application pool identity is mapped to a special `SPUser` account known as SHAREPOINT\system. If you log into SharePoint using the application pool identity account, you will be welcomed as SHAREPOINT\system. Additionally, you will have significant rights while running under the SHAREPOINT\system account. Because of the special nature of the application pool identity in SharePoint, it is important to protect the account credentials. For this reason, `RevertToSelf` is initially disabled and must be explicitly enabled using the following PowerShell script.

```
$bdc = Get-SPServiceApplication
  | where {$_ -match "Business Data Connectivity Service"}
$bdc.RevertToSelfAllowed = $true
$bdc.Update();
```

UNDERSTANDING THE SECURE STORE SERVICE

The Secure Store Service (SSS) is a service application that provides for the storage, mapping, and retrieval of credential information. The credentials stored by SSS are used to access External Systems when the credentials of the current user cannot be used. This might be the case with, for example, impersonation beyond the IIS server, trusted subsystem strategies that use a single account for access, and attempts to access External Systems that use simple username/password schemes.

Credential sets are stored by SSS in a secure database under an application, which is a plain-text name used to represent the context or usage of the credential sets. SSS responds to requests for credentials by providing the credentials associated with a Windows account for a given application name.

Because SSS contains sensitive credential information it should run in its own application pool using a unique identity account. SSS should also run on its own dedicated application server. Finally, the SSS database should reside on a separate database server from the one containing SharePoint content databases. Note that using the service application setup wizard during the initial SharePoint installation does not meet the best practices for SSS. Therefore, a new instance should be created manually and configured as described earlier.

Once the SSS service application is created, it can be managed in the standard way. From Central Administration click Manage Service Application under the Application Management section. On the Manage Service Applications page, clicking the Administrators button in the ribbon will open a dialog for defining rights to create and manage applications within SSS.

Clicking the Manage button in the ribbon will open a page for managing the SSS. If this is your first time visiting the management page, you will have to define a new encryption key before applications can be defined. The encryption key is used to encrypt the credentials in the SSS database, which should be backed up after the service is configured.

In order for credential sets for an External System to be stored, a new Target Application must be created in SSS. The Target Application acts as a container for credential sets mapped to an External

System. The Target Application settings page contains a name for the application and a setting to specify whether each individual user will have a separate set of mapped credentials, or every user will map to a single common set of credentials. Figure 8-7 shows application settings mapping a single set of credentials to an Active Directory group.

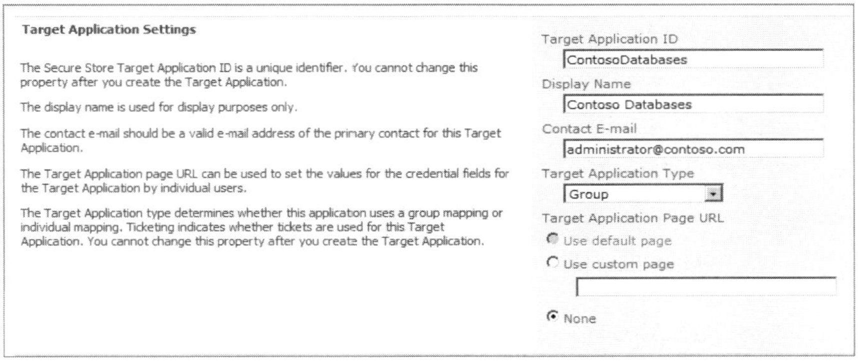

Target Application Settings

The Secure Store Target Application ID is a unique identifier. You cannot change this property after you create the Target Application.

The display name is used for display purposes only.

The contact e-mail should be a valid e-mail address of the primary contact for this Target Application.

The Target Application page URL can be used to set the values for the credential fields for the Target Application by individual users.

The Target Application type determines whether this application uses a group mapping or individual mapping. Ticketing indicates whether tickets are used for this Target Application. You cannot change this property after you create the Target Application.

Target Application ID: ContosoDatabases
Display Name: Contoso Databases
Contact E-mail: administrator@contoso.com
Target Application Type: Group
Target Application Page URL
Use default page
Use custom page
None

FIGURE 8-7

When creating a Target Application you may choose either an individual or a group type. Furthermore, you can enhance these options to include ticketing or restricted accounts. An individual account maps a separate account for each user. A group account maps all users to a single account. So an individual application type implements the Impersonation and Delegation model, while a group application type implements the Trusted Subsystem model.

For either individual or group you may elect to include ticketing. Ticketing creates a ticket for each credential request that is good for the period of time you specify in the Target Application definition. This period should be long enough for the client to use the ticket to access the External System. Tickets should be associated with a Secure Store Ticket (`SsoTicket`) filter in the BDC Metadata Model that will limit the results returned from the External System based on the ticket.

For either individual or group, you may also specify that the account is restricted. Restricted accounts are sensitive accounts stored separately from other accounts and managed through a separate API. This further protects the credentials from compromise.

The Target Application page specifies the page to which a user will be redirected if his or her credential mapping has not yet been added to the Target Application. This page is automatically generated based on the fields required for the login. Setting up an individual type application, for instance, requires that each user have stored credentials. However, there is no way that the administrator can enter these credentials when the Target Application is created. Therefore, the SSS must prompt each user to enter credentials the first time he or she uses the Target Application. These credentials can then be stored for future use. As an alternative, the SSS API could be used to load credentials in bulk.

In most cases the Target Application will save a user name and password for the credentials, but it is important to point out that SSS can save any text-based information. For example, a passcode field could be used in lieu of a password field. Figure 8-8 shows typical user name and password fields defined for an application.

Add Field

Field Name	Field Type	Masked	Delete
Windows User Name	Windows User Name	☐	×
Windows Password	Windows Password	☑	×

Important: The field names and field types cannot be edited later.

Next Cancel

FIGURE 8-8

Once the application and credential fields are defined you must enter the actual credential information. For each user or group that will access the External System, a set of credentials must be created with the field definitions for the application. Figure 8-9 shows credentials being entered for an application. Once the credentials are in place the application can be used during the definition of an External Content Type to allow access to the External System using the credentials stored in the SSS. If an end user should attempt to access the system without proper credentials in SSS, that user will be directed to a login page so the credentials can be entered and stored.

Set Credentials for Secure Store Target Application (Group)

Set values for the credential fields that are defined for this Secure Store Target Application. Help

Warning: this page is not encrypted for secure communication. User names, passwords, and any other information will be sent in clear text. For more information, contact your administrator.

Target Application Name: Contoso Databases
Target Application ID: ContosoDatabases

Credential Owners:

Name	Value
Windows User Name	Contoso\MasterDbAccount
Windows Password	••••••
Confirm Windows Password	••••••

Note: Once the credentials are set, they cannot be retrieved by the administrator. Any existing credentials for this credential owner will be overwritten.

FIGURE 8-9

Along with the interface provided by Central Administration, SSS can also be maintained through PowerShell commands. Using these commands you can manage Target Applications and credentials. The following table lists the PowerShell commands supported by SSS.

COMMAND	DESCRIPTION
`Clear-SPSecureStoreCredentialMapping`	Deletes a credential mapping for a Target Application
`Clear-SPSecureStoreDefaultProvider`	Clears the assembly information for the default pluggable SSO provider used in the `SsoProviderImplemenation` element
`Get-SPSecureStoreApplication`	Gets an SSS application
`New-SPSecureStoreApplication`	Creates a new SSS application
`New-SPSecureStoreApplicationField`	Creates a new field in a Target Application
`New-SPSecureStoreServiceApplication`	Creates a new SSS service application (which is a configured instance of SSS in the farm)
`New-SPSecureStoreServiceApplicationProxy`	Create a new SSS application proxy (which is used by the server to communicate with the SSS service application)
`New-SPSecureStoreTargetApplication`	Creates a new Target Application
`Remove-SPSecureStoreApplication`	Deletes an SSS application
`Set-SPSecureStoreApplication`	Sets properties for an SSS application
`Set-SPSecureStoreDefaultProvider`	Sets the assembly information for the default pluggable SSO provider used in the `SsoProviderImplemenation` element
`Set-SPSecureStoreServiceApplication`	Sets properties for an SSS service application
`Update-SPSecureStoreApplicationServerKey`	Updates the SSS encryption key
`Update-SPSecureStoreCredentialMapping`	Updates a credential mapping in a Target Application
`Update-SPSecureStoreGroupCredentialMapping`	Creates a new group credential mapping in a Target Application
`Update-SPSecureStoreMasterKey`	Updates the SSS encryption key

USING THE SECURE STORE SERVICE FOR AUTHENTICATION

When you're using the SSS as part of an authentication strategy, your first concern is the protocol used by the External System for authentication. If the External System supports Windows authentication, the SSS Target Application will have a different configuration from that of an External System using a proprietary user name/password scheme. The next concern is whether to implement the Impersonation and Delegation model or the Trusted Subsystem model. This choice is largely based on whether users need to authenticate individually to the External System, and you make it by creating an individual or group type Target Application. Once you know the type of Target Application you need, you can create it in SSS.

Using WindowsCredentials Authentication

`WindowsCredentials` authentication is used when the External System supports Windows authentication. Setting the value of the `AuthenticationMode` element to `WindowsCredentials` causes BCS to use the SSS credentials as Windows credentials to access the External System. The following code shows a model with the `AuthenticationModel` element set to `WindowsCredentials`. The `SsoApplicationId` element contains the name of the Target Application in SSS where the credentials are stored.

```
<LobSystemInstances>
  <LobSystemInstance Name="Adventureworks Data Warehouse">
    <Properties>
      <Property Name="AuthenticationMode" Type="System.String">
        WindowsCredentials
      </Property>
      <Property Name="DatabaseAccessProvider" Type="System.String">
        SqlServer
      </Property>
      <Property Name="RdbConnection Data Source" Type="System.String">
        AWSQL
      </Property>
      <Property Name="RdbConnection Initial Catalog"
       Type="System.String">AdventureworksDW</Property>
      <Property Name="RdbConnection Integrated Security" Type="System.String">
        SSPI
      </Property>
      <Property Name="RdbConnection Pooling" Type="System.String">true</Property>
      <Property Name="ShowInSearchUI" Type="System.String"></Property>
      <Property Name="SsoApplicationId" Type="System.String">
        AdventureworksDW
      </Property>
      <Property Name="SsoProviderImplementation" Type="System.String">
            Microsoft.Office.SecureStoreService.Server.SecureStoreProvider,
            Microsoft.Office.SecureStoreService, Version=14.0.0.0, Culture=neutral,
            PublicKeyToken=71e9bce111e9429c</Property>
          </Properties>
        </LobSystemInstance>
      </LobSystemInstances>
```

You cannot select `WindowsCredentials` when initially creating a connection to an External System in SPD. Instead you must use the Connection Properties dialog afterward and set the Authentication Mode to Impersonate Windows Identity. Figure 8-10 shows the option in the SharePoint Designer.

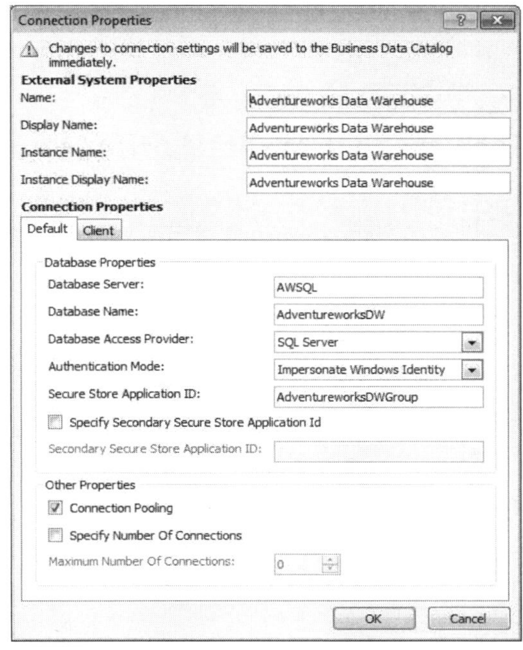

FIGURE 8-10

Using RdbCredentials Authentication

`RdbCredentials` authentication is used exclusively for database access when the database supports user name/password authentication. Setting the value of the `AuthenticationMode` element to `RdbCredentials` causes BCS to append the credentials to the database connection string when accessing the External System. The following code shows a model with the `AuthenticationModel` element set to `RdbCredentials`. The `SsoApplicationId` element contains the name of the Target Application in SSS where the credentials are stored.

```
<LobSystemInstances>
  <LobSystemInstance Name="Adventureworks Data Warehouse">
    <Properties>
      <Property Name="AuthenticationMode" Type="System.String">
        RdbCredentials
      </Property>
      <Property Name="DatabaseAccessProvider" Type="System.String">
        SqlServer
      </Property>
      <Property Name="RdbConnection Data Source" Type="System.String">
        AWSQL
      </Property>
      <Property Name="RdbConnection Initial Catalog"
       Type="System.String">AdventureworksDW</Property>
      <Property Name="RdbConnection Pooling" Type="System.String">true</Property>
      <Property Name="ShowInSearchUI" Type="System.String"></Property>
      <Property Name="SsoApplicationId" Type="System.String">
        AdventureworksDWGroup
      </Property>
      <Property Name="SsoProviderImplementation" Type="System.String">
       Microsoft.Office.SecureStoreService.Server.SecureStoreProvider,
       Microsoft.Office.SecureStoreService, Version=14.0.0.0, Culture=neutral,
       PublicKeyToken=71e9bce111e9429c</Property>
         </Properties>
       </LobSystemInstance>
      </LobSystemInstances>
```

You cannot select `RdbCredentials` when initially creating a connection to an External System in SPD. Instead you must use the Connection Properties dialog afterward and set the Authentication Mode to Impersonate Custom Identity.

Using Credentials Authentication

`Credentials` authentication is used exclusively for access to web services that do not support Integrated Windows authentication, but are using Basic or Digest authentication instead. Setting the value of the `WcfAuthenticationMode` element to `Credentials` causes BCS to use the credentials to authenticate with IIS when you're accessing the External System. The following code shows a model with the `WcfAuthenticationModel` element set to `Credentials`. The `WcfEndpointAddress` element contains the URI of the web service.

```
<LobSystemInstances>
  <LobSystemInstance Name="Adventureworks Web">
    <Properties>
      <Property Name="ShowInSearchUI" Type="System.String"></Property>
      <Property Name="SsoApplicationId" Type="System.String">
        AdventurewoksWCF
      </Property>
      <Property Name="SsoProviderImplementation" Type="System.String">
       Microsoft.Office.SecureStoreService.Server.SecureStoreProvider,
       Microsoft.Office.SecureStoreService, Version=14.0.0.0, Culture=neutral,
       PublicKeyToken=71e9bce111e9429c</Property>
      <Property Name="WcfAuthenticationMode" Type="System.String">
        Credentials
      </Property>
      <Property Name="WcfEndpointAddress" Type="System.String">
        http://awsharepoint.aw.com:5555/AdventureWorksDWService.svc
      </Property>
          </Properties>
        </LobSystemInstance>
      </LobSystemInstances>
```

You cannot select `Credentials` when initially creating a connection to an External System in SPD. Instead you must use the Connection Properties dialog afterward and set the Authentication Mode to Impersonate Custom Identity. Additionally, because Basic and Digest authentication are not considered completely secure, `Credentials` authentication should be used only with web services that implement Secure Sockets Layer (SSL), Internet Protocol security (IPSec), or both.

Using Application-Level Authentication

Business Connectivity Services supports a secondary authentication at the application level that is used in addition to the primary authentication mechanisms described previously. This secondary authentication is performed by the External System in the operation itself, and BCS supports the process by providing to a `Finder` or `SpecificFinder` operation a set of secondary credentials from SSS that are associated with input parameters.

In order to set up application-level authentication you must specify a Secondary Secure Store Application ID in the Connection Properties dialog in SPD. Then you must create a `UserName` filter and a `Password` filter on the desired read operation. The filter is created in the wizard for the read operation. Figure 8-11 shows the filter selection dialog.

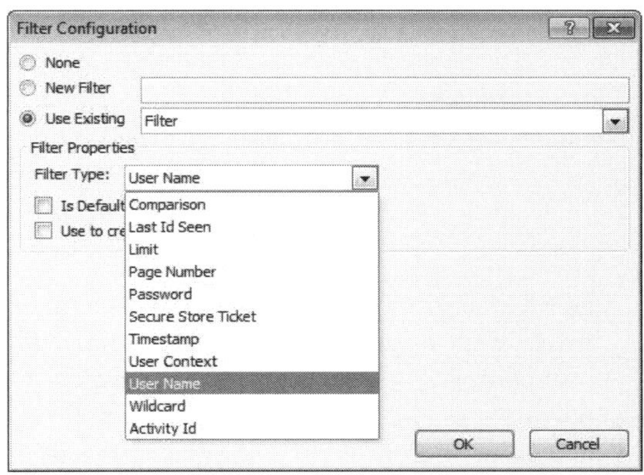

FIGURE 8-11

The `UserName` and `Password` filters must each be associated with a different input parameter for the operation. When performing the operation BCS will provide the user name and password to the designated input parameters. It is up to the application to use these parameters to perform the application-level authentication and respond appropriately. The following code shows pieces of a model with application-level authentication.

```
<LobSystemInstances>
  <LobSystemInstance Name="Adventureworks Web">
    <Properties>
      <Property Name="ShowInSearchUI" Type="System.String"></Property>
      <Property Name="SsoApplicationId" Type="System.String">
        AdventureworksWCF
      </Property>
      <Property Name="SecondarySsoApplicationId"
       Type="System.String">AdventureworksAppLevel</Property>
      <Property Name="SsoProviderImplementation" Type="System.String">
       Microsoft.Office.SecureStoreService.Server.SecureStoreProvider,
       Microsoft.Office.SecureStoreService, Version=14.0.0.0, Culture=neutral,
       PublicKeyToken=71e9bce111e9429c</Property>
      <Property Name="WcfAuthenticationMode" Type="System.String">
        Credentials
      </Property>
      <Property Name="WcfEndpointAddress" Type="System.String">
      http://awsharepoint.aw.com:5555/AdventureWorksDWService.svc</Property>
    </Properties>
  </LobSystemInstance>
</LobSystemInstances>

       <FilterDescriptors>
          <FilterDescriptor Type="Username" Name="ApplicationLevelUsername">
            <Properties>
              <Property Name="UsedForDisambiguation" Type="System.Boolean">
                False
              </Property>
              <Property Name="IsDefault" Type="System.Boolean">false</Property>
              <Property Name="CaseSensitive" Type="System.Boolean">false</Property>
```

```
        </Properties>
      </FilterDescriptor>
    </FilterDescriptors>

      <Parameter Direction="In" Name="EmployeeUsername">
        <TypeDescriptor TypeName="System.String"
         AssociatedFilter="ApplicationLevelUsername" Name="EmployeeUsername" />
      </Parameter>
```

The `SecondarySsoApplicationId` element specifies the SSS Target Application that will provide the application-level credentials. The `FilterDescriptor` element of type `Username`, named `ApplicationlevelUsername`, defines the filter, but does not actually relate it to the input parameter. The `Parameter` element defines the input parameter, and the `AssociatedFilter` attribute references the `Username` filter to complete the definition.

CONFIGURING CLIENT AUTHENTICATION

When configuring authentication for BCS solutions, you must take care to consider authentication from both the server side and the client side. While identical configuration options are given for the server and the client in the drop-down lists in the Connection Properties dialog, accessing an External System from an Office client can be very different from accessing that system from the browser. Furthermore, the authentication strategy used by the client may be different from the one used by the server.

When External Lists are synchronized to Microsoft Outlook or the SharePoint Designer, BCS directly accesses the External System from the client machine. The model contained in the BDC service is cached on the client, along with the `AuthenticationMode` element, which determines the authentication strategy used by the client. The Connection Properties dialog has tabs for both the server and the client, which enables you to configure them separately.

Using Passthrough Authentication

The Impersonation and Delegation model still has some meaning on the client, but it is not nearly as significant as on the server. This is largely because the client will always attempt to connect directly to the External System with a given set of credentials. Because there is no intermediate process like IIS, the concept of impersonation is limited to using a set of credentials other than those under which the user is logged in.

Setting the value of the `AuthenticationMode` element to `Passthrough` for the client causes BCS to attempt a connection to the designated External System using the credentials of the current client. This represents a straightforward client/server relationship. There is no intermediate system and no double-hop issue to confuse the scenario. If the current user is authenticated by the External System and authorized to perform the appropriate operations, then full CRUD operations are possible in both the Outlook and SharePoint Workspace clients as well as custom VSTO add-ins that call the BDC Runtime API.

Using RevertToSelf Authentication

Technically, `RevertToSelf` still falls under the Trusted Subsystem model of authentication, but it is virtually meaningless on the client. Setting the value of the `AuthenticationMode` element to `RevertToSelf` causes BCS to use the credentials of the current client exactly like `Passthrough`.

Using Secure Store Service Authentication

Clients support the use of credentials defined in SSS for connecting to External Systems. However, the management and storage of the credentials is handled differently from on the server. Because all access from the client is direct to the External System, the client cannot use the credential store on the server. Furthermore, passing credentials between the Secure Store Service and the Office client represents a significant security threat and is prohibited.

Because SSS cannot pass credentials to clients, a different mechanism must be used to manage and store credentials. Therefore, BCS makes use of the Credential Manager applet on the client to handle the credentials. Credential Manager is not part of BCS; it is part of the client operating system. Credential Manager is used for saving passwords for endpoints such as websites so users can be remembered when they are browsing. BCS simply takes advantage of this existing repository to save its credentials as well.

If a BCS model uses `WindowsCredentials`, `RdbCredentials`, or `Credentials` authentication, then BCS will prompt the user to enter credentials the first time it accesses the External System. After the user enters the credentials, they will be saved in the Credential Manager. Future connections will simply use the saved credentials. Figure 8-12 shows a typical login dialog presented to a user.

FIGURE 8-12

The challenge with using a separate store on each client is that the end user may not know the credentials that should be used for accessing the External System. If the BCS model calls for an individual mapping for each user, it may be reasonable to assume the end user knows what credentials to enter. However, a group mapping is problematic because a single set of credentials must be shared with many end users. It is simply unlikely that such a situation would be allowed under most organizational security policies. Therefore, the client authentication model generally should not be configured to use a group mapping.

Credentials stored in the Credential Manager may be managed by the end user. Access the Credential Manager by selecting Control Panel ➪ User Accounts ➪ Credential Manager in Windows 7. Figure 8-13 shows the Credential Manager with BCS credentials stored. If the end user deletes credentials from the Credential Manager, BCS will prompt for new credentials on the next connection to the External System.

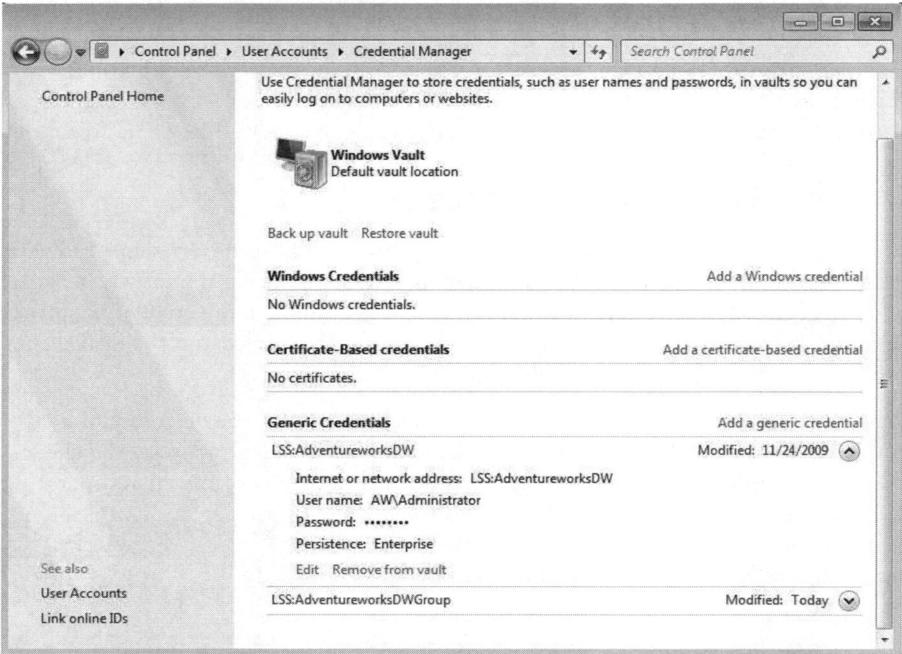

FIGURE 8-13

WORKING WITH THE SSS OBJECT MODEL

While BCS and SSS work well together out of the box to provide authentication, SSS credentials can also be used in custom solutions. In particular, there are two cases in which custom code might be used in credential management. The first involves retrieving credentials for use in a custom application, and the second involves creating your own custom credential provider.

Before you can write code against the SSO API, you must set references to the `Microsoft.BusinessData.dll`, `Microsoft.Office.SecureStoreService.dll`, and `Microsoft.Office.Server.dll`. These assemblies are all located in the ISAPI directory.

Retrieving Server-Side Credentials

Credentials stored in SSS can be retrieved programmatically for use with custom solutions. A common case involves the use of SSS credentials in a custom web part to access an External System. As an example, the following code shows a portion of a web part that builds up a database connection string based on the credentials from a Target Application in SSS.

```
protected override void OnPreRender(EventArgs e)
{
    string username = string.Empty;
    string password = string.Empty;
```

```
    try
    {

        ISecureStoreProvider p = SecureStoreProviderFactory.Create();

        using (SecureStoreCredentialCollection creds =
               p.GetCredentials(ApplicationId))
        {
            foreach (SecureStoreCredential c in creds)
            {
                switch (c.CredentialType)
                {
                    case SecureStoreCredentialType.UserName:
                        username = ConvertToString(c.Credential);
                        break;

                    case SecureStoreCredentialType.Password:
                        password = ConvertToString(c.Credential);
                        break;

                    case SecureStoreCredentialType.WindowsUserName:
                        username = ConvertToString(c.Credential);
                        break;

                    case SecureStoreCredentialType.WindowsPassword:
                        password = ConvertToString(c.Credential);
                        break;
                }
            }
        }

        SqlConnectionStringBuilder cBuilder = new SqlConnectionStringBuilder();
        cBuilder.DataSource = ServerName;
        cBuilder.InitialCatalog = DatabaseName;
        cBuilder.UserID = username;
        cBuilder.Password = password;

        messages.Text = cBuilder.ConnectionString;

    }
    catch (Exception x)
    {
        messages.Text = x.Message;
    }
}


private String ConvertToString(SecureString s)
{
    IntPtr b = Marshal.SecureStringToBSTR(s);
    try { return Marshal.PtrToStringBSTR(b); }
    finally { Marshal.FreeBSTR(b); }
}
```

The web part defines custom properties for ServerName and DatabaseName that are simply entered into the configuration pane. The user name and password, however, are retrieved from SSS. A connection to SSS is made via the Microsoft.Office.SecureStoreService.SecureStoreFactoryProvider class. Credentials are then retrieved from SSS by calling the GetCredentials method and passing in the name of the Target Application.

The credentials are returned in code as an instance of the SecureString class. The SecureString is then converted to clear text to build up the connection string, which can then be used to access the External System. The connection string generated by the web part takes the form shown in the following code.

```
Data Source = {server name};Initial Catalog={database name};
User Id={username}; Password={password}.
```

Retrieving Client-Side Credentials

Credentials stored on the client can be retrieved for use in custom solutions as well. Following the principle that is used throughout BCS architecture, an API exists for retrieving credentials from the client that parallels the API used on the server. The code for retrieving credentials is nearly identical to the server except that you must set references to the client-side components Microsoft.BusinesData.dll and Microsoft.Office.BusinessData.dll. These assemblies are both located in the Office directory on the client. Instead of connecting to the store using the SecureStoreFactoryProvider class, access to the local store is done through the Microsoft.Office.BusinessData.LocalSecureStoreProvider class. After that, the code is essentially identical to the server code.

Along with the API supplied by the BCS architecture, the Credential Manager is accessible through an unmanaged API defined in Windows\System32\credui.dll. In order to use the API, you must import it into the current VS2010 project. The following code shows how to import the CredUIPromptForCredentials method, which is used to validate credentials and prompt the user to enter them when required.

```
[DllImport("credui", EntryPoint = "CredUIPromptForCredentialsW",
          CharSet = CharSet.Unicode, SetLastError = true, ExactSpelling = true)]
private static extern CredUIReturnCodes CredUIPromptForCredentials(
    ref CREDUI_INFO creditUR,
    string targetName,
    IntPtr reserved1,
    int iError,
    StringBuilder userName,
    int maxUserName,
    StringBuilder password,
    int maxPassword,
    ref int iSave,
    CREDUI_FLAGS flags);
```

The CredUIPromptForCredentials method takes the user name, password, and target application and verifies them against what is stored in the Credential Manager. The user name and password can either contain values or be left empty to simply retrieve the current values. The following code shows how to call the CredUIPromptForCredentials method from a Windows application.

```
StringBuilder username = new StringBuilder();
StringBuilder password = new StringBuilder();
string target = targetApplication.Text;
int saveCreds = 1;
CREDUI_FLAGS flags = CREDUI_FLAGS.GENERIC_CREDENTIALS;
CREDUI_INFO info = new CREDUI_INFO();
info.hwndParent = this.Handle;
info.pszCaptionText = "Credentials";
info.pszMessageText = "Please enter your credentials";
info.cbSize = Marshal.SizeOf(info);

CredUIReturnCodes returnCodes = CredUIPromptForCredentials(ref info,
                                                           target,
                                                           IntPtr.Zero,
                                                           0,
                                                           username,
                                                           50,
                                                           password,
                                                           50,
                                                           ref saveCreds,
                                                           flags);

if (returnCodes == CredUIReturnCodes.NO_ERROR)
{
    targetUsername.Text = username.ToString();
    targetPassword.Text = password.ToString();
}
```

If the credentials exist they are simply returned. If the credentials do not exist, the user is prompted to enter the credentials. Credential Manager generates the login dialog automatically, as shown in Figure 8-14.

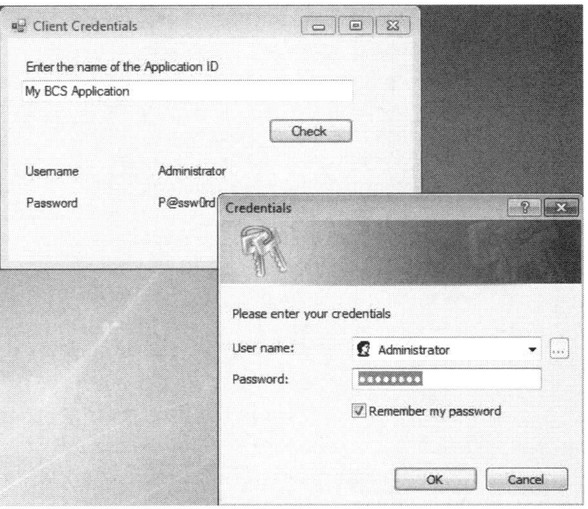

FIGURE 8-14

Creating a Pluggable Provider

While SSS provides a good core credential management capability, many organizations already have an existing single sign-on solution that is independent of SSS. Because the organization already has a significant investment in the existing solution, it may not want to move to SSS. In this case the answer is to create a custom provider so that BCS can use the credentials in the existing single sign-on solution instead of SSS. This custom solution is called a *pluggable provider.*

Pluggable providers are made possible by the `SsoProviderImplementation` element in the BCS application model. The `SsoProviderImplementation` element takes the value of a type that implements the `ISecureStoreProvider` interface. This causes BCS to call the custom pluggable provider for credentials instead of SSS.

Creating a pluggable provider is reasonably straightforward. You create a class that inherits from `ISecureStoreProvider` and install the resulting assembly in the GAC. Once the assembly is in the GAC, you may register it as the default provider by using the PowerShell commandlet `Set-SPSecureStoreDefaultProvider`. When set as the default provider, SharePoint Designer will automatically write the appropriate type into the `SsoProviderImplementation` element in the application model whenever the Connection Properties dialog specifies the use of `WindowsCredentials`, `RdbCredentials`, or `Credentials` for the `AuthenticationMode`. The following code shows a portion of an application model with a pluggable provider specified.

```
<LobSystemInstance Name="AWDW">
  <Properties>
    <Property Name="AuthenticationMode" Type="System.String">
      WindowsCredentials
    </Property>
    <Property Name="DatabaseAccessProvider" Type="System.String">
      SqlServer
    </Property>
    <Property Name="RdbConnection Data Source" Type="System.String">
      CONTOSOSERVER
    </Property>
    <Property Name="RdbConnection Initial Catalog" Type="System.String">
      AdventureworksDW
    </Property>
    <Property Name="RdbConnection Integrated Security" Type="System.String">
      SSPI
    </Property>
    <Property Name="RdbConnection Pooling" Type="System.String">true</Property>
    <Property Name="ShowInSearchUI" Type="System.String"></Property>
    <Property Name="SsoApplicationId" Type="System.String">DBCREDS</Property>
    <Property Name="SsoProviderImplementation" Type="System.String">
     PluggableSSO.CustomSecureStoreProvider, PluggableSSO,
     Version=1.0.0.0, Culture=neutral,
     PublicKeyToken=0b59646182efb774</Property>
  </Properties>
</LobSystemInstance>
```

The `ISecureStoreProvider` interface defines the methods `GetCredentials`, `GetRestrictedCredentials`, `GetCredentialsUsingTicket`, `IssueTicket`, and `DeleteCredentials`. It also defines a single property, `ProviderInformation`. The methods for retrieving credentials allow the implementation of different methods for generic, secure, and ticketed credential types. The following code shows the implementation of the `GetCredentials` method using a custom database to store the application and credential information.

```
public SecureStoreCredentialCollection GetCredentials(string appId)
{
        CredentialStore store = new CredentialStore();

        var q = from ac in store.ApplicationCredentials
             where ac.ApplicationName.Equals(appId,
```

```
                  StringComparison.CurrentCultureIgnoreCase)
               select ac;

        SecureUsername userName = new SecureUsername();
        userName.UnsecureString = q.First().Username;

        SecurePassword password = new SecurePassword();
        password.UnsecureString = q.First().Password;

        List<ISecureStoreCredential> evidence = new List<ISecureStoreCredential>();
        evidence.Add(userName);
        evidence.Add(password);

        SecureStoreCredentialCollection creds =
          new SecureStoreCredentialCollection(evidence);

        return creds;
}
```

The `GetCredentials` method returns a `SecureStoreCredentialCollection` object, which contains objects that implement the `ISecureStoreCredential` interface. In the sample code, the credentials are retrieved from a database by means of Language Integrated Query (LINQ) calls through an Entity Framework model. The retrieved credentials are then placed in new instances of classes that inherit from `ISecureStoreCredential` and returned to BCS. The following code shows a class that implements `ISecureStoreCredential` to hold the returned user name.

```
class SecureUsername : ISecureStoreCredential
{
    private string unsecureString;

    public string UnsecureString
    {
        set { unsecureString = value; }
    }

    #region ISecureStoreCredential

    public System.Security.SecureString Credential
    {
        get
        {
            char[] chars = unsecureString.ToCharArray();
            SecureString s = new SecureString();
            foreach (char c in chars)
                s.AppendChar(c);
            return s;
        }
    }

    public SecureStoreCredentialType CredentialType
    {
```

```
            get { return SecureStoreCredentialType.UserName; }
        }

        public void Dispose()
        {
            unsecureString = null;
        }

    #endregion

    }
```

UNDERSTANDING CLAIMS AUTHENTICATION

Although Windows authentication is still the most widely used mechanism for authenticating users, it presents several challenges to developers and IT professionals. As users increasingly need to cross system and network boundaries, new standards are emerging to simplify authentication and identity management. These standards are embodied in claims authentication.

Understanding Authentication Challenges

Each of the classic authentication mechanisms, such as NTLM, Kerberos, and forms, has limitations that directly affect the design and implementation of BCS solutions. Furthermore, these limitations have a larger impact on the maintenance and operation of SharePoint sites in general. Specifically, classic authentication mechanisms present the following challenges, which are explained in more detail in the following sections.

- Multiple user repositories often exist within the enterprise.
- Individual applications must run queries directly against a user repository for authentication.
- Identity exists only within a given network, and delegation of identity is not widely supported across systems.

Within any organization, custom ASP.NET web applications, services, and SharePoint extranets often use forms-based authentication and have their own SQL database acting as a user repository. As a result, multiple user repositories can exist throughout an organization, which severely limits the interoperability of these systems. Furthermore, user maintenance can be extremely challenging, as users must be added and removed from multiple repositories when staff changes.

In response to the challenges of multiple user repositories, many organizations have implemented Active Directory as a single-user repository. Active Directory improves user management, but still presents several limitations. These limitations involve the efficiency of querying Active Directory and the management of identity between systems.

If Active Directory is set up as the single-user repository in an organization, then every application must query Active Directory directly to authenticate users. Hopefully, these queries are efficient, but it would be easy for developers to write custom code against the Active Directory API that causes performance problems for other applications. Additionally, significant code rewrites may be necessary if directories from other organizations come into play, such as through a merger or an acquisition.

Beyond simply querying for authentication, it can be difficult to manage user identity across systems and networks. Earlier in the chapter, the limitations of impersonation were presented. This problem is compounded when the scope of interoperability extends beyond the current network. It is quite common, for example, to see SharePoint use Windows authentication for users inside the firewall, but forms-based authentication for users outside the firewall. This is problematic because each authentication mechanism results in a separate identity. So if an employee logs in from home, he or she will not be the same user as when logging in from work.

Several workarounds exist today to solve various identity problems. Organizations can make use of a virtual private network (VPN) to allow users at home to access SharePoint using their Windows credentials. Organizations can also set up an Internet Security and Acceleration (ISA) server that provides a forms-based login while creating a true Windows identity. Third-party solutions such as Citrix can also be used to give remote users access to the network. These workarounds, however, fall short of a comprehensive solution to identity management across systems and networks. The answer to all of these problems lies in the implementation of claims authentication.

Understanding Claims Concepts

Claims authentication is a new form of authentication available in SharePoint 2010. When a new web application is created through Central Administration that uses *Claims Mode authentication*, the resulting IIS website is configured to be *claims-aware*. Claims-aware websites can still make use of classic repositories such as Active Directory or SQL Server, but the user is also issued an additional claims token as part of the authentication process.

Claims authentication overcomes the current limitations of multiple repositories and centralized repositories by moving the task of authentication out of the application altogether. Under a claims authentication model, applications no longer need to worry about querying a user repository. Instead, the user arrives at the application with authentication already completed. This is the single biggest advantage of claims authentication; the authentication mechanism is abstracted out of the application.

Earlier in the chapter, metaphors were presented for both NTLM and Kerberos authentication. NTLM was likened to a carnival where a ticket must be presented for each ride, while Kerberos was likened to a theme park where payment is made once at the gate. A common metaphor for claims authentication involves the issuing of a license and the purchase of alcohol. In this metaphor a person (the end user) wants to purchase alcohol from a store (the application). In order to purchase the alcohol, the person must be 21 years old (the claim). At the point of purchase, the user presents a license (the token) to the clerk, who verifies the person's age and sells him or her the alcohol.

The key to understanding this metaphor is recognizing that the license was issued not by the store, but by the state. The authentication authority is completely independent of the application that uses the token to allow access. Of course, the entire transaction hinges upon the fact that the store trusts the state to issue a valid license with a correct birth date. Furthermore, the license can be used for authentication in multiple scenarios like cashing a check, boarding a plane, and of course driving.

There are several advantages to this authentication model over the current models. First, a single authentication authority can be used across multiple applications. Second, applications do not have to query a repository. Third, the authentication authority can span systems and networks. Fourth, new authorization scenarios are supported that are simply not possible with current models.

Consider the following metaphor to understand how new authorization scenarios are enabled by claims authentication. Instead of purchasing alcohol at a store, imagine that the person wants to gain access to a club that sells alcohol. In this case the person presents the license to the bouncer, who trusts the license and its claim that the person is 21. In response the bouncer stamps the person's hand upon entry. Now the person can simply show the hand stamp to the bartender when ordering a drink.

The key to understanding this metaphor is that the hand stamp now represents a new claim added to the user upon authentication. The point here is that the central authority cannot know all the claims every application wants to retain about a user. So the claims model allows for new claims to be added to the user after authentication. In subsequent resource requests the application can simply look for the presence of the new claim and grant access.

Understanding Claims Architecture

Microsoft's claims authentication architecture is based on the Windows Identity Foundation (WIF). WIF is a set of managed classes available in .NET Framework 3.5 SP1. WIF provides the foundation for creating Security Token Services (STS). An STS authenticates a user and issues the claims token that will be used to gain access to resources with which a trust has been established. WIF can also be used to create claims-aware sites and services.

At the enterprise level, an organization can implement Active Directory Federation Services 2.0 (AD FS). AD FS 2.0 can issue tokens and establish trust with other organizations and systems. Organizations that share trusts can share identities across network boundaries. AD FS also supports existing authentication mechanisms, so a move to claims authentication does not stop existing applications from functioning.

The claims-aware capabilities in SharePoint 2010 are built on WIF. SharePoint can use tokens issued by an STS to grant access to sites. Additionally, SharePoint has its own STS that can add claims to a token. This is the SharePoint version of the hand stamp discussed earlier. Figure 8-15 shows a complete diagram of the authentication process.

Authentication begins when the end user makes a request to access a resource inside SharePoint. SharePoint responds by redirecting the user to authenticate with the appropriate identity provider. Authentication could be done via a forms-based login screen or a Live ID login, or Windows authentication could authenticate the user, as described earlier in the chapter. In any case, successful authentication results in the identity provider's issuing a token to the user with a given set of claims. Once this token is issued, a service request is made to the SharePoint STS, which responds by adding claims to the token. The token is then used to access the requested resource and the response is sent to the user. Future requests for resources can simply use the issued token.

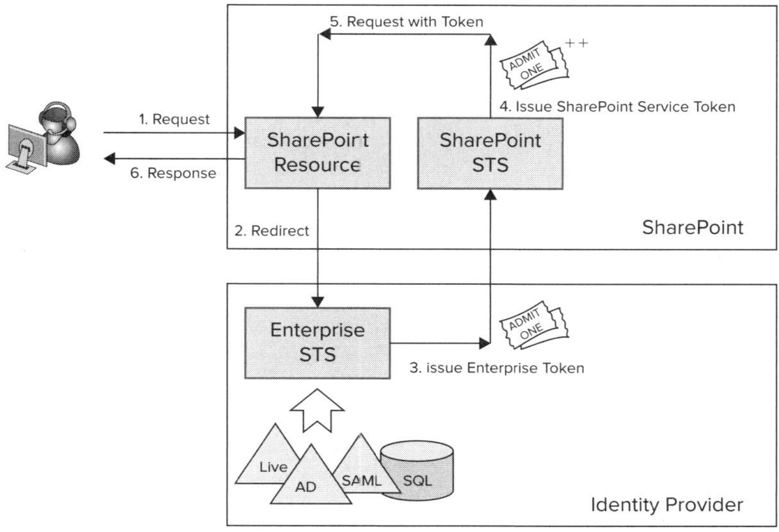

FIGURE 8-15

CONFIGURING CLAIMS AUTHENTICATION

Claims authentication is really designed to be used in a delegation environment in which the identity of the current user is always used to access resources. This is a far more secure setup than using the BDC identity or transforming credentials with SSS. For that reason, `Passthrough` authentication is the only strategy that makes any sense. In this scenario the token used to access SharePoint resources will be used to access the External System.

While `Passthrough` authentication is ideal in theory, the reality is that many External Systems are not *claims-aware*. This means that they have no mechanism for accepting the claims token passed by SharePoint. In these cases, you may use SSS to provide a set of credentials for the External System, make use of the Claims-to-Windows Token Service (c2WTS), or create a claims-aware web service to wrap the External System.

Understanding the Claims-to-Windows Token Service

The Claims-to-Windows Token Service creates Windows security tokens from claims tokens so that applications may impersonate the current user when accessing a system that does not support claims. Note, however, that this is only possible for Windows identities. The c2WTS cannot create Windows security tokens for users authenticated by non-Windows mechanisms such as LiveID or forms-based authentication.

The c2WTS is part of WIF, but may be started and stopped through Central Administration in the list of services. The c2WTS must be configured with a list of the accounts that are allowed to transform tokens. This is accomplished by adding the accounts to the `c2wtshost.exe.config` file located in `Program Files\Windows Identity Foundation\v3.5`. SharePoint 2010 installs with the service stopped and includes the WSS_WPG group in the authorization list. The following code shows the configuration file.

```
<?xml version="1.0"?>
<configuration>
  <configSections>
    <section name="windowsTokenService"
 type="Microsoft.IdentityModel.WindowsTokenService.Configuration
.WindowsTokenServiceSection, Microsoft.IdentityModel.WindowsTokenService,
 Version=3.5.0.0, Culture=neutral, PublicKeyToken=31bf3856ad364e35" />
  </configSections>
  <startup>
    <supportedRuntime version="v4.0" />
    <supportedRuntime version="v2.0.50727" />
  </startup>
  <windowsTokenService>
    <!--
        By default no callers are allowed to use the Windows Identity
        Foundation Claims To NT Token Service.
        Add the identities you wish to allow below.
      -->
    <allowedCallers>
      <clear />
      <add value="WSS_WPG" />
    </allowedCallers>
  </windowsTokenService>
</configuration>
```

The c2WTS is used by BCS to create Windows security tokens automatically when the SQL Connector is used, provided that Kerberos is implemented. Additionally, you can use code to create a Windows security token for use in .NET Assembly and Custom connectors. The process involves extracting the Windows claim from the current token and calling c2WTS to return the Windows identity. Once the Windows identity is obtained, it can be used through impersonation to access the External System. The following code shows a simple web part that displays the Windows identity for the current user who is logged in to a SharePoint site operating in claims mode.

```
public class Claims2WindowsTokenPart : WebPart
{

    protected override void RenderContents(HtmlTextWriter writer)
    {
        //Get Windows claim from token
        IClaimsIdentity identity =
        (ClaimsIdentity)Thread.CurrentPrincipal.Identity;
        string upn = null;
        foreach (Claim claim in identity.Claims)
        {
            if (StringComparer.Ordinal.Equals(
                System.IdentityModel.Claims.ClaimTypes.Upn,
                claim.ClaimType))
```

```
                {
                    upn = claim.Value;
                }
            }

            //Get the Windows Identity
            WindowsIdentity windowsIdentity = null;
            if (!String.IsNullOrEmpty(upn))
            {
                try
                {
                    windowsIdentity = S4UClient.UpnLogon(upn);
                }
                catch (SecurityAccessDeniedException)
                {
                    writer.Write("<p>Access to c2WTS denied.</p>");
                    return;
                }
            }
            else
            {
                writer.Write("<p>No Windows claim found</p>");
            }

            //Use the Windows Identity
            using (WindowsImpersonationContext ctxt =
                   windowsIdentity.Impersonate())
            {
                writer.Write("<p>Windows identity is: " +
                             windowsIdentity.Name + "</p>");
            }
        }
    }
```

The first step in the code is to obtain the `Microsoft.IdentityModel.Claims.IClaimsIdentity` for the current user. The `IClaimsIdentity` interface gives access to all of the claims in the current user's token. Using this interface, the set of claims can be examined looking for the `Upn` claim type, which represents the Kerberos Unique Principal Name for the current user.

If the `Upn` claim is found, then the `Microsoft.IdentityModel.WindowsTokenService.S4UClient` class can be used to call the c2WTS. The `UpnLogon()` method creates a `WindowsIdentity` from the Kerberos UPN. This `WindowsIdentity` may then be used to create a `WindowsImpersonationContext` for accessing the External System.

Creating a Claims-Aware Service

Another option for handling systems that are not claims-aware is to simply wrap them in a claims-aware WCF service. This approach is superior to solutions that rely on the c2WTS because they may easily be moved between environments without worrying about the availability of the c2WTS. A claims-aware service can be written quite simply with WIF and the WIF SDK. Once installed, the WIF SDK supplies project templates in Visual Studio for claims-aware websites and services. Figure 8-16 shows the New Web Site dialog in Visual Studio 2010.

FIGURE 8-16

When a new claims-aware WCF service is created, it will initially accept tokens from any provider. In this configuration the SharePoint token can be passed to the service, which then uses information from the token to perform authentication and authorization. As a simple sample, the following code shows a WCF service that implements two methods: `GetClaims` and `GetClaim`. These methods are used to return the current set of claims for display as an External List, which is an excellent way to see the set of claims in the SharePoint token.

```
public List<ClaimDatum> GetClaims()
{
    List<ClaimDatum> claimData = new List<ClaimDatum>();

    try
    {
        IClaimsIdentity identity =
       (IClaimsIdentity)WindowsClaimsIdentity.GetCurrent();

        foreach (Claim claim in identity.Claims)
        {
            ClaimDatum claimDatum = new ClaimDatum();
            claimDatum.Key = claim.ClaimType;
            claimDatum.Value = claim.Value;
            claimData.Add(claimDatum);
        }

        return claimData;
    }
```

```
        catch (Exception x)
        {
            ClaimDatum claimDatum = new ClaimDatum();
            claimDatum.Key = "Error";
            claimDatum.Value = x.Message;
            claimData.Add(claimDatum);

            return claimData;
        }

    }

    public ClaimDatum GetClaim(string Key)
    {

        IClaimsPrincipal principal = (IClaimsPrincipal)Thread.CurrentPrincipal;
        IClaimsIdentity identity = (IClaimsIdentity)principal.Identity;

        ClaimDatum claimDatum = new ClaimDatum();

        foreach (Claim claim in identity.Claims)
        {
            if (claim.ClaimType.Equals(Key,
                System.StringComparison.CurrentCultureIgnoreCase))
            {
                claimDatum.Key = claim.ClaimType;
                claimDatum.Value = claim.Value;
            }
        }

        return claimDatum;
    }
```

The methods `GetClaims` and `GetClaim` are intended to be used to support a `Finder` and `SpecificFinder` operation respectively in an External List. The methods return `ClaimDatum` objects, which are created by means of a simple custom class not shown in the code. Once created, the External List will simply display an item for each claim in the token. In a more sophisticated implementation the claims could be used to support authentication and authorization to the External System.

Using an STS with a Claims-Aware Service

Creating a service that accepts all tokens is simple and educational, but a production system will likely require more stringent controls. In this case you can choose to create a custom STS or install ADFS 2.0. A custom STS can be easily created using the WIF SDK, and AD FS 2.0 can be installed in the enterprise and configured to be trusted by both SharePoint and the WCF service. While the complete creation of a custom STS and the setup of AD FS 2.0 is beyond the scope of this book, the basic approach is to establish trust with the SharePoint 2010 installation and then configure the BCS model to use the STS when accessing the External System.

In order to configure the BCS model to use a given token when accessing an External System, you must create a *binding provider*. A binding provider is a class that creates a binding referencing the desired STS. The assembly information is then entered into the `WcfBindingProviderImplementation` element of the BCS model. The following code shows a sample model.

```
<LobSystem Type="Wcf" Name="ShowClaimsService">
  <Properties>
    <Property Name="WcfBindingProviderImplementation"
     Type="System.String">ClaimsAwareExternalSystemBinding.BindingProvider,
     ClaimsAwareExternalSystemBinding, Version=1.0.0.0, Culture=neutral,
     PublicKeyToken=9e5b30f344ec8fef
    </Property>
    <Property Name="WcfMexDiscoMode" Type="System.String">Disco</Property>
    <Property Name="WcfMexDocumentUrl"
     Type="System.String"> http://contososerver:1234/Service.svc?wsdl
    </Property>
    <Property Name="WcfProxyNamespace"
      Type="System.String">BCSServiceProxy
    </Property>
    <Property Name="WildcardCharacter" Type="System.String">*</Property>
    <Property Name="WsdlFetchAuthenticationMode" Type="System.String">
      PassThrough
    </Property>
  </Properties>
...
</LobSystem>
```

You build the binding provider by creating a class that inherits from `IWcfBindingProvider`. In this class the `CreateBinding` is overridden and a binding is created to the STS. The following code shows a sample implementation.

```
public class BindingProvider : IWcfBindingProvider
{
    static readonly string CertificateName = "CN=STSTestCert";

    public Binding CreateBinding(
      Microsoft.BusinessData.MetadataModel.ILobSystemInstance lobSystemInstance,
      Binding existingBinding)
    {
        //The STST binding
        WS2007FederationHttpBinding stsBind =
            new WS2007FederationHttpBinding(WSFederationHttpSecurityMode.Message);

        stsBind.Security.Message.IssuerAddress =
            new EndpointAddress("http://awsharepoint:5678/SimpleSTS");
        stsBind.Security.Message.IssuerMetadataAddress =
            new EndpointAddress("http://awsharepoint:5678/SimpleSTS/mex");

        //Don't use Security Context Token binding
        WS2007HttpBinding noSCT = new WS2007HttpBinding(SecurityMode.Message);
        noSCT.Security.Message.EstablishSecurityContext = false;

        stsBind.Security.Message.IssuerBinding = noSCT;

        return stsBind;
    }
}
```

UNDERSTANDING TOKEN AUTHENTICATION

Today many web-based applications use a token-based authentication system. These systems typically have a log-on mechanism that is separate from the applications that they support. For example, Windows Live has a log-on system that uses a Windows Live ID. This ID is used for many applications, including HotMail, SkyDrive, and LiveMesh. Regardless of the application, however, the end user always uses the same log-on screen to authenticate and receive a token that is trusted by the applications. Figure 8-17 shows the Windows Live ID login for access to MSDN subscriptions.

FIGURE 8-17

For these types of BCS solutions, the SharePoint SDK provides some starter code in the form of a Netflix sample. The SDK has good setup instructions for the sample, which requires the creation of a Netflix account. The Netflix sample uses OAuth, which is a protocol that establishes support for using APIs associated with services. In the case of the Netflix sample, OAuth allows BCS to consume Netflix movie queues and expose them as ECTs. Figure 8-18 shows a Netflix movie queue displayed in the Business Data List web part. Custom XSLT is used to transform the URL for the box art into an image.

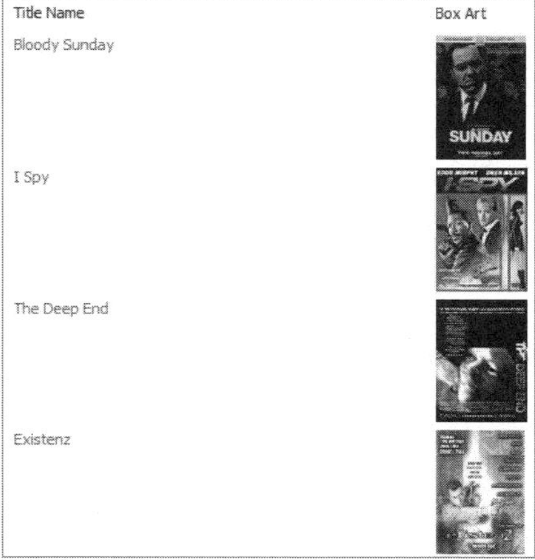

FIGURE 8-18

Because BCS does not provide out-of-the-box support for token-based authentication systems, a custom Secure Store provider must be created. Additionally, a custom authorization handler must be created to redirect users to the appropriate logon page for the system. The Netflix sample implements both of these components, which can be used as a basis for your own solutions. Figure 8-19 shows the basic architecture for the Netflix sample.

Custom Secure Store providers were discussed earlier in the chapter. The Netflix sample uses such a provider to work with OAuth tokens. In the case of the Netflix sample, however, the Secure Store provider requires fields that are particular to OAuth and the Netflix API. In particular, there are three pieces of information required to allow access to the Netflix API: `ConsumerKey`, `ConsumerSecret`, and `ConsumerApp`. All of these fields are provided by Netflix when registering for API access as described in the sample setup.

The custom authorization handler implemented in the Netflix sample is responsible for acquiring and persisting tokens. If the custom Secure Store provider does not have valid credentials for the Netflix service, then the user must be redirected to the Netflix login. Once logged in, the OAuth token can be persisted and used in subsequent operations. Figure 8-20 shows the Netflix login for the sample.

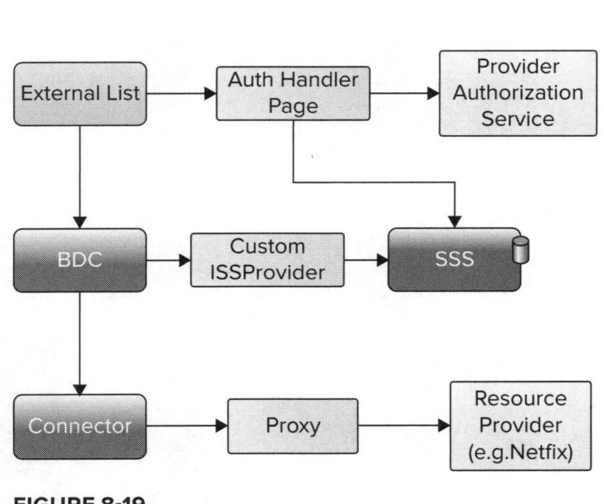

FIGURE 8-19

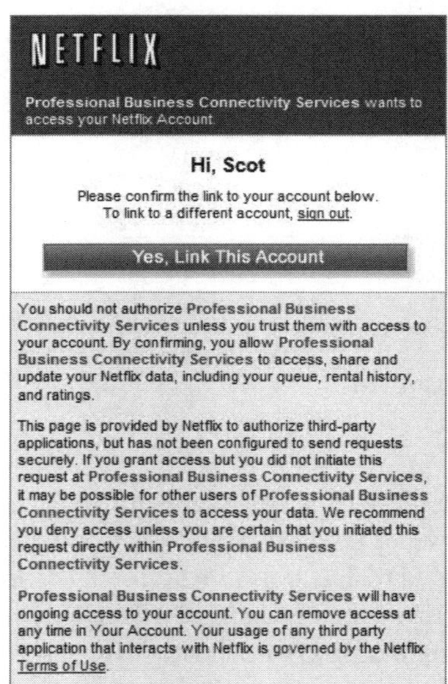

FIGURE 8-20

SUMMARY

Security considerations in BCS solutions are significant. Authentication and authorization are affected by the security protocols in use on the network, the External System, SharePoint, and the BDC service application. In order to successfully create BCS solutions, you must carefully consider all of these factors in the design. While most solutions will be written using Windows authentication against databases, BCS provides the capability to access External Systems that implement more sophisticated capabilities such as claims and OAuth. Because there are so many combinations of authentication for SharePoint, External Systems, and BCS solutions, developers can easily become confused as to which combinations are valid. As a summary, Table 8-1 shows the various authentication combinations and the available BCS authentication modes.

TABLE 8-1: BCS Authentication Matrix

<table>
<tr><th rowspan="3">CONNECTOR</th><th rowspan="3">EXTERNAL SYSTEM AUTHENTICATION SCHEME</th><th colspan="4">SHAREPOINT 2010 AUTHENTICATION SCHEME</th><th rowspan="3">MICROSOFT OUTLOOK 2010</th></tr>
<tr><th colspan="2">CLASSIC MODE</th><th colspan="2">CLAIMS MODE</th></tr>
<tr><th>NTLM</th><th>KERBEROS</th><th>NTLM OR FBA</th><th>KERBEROS</th></tr>
<tr><td rowspan="2">SQL</td><td>Windows</td><td>RevertToSelf
Windows Credentials</td><td>Passthrough
RevertToSelf
Windows Credentials</td><td>Windows Credentials</td><td>Passthrough (c2WTS)
RevertToSelf (c2WTS)
Windows Credentials</td><td>Passthrough
Windows Credentials</td></tr>
<tr><td>Username/ Password</td><td colspan="5">RdbCredentials</td></tr>
<tr><td rowspan="5">WCF</td><td>Windows</td><td>RevertToSelf
Windows Credentials</td><td>Passthrough
RevertToSelf
Windows Credentials</td><td>Windows Credentials</td><td>Passthrough (c2WTS)
RevertToSelf (c2WTS)
Windows Credentials</td><td>Passthrough
Windows Credentials</td></tr>
<tr><td>Username/ Password</td><td colspan="5">Credentials</td></tr>
<tr><td>Claims</td><td colspan="2">Custom Pluggable Provider and Authentication Handler</td><td colspan="2">Passthrough</td><td rowspan="2">Custom VSTO Application with code to create required connection</td></tr>
<tr><td>OAuth</td><td colspan="4">Custom Pluggable Provider and Authentication Handler</td></tr>
<tr><td>Application-Level</td><td colspan="5">Secure Store Service Secondary Application ID</td></tr>
<tr><td>.NET Assembly or Custom</td><td>Any</td><td colspan="5">Custom code to create the required connection</td></tr>
</table>

Working with Enterprise Search

WHAT'S IN THIS CHAPTER?

- Understand Search Architecture
- Learn to enable BCS search support
- Learn to create connectors for search
- Learn to trim search results

Business Connectivity Services and Enterprise Search are intimately related in SharePoint 2010. External Systems may be crawled and searched through BCS by defining just a couple of simple properties in the BDC Metadata Model. Similarly, BCS connectors have replaced the Protocol Handler (used in Microsoft Office SharePoint Server 2007) as the primary mechanism by which the search indexing engine accesses system data. All of this means that you should think of BCS as a part of the search architecture in SharePoint 2010. This chapter covers the search architecture and BCS components in detail so that you can create solutions with powerful capabilities to search for data in External Systems.

UNDERSTANDING SEARCH OFFERINGS

When it comes to Enterprise Search, the number of choices offered under the SharePoint 2010 umbrella can easily confuse you. The offerings include Microsoft SharePoint Foundation 2010 Search, Microsoft Search Server Express, Microsoft Search Server 2010, Microsoft SharePoint Server 2010, and FAST Search Server 2010 for SharePoint. Each of these options is intended for use in different situations, provides different levels of functionality, and has different licensing requirements.

Microsoft SharePoint Foundation 2010 Search is the search engine that ships with SharePoint Foundation 2010. This search engine works only on a single site collection at a time and cannot crawl External Systems. This engine is intended for team or departmental installations of SharePoint that do not require Enterprise Search.

Microsoft Search Server Express is an Enterprise Search engine that is a free downloadable product. This engine can crawl External Systems and supports search federation. It is intended for organizations that want an Enterprise Search capability, but that do not require significant scalability.

Microsoft Search Server 2010 is an Enterprise Search engine that can scale across multiple servers and tens of millions of items. This product is the upgrade for Microsoft Search Server Express. It is intended for organizations that need a scalable search engine, but that are not using Microsoft SharePoint Server 2010.

Microsoft SharePoint Server 2010 includes all the capabilities of Microsoft Search Server 2010 as well as the integration of people search, taxonomy, and social networking. This is the Enterprise Search engine that is built into SharePoint Server 2010, and the one most readers will be using. Therefore, this engine will be the basis for all architectural discussions in this chapter. Additionally, all the BCS solutions in this chapter will work with this engine.

FAST Search Server 2010 for SharePoint is the most powerful of all the search offerings. FAST provides scalability beyond that of any other offering and supports additional customizations and configurations. While a complete discussion of FAST is beyond the scope of this book, the BCS solutions presented in this chapter will also work with the FAST search engine.

UNDERSTANDING SEARCH ARCHITECTURE

The search architecture for Microsoft SharePoint Server 2010 is complex. It includes components for crawling and indexing content, administration, and search query execution. Figure 9-1 shows a diagram of the search architecture. This diagram is explained in the following sections.

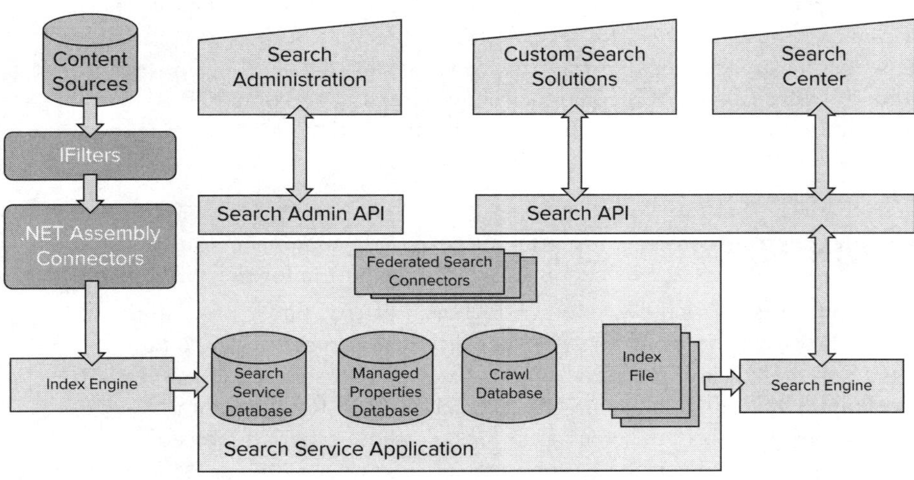

FIGURE 9-1

Understanding the Search Service Application

In the center of the search architecture is the Search Service Application (SSA). The SSA is one of the many shared services available in SharePoint Server. This means that you can create and share instances of the SSA across farms just as with any other service application. From the Central Administration website you can access the SSA by selecting Manage Service Applications. From the list of service applications you can then select the SSA, set its properties, designate administrators, and enter the administration pages. Figure 9-2 shows the SSA in the list of service applications.

FIGURE 9-2

Within the SSA are three databases: the Search Service database, the Managed Properties database, and the Crawl database. The Search Service database maintains configuration data for the SSA. The Managed Properties database contains the definitions for Managed Properties that are defined and mapped to crawled properties. The Crawl database contains configuration information related to content sources to be crawled. The SSA also maintains the index file that is built during the crawl, and support for Federated Search connectors. Each of these components supports search administration, which you can perform by clicking the Manage button for the SSA.

Understanding the Indexing Process

The indexing process is responsible for building the index file. The index file contains properties from content sources along with access control information that ensures that search results display only content to which the user has rights. The process of building the index file involves crawling the designated content sources.

A content source is a repository that you want to search. Content sources can be SharePoint sites, websites, external file systems, Exchange public folders, External Systems, or other custom repositories. The Index Engine gains access to these repositories through .NET Assembly Connectors and access to the contents of individual items through IFilters.

Chapter 8 presented the fundamentals of .NET Assembly Connectors, which are used by BCS to connect with External Systems. The indexing process makes use of these same components to connect with content sources. In previous versions of SharePoint, Protocol Handlers were the primary means of connecting with content sources, but they were difficult to create in managed code and are deprecated. In SharePoint 2010, Protocol Handlers are still supported, but .NET Assembly Connectors should be created whenever a custom repository is used as a content source.

Just as in previous versions of SharePoint, IFilters are used to allow the indexing process to access the body of an item. For example, IFilters are used to allow the indexing process to access the body of Office documents so that a full-text search can be performed. While SharePoint 2010 ships with IFilters for Office documents, you may need to install additional IFilters for other types such as PDF documents. Generally IFilters are available from the appropriate manufacturer, such as Adobe, and require a simple installation on the server on which the indexing process runs.

Understanding the Query Process

Once the index file is created, it may be used to support query execution. Query execution begins when an end user navigates to the Search Center and enters a query. The query in the Search Center may take the form of a simple keyword or an advanced search with multiple values against multiple Managed Properties.

When the user issues the search, the query is sent to the search engine. Within the search engine the query processor accepts the query and also retrieves any required information from the Managed Properties database. Information from the Managed Properties database is required whenever a query is issued against a specific Managed Property, such as Title. The combination of the user query and Managed Property information is then sent to the query server, which executes the query and returns the results. The results are returned as XML to the Search Center, where they are formatted by means of the XSLT contained in the Core Search Results Web Part.

Along with performing a query on its own index, SharePoint can send the query out to other *federated search locations*. Federated search locations are connections to other search services that independently run the query and return the results to the Search Center for display separately. Communication with federated locations is based on the Open Search protocol, so any search service that supports Open Search can be used as a federated location.

The primary way in which users interact with the search engine is through a set of search Web Parts that ships with SharePoint. These search Web Parts may be used independently, but are most often used as part of an Enterprise Search site created via a site template. The Enterprise Search template contains Web Parts for issuing queries and returning results.

USING BASIC BCS SEARCH SUPPORT

Throughout the book you have seen that BCS solutions can range from simple, no-code solutions to complex solutions created in Visual Studio 2010. All BCS solutions, regardless of their complexity, can provide support for indexing and search as long as they define a `Finder` and `SpecificFinder` method to support indexing the External System.

Enterprise Search uses the Finder and SpecificFinder methods to query the External System and build up the search index file. During the indexing process the crawler calls to the Finder method designated as the RootFinder in the BDC Metadata Model. This call returns information about the entity instances in the External System.

If the information returned from the Finder method is sufficient to build the index, no further calls are made. If, however, the call to the Finder method does not return all the required metadata, additional calls are made to the SpecificFinder method for each entity instance.

Enabling Search Support

When creating no-code solutions in SharePoint Designer, you are required to define Finder and SpecificFinder methods to support the creation of External Lists. Additionally, these methods are used to support indexing and search. In order to see how these solutions support indexing and search, you can export an ECT that was modeled in SPD. Opening the file as text will enable you to locate the RootFinder in the model. The following code shows a Finder MethodInstance designated as the RootFinder:

```
<MethodInstances>
 <MethodInstance Type="Finder" ReturnParameterName="Read List"
  Default="true" Name="Read List" DefaultDisplayName="Product Read List">
  <Properties>
   <Property Name="RootFinder" Type="System.String"></Property>
  </Properties>
 </MethodInstance>
</MethodInstances>
```

Notice that the RootFinder property has no value. If you include a value for this property it is simply ignored. Sometimes you may see a value of x in the property, but this is simply a style choice. The presence of the property is enough to designate the Finder method as the RootFinder.

Although the RootFinder property is the only one necessary to support indexing the External System, an additional property is required to allow the ECT to be selected as a content source in the SSA. The ShowInSearchUI property must be present on the LobSystemInstance for the ECT to be selectable as a content source. The following code shows the property:

```
<LobSystemInstances>
 <LobSystemInstance Name="AWProducts">
  <Properties>
   <Property Name="AuthenticationMode" Type="System.String">
    PassThrough
   </Property>
   <Property Name="DatabaseAccessProvider" Type="System.String">
    SqlServer
   </Property>
   <Property Name="RdbConnection Data Source" Type="System.String">
    AWSERVER
   </Property>
   <Property Name="RdbConnection Initial Catalog" Type="System.String">
    AdventureworksProducts
   </Property>
```

```
      <Property Name="RdbConnection Integrated Security" Type="System.String">
       SSPI
      </Property>
      <Property Name="RdbConnection Pooling" Type="System.String">
       True
      </Property>
      <Property Name="ShowInSearchUI" Type="System.String"></Property>
     </Properties>
    </LobSystemInstance>
   </LobSystemInstances>
```

Just like the `RootFinder` property, the `ShowInSearchUI` property does not require a value. Its presence is enough to allow the ECT to appear as a content source in the SSA. Again, as with the `RootFinder` property, you may occasionally see examples in which this property has a value of `x`.

Once the `RootFinder` and `ShowInSearchUI` properties are added to the model, you may configure the ECT as a content source. Simply create a new content source in the SSA and select Line of Business Data as the type. All the ECTs with the `ShowInSearchUI` property will appear next to checkboxes. Check the ECT and you can immediately begin a full crawl of the External System provided the account performing the crawl has permission to use the BDC Metadata Model and access the External System. Figure 9-3 shows the Add Content Source page with some ECTs visible.

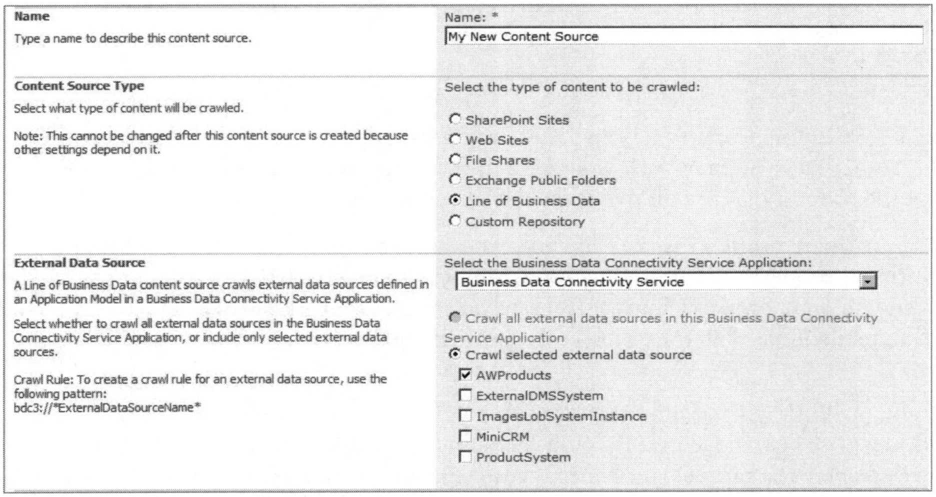

FIGURE 9-3

In addition to full crawls, BCS solutions can also support incremental crawls with the `LastModifiedTimeStampField` property. This property has a value that refers to a `DateTime` field, which indicates the last time the item was modified. If the item has not been modified since the last incremental crawl, it will not be included in the current incremental crawl. The following code shows an example of the property mapping to a field in the ECT named `ChangedDateTime`. This mapping specifies that the `ChangedDateTime` field in the External System will be used to determine whether the row of data has changed since the last crawl.

```
<MethodInstances>
 <MethodInstance Type="Finder" ReturnParameterName="Read List"
  Default="true" Name="Read List" DefaultDisplayName="Product Read List">
  <Properties>
   <Property Name="RootFinder" Type="System.String"></Property>
   <Property Name="LastModifiedTimeStampField" Type="System.String">
    ChangedDateTime
   <Property Name="UseClientCachingForSearch"
            Type="System.String"></Property>
  </Properties>
   </Property>
  </Properties>
 </MethodInstance>
</MethodInstances>
```

When defining an ECT in the SharePoint Designer, you may designate a field that will support incremental crawls by checking the Timestamp Field box when defining the `Finder` method in the wizard. Checking this box will add the `LastModifiedTimeStampField` property to the model and set the property value to that of the designated field.

Along with the `LastModifiedTimeStampField` property, note the use of the `UseClientCachingForSearch` property in the Metadata Model. The presence of this property indicates that the `RootFinder` is capable of returning all content for an entity instance within an 8K data block. This tells the crawler that it does not need to make a subsequent call to the `SpecificFinder` method because all required data was returned from the `RootFinder`. Note that the cache size is fixed and works on a per-item basis, so only those items that cannot return all required data will result in an additional call. If the `UseClientCachingForSearch` property is not present, the `LastModifiedTimeStampField` property must also be included under the `SpecificFinder` method instance because it will be called for each item crawled. It is generally a good idea to use the `UseClientCachingForSearch` property whenever possible, as this makes crawling more efficient.

Working with Search Results

As soon as a full crawl of the External System is complete, you may execute searches against the ECT from an Enterprise Search Center. If you have defined a profile page for the ECT, clicking a search result will display the profile page for that entity instance. This approach rounds out the no-code solution by ensuring all aspects of BCS are supported through SPD. As with all BCS solutions, however, you'll be able to take more control of the search behavior later by writing custom code.

Creating and Using Scopes

Search Centers typically have tabs that represent different search scopes. The out-of-the-box All Sites scope encompasses all the BCS content sources that you have defined, but usually you will want to create a separate search scope and tab for the External System. Typically end users will be interested in particular results from an External System and will not want these results mixed with results from SharePoint sites.

You create a search scope through the Search Service Application. Within the SSA you will find a Scopes link. Here you may define a new search scope based on web address, property, or content source. For BCS solutions you use the content source option to reference the content source related to the ECT.

Once you have defined the scope in the SSA, you can make the scope available to a site collection. Start by going to Site Settings ⇨ Site Collection Administration ⇨ Search Settings and enabling custom scopes, for which you will have to enter the URL of the associated Search Center. After that you can go to Site Settings ⇨ Site Collection Administration ⇨ Search Scopes and decide whether or not to use the new scope in the scopes drop-down list. You may then create a new tab in the Enterprise Search Center and associate the new scope with the search tab.

A Search Center is a publishing site that has a Pages library, a Site Pages library, and a Site Assets library. When creating a new search tab for a scope, you will typically add pages to the site using one of the following four-page layouts associated with the Pages library:

- **Search Box:** This is the page layout used for the initial search page. It contains the Search Box Web Part.
- **Search Results:** This is the page layout used to show search results and initiate subsequent searches. This page layout contains several Web Parts for displaying and manipulating search results.
- **Advanced Search:** This is the page layout used to display the Advanced Search Web Part, which enables the selection of multiple search parameters.
- **People Search Results:** This is the page layout used to show search results for the People tab in the Search Center. This page layout contains several Web Parts for displaying and manipulating search results.

By default the Search Center has an All Sites tab and a People tab, which correspond to the out-of-the-box search scopes. What's interesting, and potentially confusing, about the Search Center template is that it actually has two sets of tabs. One set is used to render initial tabs before a search is executed. The other set is used to render tabs that appear in the search results. However, both sets of tabs are given the same names in order to make it appear as though only a single set of tabs exists. The Tabs in Search Pages list contains the first set of tabs and the Tabs in Search Results list contains the second set of tabs. This means that adding a new tab is a multistep process involving the creating of page layouts and tabs.

Once the scope is defined and available, you may go to the Search Center to define search and search results pages. The best way to add the required pages is simply to select View All Site Content from the Site Actions menu in the Search Center. From the All Site Content page, click the Pages library link. Within the Pages library, click the Documents tab, and finally the New Document button in the ribbon, which will present the Create page.

On the Create page you will see the four different page layouts available for the Search Center. For a typical BCS solution you will create a Search Box page and a Search Results page. The exact names of the pages don't matter as long as you keep track of them. Typically, however, these pages are named *Scope*`Search.aspx` and *Scope*`Results.aspx`. Figure 9-4 shows the Create page.

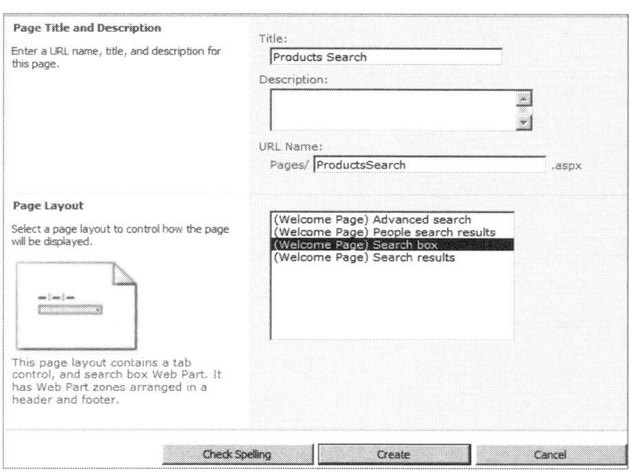

FIGURE 9-4

Once the pages are created, you can create the associated tabs. Again, the best way to do this is through the All Site Content page. In the Tabs in Search list, create a new tab with the same name as the scope and associate the search page. In the Tabs in Search Results list, create a new tab with the same name as the scope and associate the results page. At this point you should be able to see the new tab in the Search Center. Creating the tabs and pages is not enough, however, to duplicate the functionality of the other tabs in the Search Center. In order to fully implement the new scope you must make changes to several Web Parts.

First you must make a change to the Search Box Web Part on both the search and results pages. You can do this by simply putting the appropriate page in edit mode and selecting to edit the Search Box Web Part. Under the Miscellaneous category, locate the Target Search Results Page URL and change it to the name of the results page created earlier. Additionally, you must make a change to the Search Core Results Web Part on the results page. In this Web Part, under the Location Properties category, you must enter the name of the scope in the Scope property. After these changes are complete, publish both the search and results pages. The new scope will now be available in the Search Center and will show results only for the specified External System.

Displaying BCS Data in Search Results

Search results are displayed in the results page by the Core Search Results Web Part. The columns that appear in the search results are specified by the Fetched Properties property located under the Display Properties category. This property is made up of an XML chunk. The following code shows the default XML contained in the Fetched Properties property:

```
<root xmlns:xsi="http://www.w3.org/2001/XMLSchema-instance">
  <Columns>
    <Column Name="WorkId"/>
    <Column Name="Rank"/>
    <Column Name="Title"/>
    <Column Name="Author"/>
    <Column Name="Size"/>
    <Column Name="Path"/>
    <Column Name="Description"/>
    <Column Name="Write"/>
    <Column Name="SiteName"/>
    <Column Name="CollapsingStatus"/>
    <Column Name="HitHighlightedSummary"/>
```

```
    <Column Name="HitHighlightedProperties"/>
    <Column Name="ContentClass"/>
    <Column Name="IsDocument"/>
    <Column Name="PictureThumbnailURL"/>
    <Column Name="ServerRedirectedURL"/>
  </Columns>
</root>
```

While you can customize the list of columns that appear in search results, it is not necessary for simple BCS solutions. Fields defined in the Metadata Model may be mapped to the Title, Author, and Description fields by means of simple properties. In more complex scenarios the hyperlink in the search results can be directed to something other than the profile page.

You can map the Title field in the search results by using the `Title` property under the Entity element in the Metadata Model. The value of the `Title` property refers to the name of the ECT field that should be used for the Title field. The Title field will then be used as the header for each entity instance in the search results. The following code maps the `ProductName` field of the `Entity` to the Title field of the search results:

```
<Entity Namespace="http://aw/bcs" Version="1.0.0.0"
 EstimatedInstanceCount="10000" Name="AWProduct"
 DefaultDisplayName="AWProduct">
 <Properties>
  <Property Name="Title" Type="System.String">ProductName</Property>
 </Properties>
</Entity>
```

When creating ECTs in SPD you can set the `Title` property through the ribbon. You can display the ECT in SPD and then select from the list of available field names. Figure 9-5 shows an example.

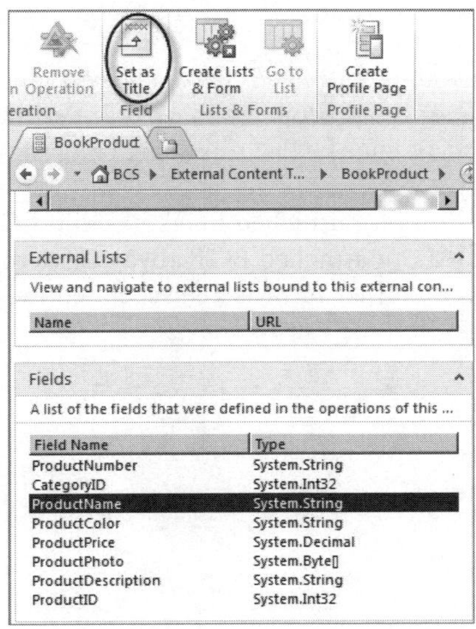

FIGURE 9-5

The Author, Description, and Link fields in the search results are mapped through the `AuthorField`, `DescriptionField`, and `DisplayUriField` properties respectively. The values of these properties map to fields in the ECT. The SharePoint Designer does not support the creation of these properties through its tooling; they must be manually added to the Metadata Model, as in the following example:

```
<MethodInstances>
 <MethodInstance Name="ReadAllItems" Type="Finder"
  ReturnParameterName="documentList"
  ReturnTypeDescriptorPath="DocumentList"
  DefaultDisplayName="Read All Items" Default="true">
  <Properties>
   <Property Name="RootFinder" Type="System.String"></Property>
   <Property Name="LastModifiedTimeStampField" Type="System.String">
    Modified
   </Property>
   <Property Name="DisplayUriField" Type="System.String">
    Url
   </Property>
   <Property Name="DescriptionField" Type="System.String">
    Description
   </Property>
   <Property Name="AuthorField" Type="System.String">
    Author
   </Property>
   <Property Name="UseClientCachingForSearch"
            Type="System.String"></Property></Properties>
 </MethodInstance>
</MethodInstances>
```

As in previous examples, if the `UseClientCachingForSearch` property is present, the `AuthorField`, `DescriptionField`, and `DisplayUriField` properties need be defined only beneath the `RootFinder`. If the `UseClientCachingForSearch` property is not present, these properties must also be defined under the `SpecificFinder` method instance.

Crawling Associations

If you have created associations between ECTs, search can crawl these associations. The crawling of associations is supported in two different ways: for child ECTs and for attached ECTs. A child ECT has its own separate URL displayed in the search results, whereas an attached ECT always uses the URL of the parent ECT. This means that when a search is executed that returns an associated ECT, the child ECT will appear as a separate result, but the attached ECT will show the parent ECT as a result instead.

In order for the indexing engine to crawl an associated ECT as a child, the `DirectoryLink` property should be added to the `Association` element in the Metadata Model. In order for the indexing engine to crawl the associated ECT as an attachment, the `AttachmentAccessor` property should be added to the `Association` element in the Metadata Model. The following code shows an example of each approach:

```
<Association Name="GeographyAssociation"
 Type="AssociationNavigator"
 ReturnParameterName="GeographyAssociation"
 DefaultDisplayName="Geography Association">
 <Properties>
  <Property Name="DirectoryLink" Type="System.String"></Property>
</Properties>
 <SourceEntity Namespace="http://aw/marketing" Name="Geography" />
 <DestinationEntity Namespace="http://w/marketing" Name="Campaign" />
</Association>

<Association Name="GeographyAssociation"
 Type="AssociationNavigator"
 ReturnParameterName="GeographyAssociation"
 DefaultDisplayName="Geography Association">
 <Properties>
  <Property Name="ForeignFieldMappings" Type="System.String">...</Property>
  <Property Name="AttachmentAccesor" Type="System.String"></Property>
 </Properties>
 <SourceEntity Namespace="http://aw/marketing" Name="Geography" />
 <DestinationEntity Namespace="http://w/marketing" Name="Campaign" />
</Association>
```

Ignoring Fields

Occasionally, you will want to prevent certain fields defined in the model from being indexed. This may be because the fields have no meaningful value that can be searched or because the data is just there for validation. Fields that have no meaningful value include things like `Identitifers` that use GUIDs. Fields used for validation were shown in Chapter 7, where additional fields containing original values were added to the Metadata Model to support conflict resolution. In these cases you can cause the crawler to ignore the fields by using the `SuppressCrawl` property in the `TypeDescriptor` for the `Finder` and `SpecificFinder` methods. The following code shows an example:

```
<TypeDescriptor Name="OriginalName" TypeName="System.String" ReadOnly="true">
 <Properties>
  <Property Name="SuppressCrawl" Type="System.Boolean">true</Property>
 </Properties>
</TypeDescriptor>
```

Customizing the Search Results Display

Search results are returned to the Search Core Results Web Part as XML. XSLT contained under the Display Properties of the Search Core Results Web Part transforms the returned XML into the results displayed in the Search Center. While you have complete access to this XSLT and can customize it significantly, SharePoint provides no graphical environment for understanding how changes to the XSLT will affect the search results display. Fortunately we can use a combination of the SharePoint Designer and Visual Studio to create and analyze the XSLT.

In order to begin modifying the XSLT you must first get a copy of the raw XML sent to the Search Core Results Web Part before transformation. The simplest way to do this is to replace the XSLT with a null transformation. Doing so will cause the search results to appear as XML. The following code shows the null-transformation XSLT to use:

```
<?xml version="1.0" encoding="utf-8"?>
<xsl:stylesheet xmlns:xsl="http://www.w3.org/1999/XSL/Transform" version="1.0">
  <xsl:output method="xml" version="1.0" encoding="utf-8" indent="yes"/>
  <xsl:template match="/">
    <xmp>
      <xsl:copy-of select="*"/>
    </xmp>
  </xsl:template>
</xsl:stylesheet>
```

After you have a copy of the raw XML generated by the search, you can use this as a basis for creating the desired XSLT. The simplest way to create XSLT is to use the SharePoint Designer. This is because the Data View Web Part accepts an XML file as a data source and will generate XSLT as you use the SharePoint Designer to customize the display.

Start by opening the SharePoint Designer to any site. You will not be keeping any of the pages you create, so the exact location of the pages is irrelevant. Once inside SPD, click the Data Sources object and then select to add a new XML file connection from the New group in the ribbon. Add the raw XML file that you generated from the search results.

Next, add a Web Part page to the site and place it in edit mode. From the Edit menu, insert a Data View Web Part based on the raw XML file. Once the Data View Web Part is on the page, you can use the Add/Remove columns dialog to decide what columns to display. Additionally, you can go directly to the source view to make edits to the generated XSLT, which is contained between XSL tags in the document. Once you have the search results appearing as you want them, simply copy the XSLT out of SPD and into the Search Core Results Web Part. You can use this same approach to customize the XSLT associated with list forms and the External Data Web Parts.

Creating Ranking Models

When a user executes a query, he or she expects to have the most relevant items appear near the top when the results are displayed. The ranking engine is responsible for assigning a ranking score to each returned item based on a number of factors defined in a ranking model. The ranking model contains the rules that will be applied to the search results and determine ranking. SharePoint Server 2010 ships with several ranking models that are applied when you search different contexts such as documents or people. You can list all the ranking models with the following PowerShell command:

```
Get-SPEnterpriseSearchServiceApplication |
   Get-SPEnterpriseSearchRankingModel |Format-List
```

When you list the ranking models you will notice that one of them is designated as the default model. This is the model that is used in SharePoint searches out of the box. You'll also notice that there are several models to support people search and social networking. BCS solutions use the default ranking model unless you specify otherwise. For most solutions the default ranking model will be appropriate. However, there may be times when you need to create a custom ranking model for use with your solution. This section outlines the steps necessary to create a custom ranking model.

Understanding Ranking Models

The parameters used by a ranking model can be either *query-independent* or *query-dependent*. Query-independent parameters are computed at crawl time because they are static and will not change regardless of the query that is run. The creation date of a document is a good example of a query-independent parameter. Query-dependent parameters are computed when the search is executed because they are affected by the search that the user runs. A keyword search of a document body is a good example of a query-dependent parameter. This distinction is important because a ranking model will not be able to gain access to query-independent information if the query is formed in such a way so as not to access the static information. This can happen when an end user forms a query strictly against a Managed Property. In this case the Managed Property database is accessed and there is no need for a full search of the index. So, for efficiency, the static data is skipped. However, this can give strange results if the ranking model is highly dependent on query-independent factors.

One of the main query-independent parameters that you can affect is the proximity of an item to an authoritative page. An authoritative page is a means of specifying which pages in SharePoint are the most important. Authoritative pages are designated through the search administration interface in Central Administration. When designating authoritative pages you may specify a page as either *most authoritative*, *second-level authoritative*, *third-level authoritative*, or *non-authoritative*. The ranking of an item within search results will be based on its click distance from an authoritative page, with different multipliers being used for the various levels. Non-authoritative pages will be pushed to the bottom of the search results.

In previous versions of SharePoint, authoritative pages were the primary means of influencing the relevancy of items in search. A custom ranking model, however, enables you to specify query-independent and query-dependent factors to be used in the ranking of search results. This gives you a powerful way to influence the display of results within your BCS solutions.

Before we move on to the creation of custom ranking models, it is important that you consider the difference between ranking results and sorting results. As discussed previously, ranking results should involve both query-independent and query-dependent factors that influence the order in which results are displayed. Sorting, on the other hand, is always completely static. For example, the ranking of documents by searching the body for keywords is dynamic and depends on the keyword. The sorting of the same documents by creation date will not change no matter what keywords are used in the search. The point is that you should never use a custom ranking model when what you want is a fixed sort.

A custom ranking model is best used in situations in which the default ranking model is not returning results of interest close enough to the top and the introduction of an authoritative page does not solve the problem. This means that you will likely create few custom ranking models, but they can be very useful. You can accomplish fixed sorts, on the other hand, by using the query object model to perform a search.

Creating a Custom Ranking Model

In SharePoint 2010 not all of the internal ranking model capabilities are available to your custom ranking models, but there is enough power to have a significant impact on the search results. Custom ranking models are created as XML files that specify the query-independent and query-dependent factors to use in the ranking of search results. The following code shows a sample custom ranking model that gives extra weight to the title of an item and to Word documents. Such a model might be used if an organization's most important documents are typically in Word format and if document titles contain key information.

```
<?xml version='1.0'?>
<rankingModel
    name='NewRankingModel'
    id='11111111-65CD-4a1b-9A63-F7ECB4B6BB5E'
    description = 'Sample ranking model'
    xmlns='http://schemas.microsoft.com/office/2009/rankingModel'>
    <queryDependentFeatures>
        <queryDependentFeature
          name='Body' pid='1' weight='10.0000000000'
          lengthNormalization='2.8898552470'/>
        <queryDependentFeature
          name='Title' pid='2' weight='100.0000000000'
          lengthNormalization='0.9574077587'/>
        <queryDependentFeature
          name='Author' pid='3' weight='0.1000000000'
          lengthNormalization='1.0131509886'/>
        <queryDependentFeature
          name='AnchorText' pid='10' weight='0.1000000000'
          lengthNormalization='2.6713762088' />
        <queryDependentFeature
          name='DisplayName' pid='56' weight='0.1000000000'
          lengthNormalization='0.9713508040'/>
        <queryDependentFeature
          name='ExtractedTitle' pid='302' weight='0.1000000000'
          lengthNormalization='1.0095022768'/>
        <queryDependentFeature
          name='QueryLogClickedText' pid='100' weight='0.1000000000'
          lengthNormalization='1.6000001537'/>
    </queryDependentFeatures>
    <queryIndependentFeatures>
        <queryIndependentFeature
          name='DistanceFromAuthority' pid='96' default='5'
          weight='0.1000000000'>
            <transformInvRational  k='0.1359244473'/>
        </queryIndependentFeature>
        <queryIndependentFeature
          name='URLdepth' pid='303' default='3' weight='0.1000000000'>
            <transformLinear max='1000'/>
        </queryIndependentFeature>
        <queryIndependentFeature
          name='DocumentPopularity' pid='306' default='0'
          weight='0.1000000000'>
            <transformRational k='1.2170868558'/>
```

```
        </queryIndependentFeature>
        <queryIndependentFeature
          name='DocumentUnpopularity' pid='307' default='0'
          weight='0.1000000000'>
            <transformRational k='0.7333557072'/>
        </queryIndependentFeature>
        <categoryFeature name='FileType' pid='98' default='0'>
            <category name='Html' value='0' weight='0.1000000000'/>
            <category name='Doc' value='1' weight='100.0000000000'/>
            <category name='Ppt' value='2' weight='0.1000000000'/>
            <category name='Xls' value='3' weight='0.1000000000'/>
            <category name='Xml' value='4' weight='0.1000000000'/>
            <category name='Txt' value='5' weight='0.0000000000'/>
            <category name='ListItems' value='6' weight='0.1000000000'/>
            <category name='Message' value='7' weight='0.1000000000'/>
        </categoryFeature>
        <languageFeature name='Language' pid='5' default='1'
         weight='10.0000000000'/>
    </queryIndependentFeatures>
</rankingModel>
```

Custom ranking models begin with the `rankingModel` element. The only required attribute for this element is the `id` attribute, which is a GUID that identifies the model. The other attributes are optional and used largely for readability. Additionally, the namespace must be `http://schemas.microsoft.com/office/2009/rankingModel`. The child elements of the `rankingModel` are a set of `queryDependentFeatures` and `queryIndependentFeatures`, which specify the factors that will be used for dynamic and static ranking respectively.

The `queryDependentFeature` element has `name`, `pid`, `weight`, and `lengthNormalization` attributes. The `queryIndependentFeature` element has `name`, `pid`, `default`, and `weight` attributes. The `name` attribute is optional, not used, and primarily there for readability. The `pid` attribute is the property identifier for the Managed Property being referenced. The `weight` attribute is a relative attribute that determines the effect the factor will have on the ranking. The `lengthNormalization` attribute is a number used to account for differences in the lengths of various properties. The `default` attribute is the value to be used when an actual value cannot be determined.

The `categoryFeature` and `languageFeature` elements are children of `queryIndependentFeature`. The `categoryFeature` element enables you to specify a set of possible values for a Managed Property and give different weights to each one. The `languageFeature` element gives extra weight to an item if it is in the default language. Finally, the `transformRational`, `transformInvRational`, and `transformLinear` elements associate additional functions with the model that transform the weighting values.

Managed Property identifiers are critical to the creation of custom ranking models because both the `queryDependentFeatures` and the `queryIndependentFeatures` can use Managed Properties. When creating custom ranking models you can choose which Managed Properties you want to include in the model, whether their effect will be static or dynamic, and the weight of their impact. In order to do this, however, you must know the identifier for the Managed Property. You can use the following PowerShell script to list all the Managed Properties and their identifiers:

```
Get-SPEnterpriseSearchServiceApplication |
    Get-SPEnterpriseSearchMetadataManagedProperty
```

SharePoint Server comes with many Managed Properties already defined, but when you are creating search-based applications you will quite often need to create your own Managed Properties. Managed Properties are created through the search administration interface in the Central Administration site. Essentially, Managed Properties are properties that refer to one or more crawled properties. Managed Properties enable you to group together several different crawled properties that might refer to the same thing and to represent them as a single Managed Property. For example, the Managed Property `Title` refers to the crawled properties `Mail:5`, `People:PreferredName`, `Basic:displaytitle`, and `ows_Title`. This grouping not only simplifies working with several crawled properties at once, it also provides a more readable name.

When creating a custom ranking model you must set the weights that will be used for each of the Managed Properties. The weights you apply can have any value and they are relative to all the other weights. You can also set default values for `queryIndependentFeatures` should an item not have the specified Managed Property.

All this means that you can disregard certain properties by setting them to `0` or greatly enhance them with a large number. It is important to remember, however, that using very large or very small numbers can overwhelm your model and essentially turn it into a sorting algorithm instead of a ranking model.

Of all the pieces in the custom ranking model, perhaps none is as mysterious as the `lengthNormalization` attribute. Length Normalization is the process of accounting for the length of a string when keywords are found in it. This is necessary because longer strings have a better chance of containing a keyword, but that does not necessarily mean they are more relevant. While the `lengthNormalization` attribute is required, it can be difficult to know what value to use. As a general guide, long strings like `Body` have a number greater than `1` and shorter strings like `Title` have a value of less than `1`.

Transforms apply functions to `queryIndependentFeatures`. These functions use an additional factor as an input to the transformation function. A complete description of the effects of each transformation is beyond the scope of this chapter. Generally these transforms will not be necessary for simple ranking models.

Using a Custom Ranking Model

Once you have created a custom ranking model you can use it with SharePoint Server. The process of using the custom ranking model involves several steps. First, you must enable any associated Managed Properties for use with the model. Second, you must install the ranking model. Third, you must reference the new model in the Core Search Results Web Part.

When you create a custom ranking model you will quite often be creating new Managed Properties for use in the weighting strategy. Previously you saw how to get the identifier for a Managed Property so that it could be referenced in the ranking model. However, Managed Properties are not by default enabled for use as query-independent parameters. You must explicitly allow this. So if your model uses a Managed Property as a query-independent feature, you must set the

EnabledForQueryIndependentRank property to True. You can set the property using the following PowerShell, substituting the name of the Managed Property in question:

```
$p = Get-SPEnterpriseSearchServiceApplication |
     Get-SPEnterpriseSearchMetadataManagedProperty -Identity {PropertyName}
$p.EnabledForQueryIndependentRank = $true
$p.Update()
```

The next step is to install the custom ranking model. You do this using the PowerShell cmdlet New-SPEnterpriseSearchRankingModel. This cmdlet takes as a parameter the complete ranking model as a string. Therefore you have to "crunch" your ranking model into a single piece of text by removing all the line breaks and white space so it can be passed as a parameter. Once this is done, the following PowerShell script will install the new ranking model:

```
Get-SPEnterpriseSearchServiceApplication |
    New-SPEnterpriseSearchRankingModel
       -RankingModelXML {Crunched Ranking Model}
```

The final step in the process is to reference the custom ranking model in the Search Core Results Web Part. The Search Core Results Web Part displays the primary result set from a search and uses the default ranking model out of the box. However, it has a DefaultRankingModelID property that may be changed to reference the ID of any custom ranking model.

In order to change the DefaultRankingModelID property you must navigate to a search results page and place that page in edit mode. Now the Search Core Results Web Part may be exported as an XML file. After exporting the Web Part you can open it in an editor and search for the DefaultRankingModelID property, which will be empty. When the property is empty, the default ranking model is used. Simply change this value by hand and save it. You may then return to the search page and import the new file as an instance of the Search Core Results Web Part. Deleting the original Web Part from the page completes the process. Now when you search, the new ranking model will be used.

SEARCHING WITH .NET ASSEMBLY CONNECTORS

As mentioned earlier in the chapter, .NET Assembly Connectors have replaced Protocol Handlers as the primary means for the crawl engine to access systems. Chapter 7 covered these connectors in detail, with the exception of search support. In this section you'll learn how to search-enable a .NET Assembly Connector and add security trimming to search results.

Enabling Search Basics

In the same way that no-code solutions support search through properties in the Metadata Model, .NET Assembly Connectors also support search. Not surprisingly, the primary difference between search-enabling an ECT in SharePoint Designer and doing the same thing in Visual Studio 2010 lies in the tooling. While SPD provides a wizard interface to do most of the work, Visual Studio requires the use of the Entity Design Surface, BDC Explorer, and Method Details pane.

The .NET Assembly Connector supports all the same properties discussed earlier in the chapter, and they must be set on the same elements. In Visual Studio 2010 you can set properties on an element by using the Custom Properties associated with the element. As an example, consider the `RootFinder`, `LastModifiedTimeStampField`, `DisplayUriField`, `DescriptionField`, `AuthorField`, and `UseClientCachingForSearch` properties. All these properties must be set on a method instance for a `Finder` method.

In Visual Studio 2010 you can display method instances in the Method Details pane by selecting a method on the Entity Design Surface. When you select a method instance, the properties for that instance will appear in the Properties pane. Within the Properties pane you can click the Custom Properties to open the Property Editor dialog. In this dialog you can add custom properties to the current method instance. Figure 9-6 shows how this is done in Visual Studio 2010.

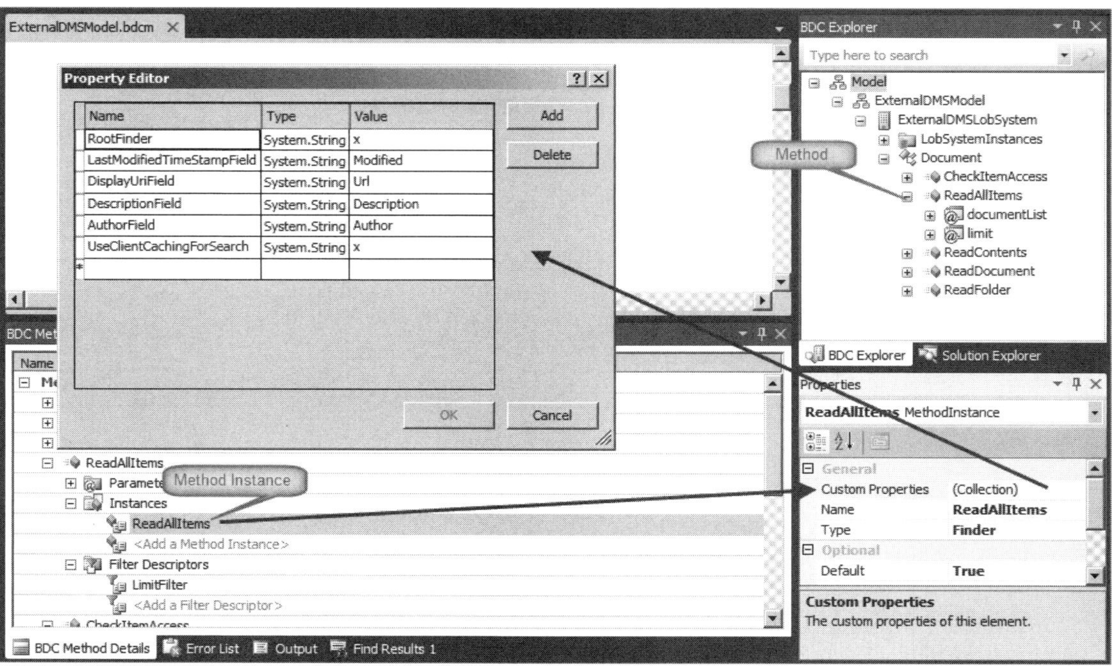

FIGURE 9-6

When you first begin working with .NET Assembly Connector properties it is easy to become confused about exactly which node you are working with. Remember that the Entity Design Surface and the BDC Model Explorer are both showing methods, not method instances. The search properties must be attached to the method instance for it to work properly. Also remember that if the `UseClientCachingForSearch` property is not included, the properties must also be defined under the `SpecificFinder` method instance. The process for defining the properties under `SpecificFinder` is identical. Finally, note that the `RootFinder` and `UseClientCachingForSearch` properties have values of `x`. As noted previously, the value for these properties is ignored, but using a value of `x` gives you something to enter in the dialog.

If you find the Visual Studio tooling confusing, remember that you can always open the model directly as text. Simply right-click the BDCM file in the Solution Explorer and select Open With from the context menu. Then select to open the model with the text editor. You may now make direct edits to the model. Figure 9-7 shows the model text generated from the dialog entries in Figure 9-6.

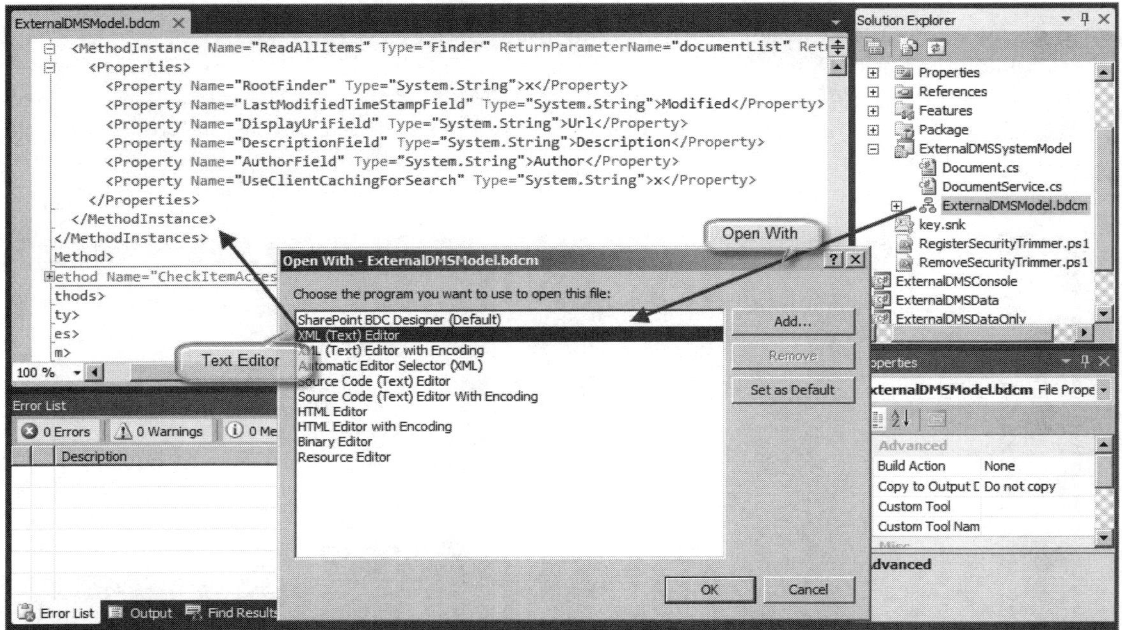

FIGURE 9-7

When you are mapping fields for properties, such as the author, title, description, and hyperlink, the values for these fields are always the name of one of the fields defined in the entity class for the ECT. Simply use the exact name of the field, which should also be the name of the `TypeDescriptor` used in the method. As always, strong understanding of the Metadata Model schema is critical for success, and you should always check your work by examining the Metadata Model XML directly.

Using Custom Hyperlinks in Search Results

While mapping a field to the hyperlink associated with a search result is a simple matter of including the `DisplayUriField` property in the Metadata Model, the impact of this property is worth a closer look. As noted earlier, the default behavior for search results links is to lead to the profile page for the BCS solution. While this works fine for simple solutions, more sophisticated ones will want to open a file or record in an External System for viewing. This means that you must construct a URL that performs the desired action.

If your search results contain documents, you will want to construct a hyperlink that opens the document in the appropriate application. The basic strategy is to create a hyperlink that navigates to a download page. The download page can then use the BDC Server Runtime to call a StreamAccessor method that can be used to access the document contents. The following code shows how to create the download page:

```
//Connect to BCS
BdcServiceApplicationProxy proxy =
  (BdcServiceApplicationProxy)SPServiceContext.Current.GetDefaultProxy(
  typeof(BdcServiceApplicationProxy));

DatabaseBackedMetadataCatalog catalog =
  proxy.GetDatabaseBackedMetadataCatalog();

IEntity ect = catalog.GetEntity("MyExternalSystem", "DocumentEntity");
ILobSystem lob = ect.GetLobSystem();
ILobSystemInstance lobi = lob.GetLobSystemInstances()["MyExternalSystem"];
IMethodInstance mi = ect.GetMethodInstance(
                          "ReadDocumentStream",
                          MethodInstanceType.StreamAccessor);

//Call BCS to get stream
object[] args = { int.Parse(Request.QueryString["DocumentId"]), null };
ect.Execute(mi, lobi, ref args);
byte[] buffer = ((MemoryStream)args[1]).ToArray();

//Download
this.Page.Response.Clear();
this.Page.Response.ClearHeaders();
this.Page.Response.AddHeader("Content-Disposition",
  "attachment; filename=\"" + Request.QueryString["fileName"] + "\"");
this.Page.Response.AddHeader("Content-Length", buffer.Length.ToString());
this.Page.Response.BinaryWrite(buffer);
this.Page.Response.Flush();
this.Page.Response.End();
```

In the code, the Identifier for the document is passed as a QueryString parameter to the download page. The download page connects to the External System through the BDC Server Runtime and calls the StreamAccessor method. The method parameters are placed into an object array and passed to the Execute method. Notice that the first parameter is the document Identifier and the second parameter is the return stream. The return stream is then downloaded using the page response stream.

While downloading is a common scenario, the hyperlink you create is not limited to document streams. You may, for example, have the hyperlink open a record in an External System. Many External Systems, such as Microsoft Customer Relationship Management System (MSCRM) and Lotus Notes databases, support hyperlink access. You should also note that any hyperlink you create is subject to the crawl rules defined within the Search Service Application, which can affect your ability to include items in the index.

Using a Changelog for Incremental Crawls

Previous examples showed that you can easily enable incremental crawls for External Systems by using the LastModifiedTimeStampField property to map a field that contains a timestamp. This is by far the simplest approach for implementing incremental crawls, but it is not the most efficient, because timestamps must be stored for every item.

The *changelog* approach is an alternative way to implement incremental crawling, in which the SSA maintains a single timestamp marking the last time a crawl was performed. This timestamp is then used as a parameter, which is passed to the .NET Assembly Connector during an incremental crawl. The .NET Assembly Connector uses the timestamp to identify entity instances that have changed or have been deleted. It then returns that information to the SSA.

The changelog approach depends on the definition of two new method stereotypes: `ChangedIdEnumerator` and `DeletedIdEnumerator`. These methods take a timestamp as an input and return a collection of `Identifiers`. The timestamp is provided by the crawl engine through a filter marked with the `SynchronizationCookie` property. This filter is then associated with an `In` parameter so it can be passed to the method implementation. The following code shows a typical definition of these methods in a Metadata Model:

```
<!-- The prototype for the ChangedIdEnumerator method -->
<Method Name="ReadChangedIds">
  <FilterDescriptors>
    <FilterDescriptor Name="LastCrawl" Type="InputOutput">
      <Properties>
        <!-- Marks this filter as the cookie -->
        <Property Name="SynchronizationCookie" Type="System.String">
         x
       </Property>
      </Properties>
    </FilterDescriptor>
    <FilterDescriptor Name="timestamp" Type="Timestamp" />
  </FilterDescriptors>
  <Parameters>
    <Parameter Name="lastCrawlDate" Direction="InOut">
      <TypeDescriptor Name="LastCrawlDate" TypeName="System.DateTime"
       IsCollection="false" AssociatedFilter="LastCrawl">
        <Interpretation>
          <NormalizeDateTime LobDateTimeMode="Local" />
        </Interpretation>
      </TypeDescriptor>
    </Parameter>
    <Parameter Name="returnIds" Direction="Return">
      <TypeDescriptor Name="DeletedIds"
       TypeName="System.Collections.Generic.IEnumerable`1[System.String]"
       IsCollection="true">
        <TypeDescriptors>
          <TypeDescriptor Name="ID" TypeName="System.String"
           IdentifierName="ID" />
        </TypeDescriptors>
      </TypeDescriptor>
    </Parameter>
  </Parameters>
  <MethodInstances>
    <MethodInstance Name="ReadChangedIdsInstance" Type="ChangedIdEnumerator"
     ReturnParameterName="returnIds" />
  </MethodInstances>
```

```
</Method>
<!-- The prototype for the DeletedIdEnumerator method -->
<Method Name="ReadDeletedIds">
  <FilterDescriptors>
    <FilterDescriptor Name="LastCrawl" Type="InputOutput">
      <Properties>
        <!-- Marks this filter as the cookie -->
        <Property Name="SynchronizationCookie" Type="System.String">
         X
       </Property>
      </Properties>
    </FilterDescriptor>
    <FilterDescriptor Name="timestamp" Type="Timestamp" />
  </FilterDescriptors>
  <Parameters>
    <Parameter Name="lastCrawlDate" Direction="InOut">
      <TypeDescriptor Name="LastCrawlDate" TypeName="System.DateTime"
       IsCollection="false" AssociatedFilter="LastCrawl">
        <Interpretation>
          <NormalizeDateTime LobDateTimeMode="Local" />
        </Interpretation>
      </TypeDescriptor>
    </Parameter>
    <Parameter Name="returnIds" Direction="Return">
      <TypeDescriptor Name="DeletedIds"
       TypeName="System.Collections.Generic.IEnumerable`1[System.String]"
       IsCollection="true">
        <TypeDescriptors>
          <TypeDescriptor Name="ID" TypeName="System.String"
           IdentifierName="ID" />
        </TypeDescriptors>
      </TypeDescriptor>
    </Parameter>
  </Parameters>
  <MethodInstances>
    <MethodInstance Name="ReadDeletedIdsInstance" Type="DeletedIdEnumerator"
     ReturnParameterName="returnIds" />
  </MethodInstances>
</Method>
```

As with all methods defined by means of Visual Studio tooling, a stub is created automatically for implementing the method. Within the service class two new function signatures are created that have a `DateTime` input and a collection return value. The following code shows the function signatures associated with the Metadata Model. All that is required is the implementation code to return the `Identifiers` based on the timestamp.

```
public static IEnumerable<string> ReadChangedIds(ref DateTime lastCrawlDate)
{
}

public static IEnumerable<string> ReadDeletedIds(ref DateTime lastCrawlDate)
{
}
```

Debugging Search Connectors

When working with .NET Assembly Connectors to enable search and crawling capabilities, you will undoubtedly need to debug your code. You can easily debug in Visual Studio 2010 by attaching to either the `w3wp.exe` process or the `mssdmn.exe` process. You will want to attach to the `w3wp.exe` process for debugging scenarios in which the search results are displayed and the user clicks a particular item. You will want to attach to the `mssdmn.exe` process to debug crawling operations.

When debugging, you may experience situations in which the latest version of your .NET Assembly Connector is not loaded into memory. This may happen if you deployed from Visual Studio, but your changes were not properly merged with the existing Metadata Model. In these situations you should delete the BDC model from the BDC service application and redeploy your project. You may also experience this problem if the crawler still has an old version of your assembly in memory. In these cases you can simply restart the SharePoint Server Search service.

Trimming Search Results

As you saw previously, .NET Assembly Connectors give you significant control over how BCS interacts with External Systems. In the case of Enterprise Search, the .NET Assembly Connector also provides significant control over how search results are trimmed so that you can guarantee end users will see only those search results that map to items for which they have permissions.

When it comes to trimming search results there are two approaches: you can trim during crawl time or during query time. Trimming search results during crawl time is the preferred approach because you can build up an access control list (ACL) during the crawl that becomes part of the search index. During query time, the ACL in the index is used to exclude items that the current user is not allowed to view. Trimming search results at query time requires that the permissions for the current user be checked against every item returned from the search query after the query is complete. This is potentially a very expensive process, but, it may be required because of the design of the External System or because SharePoint is using something other than Active Directory for security.

Implementing Crawl-Time Security

Implementing crawl-time security in your .NET Assembly Connector requires the definition of a `BinarySecurityDescriptorAccessor` method. A `BinarySecurityDescriptorAccessor` method accepts at least an `Identifier` and returns a `byte` array. The `Identifier` identifies a particular entity instance and the `byte` array represents a set of security principals and their associated permissions for the entity instance. The security descriptor returned from the method becomes part of the search index and can be used to trim search results. As an example, consider the following XML file, which defines a security policy associated with some External System:

```
<?xml version="1.0" encoding="utf-8" ?>
<Policy>
  <Grant>
    <Account Name="AW\Scoth"/>
  </Grant>
  <Deny>
    <Account Name="AW\Brianc"/>
  </Deny>
</Policy>
```

If you want to use the policy file as a source for trimming search results, you first define a new `BinarySecurityDescriptorAccessor` method in the .NET Assembly Connector. At a minimum an `In` parameter must be defined as the `Identifier` and a `Return` parameter as the `byte` array. In the preceding example a filter was also defined to pass in the user name of the current user. Figure 9-8 shows the Method Details pane with the new method instance defined.

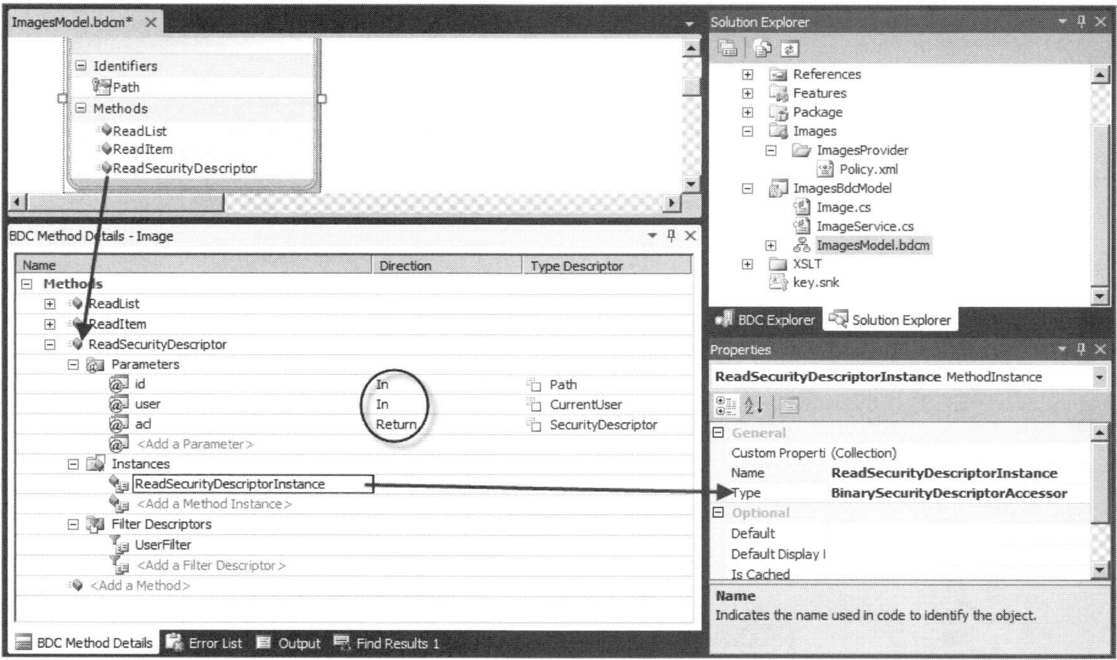

FIGURE 9-8

In addition to defining the new method, you can also map the security descriptor to a field of the entity. You map the field using the `WindowsSecurityDescriptorField` property. If the `WindowsSecurityDescriptorField` property is not present, the `BinarySecurityDescriptorAccessor` method will be called whenever the security descriptor for the entity instance is needed. The following code shows a complete definition for a `BinarySecurityDescriptorAccessor` method and `WindowsSecurityDescriptorField` property in the Metadata Model:

```
<Method Name="ReadSecurityDescriptor">
 <FilterDescriptors>
  <FilterDescriptor Name="UserFilter" Type="UserContext" />
 </FilterDescriptors>
 <Parameters>
  <Parameter Name="id" Direction="In">
   <TypeDescriptor Name="Path" TypeName="System.String"
    IdentifierName="Path" IsCollection="false" />
  </Parameter>
  <Parameter Name="user" Direction="In">
   <TypeDescriptor Name="CurrentUser" TypeName="System.String"
```

```
        AssociatedFilter="UserFilter" />
      </Parameter>
      <Parameter Name="acl" Direction="Return">
       <TypeDescriptor Name="SecurityDescriptor" TypeName="System.Byte[]"
        IsCollection="true">
        <TypeDescriptors>
         <TypeDescriptor Name="SecurityDescriptorByte" TypeName="System.Byte" />
        </TypeDescriptors>
       </TypeDescriptor>
      </Parameter>
     </Parameters>
     <MethodInstances>
      <MethodInstance Name="ReadSecurityDescriptorInstance"
       Type="BinarySecurityDescriptorAccessor" ReturnParameterName="acl">
       <Properties>
        <Property Name="WindowsSecurityDescriptorField" Type="System.String">
         SecurityDescriptor
       </Property>
       </Properties>
      </MethodInstance>
     </MethodInstances>
    </Method>
```

After the method is defined, Visual Studio will automatically stub out the implementation. As always, your job is to code the implementation. In this case you must create an ACL based on the information contained in the XML policy file. The following code shows the complete implementation for the method:

```
public static byte[] ReadSecurityDescriptor(string id, string user)
{

    XDocument policyFile = XDocument.Load(
    GetImagesDirectory() + "\\ImagesProvider\\Policy.xml");

    NTAccount workerAcc = new NTAccount(
                          user.Split('\\')[0],
                          user.Split('\\')[1]);

    SecurityIdentifier workerSid =
    (SecurityIdentifier)workerAcc.Translate(typeof(SecurityIdentifier));

    CommonSecurityDescriptor csd =
           new CommonSecurityDescriptor(
                                        false,
                                        false,
                                        ControlFlags.None,
                                        workerSid,
                                        null,
                                        null,
                                        null);

    //Grant
    var grant = from account in
```

```
            policyFile.Descendants("Grant").First().Descendants("Account")
            select account;

        foreach (var acc in grant)
        {
            NTAccount ntacc = new NTAccount(
                              acc.Attribute("Name").Value.Split('\\')[0],
                              acc.Attribute("Name").Value.Split('\\')[1]);

            SecurityIdentifier sid =
            (SecurityIdentifier)ntacc.Translate(typeof(SecurityIdentifier));

            csd.DiscretionaryAcl.AddAccess(
                                           AccessControlType.Allow,
                                           sid,
                                           unchecked((int)0xffffffffL),
                                           InheritanceFlags.None,
                                           PropagationFlags.None);
        }

        //Deny
        var deny = from account in
            policyFile.Descendants("Deny").First().Descendants("Account")
            select account;

        foreach (var acc in deny)
        {
            NTAccount ntacc = new NTAccount(
                              acc.Attribute("Name").Value.Split('\\')[0],
                              acc.Attribute("Name").Value.Split('\\')[1]);

            SecurityIdentifier sid =
            (SecurityIdentifier)ntacc.Translate(typeof(SecurityIdentifier));

            csd.DiscretionaryAcl.AddAccess(
                                           AccessControlType.Deny,
                                           sid, unchecked((int)0xffffffffL),
                                           InheritanceFlags.None,
                                           PropagationFlags.None);
        }

        byte[] secDes = new byte[csd.BinaryLength];
        csd.GetBinaryForm(secDes, 0);
        return secDes;

    }
```

The first thing that happens in the `BinarySecurityDescriptorAccessor` method implementation is that the XML policy file is loaded and a new `NTAccount` object is created based on the identity of the current user. During crawl time, the identity of the user will be the account used to crawl the External System. The implementation code will make this account the owner of the security descriptor for the entity instance. It will do this by creating a `SecurityIdentifier` and setting that as the owner for the `CommonSecurityDescriptor`. The `CommonSecurityDescriptor` is the object that will hold the access control list.

The next step is to run a LINQ query on the policy file and return all the accounts that will be granted access. For each of these accounts an entry is made in the access control list to grant access. Similarly, entries are made in the access control list to deny access for designated accounts in the policy file. Finally, the `CommonSecurityDescriptor` is transformed into a byte array and returned from the method.

Once the method implementation is complete, the .NET Assembly Connector may be deployed to SharePoint. From here it can be used as a content source in search, and a full crawl can be performed. The ACL will be built during the crawl and used to exclude results from the search.

Implementing Query-Time Security

While trimming search results during crawl is the best practice, there are times when it is simply not possible to create an access control list at this time. This is most often because of SharePoint's implementing a security model based on something other than Windows authentication. In these cases you will have to trim the search results at query time.

Implementing query-time trimming requires the definition of an `AccessChecker` method in the Metadata Model. This method typically has parameters that pass in the `Identifier` of the entity instance requested, along with the identity of the current user. The `Return` parameter is then either a `0` or `1`, where `0` is unauthorized and `1` is authorized. The following code shows a typical definition in the Metadata Model:

```
<Method Name="CheckItemAccess" DefaultDisplayName="Check Item Access">
 <FilterDescriptors>
  <FilterDescriptor Name="CurrentUser" Type="UserContext"
   DefaultDisplayName="CurrentUser" />
 </FilterDescriptors>
 <Parameters>
  <Parameter Name="id" Direction="In">
   <TypeDescriptor Name="ID" TypeName="System.Int32"
    IdentifierName="ID" IsCollection="false" />
  </Parameter>
  <Parameter Name="result" Direction="Return">
   <TypeDescriptor Name="Access" TypeName="System.Int64"
    IsCollection="false" />
  </Parameter>
  <Parameter Name="user" Direction="In">
   <TypeDescriptor Name="User" TypeName="System.String"
    AssociatedFilter="CurrentUser" />
  </Parameter>
  </Parameters>
  <MethodInstances>
   <MethodInstance Name="CheckItemAccess" Type="AccessChecker"
    ReturnParameterName="result" />
  </MethodInstances>
</Method>
```

Once the method is defined, you have complete freedom to implement it as necessary to support the External System. This will enable you to take into account any peculiarities associated with the system, as long as your implementation returns the required `0` or `1`. The following code shows a simple implementation of the `AccessChecker` method in which permissions are stored in a database table accessed through LINQ:

```
public long CheckItemAccess(int id, string user)
{
    long rVal = 0;

    DMSEntities ctx = new DMSEntities();

    var q = from perms in ctx.Permissions
            where (perms.Document.Id == id) &&
            (perms.User.Username.Equals(user))
            select perms;
    if (q.Count() > 0)
        rVal = 1;

    return rVal;
}
```

Implementing the `AccessChecker` method is not enough to actually make query-time trimming operational. In addition to the method, you must also create a crawl rule and associate a security trimmer with it. The security trimmer is an assembly that looks at all items defined in a crawl rule and applies the actual trimming logic.

You define a crawl rule for the .NET Assembly Connector within the SSA. From the Enterprise Search administration home page click Crawl Rules. On the Manage Crawl Rules page click New Crawl Rule. On the Add Crawl Rule page you must specify the path to the External System and select to include all items in the path. The path definition takes the form `bdc3://`*`LobSystemName_LobSystemInstanceName`*`/*`. Figure 9-9 shows a new crawl rule definition in Central Administration.

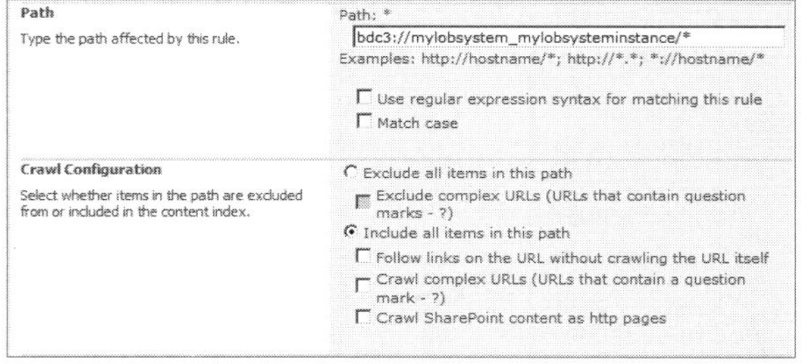

FIGURE 9-9

You associate the security trimmer with the crawl rule using a PowerShell script. While it is possible to create your own custom security trimmer (covered later), you can also use the default BDC security trimmer, which works well for most applications. The following code shows how to register the default BDC security trimmer against a crawl rule:

```
$ssa = Get-SPEnterpriseSearchServiceApplication
       -Identity "Search Service Application"

New-SPEnterpriseSearchSecurityTrimmer
       -Id 1
       -SearchApplication $ssa
       -TypeName
 "Microsoft.Office.Server.Search.Connector.BDC.SPBDC.SPBdcSecurityTrimmer,
```

```
Microsoft.Office.Server.Search.Connector, Version=14.0.0.0,
Culture=neutral, PublicKeyToken=71e9bce111e9429c"
     -RulePath bdc3://mylobsystem_mylobsysteminstance/*
```

The `New-SPEnterpriseSearchSecurityTrimmer` cmdlet takes several parameters. The `Id` parameter is the unique ID for the security trimmer. If the `Id` used in the PowerShell script already exists, it overwrites the existing trimmer registration. The `SearchApplication` parameter is the SSA in which the trimmer should be registered. The `TypeName` is the full, strong name of the class in which the custom security trimmer is implemented. The `RulePath` parameter is the crawl rule with which the custom security trimmer is associated. Additionally, the cmdlet supports the inclusion of custom properties, which are covered later in the chapter.

Once the security trimmer is registered, query-time trimming is complete. The External System can now be crawled and searched. Remember that query-time trimming is not very efficient, so large result sets can be problematic. In these cases you may want to create a custom security trimmer.

Creating a Custom Security Trimmer

Creating a custom security trimmer is appropriate when you want more control over the trimming process. The procedure is reasonably straightforward. It requires the creation of a class that implements the `Microsoft.Office.Server.Search.Query.ISecurityTrimmer2` interface. The class must then be registered against a crawl rule.

The `ISecurityTrimmer2` interface consists of the `Initialize()` method and the `CheckAccess()` method. The `Initialize()` method runs when the custom security trimmer is first loaded and gives you the opportunity to configure aspects of the trimming process. The `CheckAccess()` method runs for each result returned from the search query in order to trim out the unauthorized search results.

The `Initialize()` method receives two parameters when it runs. The first is a `System.Collections.Specialized.NameValueCollection` object containing configuration properties that were defined when the security trimmer was registered against the crawl rule. The second is a `Microsoft.Office.Server.Search.Administration.SearchServiceApplication` object containing a reference to the SSA.

One of the main reasons to create a custom security trimmer is to better manage the performance aspects of query-time trimming. Because of this, it is advisable to always have a limit on the number of checks the trimmer will perform. If, for example, a user runs a query that returns hundreds of thousands of documents, the trimmer will have to query each one and the result will be unacceptable performance. To work around this problem, custom security trimmers should always define a check limit as a configuration property. This check limit will be used in the `CheckAccess()` method to stop the trimmer from processing results and to cause the method to return a message telling the end user to narrow the search. The `Initialize()` method will get the value for this setting, as shown in the following code:

```
private int intCheckLimit = 200;

public void Initialize(NameValueCollection staticProperties,
                       SearchServiceApplication searchApplication)
{
```

```
        //The CheckLimitProperty is added when the trimmer is registered
        if (staticProperties["CheckLimitProperty"] != null)
            intCheckLimit =
            Convert.ToInt32(staticProperties["CheckLimitProperty"]);
    }
```

The number of times that security trimming has been called is tracked by a helper function. This function uses a property to store the current count of security checks and returns a `bool` indicating whether the check limit has been exceeded. The following code shows a typical implementation of the helper function:

```
    private bool CheckLimit(IDictionary<String, Object> sessionProperties,
                            int numChecks)
    {
        //Checks to see if the access check limit is exceeded
        Object count;

        //Session properties can hold values between calls to the trimmer
        sessionProperties.TryGetValue("currentCheckCount", out count);

        if (count == null)
        {
            sessionProperties["currentCheckCount"] = numChecks;
            return (true);
        }

        int countInt = Convert.ToInt32(count);
        countInt += numChecks;

        sessionProperties["currentCheckCount"] = countInt;

        if (countInt <= intCheckLimit)
            return true;
        else
            return false;
    }
```

The `CheckAccess()` method takes three parameters. The first is an `IList<string>` containing a collection of the crawled URLs to check. The second is an `IDictionary` collection of the properties for the current session. The third is a `System.Security.Principal.IIdentity` object containing the identity of the user running the search. The return value from the method is a `BitArray` containing `bool` values indicating whether the current user is authorized to see the search results. The following code shows a sample implementation that uses claims-based security to determine what results the current user can see:

```
    public BitArray CheckAccess(IList<string> documentCrawlUrls,
                                IDictionary<string, object> sessionProperties,
                                IIdentity userIdentity)
    {
        //Check to see if the access check limit has been exceeded
        if (!this.CheckLimit(sessionProperties, documentCrawlUrls.Count))
```

```
            throw (new PluggableAccessCheckException(
                   "Too many results, please narrow your search."));

        //Get identity of current user
        IClaimsIdentity claimsIdentity = (IClaimsIdentity)userIdentity;

        //Construct a claim for the "Developer" role
        Claim permClaim =
          new Claim(Microsoft.IdentityModel.Claims.ClaimTypes.Role, "Developer");

        //Grant access to anyone with the "Developer" role claim
        BitArray retArray = new BitArray(documentCrawlUrls.Count);

        for (int x = 0; x < documentCrawlUrls.Count; x++)
        {
            if (claimsIdentity.Claims.Contains(permClaim))
                retArray[x] = true;
            else
                retArray[x] = false;
        }

        return retArray;
    }
```

Once the custom security trimmer is complete, it needs to be given a strong name and deployed to the GAC. Once in the GAC it must be registered against a crawl rule. The PowerShell script uses the `properties` parameter to define the custom property used to limit the number of access checks. The following PowerShell script shows how the custom security trimmer might be registered:

```
New-SPEnterpriseSearchSecurityTrimmer
   -SearchApplication "Search Service Application"
   -typeName "SecurityTrimmer.Trimmer, SecurityTrimmer, Version=1.0.0.0,
              Culture=neutral, PublicKeyToken=0005979aa8d60a1a"
   -RulePath file://FileServer1/*
   -id 1
   -properties CheckLimitProperty~200
```

SEARCHING WITH CUSTOM CONNECTORS

Chapter 7 covered the fundamentals of creating custom connectors. This section goes further by showing how custom connectors can support crawling and searching. Creating a custom connector for searching is a good choice when the schema of the External System is dynamic, has custom or complex data types, or is large. As detailed in Chapter 7, you will find that tooling support for custom connectors is minimal. Most of the development effort must be made by hand.

Implementing Required Interfaces

In Chapter 7 you learned about the fundamentals of custom connectors by implementing the `Microsoft.BusinessData.Runtime.ISystemUtility` interface. Additional interfaces must be implemented to add support for search. Specifically, you must create additional classes that inherit from the Microsoft.Office.Server.Search.Connector.BDC.LobUri interface and implement the Microsoft.Office.Server.Search.Connector.BDC.INamingContainer interface.

When content sources are created in search, each must have a protocol associated with them. Most commonly these are http protocols, but you have also seen that BCS can use bdc3 protocols. However, the data in an External System may be stored in a repository such as a database that does not support access through any standard protocol that can be used with a content source. In these cases a protocol is created for the SSA to use, but the URLs associated with this protocol must be transformed into something that can access the External System for crawling. This is where the LobUri class and INamingContainer come into play.

The LobUri class is an implementation of the ILobUri interface. This class is used to map the URLs that are passed from the SSA to URLs in the External System. The INamingContainer interface is used to map the URLs from the External System to the URLs expected by the SSA.

The LobUri class consists of an Initialize() method and the properties Entity, Identity, LobSystem, LobSystemInstance, and SourceUri. The Initialize() method is called once for each item being crawled and is used to set the properties to appropriate values for transforming the URLs. The following code shows a simple implementation of the LobUri class:

```
private Uri sourceUri;
private IEntity entity;
private Microsoft.BusinessData.Runtime.Identity identity;
private ILobSystem lobSystem;
private ILobSystemInstance lobSystemInstance;

public override IEntity Entity
{
    get { return this.entity; }
}

public override Identity Identity
{
    get { return this.identity; }
}
public override ILobSystem LobSystem
{
    get { return this.lobSystem; }
}

public override ILobSystemInstance LobSystemInstance
{
    get { return this.lobSystemInstance; }
}

public override Uri SourceUri
{
    get { return this.sourceUri; }
    set { this.sourceUri = value; }
}
```

```
public override void Initialize(IConnectionContext context)
{
  Uri sourceUri = context.Path;
  string accessPath = sourceUri.AbsolutePath.Replace('/', '\\');
  this.lobSystemInstance = this.lobSystem.GetLobSystemInstances()[0].Value;
  this.entity = this.Catalog.GetEntity("MyNamespace", "MyEntity");
  this.identity = new Identity(accessPath);
}
```

The `sourceUri` is the URL provided by the SSA. This value is used as an input to the transformation process to generate an `accessPath` for the External System. The `LobSystem` and `LobSystemInstance` properties represent the External System as defined in the Metadata Model. The `Entity` and the `Identity` represent the entity instance to be crawled in the External System.

The `INamingContainer` interface consists of `Initialize()`, `GetAccessUri()`, and `GetDisplayUri()` methods, along with a `PropertySet` property. The `Initialize()` method receives the `Uri` from the External System. The `GetAccessUri()` method has several overloads and maps the `Uri` from the External System to the `Uri` used by the SSA. The `GetDisplayUri()` method has several overloads and maps the display URL for the SSA. The `PropertySet` property is a GUID that sets a unique category for the properties included in the crawled system. The following code shows a simple implementation of the `INamingContainer` interface:

```
private Uri sourceUri;
private Uri accessUri;
private static Guid propertySetGuid =
        new Guid("{AC0E43DF-52CF-401f-97BD-912CE683FE1C}");


public void Initialize(Uri uri)
{
    this.sourceUri = uri;
}

public Uri GetAccessUri(IEntityInstance entityInstance,
                        IEntityInstance parentEntityInstance)
{
    return this.GetAccessUri(entityInstance);
}

public Uri GetAccessUri(IEntityInstance entityInstance)
{
    object[] ids = entityInstance.GetIdentity().GetIdentifierValues();
    string idString = ids[0].ToString();
    idString = idString.Substring(idString.LastIndexOf('\\') + 1);
    this.accessUri = new Uri(this.sourceUri + "/" + idString);
    return this.accessUri;
}

public Uri GetDisplayUri(IEntityInstance entityInstance,
                         IEntityInstance parentEntityInstance)
```

```
{
    return this.sourceUri;
}

public Uri GetDisplayUri(IEntityInstance entityInstance,
                         string computedDisplayUri)
{
    if (string.IsNullOrEmpty(computedDisplayUri))
        return this.sourceUri;
    return new Uri(computedDisplayUri);
}

public Uri GetDisplayUri(IEntity entity,
                         ILobSystemInstance lobSystemInstance)
{
    return this.accessUri;
}

public Uri GetDisplayUri(ILobSystem lobSystem)
{
    return this.sourceUri;
}

public Guid PropertySet
{
    get { return propertySetGuid; }
}
```

Once the coding is completed, the BDC Metadata Model must be updated to reference the new classes. The entries consist of an `InputUriProcessor` property and an `OutputUriProcessor` property associated with the `LobSystem` element. These properties must refer to the class that implements the `LobUri` and the class that implements the `INamingContainer` respectively. The following code shows a section from the custom connector created in Chapter 7, with the properties defined:

```
<LobSystem Name="MyFileSystem" Type="Custom">
 <Properties>
  <Property Name="SystemUtilityTypeName"
   Type="System.String">MyFileConnector.MyFileConnector, MyFileConnector,
   Version=1.0.0.0, Culture=neutral,
   PublicKeyToken=15865f58b9878bf8</Property>
  <Property Name="InputUriProcessor"
   Type="System.String">MyFileConnector.MyFileLobUri, MyFileConnector,
   Version=1.0.0.0, Culture=neutral,
   PublicKeyToken=15865f58b9878bf8</Property>
  <Property Name="OutputUriProcessor"
   Type="System.String">MyFileConnector.MyFileNamingContainer,
   MyFileConnector, Version=1.0.0.0, Culture=neutral,
   PublicKeyToken=15865f58b9878bf8</Property>
 </Properties>
```

Deploying the Connector

After the required interfaces are implemented and the model updated, the connector assembly needs to have a strong name and be deployed to the GAC. The BCS Model should be deployed to the BDC service application so that External Lists can be created, but it must also be copied to a file share on the server so that it can be referenced by PowerShell when the connector is registered. A PowerShell command is needed to register the custom connector with the SSA and declare the protocol that will be used by the SSA to access the External System. The following PowerShell code shows how to register the custom connector with the SSA:

```
$searchapp = Get-SPEnterpriseSearchServiceApplication
New-SPEnterpriseSearchCrawlCustomConnector
   -SearchApplication $searchapp
   -protocol {protocol}
   -ModelFilePath {path to model}
   -Name {name for connector}
```

The protocol can be anything you want as long as you are consistent throughout the creation of the connector. You can use values such as `myfile`, `abc`, or `xyz` to define the protocol for your system. The path to the model is the complete path to the model in the file share you created to support the registration process. The name of the connector is what will appear in the SSA when you make a new content source based on the connector.

While working with custom connectors you may need to unregister them as well. You can do this with a simple PowerShell command. The following code shows how to unregister a custom connector:

```
$searchapp = Get-SPEnterpriseSearchServiceApplication
$crawler = Get-SPEnterpriseSearchCrawlCustomConnector
          -SearchApplication $searchapp
          -Protocol {protocol}
Remove-SPEnterpriseSearchCrawlCustomConnector
      -SearchApplication $searchapp
      -Identity $crawler
```

Along with registering the custom connector, you must also add a new registry key to the server where the crawling will take place. The key takes the form `[HKEY_LOCAL_MACHINE]\SOFTWARE\Microsoft\Office Server\14.0\Search\Setup\ProtocolHandlers\{protocol}`. The value of this key must be set to `OSearch14.ConnectorProtocolHandler.1`, which references the COM component `ConnectorPH.dll`.

Using the Connector

Once the custom connector is properly deployed you can use it to create new content sources for searching. From the SSA, select to create a New Content Source. In the Content Source Type section choose Custom Repository, which will display the name of the available custom connectors. After selecting the custom connector, specify a start address that uses the protocol defined for the connector and provides a starting path that is meaningful for the custom connector. Figure 9-10 shows an example content source creation page for a custom connector that searches file shares.

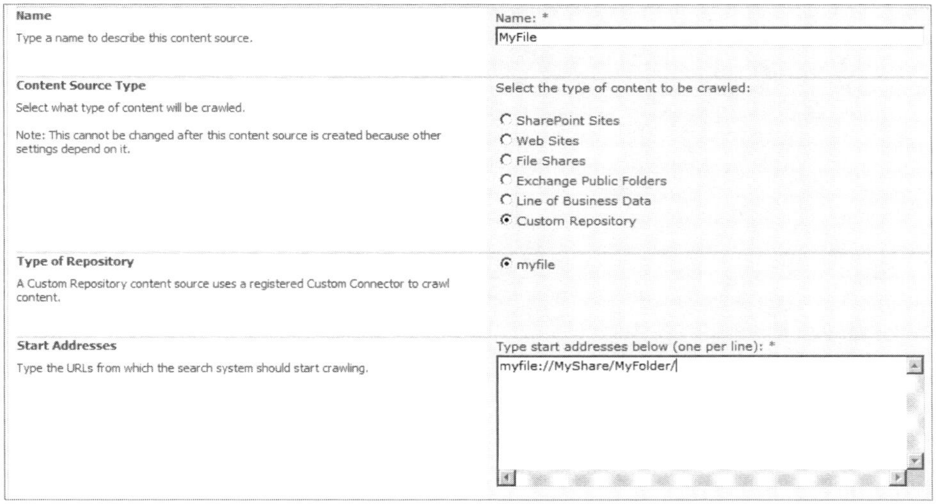

Name

Type a name to describe this content source.

Name: *

MyFile

Content Source Type

Select what type of content will be crawled.

Note: This cannot be changed after this content source is created because other settings depend on it.

Select the type of content to be crawled:

- SharePoint Sites
- Web Sites
- File Shares
- Exchange Public Folders
- Line of Business Data
- Custom Repository

Type of Repository

A Custom Repository content source uses a registered Custom Connector to crawl content.

myfile

Start Addresses

Type the URLs from which the search system should start crawling.

Type start addresses below (one per line): *

myfile://MyShare/MyFolder/

FIGURE 9-10

SUMMARY

Implementing search capabilities in your BCS solutions makes them more powerful and valuable to the end user. While many custom applications implement some form of querying, very few can claim to have a search engine as powerful as the one offered by SharePoint Server 2010. As a result, you should give strong consideration to making search an integral part of every BCS solution.

INDEX

INDEX

A

B

D

G

H

I

J

K

L

M

S